Management in the Financial Services Industry
Thriving on Organizational Change

Liz Croft, Ann Norton and
Ian Whyte

The Chartered Institute of Bankers

CIB Publishing
c/o The Chartered Institute of Bankers
Emmanuel House
4-9 Burgate Lane
Canterbury
Kent
CT1 2XJ
United Kingdom

Telephone 01227 762600

CIB Publishing Publications are published by The Chartered Institute of Bankers, a non-profit-making registered educational charity.

Typeset by Kevin O'Connor
Printed by Thanet Press Limited, Margate, K

ISBN 0-85297-502-3

Contents

Introduction   v

Section One – Introduction   **1**
1   The changing nature of the financial services industry   3
2   Managing the strategy process in financial services organisations   29
3   The internal environment   54
4   Managing change in financial services organisations   93
5   Managing customer relations   114

Section Two – Introduction   **143**
6   The history of management   145
7   Elements of management   167
8   Control in organisations   192
9   Self-management   217
10   Managing groups   244
11   Communication   273

Section Three – Introduction   **293**
12   Human resource management   294
13   Human resource plans and their implementation   315
14   Training, development and appraisal   348
15   Motivating employees   371
16   Employment legislations and policies   392

Index   408

Acknowledgements

The authors and The Chartered Institute of Bankers would like to thank Barclays Bank plc for the kind permission to reproduce some of their specimen documents.

They would also wish to thank the following for their helpful comments.

Peter Bamber - CIB Information Services
Colin Bower - National Westminster Bank
Dr David Goacher - Sheffield Hallam University
Simon Hyde - NCM Leeds Office
Ken Moss - Sheffield Chamber of Commerce and Industry
Ian Quinn - Barclays Bank
Peter Regan - NCM Cardiff

Introduction

This book aims to present a managerial approach to the study of financial services organisations. It focuses on the formation of strategy and structure, and examines the process of managing both people and resources within the context of the financial services sector. It is hoped that the book will appeal to students and practitioners alike studying management in this industry.

The book is clearly structured into three sections: the first focuses on the external and internal environment of the firm, structure and strategy; the second on managerial processes and the role of the manager; and the third on the management of people. Within each chapter there are learning objectives, a short introduction, summary and references.

No single book could adequately cover all aspects of such a wide and multidisciplinary field, which includes strategy, management, organisational behaviour and human resource management. Some topics are given only limited coverage within the book. This is because the book attempts to concentrate on topics which are of particular relevance to the problems of organisations and management in the financial services sector, and which are cited in the syllabus for management and organisation in the CIB/UMIST degree.

The book has been written by authors who have specialised knowledge of the industry through work experience, teaching and examining at undergraduate, postgraduate and professsional level in the fields of management and organisations. Chapters 1-7, 10, 12, 15 and 16 have been co-authored by Ann Norton and Liz Croft and Chapters 8, 9, 11, 13 and 14 by Ian Whyte.

Introduction to section one

This first section examines the changing nature of the financial services industry by looking at the following distinct areas:

- the analysis of the external and internal environment;

- the consideration and evaluation of the different paths of action open to the organization;

- the implementation of the chosen strategy.

However these areas cannot in practice be considered isolated and independent stages but rather interdependent steps, and are all part of a total integrative strategic planning process.

Although each chapter deals with a specific aspect of managing financial service organizations, there are certain common themes which run throughout.

The first theme evident in all chapters is the requirement that management must be aware of the business environment, how it is changing and the influences it can exert. Chapters 1, 2 and 4 focus on this in terms of the importance and impact of external environmental influences.

The second theme apparent in this section is that it is not enough for organizations to be aware of these influences, they must be seen to respond to them in a flexible and appropriate way. Chapters 2, 3, 4 and 5 all reflect this theme. Chapter 2 focuses on the development of appropriate strategies. Chapter 3 examines how organizations might structure operations to reflect external influences and provide the most effective and flexible means of production. Chapter 4 examines the issues involved in implementing strategies and managing change. Chapter 5 explores the responses organizations have provided to customers and the strategies adopted.

The final theme is the requirement that organizations evaluate the impact of various strategies and decide upon possible courses of action. In Chapter 1 it is stressed that the relative impact of the different environmental influences should be evaluated, whilst in Chapter 2 the relative effectiveness of the different strategies is considered. The advantages and problems of different internal structures and internal labour markets are also examined in Chapter 3. Chapter 4 considers and evaluates the different approaches to managing change. The appropriate strategy must be chosen by the organization in the light of external and internal factors if the organization is to function effectively. Finally in Chapter 5 the benefits of customer relationship strategies are evaluated.

1 The changing nature of the financial services industry

Objectives

This chapter introduces the external environment in which financial services organizations operate. It sets out a number of frameworks which can be used to analyse the business environment in order to allow an improved understanding of the organization's situation.

The detailed objectives of this chapter are:

- to analyse and evaluate the external influences on business;

- to identify the legal, ethical, political, economic, social, technological and competitive environments within which organizations and management operate;

- to appreciate the legal and political nature of the business environment and the agencies affecting decision making;

- to understand the consequences of economic deregulation and increased competition.

Introduction

Environmental analysis is fundamentally concerned with understanding what is going on in the external environment and how this in turn may impact on the organization and its activities. In order to manage effectively, the external environment must be analysed and understood. Without this, a strategy cannot be developed which will fit the capability of the organization and the environment in which it operates.

This chapter begins by exploring the general environment in which financial services organizations operate and the influence of turbulent as opposed to stable business conditions. It then proceeds to explore specific factors influencing the operation of organizations under the headings of legal, ethical, political, economic, social, technological and competitive.

Why analyse the environment

Over the last twenty years the rapid pace and rate of change within the financial services sector has created the need for accurate assessment of the environmental forces. Failure to anticipate and react to changes in these external circumstances can lead to inappropriate services and products being developed with structures, costs and systems unable to meet customer demand and expectations.

The external environment encompasses many different influences and can be considered to consist of everything outside the organization that may affect performance either directly or indirectly. Although it is easy to assert that the changing environment has a major impact on organizations and the actions they take, this statement simplifies the complex nature of the environment and the difficulty of the task. It is not enough just to list the environmental influences that may have an effect, it is important to adopt a structured approach by evaluating the influences and prioritising them. The key stages to making this evaluation feasible is to try to categorize the factors, to understand the nature of the influences, and to reach conclusions which will provide an insight into the position of the organization and how it should respond.

While some of the environmental factors are beyond the control of the organization, success or failure will depend on how the organization anticipates and reacts to the opportunities and threats that emerge. Thus, undertaking an environmental analysis can:

- enhance self-understanding, that is develop an awareness of the organization's own position *vis-à-vis* the environment both now and in the future;

- help the organization avoid surprises by anticipating major changes in the business environment;

- help with swifter identification of opportunities and threats;
- improve planning and decrease reaction time – a good understanding of the environment should allow an organization to act more effectively once opportunities and threats have been identified.

The nature of the environment

Before exploring specific aspects of the environment it is important to understand the basic conditions surrounding the organization. Lynch (1997) proposes that consideration should be given to the degree of turbulence in the environment. This can be explored in terms of changeability (that is the degree to which the environment is likely to change), and predictability (which is concerned with the degree to which change is predicted). Where turbulence is high the organization will need to structure itself so it is adaptable and flexible, and so can cope with rapidly changing circumstances.

Ansoff (1987) devised a model which identifies the factors which determine the level of turbulence in the environment. The factors he identified include:

- the changeability of the market environment;
- the speed of change;
- technological advancements;
- discrimination by customers;
- pressures from government and interest groups.

Johnson and Scholes (1997) also suggest that an initial assessment of the nature of the environment is needed when clarifying how uncertain the environment is. This can be determined by examining the degree of complexity within the environment and the degree of dynamism. In other words, is the environment simple or complex to understand and is it static or dynamic with rapid change? Johnson and Scholes propose that uncertainty increases when environmental conditions are more complex and dynamic.

At present, the environment for financial services can be characterized as being complex and dynamic and thus highly uncertain. The consequence of this is that organizations operating in the industry are facing constant challenges. Environmental analysis must be an iterative process, not only analysing the current situation but anticipating how the environment might change in the future.

Environmental influences

The next step in understanding the environment is to identify the environmental influences which are likely to affect organizations. This can be revealed by undertaking an audit of the environmental influencers and drivers of change.

The environment can be divided into the macro-environment, which includes developments in the wider business environment, and the micro-environment, which is of more immediate concern and encompasses competitive pressures within the industry and demands from customers and suppliers. Another categorization is that between the near environment, which the organization can influence, and the far environment, which is harder to influence. In reality, organizations will be affected by a number of environmental forces and any analysis must be guided by what is relevant for each particular organization.

The external forces driving change can be usefully categorized under the headings legal, ethical, political, economic, social, technological and competitive environments and provide a useful starting point for analysis. This is sometimes referred to as a Le Pest & Co analysis. Factors within each of these dimensions can affect, either directly or indirectly, the organization's business strategy and performance, hence management policies.

Figure 1.1 provides an illustration of some of the key issues pertaining to each of the dimensions. These issues are particularly relevant to the financial services sector and, although not exhaustive, indicate some of the major factors. The headings can be used as a checklist to assess the relative importance of the different influences in order to identify the *key* drivers of change.

Figure 1.1: Factors in a Le Pest & Co Analysis

Legal

- Employment law
- Monopolies legislation
- Industry regulatory framework
- Consumer legislation

Ethical

- Minority groups
- Social accountability & responsibility

Economic

- Inflation levels
- Consumer income & expenditure
- Interest rate levels
- Investment
- Unemployment
- Exchange rate & currency fluctuations

Technological

- Technological developments
- Speed of change
- Rate of adoption of new technologies
- Cost of technologies

- Green issues

Political

- Government stability
- Political parties at national, European or trading block level
- Relations between government & organization
- Government attitudes towards competition

Social

- Shifts in values
- Changes in lifestyles
- Attitudes to work
- Education & health
- Demographic changes
- Distribution of income

Competition

- Market structure
- Intensity of competitive rivalry
- Market growth
- Stage in life cycle of products & services

Using the Le Pest & Co framework the following section explores some of the key factors which have influenced or might, in the future, influence the strategies of financial services organizations.

Legal influences

The legal influences exerted on the financial services sector can be discussed from a number of different perspectives because of the unique nature and role of the industry:

- legislation governing customer relations and business operations;
- legislation governing the recruitment and employment of individuals;
- legislation regulating the activities of financial institutions.

UK organizations are directly controlled by both the European Community and UK Parliamentary legislation. There are also a series of local regulations and custom and practice which set guidelines and which must be respected.

Legislation governing the employment of individuals will be more fully explored in Chapter 16 when reviewing Human Resource (HR) policies and systems. However, it should be noted at this stage that statutes or codes of conduct govern all aspects of employment from advertising jobs, recruitment, and terms and conditions of employment to severance of employment, grievance and disciplinary procedure, and equal opportunities.

Similarly legislation aimed at regulating the customer relationship and protecting the customer is covered briefly in Chapter 5. While both these key legislative areas will clearly exert influences on the activities of the financial services sector, this part of the chapter will concentrate on legislation that regulates the activities of financial institutions.

Over recent years changes in the regulatory framework have encouraged alterations in the operations and strategy of financial institutions. Some of these changes could be classified as deregulation, affecting opportunities for additional activities. However, reregulation, restricting activities, could also have been said to occur.

Some examples of official deregulation are:

- Building Society Act 1986;

- EU Second Banking Co-ordination Directive 1993.

Examples of official reregulation are:

- Financial Services Act 1986;
- Basle Capital Adequacy Accord 1988;
- EU Capital Adequacy Directive 1996.

There are also examples of unofficial regulation and deregulation, applied by professional bodies, trade associations and cartels. Most of these have tended to be deregulatory in nature, e.g. abandoning building society interest rate cartel (1992) and changes in the membership rules and allowable activities of London Stock Exchange (1986).

Until the 1970s there were clear divisions between the operations of different types of financial institutions. The main reason for this was the regulative restrictions on the scope of activities of particular types of institutions.

However, with the deregulation of the industry, since the beginning of the 1980s, the competitive pressures within the UK financial system have ensured that organizations provide a broader range of financial services. This influence of deregulation is clearly reflected in the strategies adopted by organizations operating in the financial services sector. For example government policy in respect of free competition and market forces generated demand for regulatory change, leading to the removal of monetary control on banks. This has increased competition between banks, building societies and insurance companies and has led to new entrants (e.g. Marks and Spencer, and Virgin) and to partnerships and mergers between organizations (Lloyds-TSB, and Cheltenham and Gloucester Building Society, and Halifax and Leeds Permanent Building Society).

The following section examines in more detail the main acts mentioned above and considers their effects. These acts have been selected because of their influence in altering the nature and composition of the financial services sector.

Deregulation

Building Society Act 1986

This Act formalized and further encouraged the changes that had been happening in this area since the 1980s.

Building societies are mutual institutions owned by members. The bulk of their funds are raised by members via the purchase of shares, and are effectively the same as deposits although deposits can be raised from individuals, other institutions, organizations and businesses. The changes that had been occurring over this period of time were several.

1. Until the 1980s building societies had specialized in raising funds from members and in lending to other members via mortgage loans for homes. The provision of other financial services had been very limited and was mainly related to housing facilities, home insurance, etc. During the early 1980s the building societies broadened the services offered, including very basic banking services in collaboration with banks.

2. The number of individual institutions had diminished substantially since 1900 with the period from 1970 onwards being one of rapid consolidation.

3. There was the establishment of a large and expanding branch network from the 1970s until the late 1980s.

4. A small number of building societies had grown into very large institutions although the majority remained small.

5. There was almost continuous growth in terms of the number of share, deposit and borrower accounts, with particularly rapid growth between 1970 and 1989.

6. The value of the assets controlled by the building societies had grown continually but was changing as a result of restructuring the sector.

This rapid growth could be explained in terms of the high demand for mortgages (encouraged by the tax relief scheme introduced by the government), the ability of the banks to compete with the building societies because of changing monetary controls, and the lower cost/income ratio of building societies due to the simplicity of their operations and smaller branch networks.

In January 1987 the Building Society Act came into force, and was designed to update the legislative framework for building societies. It gave the societies, especially the larger ones, more flexibility to manage their affairs and more opportunities to provide a better quality of service for customers. It was not intended that the societies should fundamentally change their role but be able to offer complementary services to the customer.

In particular the Act:

● allowed societies to take limited powers to make unsecured loans;

● allowed societies to offer a range of financial and banking services hitherto forbidden;

● formalized the position on societies raising wholesale funds;

● provided a mechanism for societies to relinquish their mutual status and become PLCs (convert to banks);

● established the Building Society Commission to supervise their activities.

In February 1988 it was announced that the powers of the building societies should be widened further. Building societies could now take equity stakes in life and general insurance companies, undertake fund management, and establish and manage personal equity plans and unit trusts through associated bodies and stockbroking firms offering a wider range of bank and related services. As a result many organizations extended their range of activities.

The limits set on non-trading lending activities were also raised and these came into effect in summer 1988. There was also further relaxation of the restrictions announced by the Treasury in July 1994. This allowed societies to set up subsidiaries to make loans not secured on land and also allowed 100% ownership of general insurance companies. Rules were also introduced to make societies more accountable to their members. Many building societies have now moved to plc status with approval from members and the Commission, and authorization from the Bank of England.

There is no doubt that the Building Society Act 1986 fundamentally altered the sector, and although further relaxation of the restrictions is proposed it is unlikely to have the same dramatic effect.

EU Second Banking Co-ordination Directive 1993

Prior to the late 1980s the EU had little impact on bank activities in the UK. However, the single European Market Initiative (1992) gave a major boost to the relevance of EU legislation.

The Second Banking Directive was adopted in January 1988. It introduced the concept of a single European bank licence whereby any bank authorized in any European state could operate freely in any other state without further authorization. This authorization gave the home country the responsibility for the overall supervision of the EU-wide operations of banks based in the respective countries. The Directive came into force on the first of January 1993.

For this mutual recognition to be acceptable to the EU member states there was a harmonization of key supervisory standards with requirements for:

● capital bases;

● major shareholders in banks;

● bank's participation in the non-bank sector;

● accounting and internal control mechanisms.

On the first January 1996 the EU Capital Adequacy Directive became effective which set the minimum capital requirements for market risks in the trading books of banks and investment firms. This will be discussed later in the chapter.

Reregulation

As referred to earlier reregulation of the financial services industry has occurred through several other acts.

Financial Services Act 1986

This Act made the Department of Trade and Industry (DTI) responsible for the regulation of investment business in the UK. In turn the Secretary of State for Trade and Industry delegated operating powers to the Securities and Investment Board (SIB).

In 1992 the DTI's responsibility in respect of the Financial Services Act was transferred to the Treasury to consolidate a wide range of financial regulations under one ministry.

The Financial Services Act explicitly made the Bank of England responsible for the regulation of the gilts bullion market and wholesale money markets and foreign exchange. The DTI also has considerable power over the operations of insurance companies and unit trusts although marketing activities rest with the Treasury.

The SIB formulated the rulebook with codes of conduct and regulations for those involved in the investment business. Once this rulebook was approved by the Director General of Fair Trading and the Secretary of State at the DTI the formal powers were transferred to the SIB who then delegated to the Self Regulatory Organizations (SROs) their responsibility. Each SRO produced their own rulebook, which again had to be approved. Although initially there were five new boards there are now only three:

- Securities and Futures Authority;

- Investment Management Regulatory Organization;

- Personal Investment Authority.

Originally the boards were very legalistic and detailed and were criticized because of the increasing costs, but now they have been rationalized and follow certain core rules. The SIB structure also includes recognized professional bodies (chartered accountants and recognized investment exchanges).

In July 1998 the Government published the draft Financial Services and Markets Bill, which proposed giving wide-ranging powers to the Financial Services Authority (FSA). Included in this bill was confirmation of the Labour Government's desire to bring under a single authority the regulation and supervision of virtually all banking and financial services activities and products in the UK. The main exceptions being mortgage loans, bank and banking and building society deposits and general insurance. Even with these products the bill proposes reserve powers to allow the government to bring them under FSA control without further recourse to Parliament.

The FSA will receive all of the powers currently available to the existing regulatory bodies, plus additional powers to deal more effectively with market abuse. This is explored more fully in Chapter 8.

Basle Capital Adequacy Accord 1988

This Accord is also referred to as Bank for International Settlements (BIS) Requirements on the Harmonization of Capital Adequacy Standards.

This strictly applies only to banks with international activities after

1992, but the Bank of England has applied it to all UK registered banks since 1989.

The requirements give specific weightings to the broad classes of assets set according to their risk. The greater the risk the greater the weight attached. Capital is also divided and the bank should hold capital equal in value to 8% of the total risk weighted assets. The regulation was designed to strengthen individual banking systems and to create a more equitable base for regulation between countries.

Currently the FSA applies the regime inherited from the Bank of England and uses the BIS capital adequacy requirements as a minimum level for individual banks. These requirements are largely compatible with the European Union regulations, referred to in the next section.

EU Capital Adequacy Directive 1996

On the first of January 1996 this directive became effective. The directive sets minimum capital requirements for market risks in the trading books of banks and investment firms. The authorities have however agreed that banks, subject to certain conditions, can use their own in-house value at risk models to calculate the relevant capital charges.

In summary, recent legislation has to some extent restructured the financial services sector in the UK. Many building societies have sought conversion to plcs (e.g. Abbey National in July 1989 and Halifax in 1997), with several other applications pending.

The conversion provides building societies with a number of advantages in terms of lifting restrictions on unsecured lending, transactions with the corporate sector and wholesale funding. It also means the organizations can engage in a wider range of financial services, including lending to corporate and overseas customers. They have the ability to raise capital in the open markets and take over and merge with other institutions.

The disadvantages include more rigorous supervision by the Financial Services Authority and pressure from shareholders to increase dividends at the expense of longer term development of business, whilst at the same time incurring increased costs as commercial pressures drive up salaries.

There is also the danger of take-over from other institutions and institutional investors attempting to influence business policy.

At the moment it appears likely that the smaller societies will not convert but rather concentrate on niche markets, by specialising geographically and in terms of services.

Similarly the EU Second Bank Directive 1993 has meant some bank markets in Europe have become far more competitive with opportunities for expansion presenting themselves. UK banks cannot ignore the competitive threat to the domestic market from other EU banking institutions.

Ethical influences

Ethics is concerned with the distinction between what is right and what is wrong, and with the way in which humans arrive at such judgements. Business ethics has to do with the application of ethical principles to business issues.

One of the difficulties in dealing with ethics in any practical sense is that determining what is 'right behaviour' in a way which is universally applicable is not a reasonable objective. This is because what is ethical is dependent, to a great extent, upon the context in which the issue arises. For example, for those of us who have been raised in 'Western society' our thinking about ethics is rooted in two traditions: the ideas on what constitutes moral behaviour as expounded by Greek philosophers from the Stoics to the Epicureans, and the Judaeo/Christian concept of a moral code as an exposition of divine law. Westerners are thus deprived in that they probably lack an understanding of the developments in Western moral philosophy which have taken place during the past thousand years, and are almost certainly ignorant of approaches to ethics which have been developed in other parts of the world.

What any individual regards as ethical will be determined by a combination of genes, upbringing, education and development. That is to say, by the influences to which that individual has been exposed and by the decisions which he or she has had to make. In a more general sense ethical thought depends on the body of tradition which supports it and the problems with which it is asked to grapple. Not many of the world's great philosophers have addressed the question of whether cloning is morally defensible or whether the development of genetically modified vegetables is ethically correct behaviour.

Johns and Connock (1995) outline three broad approaches to ethics:

a) *Social Ethics*: which describe the basic rules for existence within a given society. A 'society' could be a group as large as a nation or one as small as a family unit. It includes a commercial organization in which social ethics will probably manifest themselves as underpinning the organization's vision statement, its codes of conduct and its corporate values. Social ethics, as a foundation for business ethics, suffer from inherent insularity and tend to break down in situations which involve competition between differing groups (such as employees as a group, or 'society', and customers as a group).

b) *Transcendental ethics*: which are founded on the concept that there is a set of absolute standards of right and wrong behaviour which have universal applicability. Whilst this is an appealing concept it is of little practical benefit because it ignores the essentially contextual nature of ethics and the idea that different cultures will operate from different ethical bases.

c) *Tactical ethics*: whereby what may be regarded as ethical standards are observed not because such observation is 'right' but primarily because such observation is in the best interests of the individual, or group of individuals, concerned.

Carroll (1990) suggests that there are eleven different ethical criteria which managers may use as a basis of judgement in relation to business issues:

1. The **categorical imperative** – whereby principles of action will only be adopted if they can be adopted without inconsistency by everyone else, i.e. the principles are transcendental in nature.

2. The **conventionalist ethic** – whereby acting in your own self-interest is permissible provided that the laws imposed by society are not thereby infringed.

3. The **golden rule** – do unto others as you would have them do unto you.

4. The **hedonistic ethic** – if it feels O.K. then it probably is O.K.

5. The **disclosure rule** – whereby the rectitude of any particular

action is judged by reference to one's projected feelings should it happen to be reported on the front page of a tabloid newspaper.

6. The **intuition ethic** – do whatever your emotional as opposed to your rational decision-making machinery tells you to do.

7. The **means to an end ethic** – whereby it is permissible to act if the end result is defensible.

8. The **might equals right ethic** – whereby acting in accordance with the strength of your power base, even though this runs contrary to social convention, is permissible.

9. The **organization ethic** – whereby loyalty to the organization takes precedence over all other considerations.

10. The **professional ethic** – whereby adherence to the code of your profession transcends other considerations.

11. The **utilitarian principle** – whereby the guiding principle is attaining the 'greatest good of the greatest number'.

The fact that there are so many possible approaches to the determination of what in a given set of circumstances would constitute 'right' behaviour only serves to show how difficult the translation of anything which could be regarded as an ethical principle into the world of commercial activity can be. Yet is becoming increasingly important for commercial organizations to grapple with this problem.

Increasingly business is judged by those with whom it comes into contact, be they customers, regulators, suppliers or others, who expect it to exhibit 'right' behaviour even though each group may have a different slant on what constitutes rectitude. As we approach the 21st century we must recognize that in many aspects of human existence there is an increased awareness of the need to consider ethics. Genetic engineering, pollution, environmental friendliness, nuclear waste and space debris are but a few of the topics on which the ethical debate can be said to have grown up in the past ten to twenty years. This impacts upon the business world where the ethical agenda includes not only the above topics but also the relationship between business and its various counterparties including issues of remuneration policy, questions of excess profits, the impact on the community at large of inadequate business systems (such as led to pensions miss-selling), the exploitation of third world labour, etc. For many of these topics there is no long tradition of philosophical thought. This means that organizations are having to determine on the hoof approaches to unexplored issues. So, having an ethical framework in place makes it easier for business to choose the 'right' behaviour, even if that ethical framework is contextual.

There are two basic approaches to developing an ethical organization:

a) compliance-based;

b) integrity-based.

A compliance approach seeks not so much to promote ethical behaviour but to eradicate that which is unethical. It is designed fundamentally to eliminate competitive disadvantage. Compliance approaches have the virtue of being readily manageable. They can also be actively promoted by forces external to the organization either by punishing non-compliant behaviour (as is happening in the UK in respect of the rectification of pension miss-selling) or by encouraging compliant behaviour through tax breaks and sentencing policy (as is happening in the USA).

Integrity strategies aim to integrate into day-to-day activities the organization's guiding values, hopes and patterns of behaviour. Elaborate programmes exist to achieve such ends involving among other things orientation, consultation on the articulation of values and standards, integrated systems and feedback channels for employees.

Such programmes are important, but are likely to fail unless the organization's leadership is prepared to 'walk the talk'. Thus, for example, remuneration systems must be designed to give credit to – or at least not to discourage – ethical behaviour. Similarly the organization should strive to establish a climate of trust whereby mistakes can be openly discussed and worries regarding the ethical credentials of a product or service can be shared internally.

The importance of communication channels which allow employees to voice their concerns cannot be overstated.

Initially, consultation with those who are required to exhibit ethical behaviour seems to be crucial to the success of the programme.

It is interesting to note that the most successful programmes are those established in companies which have workforces drawn from many cultures (multinationals or those which operate in areas of cultural diversity). Such companies, in developing their distinctive cultures, have had to accommodate a range of values and have thus distilled sets of values which can be truly shared by the employees whatever their socio-economic/ethnic background. In this way a 'transcendental ethic' begins to emerge from an amalgam of various 'social ethics'.

An absence of feedback channels sets up a dilemma for the concerned employee who, on the one hand, has doubts about the ethics of some aspect of work but on the other hand has to act ethically. Faced with this situation the employee will either be forced to compromize his ethical principles or blow the whistle on his employer.

Whistle-blowing is a matter of major concern to those interested in the introduction of ethical programmes to organizations. It is the organization's attitude to actual or potential whistle-blowers, depending as it does on the level of mutual trust which exists between employer and employee, which is primarily indicative of the viability of such programmes.

It is interesting to note that in the UK whistle-blowing has now moved from the sphere of ethical influences on corporate behaviour into that of legal influences through the passage of the Public Interest Disclosure Act 1998. This imposes on many commercial organizations operating in the UK an obligation to establish an internal system whereby employees can draw attention to behaviour which is or may be unethical.

Political influences

Inevitably political influences are closely linked with legal ones since the government of the day determines in part the legislation which reflects their own areas of interest and policy. The fundamental changes to the regulatory and supervisory framework were explored in the previous section and have been set against a background of widespread dissatisfaction with the quality of supervision and investor protection in the UK. A number of high profile cases (Maxwell pension scandal, personal pension miss-selling, etc.), combined with confusion about the split responsibilities of the SIB/SRO structure makes an attractive case for a single regulator with statutory powers.

The increasingly complex nature of financial services business at domestic and international levels, together with the trend towards diversified financial institutions, makes the inclusion of all financial service organizations into a single framework logical. The draft Financial

Services and Markets Bill referred to earlier in this chapter will address the issue of a single regulatory authority.

Another area of influence for the government of the day includes international relations between powers. This can have a profound effect on investment and trade. For example, unrest in the Middle East, recession in the Far East, and the recent changes in Hong Kong with the reversion to Chinese rule can variously alter the investment strategy of foreign powers and inhibit growth by multinationals.

The issue of lending to less developed countries and the issue of country risk will continue to be strategic issues.

The policies of governments and local authorities can also influence banking activities, e.g. policies of regeneration in areas of high unemployment.

Other political influences on financial services organizations include government policies on interest rate control, alignment of rules such as the employee's rights under Maastricht, rationalization of the European Stock exchange and the continued policy of privatization.

The relations between employers and representative groups of employees are also affected by the political climate. This issue will be explored in greater detail in Chapter 16.

Economic influences

It is sometimes difficult to distinguish between economic and political influences. Economics can be defined as the complex network of human and other resources which are involved in the production, distribution and consumption of goods and services.

Changing levels of disposable income, rates of inflation, fiscal policy, unemployment and the availability of raw materials affect many markets. The recessions of the early 1990s in the UK resulted in many defaults on loans and a move from borrowing towards saving. Other issues include changes in employment trends, income/wealth distribution and goods ownership.

Over recent years the economic changes in the UK have resulted in the decline of manufacturing industries and the growth of service industries, differences in the distribution of wealth and economic recession with high unemployment. These factors have led to the emergence of giant multinational firms which have a political influence because of the transfer of tax and funds between countries. There is far greater competition for the UK banks from overseas companies and other organizations extending or moving into financial service activities. Also playing a part are quasi-legal entities, e.g. rating agencies, which by ascribing a credit rating to banks could have serious implications for their stock market rating.

By relinquishing control of interest rates to the Bank of England in May 1997 the Labour government tried to introduce distance between the government and the body charged with fixing interest rates. The Bank of England has operational freedom in respect to the implementation of the government's monetary policy. The Bank's monetary policy committee now determines whether or not changes should be made in the short term interest rates in pursuit of the goal of maintaining a target rate of inflation (+/-1%) as specified by the government.

Social influences

Social influences encompass a range of different factors. The trends that can be discerned which will impact on the financial services industry include changing customer needs, demographic trends, household and family structure and the nature of the workforce.

Customers' needs and attitudes

Customer expectations, aspirations, behaviours and attitudes are all changing. The population is generally better educated and their needs more sophisticated. In total the marketplace is more demanding and discerning in terms of their financial services requirements with expectations of high quality, a more personalized service and competitively priced products.

Society's attitudes to business are also changing. Increasingly society is expecting greater social responsibility from organizations with regard to ethical conduct towards employees, customers and ethical protection.

Demographic

The changing demographic structure in the UK, and in most other industrialized countries, can be characterized by falling birth rates and longer life expectancy, with an increasing average age of the population. A consequence of this will be that the number of young people entering the workforce will decline whilst at the same time there will be an increase in the proportion of people over retirement age. Changes to the government welfare system mean that individuals are now having to accept increasing responsibility for their financial well being in the future in terms of provision of health care and retirement.

These demographic changes will all have significant implications for financial services organizations in terms of their recruitment strategies for staff as well as in the design of the products and services they deliver.

Household and family structure

A household can be defined as the basic social unit. There have been substantial changes in the socio-economic profile of the family unit in the UK and the number and structure of households. An increasing divorce rate has led to the decline of the traditional family unit (i.e. working husband, wife and dependent children) and a growth in single parent households.

Another trend which has impacted on the structure of households has been a move toward later marriage and delayed child bearing with an increase in the economic activity of women. This has brought greater financial independence for women and an increase in single person households. In addition there has been an increase in the number of household with joint incomes.

Nature of the workforce

There have been major changes in the structure of UK industry with a decline in the manufacturing base and a massive growth in the services sector. This has led to a decline in blue collar work, whilst at the same time there has been an increase in white collar, supervisory and management jobs.

The restructuring of UK industry has seen a corresponding change in work patterns with an increase in women working and a growth in part-time and temporary work. These changes have contributed to the development of a more casual and flexible workforce (this theme will be explored in greater depth in Chapter 3).

All the above social factors have implications for the strategies of financial services organizations in terms of the customer base they serve, the product range they offer, their delivery channels and the quality of service. In addition, organizations will have to explore alternative recruitment markets and look at the induction, career development, performance and reward systems to ensure that they attract and then retain the best employees.

Technological influences

Developments in technology over the last two decades have had far reaching implications for financial services organizations in terms of the nature of their work, the structure of the organization and the way they design and deliver their products and services to customers. The miniaturization of technological solutions, the falling cost of computer power, and the growth of computer literacy and software applications have all contributed to the transformation of the way in which work is undertaken in the financial services sector.

These developments in information technology have signalled changes in:

- processing and money transmission activities;
- the nature of work;
- product design and delivery channels.

Changes in processing and money transmission

Technology has had a major impact on one of the core banking activities: the money transmission and payments business. Systems have been developed which have speeded up the transfer of money from one place to another. Examples of such systems include:

- CHAPS (Clearing House Automated Payment System);
- BACS (Bankers Automated Clearing Systems);
- SWIFT (Society for World Wide InterBank Financial Telecommunications).

In addition IT solutions have changed the way consumers pay for goods with an increased reliance on credit and debit card payments, and more recently, the introduction of alternative methods such as smart cards. The decrease in 'physical' payment methods such as cash and cheques in favour of electronic methods presents a challenge to the traditional middleman role of the banks. In addition, the emergence of PC banking and banking on the Internet will further transform the industry.

Changes in the nature of work

Advancements in technology have fundamentally changed the nature of work and employment patterns as new jobs are created and others become obsolete. Technology has reduced the amount of basic administrative and routine tasks, particularly in the area of processing. The introduction of image scanning may eventually lead to a paperless environment. Many organizations are now moving towards centralized processing centres, often 'greenfield' sites, employing 'factory' type workers who do not necessarily have or need any knowledge of the financial services sector.

Technological changes have also encouraged the de-layering of the organizational hierarchy with the reduction in management layers, the skills required and working methods. Development in credit scoring and risk analysis technology systems have led to a de-skilling of the traditional lending role. Unskilled staff supported by expert systems are now able to sanction loans to the personal and small business markets.

There has been a revolution in communication methods as a result of technological advancements which have implications for work practices. E-mail, intranet and indeed the Internet are all examples of modern communication methods.

Changes in delivery and product design

Technology has facilitated the provision of new products and services and delivery channels. As automation has allowed for traditional back-office branch work to be undertaken at centralized processing and service centres, many organizations have invested in re-designing branches to be more customer-orientated.

Advancements in technologies have impacted more fundamentally on the customer interface. The emergence of 'self service banking' means that there is no need to go to the traditional outlet. Remote sites can be found at more convenient locations such as in supermarkets, shopping malls and train stations. Telephone banking, PC banking and smart card technology have all contributed to the change in the way financial services transactions are enacted. The advent of digital TV will further revolutionize the delivery of financial services.

Technological developments have also impacted on the way in which markets can be identified. Sophisticated database systems provide organizations with tools to analyse customer information and to provide a better understanding of the marketplace. This enables them to more accurately predict consumer needs and to identify cross-selling opportunities.

The influences of technological advancements have clearly had an impact on organization's business strategies. They have enabled organizations to seek greater operating efficiencies, productivity and service quality in their quest to sustain profitability. Advancements in technology may also provide more reliable security to cut down on fraud and improve risk assessment utilising expert modelling techniques. There are of course risks associated with this heavy reliance on technology support. For example at the mechanical level there is the risk of systems going down, along with the dangers of computer viruses and possible sabotage by disgruntled staff or customers.

Competitive influences

Understanding the nature of the competitive environment at the present time, and anticipating what are likely to be the major competitive forces in the future, is crucial in the design of the organization's strategies. Increased competition has become a dominant feature for those operating in the financial services sector. As mentioned earlier deregulation has resulted in intense rivalry at national, international and global levels, with sources of competition coming from:

- existing players who provide similar services. Banks, building societies and insurance companies are now all offering very similar product ranges and are competing in the same markets;

- niche players who offer a more restricted range of products, but who are strong competitors in their specialist field;

- non-financial services organizations who have diversified into the financial services arena (notably supermarkets such as Tesco and Sainsbury's, and other well established names such as Marks and Spencer, Virgin, General Motors, the AA and SAGA);

- foreign competition.

A well-established technique for analysing and understanding the nature of the competitive environment is Porter's five forces model (Porter 1980). This analytical framework proposes that there are five basic competitive forces which influence the state and structure of competition in an industry, and which will collectively determine the long run return on capital and the profit potential of the industry as a whole. These five competitive forces are:

1. The threat of new entrants to the industry;

2. The threat of substitute products or services;

3. The bargaining power of customers;

4. The bargaining power of suppliers;

5. The rivalry amongst current competitors in the industry.

The threat of new entrants is concerned with assessing the extent to which it is easy or difficult for other organizations to enter the industry. This in turn will depend on the extent to which there are high barriers to entry. Barriers to entry could include economies of scale, differentiated products, capital requirements (e.g. major investment in technology), switching cost (i.e. the cost and inconvenience which customers would experience by changing supplier), access to distribution channels (e.g. branch networks), government policy and legislation, and other factors such as access to key skills/experience and competencies.

New entrants bring extra capacity to the marketplace and therefore pose a threat to established players. This could lead to them losing market share with a consequent loss of economies of scale.

Within the financial services sector deregulation and consumer acceptance of technology-based delivery channel developments have significantly reduced barriers to entry. Non-bank retailers, such as Marks and Spencer and Sainsbury's, view the financial services sector as an attractive business to enter allowing them to capitalize on their strong brand image and exploit their large customer data bases.

Traditional providers must appreciate that these new players bring different marketing skills and are playing by different rules. They must therefore be willing to adapt their strategies if they are going to survive.

The threat from substitute products and services will be determined by the ease with which a product or service can be substituted. Within the financial services sector this is a major threat since products can be easily copied. Many financial services products essentially satisfy the same customer needs and customers can easily move to alternatives that offer better rates of interest for loans and savings products, or which have cheaper premiums in the case of some general insurance products.

Readily available substitutes pose a threat because they limit the ability of an organization to charge high prices for its products/services.

The bargaining power of customers is concerned with the extent to which customers are able to exert power on organizations to reduce prices or improve/change products and thus force down the profitability of the industry.

The need to focus on how to better meet customer needs and improve customer retention have both been central themes of most financial services organizations' strategies. Legislation has increased customer rights whilst at the same time competition has increased the choice of both products and suppliers. Customers have greater access to information on competitor offerings and, as switching between organizations becomes easier, the customers' traditional inertia will decline. All these factors have led to a rise in consumerism with customers in a strong position to exert power expecting better quality products and service at lower prices. This theme will be explored in Chapter 5.

The bargaining power of suppliers is a mirror image of the bargaining power of customers. Identification of suppliers involves not only the supply of raw material but also the resources needed to provide the service. The supply chain for financial services is complex but involves getting the right staff, skills and technology. In addition a further complexity is that along with the money markets, customers could also be classed as suppliers of raw material. Suppliers can influence profitability by exerting pressure for higher prices of the raw materials or by reducing the quality of services they supply.

The intensity of competitive rivalry is concerned with examining the level of direct rivalry and anticipating whether this is likely to increase or decrease. The intensity of competitive rivalry will affect the profitability of the industry as a whole.

Competitive rivalry within the financial services sector is intense, and is likely to increase as organizations fight for their share of the marketplace and as more new entrants from the telecommunications and computer technology industries join the marketplace. This is likely to result in a continued squeeze on profit margins and a continued search for cost reductions and sources of new revenue.

Summary

This first chapter has explored the environment in which financial services organizations operate. The rapidly changing nature of the environment has meant that firms need to be flexible and adaptable, especially in view of the influences which are exerted in the areas of legal, economic, political, social, technological and competitor factors. The next chapter goes on to explore the importance of understanding these factors when determining business strategy.

References

Ansoff H (1987) *Corporate Strategy*, Penguin
Carroll (1990)
Johns T and Cannock S (1995) *Ethical Leadership*, Institute of Personnel and Development
Johnson J & Scholes K (1997) *Exploring Corporate Strategy*, 4th ed. Prentice Hall
Lynch R (1997) *Corporate Strategy*, Pitman Publishing
Porter M E (1980) *Competitive Strategy, Techniques for Analysing Industries and Competitors*, Free Press

2 Managing the strategy process in financial services organizations

Objectives

Having explored the influences the external environment can exert on financial services organizations in the previous chapter, this chapter goes on to examine the process of how organizations can formulate strategies to respond to those pressures. It seeks to provide an introduction to the strategic management process and to show how an understanding of the process can help financial services organizations in the development and implementation of appropriate strategies for business growth and survival.

The overriding aims of this chapter are to:

- provide an understanding of the concept of strategy and corporate goals;
- examine the need for strategic management and planning;
- identify the different stages of the strategic management process;
- investigate alternative approaches to strategic management;
- consider the different levels of strategy and planning;
- explore stakeholder influences on strategy development.

Introduction

The dynamic, unpredictable and complex environment in which financial services organizations operate has already been discussed in Chapter 1. This climate makes it essential that financial services organizations plan for the future.

The strategic management process is concerned with mapping out the organization's future direction by devising and implementing strategies which will enhance the competitiveness of the organization, and which will thus deliver long-term added value. Whilst there are many approaches to strategic management, they all have the aim of establishing a business purpose and guiding managers on how to implement strategies to achieve organizational goals.

The corporate strategy of an organization can be viewed as the linking process between the management of the internal resources and the external environment. The strategies adopted will determine the internal character of the organization and how it relates to the outside world, the range of its products, the markets in which it operates and its intentions for the future.

How strategy is formulated and the quality of the strategies developed are critical to successful implementation, and ultimately determine the future success of the organization.

The concept of strategy

Strategy has many different interpretations and dimensions. Whilst there is no universally accepted definition, Johnson and Scholes (1997) offer the following, "strategy is the direction and scope of an organization over the long term: ideally, which matches its resources to its changing environment, and in particular its markets, customers or clients so as to meet shareholder expectations".

Andrews (1971) proposes strategy to be "the pattern of major objectives, purposes or goals and essential plans for achieving those goals, stated in such a way as to define which business the company is in or is to be in and the kind of company it is or is to be".

So strategy is essentially concerned with the scope of the organization's activities and the actions required to achieve its objectives.

Mintzberg (1991) argues that strategy has been used in many different ways and his contribution is to suggest that it can be characterized by five Ps:

- Strategy as a Plan;
- Strategy as a Ploy;

- Strategy as a Pattern;
- Strategy as a Position;
- Strategy as a Perspective.

Strategy as a *plan* is a consciously intended course of action or a guideline to deal with a situation. It is made in advance and it is developed for a specific purpose. As a *ploy*, strategy can be likened to a manoeuvre in a competitive game. Strategy can also be seen as a *pattern*. This means a realization of actions and not merely the intention to pursue actions. As a *position*, strategy is concerned with the place in the market and defines the organization's position in the marketplace relative to the competition. Finally, as a *perspective*, strategy is concerned with how the company sees itself and as such can refer to the organizational culture. For example, some organizations will see themselves as being strongly finance-orientated, others may view themselves as being at the leading edge of technology, alternatively some may focus on being customer orientated.

Whatever interpretation is put on strategy, the strategic actions of an organization will have widespread long-term consequences in terms of its position in the marketplace, its relationship with its different stakeholders and of course its business performance. A clear strategy should ensure that the organization's efforts are channelled in the same direction.

The need for strategic management and planning

Although the terms strategic management and planning are often used interchangeably, both imply a considered and analytical approach to making decisions within an organization and are concerned with the deliberate and systematic determination of what an organization needs to do in order to achieve its goals and objectives. This involves analysing the environment, the internal resources, the alternative options and managing the implementation of the strategies chosen.

Strategic management and planning are important activities because they are concerned with the critical issues that will fundamentally impact on the future survival of the organization. Strategic management provides specific guidelines for management actions in terms of identifying the resources needed and the efficient allocation of these resources to achieve organizational goals and objectives. Without planning an organization may find itself becoming out of touch with its environment, leaving itself vulnerable to competitor activity.

A formal system of strategic management will help the organization cope with uncertainty and managing risk by:

- anticipating the opportunities and threats presented by the external environment;

- providing a sense of purpose for the employees of the organization and an understanding of their own roles and responsibilities.;

- drawing attention to the need to keep changing and adapting;

- encouraging co-operation and co-ordination of efforts at all levels;

- evaluating the implications of future decisions;

- helping to improve the quality of decision-making;

- improving the consistency of actions across the organization.

Strategic planning can be characterized by its long-term nature. It looks not only at what is happening now but what the organization may want to be in the future and must be viewed as a continuous activity. The world does not stop changing whilst plans are drawn up and implemented. Whilst it is becoming increasingly difficult to predict and forecast the future with any certainty, planning should help the organization adapt to environmental changes and minimize crisis. The value of the planning activity lies in the organization being in a position to control, as far as it is feasible, its own future. This is because it will be consistently in touch with the changing environment.

The process of strategic planning can be considered by way of the analogy of a journey. Before embarking on a journey you need to know first where you are now and where you want to get to (i.e. goals and objectives). This will allow you to consider the alternative routes you could take and to decide how are you going to get there (i.e. alternative strategies and actions). Finally, having set out on the journey you need to check progress. You need to know where you are going in order to determine when you have arrived. These stages are all key stages in the strategic management process:

- where are we now?
- where do we want to be?
- how are we going get there?
- have we arrived?

Whilst the process of strategic management has been presented as a set of clear steps and activities, it is, in reality, a far more complex process because of the changing nature of the environment. The unpredictability of environmental forces means there can be no simple recipe for success for any one organization.

The process of strategic management

The traditional approach to strategic management is often termed the formal or rational approach, and can be described as a series of logical steps including:

- the determination of an organization's mission;
- the setting of goals and objectives;
- the formulation of specific strategies;
- the commitment of resources.

This suggests that a continuous analysis of the environment and the organization's resources is needed to plan for the future development and survival of the business. The rational model involves a number of interrelated stages that can be viewed as the building blocks of the strategic management process. The four core elements of the process are:

- strategic analysis;
- strategic choice;
- strategy implementation;
- review, evaluation and control.

All of these elements comprise a number of different stages as illustrated in Figure 2.1.

Figure 2.1: The Process of Strategic Management

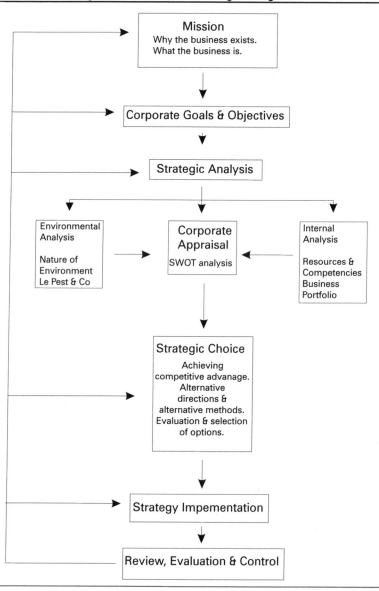

Each of these stages will now be examined.

Strategic analysis

Strategic analysis is designed to give a better understanding of the strategic position of the organization relative to the competition, by forming a view of the key influences which may impact on the present and future strategies. It involves an analysis of the organization's mission and objectives as well as an examination of the external environment and internal resources.

The process will start with an analysis of the organization's present situation. The first step is to determine the purpose of the organization. This is concerned with understanding and determining why the organization exists and what business it is in. Any business must have a clear 'raison d'être'. Without a clear knowledge of its purpose the business will drift, falter and may eventually fail.

Traditionally the banks would probably have identified 'banking' as their business domain. However this is now perhaps too restrictive a definition given the merging of boundaries of financial services suppliers and the emergence of new entrants.

The parameters of 'what business are we in' is often summarized in a mission statement which should encapsulate the long term vision of what the organization wants to be and what it wants to achieve. Bowman and Asch (1987) suggests it should include reference to:

- how the business will gain and sustain competitive advantage;

- how competitive advantage will be translated into superior profitability;

- how success will be measured.

"To be the UK's leading provider of personal financial services" and " To be the first choice of financial services for customers, shareholders and staff" are examples of financial services organizations mission statements.

The sentiments of the mission must then be translated into goals and objectives. Whilst there is no 'correct' list of goals and objectives they must relate back to the mission. Ultimately they are the means by which the performance of the organization is judged.

Goals and objectives are concerned with the outcomes that the organization seeks to achieve. They are usually specified in terms of business achievements, and are often specific statements which can be quantified and measured. For example, profit targets, return on investment (ROI), return on capital employed (ROCE), growth rate targets, size of market share, sales volume, etc. However, some goals and objectives may not lend themselves to quantifiable measures and are more qualitative in nature, for example, creating a favourable image in order to attract funds.

Goals and objectives are important because they provide:

- a basis for strategy formulation;

- a standard of performance;

- guidelines for decision-making and providing justification for action taken;

- some indications as to the priorities for the organization.

Having established where the organization is, it must then determine where it wants to go in the future. This will be influenced by the nature of the external environment and the organization's own distinctive competencies.

(i)   Analysis of the external environment

An examination of the external environment is a critical part of the strategic analysis stage. When setting out to determine its future strategies an organization must have a clear understanding of the environment it operates in and the competition it faces. The ultimate purpose is to gain an understanding of the position of the organization since the strategy of an organization should fit its environment by taking advantage of opportunities and countering threats.

The analysis requires an external appraisal to be undertaken by scanning the business environment for factors relevant to the organization's current and future activities. An analysis of environmental factors should explore the legal, ethical, political social, technological and competitive influences, perhaps using the Le Pest & Co and Porter's five forces frameworks described in Chapter 1.

(ii) Internal analysis

Internal analysis is required in order to determine the possible future strategic options by appraising the organization's internal resources and capabilities, and by identifying its strengths and weaknesses. The process is concerned with identifying the 'distinctive competencies' of the organization. This involves the identification of those things which the organization is particularly good at in comparison to its competitors, and which enable the organization to survive and flourish against its competition (Lynch 1997).

The analysis will involve undertaking a resource audit to evaluate the resources the organization has available and how it utilizes those resources, for example an appraisal of financial resources, human skills, physical assets, technologies, etc.

The internal analysis should also consider cultural issues and the structure of the organization. Additionally it may involve benchmarking exercises in terms of financial measures of performance, ranking against the competition, and market shares for different product/ service areas.

The outcome of the analysis should assist in providing an understanding of the organization's core competencies and strategic capability relative to the competition. It should help in identifying what the organization is particularly good at and which of its activities are difficult to copy. This can give it an advantage over its competitors.

Having analysed the internal resources and competencies, it is also important to examine the strategic capability in terms of the balance of different business units and product areas. One method which can be used for this analysis is the Boston Consulting Group (BCG) growth share matrix which is identified in Figure 2.2.

According to this matrix two factors define a business or product's strategic stance in the marketplace:

- the relative market share compared to their competitors;

- market growth, which is concerned with the rate of growth of the product category in the market as a whole.

This leads to four categories:

The **question mark**, sometimes referred to as problem child, which has a small market share but is in a high growth market. A question mark business requires high investment and resource allocation in the hope that the business or product is viable and will become a star in the future.

A **star** is a business unit with a high market share in a high growth market and by implication has the potential for

Figure 2.2:   The Boston Consulting Group Growth/Share Matrix

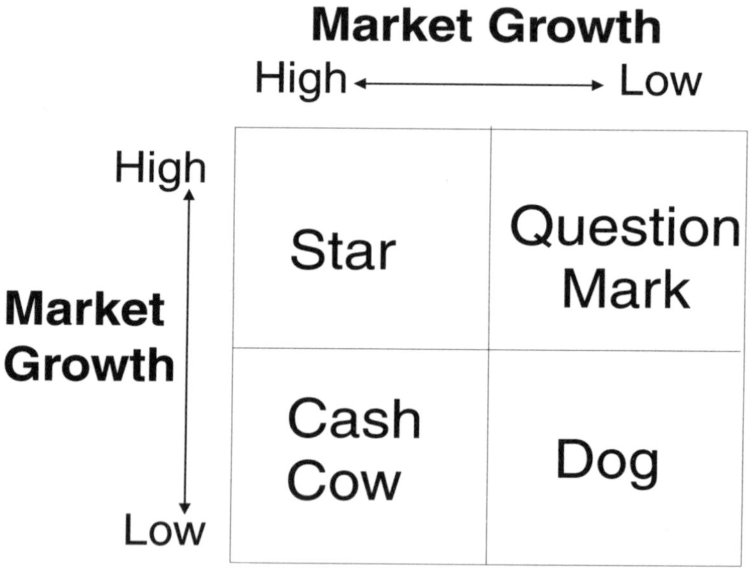

Market Growth
High ←——————→ Low

	Market Growth High ←——→ Low	
High ↑ **Market Growth** ↓ **Low**	Star	Question Mark
	Cash Cow	Dog

generating significant earnings both now and in the future.

The **cash cow** has a high market share but is in comparatively mature and slower growing markets. There is less need for heavy investment and therefore the cash cow should make a substantial contribution to overall profitability.

A **dog** can be characterized by low market shares and low growth rates in a static market and may be a drain on resources leading to cost disadvantages.

Portfolio analysis provides a picture of the balance on an organization's strategic capability. It can be used within the strategic planning process to determine the relative position of business units and inform decisions relating to resource allocation. An organization should be seeking to maintain a balanced and strong portfolio, ensuring that there are enough cash generating products/business to match those requiring investment.

(iii) Corporate appraisal

Having undertaken an analysis of the trends and possible external and internal environmental developments that may be of strategic significance now or in the future, the next step is to bring together the results. This step of the process is often referred to as corporate appraisal. A useful framework to assess the various factors is SWOT analysis, which is essentially an inventory of key external environmental opportunities and threats and strategically important internal strengths and weaknesses. The analysis should not simply be a list of the factors but requires some evaluation of the relative importance of the factors. This is often presented as a matrix of strengths, weaknesses, opportunities and threats:

- a strength is a particular skill or distinctive competence which the organization possesses and which gives it an advantage over competitors;

- a weakness is something which may hinder the organization in achieving its strategic aims, such as a lack of resources, expertise or skills;

- an opportunity is something happening in the environment which is favourable to the organization and which may be exploited to obtain benefits;

- a threat is something happening in the organization's environment which is unfavourable to the organization and which must be overcome or circumvented.

Adapting to the environment means responding to environmental opportunities while coping with threats. A strength is potentially of strategic importance because it can be used either to take advantage of an opportunity or as protection against a threat. The SWOT analysis is useful in helping to establish the organization's position prior to the preparation of a long-term strategic plan.

Having determined the organization's present situation in conjunction with its objectives (i.e. where are we now and where would we like to be), specific strategies must be developed to close the 'gap'. This is often referred to as 'the planning gap' and represents what needs to be done, in other words the corporate strategy.

Strategic choice

Strategic choice is the process by which the vast range of alternative strategic options which are available to an organization are identified and evaluated in order to allow a selection to be made. It involves the generation of strategic options in order to bridge the planning gap, and is important since it is concerned with how an organization develops.

The strategic choice process involves making decisions on:

- what basis should the organization compete and on what basis can it achieve competitive advantage?

- what are the alternative directions available and which products/markets should the organization enter or leave?

- what alternative methods are available to achieve the chosen direction?

Achieving competitive advantage

When developing a corporate strategy the organization must decide upon which basis it is going to compete in its markets. This involves decisions on whether to compete across the entire market or only in certain market segments. This can be referred to as the competitive scope. A further consideration concerns how to gain competitive advantage. Competitive advantage is anything that gives one organization the edge over its rivals which can be sustained over time. The competitive advantage allows an organization to add more value than its competitors in the same market.

Sources of competitive advantage can be found in every aspect of the way an organization competes, for example, prices, products, service levels, low cost production, etc. However, for the competitive advantage to be sustainable, organizations must seek to identify the activities which competitors cannot easily copy and imitate. In the financial services sector many products and services are easily copied, so organizations must seek other ways to achieve competitive advantage and add value.

Value has to be defined by the customer because ultimately value is judged by customers in terms of the amount they are willing to pay for the product/service. Therefore, organizations must assess why customers choose to purchase from one organization rather than another and what constitutes value in their terms. The answer to this question can be broadly categorized into two reasons:

1. The price of the product/service is lower.

2. The product service is perceived to provide better added value.

These general terms represent the generic strategy options for achieving competitive advantage, An organization can, for example, compete on price-based strategies by focusing on price sensitive market segments and portraying a cheap and cheerful image. Alternatively, they can choose to pursue a differentiation strategy which seeks to be unique on dimensions valued by buyers and which is also different from competitors, for example in terms of product design, performance, or quality of service.

Porter (1985) believes there are three generic strategies for achieving competitive advantage:

1. *Cost leadership*: which means being the lowest cost producer in the industry as a whole. By being the lowest cost producer the organization can compete on price with others in the industry by earning higher unit profits.

2. *Differentiation*: which is the exploitation of a product or service that the industry as a whole believes to be unique and which could be based on product design, branding/image, product performance, and service levels.

3. *Focus*: which involves concentrating activities on one or more particular segments or niches, and which could involve either cost focus or differentiation/focus.

Alternative strategic directions

Having looked at the basis for achieving competitive advantage, the second element is to consider the alternative directions for strategic development.

Ansoff (1988) provides a useful framework for setting out the alternative directions. The matrix illustrated in Figure 2.3 suggests that the strategy decisions are based on the fact that an organization can choose to develop by utilising existing products or new products, and by operating in existing or new markets. This produces a number of possible strategy options.

Figure 2.3: Growth Vector Matrix

Product

	Present	New
Present	Strategies based on existing markets and products (e.g. market penetration for growth; or consolidation to maintain position; or withdrawal)	Strategies based on launching new/or improved products into existing markets (e.g. product development)
New	Strategies based on finding new markets for existing products (e.g. market development)	Strategies based on launching new products in new markets (e.g. related or unrelated diversification)

Market

Market penetration is where the organization seeks to maintain or increase its share of existing markets with existing products and is the least risky option. This could involve developing explicit strategies to attract customers from the competition. This has happened in a number of financial service product areas, for example, savings, insurance and mortgages through competitive pricing and promotional activities. Alternatively, the organization may try to increase the usage of products by existing customers through the introduction of incentive schemes such as loyalty bonuses. This strategy has been pursued by a number of credit card issuers, such as Barclaycard Profile points and Midland Choice points for their MasterCard and Visa cardholders.

Product development requires the organization to develop new products or to make product enhancements which are offered to its existing markets. Development of products in the mortgage market is a good illustration of this growth strategy. Traditional mortgage products have been re-designed and supplemented with variants, for example, flexible repayments, lower starting interest rates, etc.

Within the financial services sector much of the product development activities are aimed at enhancing and modifying products.

Market development entails expanding into new markets with existing products and would be appropriate where skills and competencies cannot easily be switched to new products. This could involve either identifying new markets geographically or new market segments.

At a local level market development may involve the creation of new distribution channels. This strategy is being pursued by a number of the major banks and building societies through direct channels such as telephone, PC, and Internet and Digital TV banking.

The increasingly global marketplace will also provide opportunities for market development for financial services product areas. HSBC, who are the owners of Midland Bank, are already a global player. Some UK banks and building societies have extended their mortgage and insurance business into other European countries. However, globalization may also present a threat as foreign competition enters the UK marketplace.

Diversification is the most risky of the growth strategies since it involves the organization moving into areas where it has no experience, with new products and new markets. There are two broad classifications of diversification: *related diversification* and *unrelated diversification.*

Related diversification involves development beyond the present product market but still within the main confines of the industry, and builds on the assets and capabilities which the organization has already developed. This strategy has been a feature of many financial service organizations, who have diversified beyond their traditional product and market areas. For example, the clearing banks moving into mortgage and insurance products and markets and the building societies introducing money transmission services.

Unrelated diversification is where the organization moves into products/ markets which are beyond the present industry and which may not have any close relation to the current activities of the organization. This method is one pursued by the conglomerates such as Hanson but can also be seen in the financial services arena with non-traditional suppliers, such as Virgin, entering the marketplace. It could be argued that the supermarkets, Marks and Spencer, Boots and some car manufacturers such as General Motors, are also pursuing this strategy as they move into the financial services sector.

In addition to the above strategies an organization may decide to do nothing, or consolidate or withdraw from a product market completely. To do nothing means that the organization continues to follow in broad terms existing strategies while events around it change. Consolidation is different from doing nothing in that whilst the range of products and markets remain constant, a positive approach which adapts to the changing circumstances is being taken in order to maintain market position. Withdrawal implies that the organization withdraws from a product/market combination and may be appropriate if, by selling out from one activity, funds are released to develop another area. This may be the only viable option if the market is declining rapidly.

Alternative methods

Not only must the organization consider on what basis to compete and the direction of strategic development, it must also decide how it is going to pursue its strategic direction (i.e. what method is most appropriate). The organization could pursue:

- internal development;
- takeovers/acquisition or merger;
- strategic alliances/joint ventures.

Internal development

Internal development is where the organization uses its own internal resources to pursue the chosen strategy and may involve building up a new business from scratch and developing it. This is sometimes called organic growth and is appropriate where the organization does not need resources from outside. Consequently many product developments and market developments are made through internal development. The launch of First Direct by Midland Bank in 1989 is an example of a strategy achieved through internal development.

Takeovers/Acquisitions and mergers

An alternative would be to acquire resources by taking over or merging with another organization in order to acquire knowledge of a particular product area. This might be attempted to obtain a new product range or market presence or as a means of eliminating competition.

A takeover or acquisition involves the purchase of a controlling interest in another company. On the other hand, a merger involves the joining of two separate organizations to form a single organization. Both acquisitions and mergers have been prevalent in the financial services sector. This can be illustrated by the activities of Halifax plc who merged with Leeds Permanent Building Society and has acquired interests in Clerical and Medical.

Strategic alliances

Another key route for growth involves joint ventures and alliances. This route often has the aim of increasing exposure to potential customers or gaining access to technology. There are a variety of arrangements for strategic alliances, some of which are very formalized and some are much looser arrangements. Joint ventures involve the formation of a company whose shares are owned jointly by the parent companies. Alliances are weaker than contractual agreements between different organizations who work together.

Joint ventures and strategic alliances have become increasingly popular in the financial services sector as organizations struggle to cope with environmental pressures from their internal resources alone. The move by supermarkets into the financial services industry has been facilitated by strategic alliances with the banks. For example, Tesco Personal Finance is a joint venture between Tesco and the Royal Bank of Scotland, Sainsbury's Bank is jointly owned by Sainsbury's and the Bank of Scotland, while Abbey National has opened branches in Safeway stores.

Evaluation and selection of strategic options

Having identified the alternative strategic options, these must then be evaluated and a selection made. Johnson & Scholes (1997) categorize the criteria which can be used to evaluate alternative strategies into three broad categories: *suitability*, *acceptability* and *feasibility*.

Suitability is concerned with an assessment of whether the strategy fits the situation of the firm in terms of its resources and environment. This can be done against a number of criteria, for example:

- does it increase the organization's strengths?
- does it rectify existing weaknesses?
- is it suitable for the organization's existing position, and is it consistent with other activities? In other words, does it have strategic fit?

The *suitability* of a strategy must also be evaluated in the context of the political and cultural factors operating in the organization.

Acceptability of a strategy relates to peoples' expectations of it. Therefore, it is concerned with assessing whether the strategy is acceptable to the organization's most powerful stakeholders. Evaluating *acceptability* involves assessing the financial considerations in terms of how far the strategy will meet the objectives for return on investment, profits and growth, and the level of risk involved in pursuing the strategy. The key issue here is that different stakeholders will have different expectations from any particular strategy. This issue will be explored further later in the chapter.

Feasibility refers to the extent to which the strategy can be implemented and is achievable in practice. It is concerned with the resourcing implications and capabilities of the organization. For example, are the financial, technical and other resources available and are there no obvious barriers to its implementation?

Strategic implementation

Once the strategic route has been chosen the implementation of the strategy must be planned. In other words, the strategy which determines what must be done in broad terms must be translated into more specific actions and tactics. This includes:

- the detailed specification on how the activities will be carried out and by whom;
- the targets which need to be achieved;
- resource planning (finance, human resources, physical resource) involving the allocation of resources to the key tasks.

The implementation of the strategy may require strategic change in terms of organization redesign and re-structuring and day-to-day routines. This theme will be explored in Chapter 4.

Review, evaluation and control

The purpose of this stage is to verify the extent to which the implemented strategies are fulfilling the intended mission of the organization. According to Hofer and Schendel (1978) evaluation of a strategy can focus on:

- whether the objectives are internally consistent with other objectives;

- the quality of analysis and organizational processes to develop the strategy;

- assessing the content of the strategy;

- assessing the ability of the organization to implement the strategy;

- evaluating the performance results generated by the strategy.

The organization must determine appropriate standards for measurement. The control process will be oriented to measuring performance against the standards, and taking action where there are deviations.

An effective strategic management process which follows the various stages outlined above should result in the organization having a clear view of its purpose, its goals and objectives and its strategic approach.

Different approaches to the strategic management process

The previous section outlined the formal or rational approach to strategic management. However, there are alternative views on how strategies develop and are formulated. An organization may take different approaches depending on factors such as the nature of the organization, its culture, its management style and the environment in which it operates. Some organizations may adopt a more informal or unplanned approach. This perspective suggests that strategy 'emerges' and develops over time in an incremental and continuous way. The stance here is that managers cannot and do not operate in a rational and logical manner, and that the development of corporate strategy is far more complex than the rational approach suggests. People, politics and culture all need to be taken into account in the process.

The following statement by Mintzberg (1994) captures the essential differences between the rational (planned) and emergent (unplanned) approach:

> *The popular view sees the strategist as a planner or as a visionary; someone sitting on a pedestal dictating brilliant strategies for everyone else to implement. Whilst recognising the importance of thinking ahead and especially of the need for creative vision in this pedantic world, I would wish to propose an additional view of the strategist – as a pattern recognizer, a learner if you will – who manages a process in which strategies (and visions) can emerge as well as being deliberately conceived.*

Mintzberg argues that emergent strategies are often successful and may be more appropriate than intended strategies. Ohmae (1982) also suggests that the strategic management process should not be a mechanical process as indicated by the rational approach. He states that "phenomena and events in the real word do not always follow a linear model, hence the most reliable means of dissecting a situation into its constituent parts and reassembling them into the desired pattern is not a step by step methodology such as systems analysis. Rather it is the ultimate non-linear tool the human brain."

Thus, it should be noted that not all strategies are planned, and indeed that successful strategies can emerge without prior planning. However, emergent strategies must be evaluated and any inappropriate strategies stopped. Essentially, the formulation of intended/planned strategies is a top-down approach, whereas the formulation of emergent strategies can be viewed as a bottom-up process.

The different levels of strategy and planning

So far this chapter has explored the strategic level of management planning and decision-making. However, planning and decision-making occur can occur at different levels. Hofer and Schendel (1978) and Anthony (1965) distinguish between strategic level, business level and operational/functional level plans and decision-making.

The hierarchical nature of corporate strategy creates the framework for the business strategy and the business strategy provides the framework for the functional strategies. Thus, the different levels of strategy formulation are interdependent and one level should be consistent with the strategies at the next level. The operational and functional strategies should be directed towards contributing to the overall business and corporate strategy.

Strategic level

Johnson and Scholes (1997) propose that strategic decisions are of a higher order than other management decisions. They tend to be complex and non-routine in nature because they often involve a high degree of uncertainty based on what *might* happen in the future. They require an integrated approach to managing the organization across the boundaries of different operating units, and they often involve major change for the organization.

Strategic level planning addresses issues such as what type of business or businesses the organization should be in, and are therefore concerned with decisions of scope. For example, should the organization diversify or limit its business activities? A good example of an organization that has constantly stretched the scope of its business is Virgin, which has moved into new business areas such as financial services, rail transportation and retailing. Should the organization invest in existing businesses or buy new business? This is a key question facing the building societies who have demutualized and have capital to invest. It is also concerned with structural and financial issues, including how resources should be allocated to the different business activities.

Business level

This level is concerned with how an operating unit or strategic business unit approaches a particular market and how it should compete in order to be superior to its rivals. It is therefore concerned with how to secure and sustain competitive advantage. For example:

- which products/services should be developed?

- how should it segment the markets/should it specialize in particular profitable segments?

Financial services organizations are not single businesses but a range of different businesses. Examples of how a financial services organization may divide its activities into distinct strategic business units could be illustrated by the division into the retail sector, corporate sector, capital markets, etc.

Operational/functional level

This level of planning is concerned with determining the operational strategies of the various functional areas and would include, for example, marketing strategies, production strategies, finance strategies, information systems strategies, and human resource management (HRM) strategies. These are of strategic significance in that they will all contribute to the overall success of the corporate strategy.

Whilst the corporate strategy formulation tends to be the concern of top managers (in terms of ensuring that the purpose and direction of the organization is clearly determined and stated), other levels of management will be responsible for ensuring the successful implementation of strategy. Therefore, strategic management involves the entire organization and management from all different levels will be involved in some aspect of the planning activity.

Strategy and stakeholder influences

There are a number of different individuals and interest groups both inside and outside the organization, and who will have views about the strategy of the organization, and who will have a vested interest in the behaviour of the organization. These groups or individuals are referred to as stakeholders. Freeman (1984) defines stakeholders as any group or individual who can affect or is affected by the performance of an organization. Understanding stakeholders and how they are likely to influence the organization's strategy is, therefore, an important element of the strategic management process. The stakeholders of a financial service organization could include:

- Shareholders and Owners • Competitors

- Employees
- Customers/Clients
- Regulatory Bodies
- Trade Unions
- Media
- Local Community

- Senior Management
- Government – National
- Government – European
- Pressure Groups
- Interest Groups
- Suppliers

There are different classifications of stakeholders: internal stakeholders (employees and management); connected stakeholders (shareholders, customers, suppliers); external stakeholders (the community, government, pressure groups).

In determining and formulating its corporate strategy the organization will have to balance the demands of the different stakeholder groups. For example, the demands of customers for longer opening hours versus the needs of employees, and the short-term pressure to deliver shareholder value versus management's desire to invest in longer-term developments.

In order to fulfil the organization's mission and objectives, management activities will be influenced to a greater or lesser extent by stakeholders. Stakeholders can influence and constrain the management of the organization on a number of different levels. Each of the different stakeholder groups will have invested something in the organization and will expect a return. They will also wish to influence how this is determined. Conflict may arise when the expectations of stakeholder groups differ. The organization must identify which stakeholders have priority by analysing stakeholder power since the level of power and influence will vary between different stakeholder groups.

Ultimately, according to Johnson & Scholes (1997), objectives and strategies will be influenced by:

- who are the stakeholders concerned?

- what is their relative power?

- how important to them is a particular strategy, which they will then support or oppose?

- where and how will they exert their influence and power?

In making a strategic choice management must consider their responsibilities to the different groups. For example, it has a responsibility: to shareholders to provide a good return on the risk of investment; to customers in terms of the quality of products/services, security, pricing levels, etc.; to employees in the form of reward systems, working conditions, training and career development, job satisfaction, equal opportunities; and the community in terms of creation and maintenance of employment, and providing financial assistance to charities and community activities.

Summary

This chapter has set out the framework and activities involved in the strategic planning process. It is clear that the process is complex for financial services organizations who must continually scan the external environment, and develop strategies which capitalize on opportunities presented and minimize threats. Factors such as the power and interest of different stakeholders will influence the strategic direction and decisions of an organization. Strategy will also be influenced by, and impact upon, the internal operations of the organization. The strategy will therefore have implications for the structure, culture and internal design of the organization and it is these aspects which will be explored in the next chapter.

References

Andrews K (1971) *The Concept of Corporate Strategy*, Irwin
Ansoff H (1988) *Corporate Strategy*, Penguin
Anthony R N (1965) *Planning & Control Systems: A Framework for Analysis*, Harvard University Press
Bowman C & Asch D (1987) *Strategic Management*, Macmillan Education
Freeman R E (1984) *Strategic Management: A Stakeholder Approach*, Pitman
Hofer C W & Schendel D (1978) *Strategy Formulation: Analytical Concepts*, West
Johnson G & Scholes K (1997) *Exploring Corporate Strategy*, 4th ed. Prentice Hall
Lynch R (1997) *Corporate Strategy*, Prentice Hall
Mintzberg H (1991) 'Five Ps for Strategies', in Mintzberg H and Quinn J B, eds. *The Strategy Process*, Prentice Hall

Mintzberg H (1994) 'The Fall and Rise of Corporate Planning', *Harvard Business Review*, Jan-Feb

Ohmae (1982) *The Mind of the Strategist*, Penguin

Porter M (1985) *Competitive Advantage; Sustaining Superior Performance*, Free Press

3 The internal environment

Objectives

In order to carry out successfully the organization's strategy, not only do organizations need a clear understanding of external influences they also need some comprehension of the internal environment. The internal environment involves the strategic capabilities and resources of the organization.

In this chapter the internal environment of the organization will be explored. This will involve examining the possible structures an organization can adopt and the consequences of each. The internal culture and the influence of Japanese management practices will then be explored. The different production processes that can be used will also be identified. The implications of these different systems for employees and the internal organization of labour and employment patterns will then be discussed.

The detailed objectives of this chapter are:

- to understand and evaluate the structural design of organizations;

- to analyse and evaluate the impact of different types of internal cultures on business operations including the influence of Japanese management practice;

- to explore the differing forms of organization and production systems used within and outside the industry, such as just-in-time, mass production, flexible specialization, outsourcing and the virtual organization;

- to understand changing internal systems of employment including the flexible firm model.

Introduction

The first two chapters have examined the external environment, the influence it can exert on organizations, and the importance of organizations assessing the impact of these factors in formulating strategies. In assessing the environment, the organization can make decisions about the constraints, demands and opportunities available to it. In the light of these, and mindful of the resources and history of the organization, it can then draw up its strategy. As explored in Chapter 2, this is the set of key decisions about the match of the organizations' resources to the opportunities, and the constraints and demands in the environment, which are used when determining its strategy and future direction.

In order to implement these key decisions the organization has to work within certain parameters. These parameters, which can be said to provide the focus for internal analysis, include:

a)   The formal organizational arrangement of structures and systems;

b)   The internal cultural influences;

c)   The task of the organization, the production system and process used to achieve the task;

d)   The individuals who achieve the organizational tasks.

The next section examines the first of these.

The formal arrangement of organizational structures and systems

This section will examine the formal organizational arrangement of structures and how this can aid or hinder the ultimate performance of the organization.

It is important to first distinguish between the terms organising and organization. The former is the process or management, while the latter is the social grouping. So organising is the conversion process, part of the social system of organizations. The organization is commonly depicted through the structure of the firm. The relationship described above is usefully summarized by Mullins (1997):

> *Structure makes possible the application of the process of management and creates a framework of order and command through which the activities of the organization can be planned, organized, directed and controlled.*

The process is therefore determined by the structure and ordering of the organization. Mintzberg (1979) refers to these two aspects as:

1. The building blocks of the organization.

2. The co-ordinating mechanisms.

Both aspects are needed to support an origination's strategies and can be viewed as being configured to match the strategic situation. The building blocks of organizations proposed by Mintzberg comprise:

- the operating core, where basic work is produced, for example a factory floor or branch outlet;

- the strategic apex, where general management occurs, for example the Head Office of a financial services organization;

- the middle line, who are managers situated between the strategic apex and the operating core;

- the techno-structure, comprising analysts who design the systems for work processes;

- the support staff, who facilitate the work of the operating core, for example, secretarial, catering, human resource management;

- the ideology or culture of the organization.

These building blocks of the organization are co-ordinated through supervision, informal contact, and standardization of processes and outputs. The choice of building blocks and co-ordinating mechanisms led Mintzberg to conclude that there were six major organizational configurations or structures:

1. The simple structure, which is characterized by the entrepreneurial style and which has few of the activities formalized.

2. The machine bureaucracy, following centrally established rules and principles, which is often found in mature organizations.

3. The professional bureaucracy, where power is based on expertise not formal position in the hierarchy.

4. Divisionalized structures, in which the business is divided up into autonomous regions or product businesses. Each division is configured as a machine bureaucracy.

5. The adhocracy, with few formal structures or procedures, which is highly organic.

6. The missionary organization, which is dominated by the culture of the organization, and relies little on structures and systems.

In practice the choice of configuration should be determined by a match to the organization's strategic situation.

The study of structuring work was of major interest to early writers on organizations such as Fayol (1949), Weber (1947), etc. It still features in contemporary theories of complex organizations.

When organizations have grown past a size where owners can exercise direct control, then a degree of differentiation is inevitable and issues such as the degree of specialization, the degree of standardization, the levels of authority to be established and the centralization of decision making must be decided.

Max Weber writing in the late 19th century was one of the first writers to try and develop structures which are founded on the principles of division of labour and hierarchies. Although more will be said about Weber in Chapter 6 it is fair to say that all large scale organizations will have in some measure a bureaucratic structure (i.e. one governed by rules and procedures) and a degree of specialization (i.e. the grouping together of particular types of expertise and skills). This specialization can be achieved in different ways through structures.

The external structure (the corporate status, sole trader, partnership, plc, etc.) and the internal structure (the grouping of certain activities) of an organization are not the only factors in organizational analysis. Also involved are issues concerning the division of task, function, power and authority. Child (1984) views structure as involving the formulation and implementation of managerial plans together with the procedure for decision-making, collection of information and notification of decisions, as well as the control and co-ordination of activities. Some of these aspects of structure will be explored in more detail in Chapter 7.

In the following section the different ways of organising and structuring activities will be explored. There are a number of alternative designs. The major ones are functional and product specialization, geographic divisionalization and matrix structures. It is now proposed to look at these structures in more detail.

Functional specialization

This structure can be achieved by grouping activities together on the basis of their function, e.g. personnel, marketing, finance and information systems. The advantages are that this structure groups together those with similar technical expertise, thus providing better co-ordination and promotion opportunities. However, this type of structure can create sectional conflicts and a strong sense of territorial power. It is also more difficult to judge the performance of different services and products and it can slow down the response time for new innovations.

Product specialization

In this structure the organization is grouped on the basis of the products developed, e.g. mortgage, lending or pensions products. This type of structure can encourage diversification, allowing individuals to cope better with technological change because expertise and specialized equipment are grouped together. The structure also allows units to be run as profit centres and can lead to better targets and control systems. However it can lead to the promotion of one product at the expense of others. There is also no encouragement of functional competence since each product division will employ its own marketing, human resource staff, etc. There is therefore no significant grouping of functional expertise.

Geographical

The structure is grouped geographically, allowing for decisions and control to be exercised at national or regional level. This structure enables the organization to incorporate a sound knowledge of local markets and conditions into its strategy. However, it can create difficulties associated with a loss or lack of centralized control. An example of this type of structure within the financial services sector would be the organization of the branch network.

Divisionalized structure

This structure is divided on the basis of products or geography, and each division is in a functional form. However, some control is retained at Head Office, especially if co-operation across countries is required and the business is diversified. A balance is needed between corporate control and independence at local and functional level. It is a common structure in multinational organizations or even major national ones when separate divisions are established for credit cards, retail and corporate banking.

The key benefits of this are that it allows clear accountability for the different business units. However, problems can occur in co-ordinating the activities across several different units, e.g. providing IT support for several different business areas.

Figure 3.1: Divisionalized Structure

Matrix structure

New types of structure have resulted from the difficulties of co-ordinating activities across products or functional areas, especially where the development of new products or designs is involved. The matrix structure is sometimes referred to as a project structure which has a functional base but allows a project structure to occur within it.

Figure 3.2: Matrix Structure

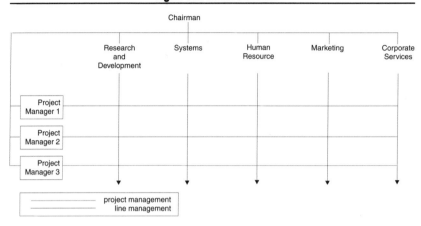

The advantages of this type of structure are that it combines lateral and vertical communication and authority so there is the efficiency of the hierarchical structure, with reporting lines to project managers and project sponsors, but the informality of the organic structure in working across product lines and functional areas. It allows the focus to fall on the requirements of the client and it clarifies who is responsible for success. It encourages managers to understand their contribution and role.

The disadvantages of this type of structure are the potential conflicts which can arise about the allocation of resources, the division of authority, the dilution of the responsibility of functional managers and the divided loyalties that can result for employees concerning their own project managers and their functional managers. It can be unclear who is responsible which may lead to delays in decision-making.

Many companies now have a mixed structure, which combines the benefits of two or more of these organizational forms. Few organizations adopt only one of the structural types mentioned earlier. The skill of management lies in balancing the structures to suit the circumstances as the company develops and evolves.

Centralization and decentralization

There are other issues concerned with structure which firms need to address. These are centred around the degree of centralization versus decentralization, and the power to delegate both responsibility and authority.

One advantage of decentralising the structure is that top management is not overloaded and they can concentrate on strategic issues, as operational decisions are made elsewhere. It can also mean that operational decisions are speeded up. The local management remains flexible and attention is centred on cost and profit centres, so the contribution of employees is clearer and responsibility is passed down.

The main disadvantage is the potential loss of control. This means there is the need for adequate control systems to avoid errors, and greater co-ordination with senior management is needed. In addition decentralization can lead to inconsistent treatment of customers. Decentralization can encourage a parochial attitude in the subsidiary units. However, it can provide a plentiful supply of managers to assume the increased levels of responsibility.

As organizations increase in size there is a pressure to decentralize. Studies at the University of Aston have shown that large size leads to less centralization but a greater amount of rules, procedures and specialization. Indeed multinational companies are an increasing feature of the financial services sector and decisions need to be taken about the degree of local independence and responsiveness versus global co-ordination.

The importance of structures

Researchers (Urwick 1952, Child 1988) are convinced of the importance of appropriate organizational structures. Poor structures can lead to:

- low morale;

- late and inappropriate decisions;

- conflict and lack of co-ordination;

- poor response to new opportunities and external changes;

- rising costs.

These hinder the implementation and achievement of strategies and effective business processes. As strategy develops and evolves so internal structures must flex and change to fit in with the requirements and demands. Whilst structure clearly influences organizational performance and must be considered in the strategy of organizations, organizational culture is also a major factor and it is this topic which is now examined.

Organizational culture

Organizational culture is an important concept, since it has a widespread influence on the behaviours and actions of employees. It represents a powerful force on an organization's operations, its strategies, structures and systems. Everyone in the organization is involved in the development and maintenance of culture. However it is also subject to influences from external environment factors.

This section will begin with an examination of the different definitions and the major dimensions and typologies of culture. It will then go on to investigate the influence of organizational culture on organizational performance.

What is culture?

As a general concept culture is a complex phenomenon and difficult to define. Many definitions are available. Schein (1992) refers to organizational culture as "the deeper level of basic assumptions and beliefs that are shared by members of the organization, that operate unconsciously and define in a basic 'taken for granted' fashion an organization's view of itself and its environment".

Moorhead and Griffin (1992) define organizational culture as "a set of values, often taken for granted, that people in an organization understand. It reflects the way work is performed; and what is acceptable and not acceptable; and what actions are encouraged and discouraged". Pettigrew (1979) offers a more straightforward definition stating that organizational culture consists of the behaviours actions and values that people in an organization are expected to follow.

So from the above definitions culture can be said to refer to the underlying values, beliefs and codes of practice that makes an organization what it is. It is the distinguishing mark between one organization and another. Culture is symbolic of what the organization is really like. Handy (1993) simplifies this by suggesting that culture is "the way things are done around here".

Different levels of culture

Culture exists at a number of different levels from the core beliefs and values to the visible manifestation of artefacts. Schein (1992) provides a model depicting the four major elements of corporate culture:

1. Basic Assumptions.
2. Values.
3. Norms.
4. Artefacts.

The next section examines these terms in more detail.

The *basic assumptions* represent the deepest level of cultural awareness and guide individuals' behaviour, determining how they should perceive, think and feel about things.

Values are often taken for granted and tell individuals what is regarded as important in the organization and what sort of behaviour is desirable. The more strongly based the values the more they are likely to affect behaviour. This does not necessarily depend on values being articulated in a written form, however, but rather the extent to which they are reinforced by the behaviours of management. *Values* are translated into reality through *norms* and *artefacts* and are often communicated through stories and other symbolic meanings.

Norms guide individuals on how they should behave in a particular situation and represent unwritten rules of behaviour. They tell people what they are supposed to do, say and believe, and are passed on by word of mouth or behaviour, for example how managers treat subordinates, the importance attached by them to status and level of formality.

Artefacts are the visible and tangible manifestations of the levels of culture and include observable behaviours, structures, systems, policies, procedures and physical aspects of the organization. Some of the physical signs of culture are more visible than others, for example:

- the working environment setting, e.g. design, reception area, building and layout;
- corporate image in brochures, literature, etc.;
- customer relations;
- methods of communication;
- degree of freedom for staff;

- what the company stresses as important, e.g. Marks and
  Spencer plc traditionally stressed their high quality goods.

Hofstede et al (1990) also offer a model of culture based on different levels, made up of *values* (the manifestation of culture at its deepest level), *rituals*, *heroes* and *symbols* which symbolize the values.

Organizations have both overt/explicit and covert/implicit constituents of culture. This can be illustrated using the organization iceberg model by French and Bell (1990). The part of the iceberg which is visible above the water constitutes the goals and strategy of the organization, the structure, systems and procedures, the products and services, all of which will both influence and be influenced by culture. The greater part of the iceberg, which is submerged, is concerned with the informal organization, for example the values, attitudes and beliefs, norms of behaviour, leadership style and behaviour all which combine to make up the 'culture'. The 'essence' of culture tends to be more about the informal or hidden part of the organization. Nonetheless it can still act to influence organizational activity.

It is important to note that culture exists at a number of different levels, for example at national level, organizational level, departmental level and team level. Thus, within an organization culture is not a uniform phenomenon. The organization will be made up of sub-cultures, for example the bank branches may have their own sub-cultures which are different from the sub-cultures in head office departments.

Development of organizational culture

The culture should help people to make sense of the organization. It provides shared meanings and signals, on how work is to be done, and how employees are to relate to each other and to other stakeholders such as management, customers and suppliers. The culture is the basis upon which managers formulate courses of action and assess the need for change and the formulation of strategies. However, each organization will have its own unique culture, which will develop over time and will be influenced by a number of variables:

- the history and nature of the business, the reason the
  organization was formed, the age and the values of the first
  owners;

- the external environment;
- the nature of the management and staff in the organization;
- the organizational goals and objectives;
- the structure, whether centralized or decentralized;
- the nature of the business environment;
- the size of the business;
- the life stage of the organization, whether it is in its youth, maturity or decline;
- the nature of the organization's business.

So whilst Abbey National, Barclays, Lloyds TSB and Nat West could be considered to operate in the same business areas and have the same corporate status in terms of being plcs, it is their own unique culture which will differentiate them from each other, derived from the variables described above.

Classifications of culture

Whilst every organization will have its own unique culture there are a number of different ways of classifying organizational cultures. Handy (1993), developing the ideas of Harrison (1992), cites four different types of culture, by organising the outward visible signs of culture into a formal framework. The four types are:

1. Power or Club culture.
2. Role culture.
3. Task culture.
4. Person culture.

Handy also classifies culture in terms of 'Greek Gods'.

1.   Power culture

Usually the Power culture, sometimes referred to as the Club Culture or 'Zeus' is highly dependent upon one or a small group of people who keep the control of all functions.

The structure is best depicted as a web where power resides at the centre and all authority and power emanate from one individual. There is little bureaucracy and few rules and procedures. Employees rely heavily on the central figure and the successor provides the key to continued success or failure.

This culture can react well to change and is excellent for speed of decision-making. People work on personal contacts rather than formal liaison. Small entrepreneurial organizations typify this type of culture and examples in the financial services sector could include investment banks and broking firms.

2.   Role culture

This culture can be depicted as a Greek temple, drawing strength from the pillars which represent functions and divisions, for example, finance, marketing, human resources. These functions are joined at the top where 'heads' form management boards. Handy also refers to this as 'Apollo'.

Bureaucracy is the major characteristic of this culture with rigid structures and clearly defined roles and reporting relationships. The organization's strength lies in its rational formal rules and procedures, which must be followed to ensure a smooth and efficient operation. The tasks of the organization are sub-divided into a system of prescribed roles.

There is a clear hierarchical structure with each stage having clearly visible status symbols attached to it. Each job is clearly defined and the power of individuals is related to their position in the hierarchy. There is a tendency for decisions to be controlled at the centre. Communications, systems and procedures are formalized.

This type of culture functions best in a stable and predictable environment because it is slow to change and react.

3.   Task culture

Task culture is job or project oriented, and can be depicted as a net with the culture drawing resources from various parts of the organizational system. Power resides at the intersections of the net. Handy uses 'Athena' to symbolize the goddess of task.

The emphasis in this culture is upon teams of people to achieve objectives and tasks and is one where the needs of the task dominate, rather than the systems and procedures. Generally people working within a task culture find themselves in a management matrix where they will be working simultaneously for more than one boss. One of the bosses will have responsibility for the tasks being performed, whilst the other may be responsible for the 'personnel' role.

The power and influence tends to be based on specialist knowledge and expert power rather than on position in the hierarchy.

Task cultures have evolved so organizations can respond to change more speedily and are most appropriate where flexibility and adaptability is needed. The culture thrives in situations where problem-solving is key and relies on team leaders and co-ordinators.

4.   Person or existential culture

A Person culture is formed when individuals work separately to serve their own interests but have a common need or work to a common purpose. In this culture the individual is the central focus and the organization is a resource for an individual's talent. Handy uses 'Dionysus' to depict this culture.

Individual talent is all-important and this is often the culture preferred by professionals where the organization is made up of a number of individuals without any real structure. Generally the organizations have a professional basis and are controlled by reference to a common professional code. There is very little central control, few interactions between participants and the pressure for the individuals to conform to an organizational norm is limited. This type of culture can be difficult to manage.

The organization is geared to satisfying individual member needs and this culture may be found when a group of individuals join together to derive the benefits from economies of scales by sharing office space, equipment and clerical support. Examples of a person culture may be found in a Barrister's Chambers or doctors' group practice, Independent Financial Services Advisors, etc.

It is not possible to say that one culture is better than another. Each culture has its own characteristics, advantages and disadvantages, and leads to assumptions about how individuals think and learn. Culture can be influenced and can change. Different cultures result in policies on how individuals are motivated and rewarded.

Pure forms of cultures in an organization are rare. In reality organizations need a mix of cultures for different activities and processes. The mix chosen is what makes organizations different and what makes them successful is getting the right mix at the right time.

Financial services organizations could traditionally be described as possessing a role culture, i.e. bureaucracies. However, many are now setting up task sub-cultures in order to achieve organizational goals. For example, in the areas of information systems development people are working as cross-functional project teams since this is essential for building and implementing new systems.

Alternative types of cultural categorization are available. Deal and Kennedy (1982) categorize corporate culture using a framework, which consists of four cultural profiles based on two factors:

- the extent of the risk connected with the activities of the organization;

- the speed of feedback on the outcome of employees' decisions.

The four generic profiles resulting are:

- tough-guy macho;

- work hard, play hard;

- bet your company;

- process.

The *Tough-guy macho* (high risk, fast feedback) type culture reflects tough, individualistic and high risk-taking organizations. This profile is likely to be an entrepreneurial firm run by the owner. The organization is made up of people working as individuals who take high risks and receive quick feedback on whether their actions were right. Financial stakes are high and the focus is on speed, resulting in a high pressure environment. Examples of this type of culture are to be found in the stock-market dealing, entertainment businesses, management consultancies and advertising agencies.

Work hard, play hard (low risk/fast feedback) cultures are where the team is all important and the customer is the key to success. Employees take few risks and any risk is relatively low. An example of this type of culture could be found the retailing industry.

Bet Your Company (high risk/low feedback) are characterized by a slow feedback culture with decision cycles taking years, for example in pharmaceutical research. However, decisions are large scale with high risk and the focus is on the future and investing in it. Examples of this type of culture would include investment banking and oil companies.

Process (low risk/slow feedback) cultures are where technical performance is of critical importance and there is a need for order and predictability. The emphasis is on how to do something. This type of culture is perhaps characteristic of traditional insurance, banking and financial services organizations.

Culture and organizational effectiveness

The interest in organizational culture as an area for study is, in part, due to the belief by some researchers that it plays a major role in determining organizational performance. In other words it can improve an organization's ability to implement new business strategies and contributes to organizational effectiveness and excellence. The creation of a strong organizational culture, they suggest, fosters organizational success and can have a direct impact on the organization's positioning and overall competitive advantage. A strong organizational culture can be a strength or a weakness.

Studies of Japanese and American management methods suggest that the relative success of Japanese companies in the 1980s can be partly explained by their strong corporate cultures which emphasize humanistic values and concern for people which may extend beyond the boundaries of the organization, e.g. Ouchi (1981), Pascale and Athos (1981). American companies adopting this type of management practice are referred to as Theory Z organizations. Whilst there are many contradictions surrounding the concept of the Japanese culture and management techniques, the characteristics of Theory Z as described by Ouchi include:

- commitment to employees, offering long-term employment often for a lifetime;

- relatively slow process of evaluation and promotion;

- development of company-specific skills, and moderately specialized career paths;

- implicit informal control mechanisms supported by explicit formal measures;

- participative decision-making by consensus but individual ultimately responsible;

- broad concern for welfare of subordinates and co-workers as a natural part of the working relationship.

In the UK, it has been suggested that organizations such as Marks and Spencer have a managerial approach, culture and characteristics similar to Theory Z organizations.

Peters and Waterman's (1982) excellence literature also draw attention to the positive benefits of having a strong corporate culture on organizational performance. From their research on what makes an 'excellent' organization they identified seven attributes as characterising the corporate cultures of 'successful' firms:

1. A bias for action and a bias for getting things done.

2. Close to the customer by listening to and learning from the people the organization serves.

3. Autonomy and entrepreneurship, innovation and risk-taking is an expected way of doing things.

4. Productivity through people, treating staff as a source of quality and productivity.

5. Simple form and lean organization, in other words, simple structural forms and systems.

6. Hands-on, value-driven management with top management keeping in touch with 'front lines'.

7. Stick to the knitting, that is staying close to what you know and do well.

Whilst the work of Peters and Waterman has received widespread attention, criticisms have been made of their research findings. There are some problems with the methodology of their research, which critics state suffers from a lack of rigour. This has led to doubt over the validity of the findings and thus the relationship between the excellence attributes and business performance. A major flaw in the work of the excellence literature, and other research advocating specific cultural attributes for achieving excellence, is that it would suggest that there is one culture which is best for all kinds of organizations. This is contrary to the growing body of research (Schein 1992 and Chandler 1962) which suggests a contingency approach to organizational culture. This proposes that the corporate culture should support the strategy of the organization, which must be uniquely tailored to the competitive situation. Thus, organizations having different strategies and operating in different competitive situations should have their own unique culture, influenced by the characteristics of marketplace, strategy, size and market position of the organization. A similar concept is reflected in the McKinsey 7S framework which is explained in Chapter 4.

Managing organizational culture

The link between culture and organizational performance assumes that culture can be managed and manipulated in pursuit of organizational effectiveness. This assumes that employees' values, norms and behaviours can be changed to support the strategic aims of the organization. Cultural management is the process of developing or reinforcing an appropriate culture, and thereby helping the organization fulfil its purpose.

However, whilst culture is built up over a period of time, a major change in an organization's situation may be impossible to handle within the existing culture. Any major new strategy will alter the 'way things are done' and some cultural change will be inevitable. There are signs that the organizational culture may not now be appropriate for all organizations. For example Braddick (1991) suggests the following could be such signs:

- no clear vision of the future;

- no widely shared beliefs or values;

- strong contrasting values held in different parts of the organization;

- leaders encourage 'divide and rule' by providing disagreement and division within the business;

- no central drive;

- internal focus, with politics and administrative detail at the expense of the workplace;

- short-term focus;

- high labour turnover, absenteeism and complaints;

- sub-cultures flourish;

- lack of emotional discipline, outburst of anger and frustration.

There is considerable debate as to whether changing such a deep-rooted phenomenon as corporate culture is possible. Where cultural change occurs it often focuses on the levels of norms and artefacts which are perhaps more changeable than the deeper elements of values and basic assumptions, and which offer a set of levers for changing managerial behaviour. However, some would say that unless the deeper values and assumptions change, the organization would eventually drift back to the customary way of 'doing things'.

To handle cultural change there are some guidelines. The organization needs:

- clear strategic vision and managers who can communicate this vision to others;

- top management commitment;

- symbolic leadership;

- the setting of high standards and insistence on achievement;

- publication of successes;

- rewarding of those who make important contributions and termination of deviants.

Where cultural change does occur it is, in reality, an extremely difficult and long-term process. This will be explored further in Chapter 4, where the topic of organizational change is discussed.

Of all the forces which impact on structure and culture one of the key ones to exert an influence is the way the task of the firm is organized. The next section considers this area.

The organizational task – processes and systems used to achieve it

The third element to be examined in the internal environment of the firm is that of the organizational production processes and systems used to develop goods and services. The systems described in this section originated in the production of tangible goods and services. However, many of the principles and work methods have been applied and continue to develop in the context of the financial services industry.

Modern production processes, whether manufacturing or service-based, are complex and costly because of the need to co-ordinate machinery, technology, materials and labour.

The production process or system begins with the planning and the setting of targets (based on forecasts of activity) to be achieved by liaising with different departments, marketing, business development, etc.

The next stage is the purchasing of materials or services at a level that is both economic and efficient. The purchasing decision is risky and can involve considerable costs. A 5% excess in purchasing costs, it has been estimated, can lead to a 25% reduction in profits (Cole 1994). Over recent years this has led to an increase in the popularity of just in time systems. This is defined in simple terms by Fincham and Rhodes (1994) as:

> A system for delivering the exact quantity and defect free quality of parts 'just in time' for each stage of production (beginning with the purchasing of stock).

This will be discussed in more detail later in the chapter. The most common classification of production systems is the division into jobbing, batch, mass, flow or process, and it is these which will be explored next.

Jobbing

This is also referred to as job or unique production. Essentially it is used to produce single items or one-offs, small tailor-made components or huge pieces of equipment. Because of the unique nature of production, planning and control is not easy in jobbing. Every stage has to be individually timed and planned and resources organized to meet the schedule. The entire process is relatively expensive compared to other methods of production. However, goods and services produced under this system meet the customer's own specification exactly.

In the financial services industry this type of production system is found most commonly when dealing with corporate clients, or in individual and personalized private banking where products are tailored to meet individual needs.

Batch production

This describes the production of standardized units in small or large lots, which is halfway between jobbing and mass production. The main difference between jobbing and batch production is in the standardized nature of the latter where production is dealt with in lots or batches, with movement only occurring when one batch has been processed.

One of the difficulties of this system is to determine the optimum size of the batch. Its key characteristics are:

1. A standardized set of operations, carried out intermittently as the work moves from one operation to the next.

2. The use of general purpose machinery which is grouped together.

3. The heavy stores of stock which are required to ensure the process remains supplied.

4. A narrower range of skills is required of employees with some consequent de-skilling.

5. The emphasis is on production plans and progress.

6. Short production runs.

Batch production is usually a well-controlled and efficient method of production. The main problem is queuing for different operations, but this problem can be overcome by the move towards flow or mass production systems.

Many financial services organizations used a type of batch system in their processing work. However like other organizations they have witnessed a move towards flow, process or mass production systems. The use of increasingly sophisticated technology can make processing the system a continuous flow through the different steps or stages.

Flow/process/mass production

This system of production first started with Henry Ford (and is frequently referred to as Fordism), who was the first to adopt a production line linked to producing a restricted range of cars. The capital costs of installing such a system are high because of the specialized nature of the machines, but once it is set up the control is simple because the products flow in an uninterrupted way from one operation to another.

The system is dependent on high demand created by the mass market so the capital invested in the machinery is returned.

In rational economic terms it is the most efficient way of producing large quantities. The greatest drawback is that it requires employees to adapt themselves to the production process because the system is regarded as generating both tedious and monotonous work.

Mass customization

A relatively new production method is that of mass customization. This involves making products which are 'tailor-made' for each individual customer but which share common components. Fundamental to the process is the idea of producing mass volumes, so still achieving economies of scale, but these are manufactured to fit the shape and needs of individual customers. It is based on mixing individualization with highly flexible and integrated manufacturing processes, and is facilitated through technological advancements in traditional production methods.

Just in time systems

Just in time systems, as mentioned earlier, have been applied to the traditional line assembly, large batch manufacturers and mass production systems. The basic features are:

1. A pull system works at given stages and only goes ahead when a signal is received from the stage in front. This is achieved using a "Kan ban" system of stock control. As the front worker empties a kan ban rack of components this activates production by the rear worker to replenish it.

2. Total Quality Management (TQM) in production means defect-free supplies of parts and materials. Because the firm is holding a minimum level of stock, the discovery of faulty parts means that the whole production process could be halted. However, the scope of TQM in a financial services organization encompasses all aspects of service production and delivery.

3. Stockless production – as mentioned earlier since there are no buffer stocks waste, and the amount of capital tied up in work in progress are reduced.

4. The supplier relations in just in time systems are extended. Deliveries go straight to production and are synchronized with the plans for production. No competing supplier can exist, and

a strong relationship develops between the supplier and producing company. It is therefore essential for financial services organizations when using this system to develop a strong relationship with their suppliers in order to meet the demands of quality of service .

Although this system can be perceived as offering an improved production method, problems can exist in terms of the impact on human resources. On the positive side as efficiency increases, morale and the willingness to accept responsibility is boosted. There is the opportunity for increased team working and a high degree of trust.

On the negative side the pace of work can be intense and can sometimes entail long overtime hours. There is much standardization of work, and deskilling is still a feature. In some ways the demands on production (with no buffer stocks) and the kan ban principles mean that there is less flexibility in production not more (Berggren 1989). This can lead to greater stress because of the sudden fluctuations in demand with little opportunity for variation.

Clearly technology has changed work processes and systems. The effect of technology on production systems and the implications for workers will now be explored in more detail.

Technology and alienation

Since technology was first introduced into the workplace environment the effect of production systems on individuals has been widely researched. Marx (1974) was one of the first writers to criticise mechanization. The competition in capitalism forced employers to increase productivity, and mechanization was the method used to achieve this. Machinery reduced the need for specialized skills so labour became easy to substitute. The machinery created standardized labour, displaced people and created unemployment.

To balance Marx's views were those opinions put forward by the sociologist Blauner (1964). He viewed technology as a liberating force, which could take on the many mundane tasks previously performed by employees, thereby upgrading the skills and status of workers. Blauner carried out his research in the printing and textile industry, the vehicle industry and the chemical processing industry. He found that alienation was at a minimum in the printing industry (where a high level of skill was retained from the traditional craft industry), and that at that time the employees had a degree of security and control over their work. Machine minding (in the textile industry) and mass assembly (in the vehicle industry) maximized alienation, and neither group of workers could dictate the pace or methods of working. There was also no sense of pride or self-esteem. However, in the process system (the chemical industry), whilst the work was routine, the employees had greater freedom, responsibility, and a sense of dignity and worth.

Blauner's conclusion was that as technology developed so alienation could decline:

> *The chemical industry shows that automation increases the workers control over his work process and checks the further division of labour and growth of large factories. The result is meaningful work in a more cohesive, integrated industrial climate.*

Technological development can thus be viewed as both a positive and a negative force, depending on individual choice and job design.

The latest writings and research continue to raise the issue of technology and alienation, and is of relevance to financial services organizations considering the latest developments in their production systems. They suggest that new flexible computer systems allow the reversal of the trend from deskilling. Similar arguments are followed in the writings of Braverman (1974) and are explored in more detail in Chapter 6. Braverman argues that deskilling is part of the capitalist process and the movement towards greater use of machinery. However, the critics MacInnes (1983) and Kelly (1985) argue that this is a limiting view of changing work patterns and that technology does in fact allow skill creation in new areas of work.

Within financial services organizations it seems that there has been a move from jobbing to batch production in serving the mass market with financial products. However with the improvements in technology there is a move towards the processing system which Blauner believes may ultimately lead to greater freedom in the workplace.

The internal organization of labour

There are a number of ways of examining the labour market and the structure of employment. It can be done by examining the external structures and to some extent this has been covered already in Chapter 1 when the social factors, structures and trends in society which determine work and employment were explored. A second approach is to look at the internal structures. This can be done by exploring the structure of the internal labour market, and the different categories of staff and the nature of their employment relationship.

Internal labour market

The internal labour market is to some extent determined by the firms themselves because they have the responsibility for the selection and allocation of employees for training, promotion, etc. They determine the extent of their recruitment from outside the organization. Within large financial services organizations there has traditionally been little recruitment from outside except at basic entry level and in specialized fields.

These firms also reflect the other divisions in the labour market in terms of primary and secondary markets. Primary markets are jobs offered by large firms who are technologically advanced and profitable. Jobs in the secondary markets are those in small firms who are not users of high technology and generally have less favourable terms and conditions of employment. However this is not always a straightforward relationship, because the primary sector can often make use of the secondary sector by sub-contracting and out-sourcing work, e.g. catering, cleaning and low-skilled roles.

It is obvious in the trends which can be observed that strategic labour policies, i.e. in terms of resourcing and the type and levels of employees, are increasing in use. These strategies are currently directed at maintaining flexibility. The next section focuses on flexible labour policies in more detail, and the trends in the labour market especially with regard to financial service organizations.

Flexible labour markets

Financial services organization are constantly searching for solutions on how to respond to external environmental pressures and internal challenges of achieving cost containment whilst at the same time improving productivity. They are looking for methods of organising labour resources in such a way that they are able to vary human resource input more easily. By doing this they will be better positioned to be flexible and responsive to the ever changing market place and turbulent business conditions. As in most service industries, staff costs in financial services organizations represent the largest overhead. There is a clear need to identify alternative approaches to reshaping the organization's labour market and the structure of the workforce so as to facilitate the most efficient use of staff, achieving labour flexibility and reducing labour costs.

Concepts and definitions – What does flexibility embrace?

Financial services organizations are employing flexible working practices so that they can adjust the size and mix of labour in response to changes in demand, thus ensuring that excess labour is not carried by the organization. Flexibility itself conveys the notions of adaptability, pliability and responsiveness to organizational change. Within the context of **labour flexibility** four sources of flexibility dominate: functional flexibility, numerical flexibility, temporal flexibility, and financial flexibility.

Functional flexibility or task flexibility is sometimes referred to as multi-skilling and is concerned with the ability to redeploy employees with appropriate training or retraining to different tasks and activities. It can be taken to refer to a "firms ability to adjust and deploy the skills of its employees to match the task required by its changing workload, production methods and/or technology" (NEDO 1986). Organizations can attempt to create greater flexibility by relaxing demarcations between different workers. It is suggested that the use of functional flexibility is increasing as skill boundaries are becoming less well defined due to the development of technology. Financial reasons in terms of the cost pressures on headcount may also lead to an increasing pressure to spread the available workforce over more tasks.

At one level functional flexibility could be viewed as a deliberate strategy to train and upgrade skill, either extending the job content horizontally (job enlargement) or vertically (job enrichment). However, it could also be argued that at another level flexibility represents work intensification with workers undertaking a variety of tasks to meet shortages. Whichever perspective is taken, the overall aim of functional flexibility is to achieve greater workforce productivity within work-time, by altering the deployment of a workforce according to tasks required across function or hierarchy.

Numerical flexibility is where adjustments are made in the number of workers to meet the demands or fluctuations in output. It is generally taken to mean the ability rapidly to increase or decrease the numbers of workers employed. This can be achieved through the deployment of part-time staff and 'hire and fire' policies aimed at temporary staff.

Another means of achieving numerical flexibility is sometimes discussed under the separate heading 'distancing', which means the employment of subcontractors, and this will again reduce the wage bill.

Temporal flexibility or working time is sometimes subsumed under the numerical flexibility heading. Both forms relate to the volume of labour supplied. However, Blyton (1992) argues that working time should be viewed as a distinct strategy within flexibility. Whilst most employees work standard blocks of time, the supply of work in not usually so regular, and is affected by seasonal pressures and varying customer demand. Temporal flexibility allows variability of labour time by varying patterns of hours worked in response to changing patterns of demand. This can be achieved through flexitime, shift work, overtime and annual hours arrangements. At a simplistic level, temporal flexibility could be viewed as a strategy employed to facilitate variability amongst those already employed by the firm, whilst other numerical flexibility strategies involve 'non-standard' workers.

Financial flexibility or wage flexibility covers both the ability to adjust labour costs, such as pay, to changes in the level of business activity (Atkinson 1984), and the linking of wages to the state of supply and demand in the external labour market.

It is also concerned with the extent to which a firm's pay and reward structure supports and reinforces the various types of numerical and/or functional flexibility. It can entail a move by the employer to seek greater flexibility by relating labour cost to output through the introduction of more individualized systems and the displacement of 'rate for the job'. Financial flexibility can take different forms, and can include a payment system which links remuneration with performance, for example performance related pay. The reward system could also be designed to encourage the development of functional flexibility through competence based pay rewards for the acquisition and practice of new skills.

The flexible firm model

One of the major contributions to labour market flexibility is the concept of the flexible firm model. The notion of the flexible firm was developed during the mid-1980s by the Institute of Employment Studies, and brought together the different forms of flexibility described in the section above. The flexible firm model identifies a framework for achieving the different forms of labour flexibility, and offers a set of suggestions whereby organizations may adopt one or more of the methods to achieve a more flexible approach to the supply and use of labour (Atkinson 1984, 1985).

The impetus for the model developed out of a need to respond to various external environmental pressures including the unstable operating conditions, intense competition, changing attitudes to work, demographic changes and skill shortages facing organizations in the UK. Other sociological influences promoting flexible working practices included the change in the labour supply, for instance the growth in the number of women who may seek or accept work on part-time or temporary basis. The largely deregulated labour market has also facilitated greater flexibility.

The model amounts to a reorganization of a firm's internal labour markets and conceptualizes employment patterns in terms of a segmentation between core and periphery labour flexibility. This is explained in Figure 3.3.

At the centre of the circle are the core employees. Organizations will have a set of *core workers* who are full-time permanent employees supplying firm specific skills. The *core workers* will carry out the most important and most unique activities of the firm, and will have skills which are highly firm specific. It is necessary to have a core workforce within an organization so that there is continuity of employment and a level of experience from which it is possible to build for the future. The employment conditions for the core should encourage retention by providing training, career development opportunities and facilitate functional flexibility for those with skills critical to the business.

The first peripheral group is made up of labour which may be given the status of full-time employees, but more vulnerable than the core

Figure 3.3: The Flexible Firm Model

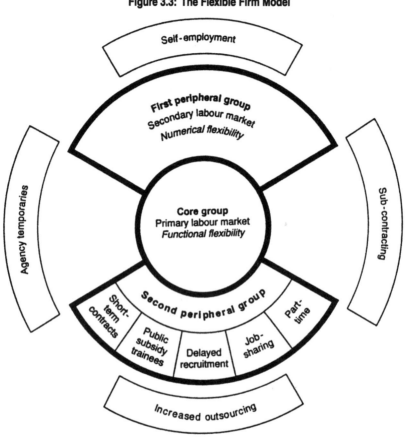

workers. They enjoy less job security, have less access to career opportunities and tend to regard their positions as more of a job than a career. Flexibility is likely to take the form of numerical and financial flexibility. There is no need to achieve functional flexibility as their jobs need little or no training and tend to be less skilled. The relatively high labour turnover of this group contributes to quick and simplified numerical adjustments.

The second peripheral group is made up of staff employed on a part-time, temporary or fixed-term contract basis to supplement the numerical flexibility of the first peripheral group. However, this part of the model could be criticized for locating part-time workers in this segment. A growing number of organizations are operating job-share systems at management levels which represent core workers.

The third group consists of external workers who are not directly employed by the firm, for example, subcontractors, self-employed, agency workers and outsourcing.

The flexible firm model suggests that organizations will adopt different approaches to labour management for different sections of the workforce. The organization of a firm's labour markets and their division into separate components will mean that workers' experiences and the employers expectations are increasingly differentiated (Atkinson and Gregory 1986).

The benefits to the employer of the flexible firm include:

- reduced labour costs as a result of lower wage and non-wage employment of the periphery;

- the ability to tailor the size of the workforce to changing levels of demand, reducing costs of carrying excess labour and achieving 'lean production';

- increased productivity from core workers.

Criticisms have been made about the value and contribution of the flexible firm model. Critics have pointed to problems in defining the core and periphery. Adopting a more flexible labour force also raises problems for the management of human resources, for example:

- which function or area should be staffed in which way?

- which management styles should apply to which groups?

- how can commitment be generated from the different groups?

Objectives of flexibility

The goals and success of labour flexibility differ between employers and employees and between the government and trade unions. Atkinson (1987) suggests that the goal for the *employer* is to promote optimal cost-effectiveness in the deployment of labour; the goal for the *government* is the reduction of unemployment; and the goal for *trade unions* is to secure terms and conditions where flexibility initiatives threaten members.

It is suggested that the major motivation for making use of the different forms of flexibility has been the focus on organizational cost-effectiveness. However, employers often do not have a single objective in mind or a consistent strategy for achieving greater flexibility. A survey undertaken by McGregor and Sproull (1992) concluded that employers have a range of reasons for employing people on different contracts. The reasons can be grouped into broad categories: traditional reasons based on demands for short-term cover, specialist skills, etc.; supply side reasons which reflect employee work-time preferences; new reasons, including the need to respond to increased product market and technological uncertainty with greater flexibility.

The results of the survey revealed that the main reason for using *temporary* staff was to provide short-term cover. Other reasons were to meet fluctuations in demand, deal with one-off tasks, to provide specialist skills and to make it easier to adjust staffing levels. There was minimal evidence to support employing temporary staff to reduce wages and non-wage costs.

The overriding reason for employing *part-time* workers was to provide cover for tasks which required limited time to complete, for example cleaning work and some catering jobs. Other reasons were to match peak times in demand, for example, extra staff cover cashier positions in banks/building societies during the busy lunch-time period. The study also identified that the use of part-time staff could be employee-driven in that there are some employees who want to work part-time.

The following figure brings together the reasons most often quoted in connection with the various types of non-standard labour:

Figure 3.4

Type of Non-Standard Labour	Dominant Reason for Use
Part-time Employees	• To cater for tasks which require a limited number of hours to complete • Matching employment levels to peaks in demand • Job applicants want to work part-time • Way of retaining valued staff who are unable to continue working full-time

Type of Non Standard Labour	Dominant Reason for Use
Temporary Employees/ Agency Staff	<ul><li>Short term cover</li><li>Meet fluctuations in demand</li><li>Deal with one-off tasks</li><li>Provide specialist skills</li><li>Easier adjustment of staffing levels</li></ul>
Self-employed	<ul><li>Provision of specialist staff</li><li>Workers preference</li><li>To match staffing levels to peaks in demand</li></ul>

Source: Adapted from McGregor and Sproull (1992)

The government's role in encouraging labour market flexibility has been in introducing policies such as reducing legal restrictions on the hiring and firing of workers and removing state intervention in pay-setting, for example, abolishing minimum wage legislation and using the law to curb trade union influence over pay and employment conditions (Beardwell and Holden 1997). These were key employment issues for the Conservative government throughout the 1980s and 1990s. However, the European Commission (1997) does recognize the dangers of flexibility for security of employment and sees the need to achieve a balance between flexibility and security as a key issue, asserting that:

> *Workers need to be assured that after the changes... they will still have a job and that this job will last for a reasonable period of time .... while there are considerable benefits for firms and workers engaged in core activities, care is needed to ensure all workers, irrespective of their contractual status, share in the potential benefits of the new work organization.*

Flexibility in the financial services sector

Increased pressures on costs, high levels of competition and new technology have all had a significant impact on the traditional working practices of financial services organizations. In the face of continued uncertainty employers are increasingly reluctant to commit to the recruitment of permanent staff.

There is evidence to suggest that organizations operating in the financial services sector are looking at alternative ways of resourcing and are adopting flexible working policies with significant changes in the structure of employment over recent years. While there has been an overall reduction in the numbers employed in the sector part-time and temporary workers have increased in number, both as a proportion of all employees and in real terms.

The following section highlights the reasons for the increased use of part-time and temporary staff and the trend to outsourcing some activities.

Part-time workers

The increased use of part-time staff within the financial services sector should be considered in the light of the restructuring and the changing nature of work. One outcome of restructuring has been the segmentation of work between branches and 'centralized' operations centres, and between administrative duties and sales staff. The segmentation of tasks has in effect divided the type of part-timers employed in terms of skill and employment relations.

The nature of the work undertaken at the operations centres was once the traditional apprenticeship work for 'bankers' on the first rung of the ladder within the hierarchy. Now it represents an increased polarity between highly skilled career orientated employees and low skill routinized jobs. A high proportion of staff employed in these areas are part-time workers and the majority are women. Any integration of workers is unlikely given the different skill requirements, and represents a move away from the tradition of natural progression within the internal labour market.

Financial services organizations also employ part-time staff to achieve numerical flexibility in the branch network in an attempt to match staff numbers to the fluctuating demand.

In the branch environment part-time staff tend to be employed to cover the busy lunch-time periods. A high proportion of part-time staff employed in branches are women returners, with organizations benefitting from retaining the skills of former employees. Research by O'Reilly (1994) indicated that almost two thirds of part-time workers had worked full-time for the organization before, rather than coming from the external labour market. Thus, part-time staff working in branches will not usually be employed from the external labour markets but are, rather, ex-employees, undertaking duties similar to full-time staff.

In the 1980s this was a deliberate policy pursued by the banks. Schemes were introduced to attract mothers back to work in order to retain skills and protect the industry against the impact of the much vocalized 'demographic time bomb' theory which predicted a fall in the number of school leavers and resultant labour shortages. The recession in the early 1990s and the overall poor performance of banks has deflected from this issue, and has been overtaken by the banks radically reducing the size of their labour force.

The law now grants equality to part-time employees in terms of entitlement to employment protection. This means that part-timers have the rights to redundancy pay, unfair dismissal, time-off for trade-union duties and longer maternity leave after two years service with their employer, in line with full-time staff. However, they can still be marginalized on other benefits, for example, access to company pension, subsidized loans and career opportunities, etc.

Within the branch banking environment part-time staff have been paid pro-rata on the same scale for the work undertaken as full-timers. However, this masks the fact that the organizations make savings from the employment of part-time staff via job reorganization. There is evidence that some of the higher responsibilities within a job have been taken out of the jobs undertaken by part-timers, so they are paid at a lower scale.

Temporary work

The nature and roles of temporary staff within the financial services sector are diverse, in terms of the length of work (short to long), level of skill (low versus high) and the way they are used both on an ad-hoc basis and in a strategic manner. Hence the concept of temporary worker can be seen to cover a wide array of experiences.

Temporary workers are employed not only to cover long-term sickness, maternity and vacancy shortfalls, but also as replacements for permanent staff. Fixed-term contract staff are being used as part of the restructuring process, as a screening device in the recruitment and selection process, and also as a means of obtaining specialist staff.

In an environment of downsizing activity and restructuring of operations by many in the industry, fixed term contract staff are being used to maintain staff levels until the service is no longer required, and to cover for those full-time staff who are redeployed or leave. For many organizations operating in this climate there is a block on recruitment so the use of temporary staff is the only way to get work done

Another phenomenon is when the organization undertakes a new area of work it may employ people on short-term contracts initially, while it judges the viability of that project.

With regard to the demand for this type of work it is apparent that within the sector there is a ready source of former employees with company specific skills, who are 'willing' to return on a temporary basis. They are usually ex-full-time employees who have left to have children. Within the temporary worker classification, the concept of 'nil hours' or 'zero hours' contracts are used by the financial services organizations. These organizations have informal arrangements with casual staff made-up of former employees. This involves keeping a register of 'on-call' staff whereby the bank will call up a worker at home and require them to work at a given time. There is no guarantee of work and no payment for being 'on-call' for the worker and the financial services organization has no contractual obligation to offer work, using those on the register on an 'as and when' basis. The registered also have the right to refuse the work if it does not fit in with their circumstances at the time.

This is cheaper than using agency staff, whilst allowing the organization to benefit from the skills of ex-employees. Thus, organizations have their own pools of 'temporary' labour and can benefit from cost advantages and existing skill levels.

Temporary staff on fixed-term contracts vary considerably in terms of the length of the contract, with some as short as a couple of days and others a couple of years. Fixed-term contract staff also vary in terms of level of skill. For example, in the case of IT where high levels of skill and expertise are required, organizations use contract staff and benefit from their skills in designing and developing systems without incurring the costs of training.

The role of agencies has been to provide temporary workers to cover for short-term holiday and sick leave. Agency staff are generally perceived as inferior to permanent staff within the context of retail banking, both in terms of quality and experience required and the constraints imposed by security. However, agency staff are increasingly being used by financial services organizations to undertake back-office duties where there is no interface with the external customer.

Subcontracting

The motivation for subcontracting is typically put forward as cost-reduction. Whilst this is certainly a key criterion for the financial services sector, there are examples to suggest that organizations are increasingly using subcontractors for an array of other reasons and as a long-term strategic plan to externalize certain tasks. Nishiguchi (1989) proposes a number of reasons to explain why organizations might subcontract including, access to specialist technology, reducing indirect control of costs, use of cheaper labour, dispersion of risk, use of subcontractors as a buffer to core production, and adaptation to technological change.

Commercial pressures have forced financial services organizations to reassess those jobs they consider to be vital to the business and those which are non-specific to the core business. Non-bank low skill jobs which have emerged as a target for outsourcing during the process of re-structuring and rationalization are ancillary work, for example, cleaning, catering and security. By outsourcing these tasks organizations are able to reduce the number of staff who are covered by their internal employment terms and conditions. There are examples of staff undertaking the same role for the organization but who are employed by the subcontractor and who therefore receive inferior pay and employment conditions. Organizations are not only able to reduce their direct costs but also the indirect costs of administration associated with the 'non-core' jobs.

Financial services organizations are also using contractors in the specialist IT and data processing area, not just for short-term projects but on a permanent basis. The rationale in this area is two-fold. Firstly to gain access to specialist staff who have skills which are not specific to the traditional banking career and secondly without having to invest in expensive training involved in 'home grown' specialists.

Some financial services organizations are subcontracting processing work or using contractors to undertake jobs which are expected to disappear as a result of new technology. This can involve recruiting a work force formerly employed by the organization to work permanently for a contractor. The staff will remain at their desks but will be employed by other companies. An example of this is at the Bank of England where Hoskyns took over both the staff and work in an IT section. This staff had formerly benefited from the employment conditions associated with working for the Bank of England.

Subcontracting to some extent impinges on financial flexibility and reduces the number of employees covered by financial services organizations' pay scales, fringe benefits and the cost of managing these services.

Shift-working and overtime

Shift-working and overtime involves changing the work patterns of employees. In the financial services industry the major force for changing work time and introducing shift patterns has been the increased length and variety of opening hours, with Sunday trading being the most recent addition. The growth of new delivery channels, for example telephone and PC banking, with seven-day and 24-hour operations, means that shift working is a necessity to do business.

Summary

This chapter has explored the internal organization of the firm in terms of its structure and culture. Both these aspects have an influence on and can in turn influence the strategic development of the organization. This chapter also examined the different production processes which are required to achieve the organizational strategies. Finally the issue of employment market structures was explored and the different approaches organizations can use to structure their workforce. All of these variables, in conjunction with the external environment, need to be considered when developing and implementing strategies. The next chapter explores how change can be introduced and maintained in the organization.

References

Atkinson J (1984) 'Manpower Strategies for Flexible Organizations', *Personnel Management*, August 1984

Atkinson J (1985) 'Flexibility: Planning for the Uncertain Future', *Manpower Policy & Practice*, Vol.1

Atkinson J (1987) 'Flexibility or Fragmentation? The United Kingdom Labour Market in the Eighties', *Labour and Society*, Vol. 12, No. 1

Atkinson J & Gregory D (1986) 'A Flexible Future. Britain's Dual Labour Market', *Marxism Today*, Vol. 30, No.4

Beardwell I & Holden L (1997) *Human Resource Management: A Contemporary Perspective*, 2nd ed. Pitman

Berggren C (1989) 'New Production Concepts in Final Assembly', in S Wood, ed. *The Transformation of Work*, Unwin and Hyman.

Blauner R (1964) *Alienation and Freedom*, University of Chicago Press

Blyton P (1992) 'Flexible Times? Recent Developments in Temporal Flexibility', *Industrial Relations Journal*

Braddick W A G (1991) *Management for Bankers*, 2nd ed. Butterworths

Braverman H (1974) *Labour and Monopoly Capital: The Degradation of Work in the 20th Century*, Monthly Review Press

Chandler A D (1962) *Strategy and Structure: Chapters in the History of Industrial Enterprise*, MIT Press

Child J (1984) *Organizations: A Guide to Problems and Practice*, 2nd ed. Chapman

Cole G A (1994) *Management Theory and Practice*, DP Publications

Deal T E & Kennedy A A (1982) *Corporate Cultures: The Rites and Rituals of Corporate Life*, Addison-Wesley

European Commission (1997) *Partnership for a New Organization of Work*, Green (Consultative) Paper COM (97) 128

Fayol H (1949) *General and Industrial Management*, Pitman

Fincham R & Rhodes P S (1994) *The Individual, Work and Organization*, Oxford University Press

French W L & Bell C H Jnr. (1990) 'Organization Development': *Behavioural Science Interventions for Organization Improvement*, 4th ed. Prentice Hall

Handy C (1993) *Understanding Organizations*, 4th ed. Penguin

Harrison R (1992) 'Understanding Your Organization's Character', *Harvard Business Review*, May-June

Hofstede G Neuijen B Ohayv D & Sanders G (1990) 'Measuring Organizational Culture: a qualitative and quantitative study across twenty cases', *Administrative Science Quarterly*, Vol. 35

Hyman R (1983) 'White Collar Workers and Theories of Class', in R Hyman & R Price, eds. *The New Working Class*, Macmillan

Kelly J E (1985) 'Management Redesign of Work', in D Knights H Wilmott & D Collinson, eds. *Job Redesign*, Gower

MacInnes J (1983) 'The Labour Process Debate and the Commodity Status of Labour'. Paper presented at *1st Aston Labour Conference* (1983)

Marx K (1974) *Capital*, Vol. 1, Lawrence and Wishart

McGregor A & Sproull A (1992) 'Employers and the Flexible Workforce', *Employment Gazette*, May

Mintzberg H (1979) *The Structuring of Organizations*, Prentice Hall

Moorhead G & Griffin R W (1992) *Organizational Behaviour*, 3rd ed. Houghton Mifflin

Mullins L J (1997) *Management and Organizational Behaviour*, Pitman

National Economic Development Office (1986) *Changing Working Patterns: How Companies Achieve Flexibility to Meet New Needs*, NEDO

Nishiguchi (1989) *Strategic Dualism: An Alternative in Industrial Societies*

O'Reilly, J (1994) *Banking on Flexibility: A Comparison of Flexible Employment in Retail Banking in Britain and France*, Avebury

Ouchi W (1981) *Theory Z: How American Business Can Meet the Japanese Challenge*, Addison-Wesley

Pascale R T & Athos A G (1981) *The Art of Japanese Management*, Simon & Schuster

Peters T J & Waterman R H (1982) *In Search of Excellence*, Harper & Row

Pettigrew A M (1979) 'On Studying Organizational Culture', *Administrataive Science Quarterly*, December

Schein E H (1992) *Organizational Culture and Leadership*, Jossey Bass

Urwick L (1952) *Notes of the Theory of Organizations*, American Management Association

Weber M (1947) *The Theory of Social and Economic Organizations*, Free Press

4 Managing change in financial services organizations

Objectives

Having explored the development of strategy in Chapter 2 and the role of structure in Chapter 3, this chapter will investigate the management of change. The implementation of strategies often involves change for people working in organizations. Change is a certainty for those operating in the financial services sector where organizations are under pressure to adapt and respond to changing business conditions. Indeed, traditional organizational structures and cultures no longer serve their purpose and can inhibit change.

This chapter recognizes the significance of change management in managing uncertainty and will:

- explore the nature of change;
- identify the forces for change;
- examine models of change;
- evaluate hard and soft approaches to change;
- discuss the implementation of change and resistance to change.

Introduction

Financial services organizations are facing a climate where the pace and scale of change is enormous and where the environment is uncertain and unpredictable. A wide range of external and internal forces face those operating in the financial services sector. These forces create a volatile environment with fierce competition at domestic and global levels. Rapid developments in new technologies and uncertain economic conditions contribute to and make change inevitable.

Change is often necessary to revitalize and improve organizational performance. Organizations must shed traditional structures and ways of working and move to more dynamic and flexible structures and processes that are responsive to change. If organizations are not prepared to change they will not be in a position to exploit successfully the strategies they choose to adopt.

Everyone in the organization is concerned with and involved in change, with change affecting all areas of the operations and functions of the organization. The organization's strategy will impact on the internal structures, culture and operations which can result in either large-scale or small-scale change. From a managerial perspective the challenge is how to best harness change to benefit the organization.

The nature of change

Change can be considered in the context of the natural ageing process of organizational resources and systems, for example the ageing of physical assets such as buildings and equipment, or of human resources in terms of skill and abilities. In contrast, some change can be deliberately initiated in order to achieve a specific strategy or to respond to particular environmental forces.

There are different types of change and therefore different approaches to managing the change process. A number of different ways of categorising organizational change can be identified. Strebel (1996) suggests that although change may be a constant it is not always the same, and can be characterized as falling along a continuum ranging from incremental change to discontinuous or fundamental change.

Incremental change occurs slowly in a systematic and predictable way. This type of change is often associated with changes as they emerge within the organization and involves fine-tuning and making adjustments to procedures which will improve the efficiency of organizational performance, but which will not fundamentally alter the organization. Most organizational changes tend to be of this type, rather than transforming the organization. Incremental change builds on skills, routines and beliefs. It can be pro-actively managed and thus ensure that the organization anticipates the need for change. Possible examples of this are succession planning and management development programmes which aim to change the skills of the organization to match its environment on an ongoing basis.

Discontinuous change, sometimes referred to as transformational or fundamental change, can be defined as large-scale change which is marked by rapid shifts in either strategy, structure or culture (Grundy 1993). External pressures which could threaten the continued existence of a firm often bring about this type of change. This is usually as a result of part of a major strategic shift, such as a merger with another organization. A number of financial services organizations have embarked on major structural change in recent years as a result of mergers and acquisitions, for example Halifax and Leeds Permanent and Lloyds/TSB, with changes to employment contracts, job roles and location of both branches and group departments, as well as marketing and product specifications.

The distinctions described above are useful in determining the strategies and methods to be employed in managing the change effort.

The forces of change

The forces that bring about change are many and varied. Triggers for change facing financial services organizations can be analysed using the Le Pest & Co framework described in Chapter 1.

The primary drivers of change are the demands of the evolving marketplace. The emergence of new technologies, swings in the economic climate, the increase in the number and quality of competitors, and shifts in the behaviour of existing competitors all represent forces for change.

Tichy and Devanna (1990) identified four main triggers for change:

1. Technology.

2. Knowledge.

3. Product obsolescence.

4. Nature of work force.

An organization needs to identify and analyse the triggers for change, but it also needs to understand the interrelationships between them. Organizations that fail to respond to these forces may decline and cease to exist.

Changes in the organization will affect the nature of work and may involve:

- changing the individuals who work in the organizations in terms of, for example, skills, values, attitudes, behaviours;
- changing organizational structures and systems;
- changing the organizational culture or style.

People, work and managers' roles are becoming increasingly complex and demanding and careers are less predictable. Stewart (1991) suggests that change will affect the kind of jobs the manager does and also the nature of their working lives and careers. This topic is explored in more detail in Chapters 6 and 9.

However, whilst strategic change is necessary in all organizations if they are to survive, managing change is not an easy task. As Machiavelli said:

> *There is nothing more difficult to plan, more doubtful of success nor more dangerous to manage then the creation of a new system. For the initiator has the enmity of all who would prohibit by the preservation of the old institutions and merely lukewarm defenders in those which should gain from the new ones.*

Managing change

As already indicated, change can happen or change can be planned. It can evolve slowly or it can be initiated deliberately by management. Planned change occurs to increase an organization's effectiveness and to improve the ability of the organization to cope with the change in its operating environment. It focuses on how change can be implemented and describes the activities that must take place to initiate and complete successful change.

Planned change within an organization is usually triggered by a need to respond to new challenges, opportunities and threats presented by the external environment. It represents an intentional attempt to improve the operational effectiveness of the organization (Mullins 1996).

Models for change

If planned change is to be adopted by the organization then models can be helpful in identifying the decisions and actions that need to be taken. Planned approaches and traditional models of managing change are based on the assumption that people have the capacity to think logically and rationally. This approach makes the assumption that clear change objectives can be identified and that the change process has discrete stages. Whilst there is no one model that can be universally applied, a simple framework for managing planned change involves the following steps:

- recognition of the need for change;

- identification of the need for change;

- identification of possible solutions;

- communication and consultations;

- selection of the solution;

- selling the solution;

- implementing the solution;

- achieving the success.

The starting point is recognising that change needs to happen and this then leads to the implementation of change.

Planned change

Lewin (1951) proposed one of the first fundamental models of planned change which encapsulates the above steps. He developed a programme of planned change to explain the change process aimed at improving performance. It involves three phases in changing behaviour:

Unfreezing

For change to take place old behaviours must be altered. This stage involves reducing those forces which maintain current behaviours and which provide recognition of the need for change and improvements to occur. It means getting rid of existing practices and of ways of working which stand in the way of change.

People therefore need to be made aware of the need for change and the benefits. Unfreezing may occur through dramatic events, such as redundancy programmes, that will lead to doubts and fears of the future. Effective communication is critical at this stage.

Movement/change

This involves the development of new attitudes or behaviours and the implementation of change.

Refreezing

This stage is where the change is stabilized at the new level and where reinforcements (through supporting mechanisms such as reward policies and structures) help establish the new norms.

It could perhaps be argued that in the current environment where change follows change, instability and uncertainty is the norm and refreezing may not always occur.

Implementation of change – hard and soft approaches

There are two major approaches to implementing change in organizations: the hard and soft approaches. The hard approach views change as needing a systematic and rigorous approach. It is typified in methodologies like business process reengineering. There are three overlapping phases involved in this approach:

1. **Description** – This stage recognizes the need to solve a problem or to take advantage of an opportunity, identifying objectives and constraints and deciding how objectives can be measured.

2. **Options** – This involves developing ideas, introducing clear options in order to achieve objectives, editing the options, and describing them in detail and what is involved in each one. There is an evaluation of chosen options versus the performance criteria.

3. **Implementation** – This involves the development of implementation strategies and carrying out any changes needed.

Business Process Reengineering

Business Process Reengineering (BPR) is typical of the methods of change associated with the hard approach. It is a management technique that aims to enhance productivity and responsiveness by changing organizational structures and the deployment of resources around key business processes. It is the term given to restructuring the way business activities, departments and entire companies operate. Many financial services organizations have instigated BPR projects as a means of identifying how to improve organizational efficiency.

The soft approach to implementing change is much less rigid and can be described as the organizational development approach. This method considers issues not always acknowledged in the hard approach such as organizational culture, power bases and leadership styles. If there is a lot of complexity and the change required is far-reaching then consideration of the soft approach or organizational development may be more appropriate. This approach:

- emphasizes the process of change rather than just the goals;
- encourages a consideration of behaviour and resistance to change;
- emphasizes participation as a way of gaining co-operation;
- expects top management's support and involvement;
- assumes people are the drivers of change and it is brought about through gaining an individual's commitment to change.

The organizational development approach therefore relies on teamwork and participative leadership styles. If a participative style is used then the changes tend to be more widely accepted and are long lasting since commitment is present. The disadvantages include the fact that this style tends to lead to slow and evolutionary change. A number of guidelines have been given to establish clear paths of action for organizational development:

1. Create an environment of trust and shared commitment and involve staff in decisions and actions affecting them.

2. Gain the full and genuine participation of staff as early as possible and well before new systems are introduced. This involves them in handling foreseen difficulties and finding solutions.

3. Through team management encourage a co-operative spirit and a feeling of involvement since this creates a willingness to change.

4. Provide a human resource management (HRM) action programme so the changes require HR planning and strategy.

5. Give consideration to the appropriate reward systems with incentive schemes providing the reward for effort and performance.

6. Social aspects must be considered in changes to work systems because job design is a key consideration in the change process.

As stated earlier, the hard approach change tends to be quicker but will only happen as long as the leader has a position of power. More time will be spent examining leadership style and its relationship with managing change in the section on cultural change.

Structure and change

In Chapter 3 the internal organization of the firm was explored along with the terms and different types of structures used in the financial services sector, and the advantages and disadvantages of each. This section examines the relationship between change, development and structure. It has often been observed that a relationship exists between the development of the organization and the structural forms it may adopt.

In the early stages of development the structure of an organization tends to be simple and focused around one individual. When this early entrepreneurial phase gives way to a more settled phase of sustained growth then the structure is likely to be formed into specialized departments or functions. As a company expands geographically and becomes global in nature then its structure will reflect this geographical expansion.

It is argued by some researchers, for example Morgan (1989), that most bureaucratic organizations are being reshaped in response to the changing demands of the world. Some changes are marginal but others are more radical and result in network structures of which the matrix organization, referred to in Chapter 3, is a forerunner. Bartol and Martin

(1994) suggest that organizations using a matrix structure have passed through four identifiable stages. These are:

1. Traditional structure normally functional in nature.

2. Temporary overlay in which posts are allocated to managers to integrate the various projects. These have cross-functional or departmental boundaries.

3. Permanent overlay in which the integrators are permanent posts with often permanent interdepartmental teams.

4. Mature matrix structures is the final stage where the matrix managers have equal power with functional managers.

Morgan (1989) perhaps sees a further development from the four stages above, whereby most activities are carried out through project teams. Although notionally there are functional departments, they only play a supporting role, hence the organization changes from a rigid bureaucracy to a loosely connected network.

The concept of the virtual organization has close links with this idea of a network organization. Although there are several ways of interpreting this term most appear to conclude that it is derived from the idea of virtual memory (Davidow and Malone 1992) rather than virtual reality. Virtual memory is described as a way of making a computer's memory capacity appear greater than it is. It could be defined as "a temporary network of companies that come together quickly to exploit fast changing opportunities" (Luthans 1995). It is different from a traditional merger and acquisition situation, as partners each contribute to the virtual organization their special skills and abilities. Virtual and network organizations are only able to offer stable, secure employment to a few from whom loyalty and commitment are expected. This links to the concept of the flexible firm, discussed in Chapter 3, and is attractive to owners and employers and to the few employed as core staff. However, it brings problems to those on short-term, temporary and low-skilled work.

Although it is possible to discern the different structures an organization can adopt as it changes and develops one issue that must be addressed is the feasibility of frequently changing structures. Mullins (1996) believes that organizations cannot change their formal structure at frequent intervals without encountering severe difficulties. For example, there has to be a considerable change in environmental factors before an organization will respond by changing its structure. There are also time lags between the factors creating the pressure to change and the change occurring.

A change in organizational structure is one of the overt signs that change has occurred. Less obvious are the cultural changes that are required. However, structural changes can also be used to facilitate changes in culture. The appropriate structure can be an important lever in achieving change but its effectiveness is dependent upon recognising the informal as well as the formal aspects of structure.

The 1990s saw a move in many financial services organizations toward flatter organizational structures that reflect and are responsive to different markets rather than functions. Customer responsiveness places a greater emphasis on horizontal processes and incorporates the concept that everyone is someone else's customer. The move to a network structure mentioned earlier facilitates the organization's responsiveness to change.

Cultural change

The concept of culture has already been explored in Chapter 3. One of the key aspects of the change process is that it will alter "the way things are done around here" so that some change in culture will be inevitable.

Changing the culture of the organization is often the most difficult change to manage. A change in culture means a change in the beliefs and values which the staff working for the organization have adopted. In seeking to develop a new corporate culture management may be either involved in making changes to a dysfunctional culture or in reinforcing or embedding an existing culture to adapt to its changing environment.

There are different views on the extent to which culture can be managed and changed. A model proposed by Silverwieg and Allen (1976) incorporates a number of steps that can be used when implementing a programme of cultural change.

Step One

Analyse the existing culture and establish the gap between the actual and desired culture in terms of:

- leadership;
- team culture;
- communication systems;
- organizational policies and structures;
- reward systems;
- training.

Step Two

Experience the desired culture by involving the employees affected in workshop sessions.

Step Three

Modify the culture through a discussion of issues and problems at work group level.

Step Four

Sustain the culture with continued measurement and evaluation.

Human Resource Management (HRM) policies and procedures play a key part in managing cultural change. All aspects of the HR system in terms of recruitment, selection, induction, training and development and reward systems can be used to both shape and reinforce the desired organizational cultural values.

Successful change can only be achieved through the involvement of employees. However, the more radical the proposed change in culture the greater the resistance to change will be. Sathe (1988) suggests that the degree of cultural resistance can be determined by the magnitude of the change in culture multiplied by the strength of the prevailing culture.

Leadership is also vital to the success of any cultural change programme. The leader has a crucial role to play in setting the vision that the organization wishes to move towards. Leaders are also responsible for allocating tasks and duties, and structuring the organization and distributing resources. Therefore, as an organization moves through different stages it may be appropriate for a leader to utilize different styles. There has already been reference to the importance of using a participative style in the soft approach or organizational development approach to managing change. In this situation the participation of staff in decision-making is vital if changes are to be widely accepted. In some situations where there is a need to drive change quickly it may be more appropriate to use an authoritative style. Different types of leadership style and their effects will be discussed more fully in Chapter 7.

Leaders can manage resistance to change through their behaviour by:

- their use of time which gives messages about priorities;
- their use of language and what they say which gives clear signals;
- meetings which can be used to give clear messages.

The 7 S Framework

Whilst structure and culture are critical aspects to managing the change process there are other important aspects. The 7 S approach, developed by the McKinsey Consultants, suggests that managing successful change is complex and should focus on the whole organization. This can be considered as consisting of seven sub-systems, all of which are important in achieving success. They all interact with one another, and if any one is changed then any or all of the others may need to be changed to achieve organizational effectiveness. The seven Ss are:

1. *Strategy* – the actions are planned in response to environmental changes in order that the organization achieves its objectives.

2. *Structure* – the issue of structure should not only be concerned with whether the organization should be of a functional/divisional or matrix form but should also consider the co-ordination between different areas operating in a changing environment.

3. *Systems* – are concerned with how the organization gets things done. This includes the formal and informal procedures that ensure the organization operates, for example accounting systems, budgeting systems, information technology systems, training, etc.

4. **Style** – relates to the management and leadership style which will be critical, because this will convey what is important in the organization.

5. **Skills** – concern the key capabilities of the organization. A change in strategic focus may mean that new skills need to be acquired as other skills become redundant.

6. **Staff** – this is concerned with the way people in the organization are managed, developed and allocated.

7. **Superordinate Goals** (Shared Values) – refers to the guiding concepts, values and aspirations of the organization that go beyond the formal statement of corporate objectives. In managing change it may be necessary to alter or introduce new guiding concepts.

The contribution of the 7 S framework is that it clearly reveals that the relationships between the different areas are important in managing change. When implementing change all aspects of the framework need attention. As mentioned in Chapter 3, this model clearly has implications for managing the culture of organizations.

Resistance to change

For management planning change there will be forces to encourage change and forces to resist change at work. Lewin's (1951) force field analysis framework is helpful to managers in predicting the likely consequences of introducing change and ways to handle resistance to change. Lewin proposes that organizations exist in a state of equilibrium which is not conducive to change and which is the result of opposing forces constantly acting upon the organization and individuals. The framework identifies forces, which push change forward, and forces which work against change. To promote the appropriate conditions for change individuals must identify the driving and restraining forces and blockages. The driving forces for change can be categorized in terms of external forces and internal forces.

Driving forces for change

1. External forces
   - Role of the state;

- Social pressures;
- Changing technology;
- Constraints from suppliers;
- Stakeholder demands;
- Competitor behaviour;
- Customer needs.

2. Internal forces
    - Organizational growth;
    - Pressures for increased performance;
    - Managerial aspirations;
    - Political coalitions;
    - Redesign of jobs;
    - Restructuring.

Driving forces against change

Resistance to change, in other words the driving forces against change, can happen at several different levels, including the individual and organizational level.

Individual level

There are different types of individual resistance to change. These are summarized as follows:

1. *Selective Perception* – where plans which propose change in the key elements of the organization meet with resistance from individuals.

2. *Habit* – where routine situations give comfort and security. Proposed changes can be resisted when the habits are ingrained and appear reasonable and rational to the people themselves.

3. *Security* – where current work practices are familiar and less threatening. Individuals therefore forego promotion because there is a need for greater security and the fear of the unknown is intense.

4. *Economic* – since any change can threaten pay and pensions benefits and potential loss of power base.

5. *Status* – if there is a change in status and esteem this can cause resistance.

6. *Fear of the unknown.*

7. *Dislike of uncertainty.*

Organization level

Organizations can also be resistant to change:

1. Most organizations have a well-defined structure and a variety of rules and procedures to consolidate the existing state.

2. Lack of organizational capability and resources. Often resources are committed to projects that cannot easily be redirected.

3. There is a perception that particular groups have power and are unlikely to concede.

4. Some parties may have contracts with a third party and there might therefore be a limit to the changes in behaviour and work practices that can be introduced.

5. Entrenched interests of stakeholders.

McCalman and Paton (1992) suggested that both individuals and organizations go through certain stages when resisting change, which include.

- *denial and confusion*, where new ideas are rejected because they do not fit in;

- *defence*, when depression and frustration with ritual behaviour and so performance sags;

- *optimism* can start to emerge which can question the commitment to the new trial behaviour;

- *adopting learning*, whereby performance starts to recover and change is assimilated;

- *Internalize and accept change* with self esteem rebuilt and new ways of doing things.

There are similarities to be found in these stages and in those found in Lewin's model of planned change theory (unfreeze, change, refreeze) which has already been explored in this chapter. Within the first three stages of the resistance model there can be further subdivisions:

Phase 1

There are only a few who see the need for change and who take reform seriously. These people are on the fringe of the organization and can be openly criticized and ridiculed as people try to get them to conform to the organizational norms.

Phase 2

As the movement for change grows the forces for and against change become identifiable. Change is discussed and more thoroughly understood. The threat associated with change is lessened because of the increased understanding and the feelings of opposition are reduced.

Phase 3

There can be direct conflict and a battle between the forces for and against change. This can still mean that the change will die as those who are enthusiastic about the change often underestimate the strength of resistance.

Phase 4

If after the battle supporters of change see the remaining resistance as a nuisance it is still possible for the resisters to mobilize support to shift the balance of power. There is a need to deal with overt opposition.

Phase 5

The resisters are few and as alienated as the advocates were in the first phase. If resistance to change is to be minimized two things need to be recognized:

1. Resistance to change can be predicted.

2. Resistance is not repressed effectively in the long run and is a sign that something is not working.

It is widely acknowledged that consideration of resistance and resulting action is vital if change is to be successful. Within this change process there are several other major factors to consider:

- the degree of change required, whether it is minor (layout of forms) or major (strategy) the greater the change the more difficult it will be to implement;

- the time frame, whether the change is happening over several months or years, since the longer the time frame the greater the degree of success;

- the impact on culture, whereby the greater the impact the greater the resistance and the greater the difficulty in implementing it;

- the evaluation of standards or levels of performance used to measure the degree of change and its impact on organizational effectiveness;

- the consultant: whether they should be internal or external to spearhead the process.

Who should manage change?

There can be a number of people involved in the implementation of change including:

- *a catalyst*, often the chief executive or managing director, who has reduced involvement in the change processes but is a key player at the beginning of the process. A catalyst will select a change agent to carry through the process of change. The catalyst occupies a prominent role in the early stages;

- *a change agent* who can be an internal or external player and who is responsible for starting up the change process;

- *the steering agent* who works with the change agent to channel change and ensures the initiative is not diverted and does not lose momentum (they act as a project manager);

- *the maintenance agent* who maintains the change achieved and the progress made.

Towards the end of the initial stages of managing change the steering agent assumes greater importance as the change agent starts to withdraw.

There can then be a need for a maintenance agent who can follow the routine process of change through rolling out the new actions and systems.

One of the key questions to be answered when identifying individuals for the roles of change and steering agents is the involvement of outside parties.

The role of the consultant in managing change

External consultants

There are a variety of opinions about the effectiveness of using an external consultant to manage the change process. Some of the issues, which may inform the final decision, are given below:

- with the use of an external consultant the issue of a thorough understanding and knowledge of corporate culture arises and the reluctance by some organizations to hand over culture specific problems;

- there are often doubts expressed about the effectiveness of standard solutions and packages frequently provided by consultants;

- consultants often appear reluctant to get to grips with the unique situations and circumstances of each company but rather offer standardization. They can have an inadequate understanding of the internal context of the client firm and 'push' their own solutions rather than work with clients to produce new ones;

- it is difficult to recruit quality practitioners who can move between corporate cultures. Consultants are technical specialists but often it is managerial problems that are at the root;

- there is a perception that much of what is provided by consultants is over-elaborate;

- finally there can be a tendency for consultants to focus on the short-term rather than try to develop longer-term relations.

In summary, the role of the consultant tends to be one of external supplier rather than network member. The advantages of external consultants are:

- they are independent and objective;

- they are invited into the firm and so have increased leverage and freedom of operations;

- they are not influenced by internal power and political issues and not dependent upon their clients for promotions pay increases, etc.;

- they have a more independent attitude to risk-taking and confrontation with clients.

The disadvantages are related to their lack of familiarity with the organization, its technology and structures, internal resistance to outsiders and their standardized solutions.

Internal consultants

Although independent external consultants can often act as a valuable initial catalyst, many organizations tend to rely on their own resources when introducing change. Companies making progress with change are more aware of their unique nature and the requirements of their own companies (Coulson-Thomas 1992).

An alternative is to use internal consultants, who have familiarity with organizational cultures and norms and behave in accordance with these.

They also know the power and structure of the organization and how to get leverage. Therefore no time is wasted. Finally there is a personal interest in the organization succeeding.

The disadvantages include:

- the internal consultant can often lack the specialist skills that may be needed;

- they can lack objectivity;

- colleagues can be influenced by the consultant's previous role;

- the internal consultant can lack power and authority.

One suggestion to combat these problems is to develop a long-term relationship with an outside consultant. Although this may provide benefits in terms of familiarity with the organization there are some factors which militate against this. A high degree of specialization means the multi-disciplinary team approach will not exist. Billing tends to be on time spent rather than tangible outcomes. Many consultants are reluctant to stray outside their own area of expertise and can resist the formation of network links.

Another solution is to use a team containing both internal and external consultants so the advantages of one offset the weaknesses of the other. This solution can offer less chance of compromise and promote greater continuity. The final section examines how to evaluate the success of organizational change.

Successful change

Given the constant change occurring within organizations it can be difficult to measure how effective strategies to achieve change have been, and what the measures used to assess the 'success' of change should be. Schein (1988) suggests that effectiveness of organizational change can be assessed as the capacity to survive, adapt, maintain and grow. Other features of successful change which can be identified include:

- appropriate organizational structure and design;
- appropriate cultures and values;
- suitable leadership and managerial style;
- supportive HR policies;
- identification and removal of blockages to change;
- effective communication systems;
- attainment of employee commitment and involvement;
- sufficient resources for implementation of change.

Summary

Change in the financial services sector is constant and unpredictable, and there is no single recipe for successfully managing change. However, in today's fast changing environment firms need to constantly consider the appropriateness of their structures, cultures and systems, and how best to plan and implement the change process within the organization if they are to survive. This chapter has explored some of the alternative approaches to planning and introducing change, and the strategies that can be used to overcome resistance.

References

Bartol K M & Martin D C (1994) *Management*, 2nd ed. McGraw Hill

Coulson-Thomas C (1992) *Transforming the Company*, Kogan Page

Davidow W H & Malone M S (1992) *The Virtual Corporation*, Harper

Grundy T (1993) *Managing Strategic Change*, Kogan Page

Lewin K (1951) *Field Theory in Social Science*, Harper & Row

Luthans F (1995) *Organizational Behaviour*, 7th ed. McGraw Hill

McCalman J & Paton R (1992) *Change Management*, PCP

Morgan G (1986) *Images of Organization*, Sage

Morgan G (1989) *Creative Organization Theory*, Sage

Mullins L (1996) *Management and Organizational Behaviour*, 4th ed. Pitman

Sathe V (1988) 'From Surface to Deep Corporate Entrepreneurship', *Human Resource Management*, Winter, 411-589

Schein E H (1988) 'Coming to a New Awareness of Organizational Culture', *Sloan Management Review*, Vol. 25, No. 1

Silverwieg S & Allen R F (1976) 'Changing the Corporate Culture', *Sloan Management Review*, Vol 17 No 3, 33-49

Stewart J (1991) *Managing Change Through Training & Development*, Kogan Page

Strebel (1996) 'Choosing the Right Path', *Mastering Management*, Part 14, Financial Times

Tichy N M & Devanna M A (1990) *The Transformational Leader*, 2nd ed. Wiley

5   Managing customer relations

Objectives

Fierce competition, along with other factors such as technological progress, deregulation and reregulation, and a demand-driven marketplace have all meant that financial services organizations are now operating in very different business conditions. One consequence of these changes is the recognition that the customer should be central to the focus of the business and its strategies. This chapter seeks to:

- define the concept of marketing;
- explore the concept of relationship management;
- examine the concepts of segmentation and mass customization;
- determine the role of service quality;
- distinguish between internal and external customers;
- examine the protection available for financial services customers.

Introduction

Traditionally, the environment for financial services could be characterized as having excess demand, with organizations being product–led and passive, and waiting for customers to come to them. However, the changed business environment has meant that an implementation of the marketing concept and a focus on the customer are crucial for business survival. This chapter will start by considering what is meant by the concept of marketing and will go on to explore why developing a customer relationship should be a key part of a financial services organization's strategy. Why many organizations are focusing on improving service quality will then be explored. Finally the protection available for customers, in cases of customer/organization dispute, is discussed.

The concept of marketing

The marketing concept holds that "the key to achieving organizational goals consists of determining the needs and wants of the target market and delivering the desired satisfaction more effectively and efficiently than competitors" (Kotler 1991). Fundamental to the marketing concept is having a customer focus and achieving profitability through customer satisfaction.

Today many organizations view marketing as a philosophy which should permeate the entire firm, encompassing the activities of the whole organization rather than just the discipline of a departmental function. Drucker (1973) encapsulates this sentiment:

> *Marketing is so basic that it is not just enough to have a strong sales team and to entrust marketing to it. Marketing is not only much broader than selling, it is not a specialized activity at all. It encompasses the entire business. It is the whole business seen from the point of view of the final results, i.e. from the customers' point of view. Concern and responsibility for marketing must, therefore, permeate all areas of the enterprise.*

This perspective elevates marketing to a strategic level so that marketing efforts must be aligned with corporate strategy and be consistent with organizational goals. It involves the continuous analysis of the business's external environment and internal capabilities.

When a business takes marketing on board as a philosophy, the central driver for the business is to create customer value. This requires a shift from an inward looking organizational focus to an outward looking customer focus. Davidson (1987) describes this as an 'outside in' perspective, which is aimed at securing business competitiveness and taking advantage of new opportunities. It involves the process of balancing the organization's need for profit against the benefits required by customers, so as to maximize long-term earnings per share.

Evolution towards the marketing concept

The development of the marketing concept within an organization is an evolutionary process. Kotler (1991) identified five distinct stages which financial services organizations pass through in the process of adopting the marketing concept and arriving at marketing enlightenment. The different phases are:

Phase 1 – Marketing is advertising, sales promotion and publicity

This first phase meant that financial services organizations realized that the increasing competition in their traditional markets required action. They looked at how the consumer goods industry had responded to competitive threats and adopted the advertising and sales promotion techniques used there. These paid off until the competition started using the same methods, and organizations found that keeping the customers gained was far more difficult than attracting them in the first place.

Phase 2 – Marketing is a smiling face and a friendly atmosphere

Whilst advertising, sales promotion and publicity made people aware of financial services organizations, this was no longer an advantage because the competition quickly followed suit. In addition, organizations faced the problem of converting consumers aware of the organization into customers.

One way to overcome this problem was by introducing customer care programmes, with staff trained in customer care techniques. However, once again competition quickly followed. The smiling and friendly atmosphere that (should) prevail in a financial services organization, therefore, now merely serves to ensure that an organization's quality of service is the same as that of its competitors.

Phase 3 – Marketing is innovation

This phase proposed that innovation is the basis of competitive advantage and differentiation. Financial services are, in the main, very easily copied, thus innovation can be very short lived. Organizations must meet the evolving needs of customers, therefore, through continuous innovation. The pressure is on financial service organizations not to be innovative occasionally, but to be always at the leading edge with continuous innovation in new products.

Phase 4 – Marketing is positioning

As financial service product developments tend to be similar (Phase 3), organizations must decide how to differentiate themselves by developing their image in a distinctive way. This involves the consideration of where to aim marketing effort. For example, should they target a particular age range, or client group? Positioning is far more than just creating an image. It also involves choosing specific target markets and serving those target markets effectively on the dimensions preferred.

Phase 5 – Marketing is analysis, planning and control

The ultimate phase of marketing is far more than a cosmetic exercise. For marketing to be a worthwhile exercise there must be effective systems installed to analyse the results of marketing campaigns, to enable a coherent planning organization to exist, and for firm control to be kept on results. If an organization fails to measure the potential of its markets, produce plans, set realistic targets and provide monitoring systems, then it cannot know where it is going. At this stage marketing becomes a philosophy, i.e. the service matches promises and is directly aligned with the organization's corporate strategy.

Businesses are usually led to embrace the marketing concept when driven by circumstances typically related to a changing business environment. Kotler (1991) identified a number of reasons which could trigger an organization to move towards adopting a market orientation, all of which are pertinent to conditions in the financial services industry:

a) *Declining sales or falling market share*;
   If a company suffers from declining sales or falling market share, then it is very likely that profits are being seriously affected. The causes of the fall may be myriad. In such cases the sudden awareness of falling profits can provide the impetus for the company to adopt the marketing concept, investigating and analysing what is happening in the market place. For traditional financial services organizations, the emergence of new competitors stealing market share has been the trigger for developing a marketing orientation.

b) *Slow growth*;
As demand for goods/services is finite, at some point market saturation will occur. Organizations must find new market opportunities. Marketing is crucial in this process of identifying, evaluating and selecting new opportunities.

c) *Changing consumer buying patterns*;
A rapid change in needs and wants, and a move to greater sophistication and quality conscious customers, may drive organizations to adopt the marketing concept. Historically, there has been little pressure for financial services organizations to respond to customers' needs. However, marketing and the marketing efforts of competitors have gradually led to customers requiring more sophisticated services. As customers become more financially aware and lifestyles change, so do consumer buying patterns.

Changes in working hours, demand for service at the customers' convenience and changes in shopping patterns are just some of the influences financial services organizations have had to address. Marketing not only identifies these ever changing trends, but also enables services and distribution systems to be created to meet the changing customer demands.

d) *Increasing competition*;
Increased competitive pressures and conditions of excess supply may force companies to learn marketing. Competition in financial services markets has grown in intensity over the last decade both at a national, an international and a global level. This has manifested itself in acquisitions and the amalgamation of organizations, and the emergence of new 'non-traditional' suppliers (for example, the launch of General Motors GM credit card, Virgin, Marks and Spencer personal financial services and supermarkets who now offer an array of financial services products).

Relationship management

An organization can take alternative directions for their business with regard to customers. The focus could be on, for example:

- acquiring new customers;

- retaining existing customers.

In periods of high growth the emphasis tends to be on *attracting* new customers. However, in an environment where many market sectors, including markets for financial services, face slow growth the focus should be on *keeping* customers. Replacing lost customers is more difficult and expensive then retaining them.

Linked to these alternative directions, an organization can choose to adopt a strategy that ranges from a transactional emphasis at one end, to a relationship strategy at the other end, with the position related to the industry and environment in which the organization operates. Transaction marketing is where the focus is on one transaction at a time and marketing revolves around creating a single transaction or exchange. Relationship management, on the other hand, is based on *continuous* buyer-seller relationships rather than on *discrete* transactions, and is aimed at developing long-term enduring relationships with customers.

For some personal financial services there have been signs of a trend towards a commodity market where price is the principal discriminator and where the emphasis is on individual transactions. An example of a transaction approach is the motor insurance industry. Here consumers are price sensitive, often reviewing their supplier and shopping around every time they receive their annual renewal. Generally a focus on individual transactions tends to be less profitable. This is because the organization is reliant on recruiting new customers, which is an expensive activity and can often result in reduced margins due to price driven competition.

There is a realization that there are not an infinite number of customers to help the organization grow. This has clearly put the focus back on developing long-term relationships, rather than customer acquisition and price based strategies. It is suggested that financial services organizations can increase earnings by maximising the profitability of total customer relationships over time, rather than by seeking to extract profit from an individual product or transaction (Moriarty 1983).

Relationship management is fundamentally concerned with recruiting and retaining customers by nurturing customer loyalty: "the attraction, maintenance and enhancement of client relationships". The rationale is that the resulting long-term retention and development of the existing customer base will lead to significantly improved financial and business performance. To achieve this, a greater emphasis must be placed upon the creation of customer value.

Within the context of relationship management the customer is viewed as an appreciating asset. Customers become partners and organizations must make long-term commitments to maintain those relationships with quality, service and innovation (Webster 1994).

The primary goals of a relationship management strategy are to:

- build and maintain a base of committed customers who are profitable to the organization;

- provide customer enhancement to develop loyal customers who will then buy more products and provide a solid base. This base represents a potential for growth which should lead to increased market share and increased profitability;

- improve effectiveness of marketing expenditure based on a cross sales focus;

- increase knowledge of customer needs.

A relationship management strategy is appropriate when the following characteristics of the marketplace are present:

- mature marketplace;

- no/slow growth;

- no clear market leader;

- competitive environment;

- declining customer loyalty;

- emergence of sophisticated delivery mechanisms.

Most, if not all of these features are apparent in the financial services industry.

Profitable segments

The process of relationship management should start with the attraction of customers who are likely to become future profitable long-term relationship customers. However, an organization is limited in terms of its resources and competencies. Therefore it must limit the markets it chooses to service through market segmentation, targeting and positioning strategies. The service delivered should be based on the overall worth of a customer. The skill is to isolate those customers with long-term profit potential. Using modelling techniques to identify those segments which yield the best potential return an assessment can be made to ensure that profitable sectors are chosen.

Customers within a market vary in terms of the needs they seek to satisfy, and it could be argued that to be fully customer-focused an organization would need to adapt its offerings to meet the needs of each individual. While for many organizations this is not economically viable, a strategy of market segmentation may be beneficial. Segmentation is essentially a concept which provides an understanding of the market and leads to the selection of target markets. It can be defined as the process of dividing a market into smaller and homogenous segments which are then targeted with different, appropriately designed, service offers. A segment describes a group of people who have broadly similar needs which differ in some definable way from the needs of other segments.

The rationale underlying a strategy of market segmentation is that, from an organization's perspective, it should be possible to increase the profit contribution when compared with using an undifferentiated approach. From a consumer perspective, market segmentation should mean that they get a product more suited to their requirements.

Within financial services the most obvious segmentation is between commercial (corporate/business) and retail (personal) markets. However, the developments of more sophisticated segmentation strategies have emerged as a response to the competitive operating conditions. The development and installation of advanced customer information systems have provided financial services organizations with access to valuable background data on customers, which can be utilized for segmentation purposes.

When determining appropriate segmentation strategies financial services organizations must consider:

- market attractiveness;

- organization's ability to serve the markets.

Once a profile of the possible target segment has been identified, it is only useful if it is within the company's capabilities to profit from targeting the segment.

There are many different ways in which a financial services organization could segment its markets. For example:

1. *Geographic segmentation*, which is based on where customers live. This could involve, for instance, a global financial services organization developing unique product portfolios for different countries because of cultural influences impacting on product design.

2. *Demographic segmentation*, which is where the market is divided into groups based on variables such as age, gender, income, occupation or stage in the family life cycle. The premise here is that the variables will provide accurate predictors of the need for different financial services. For financial services both age and the family life cycle concept have provided potent bases for segmentation on the basis that financial circumstances, needs and priorities change at different stages within the life cycle.

3. *Geo-demographic segmentation*, which is an approach which interlaces a number of dimensions based on geographic and demographic terms such as location of household, type of household, occupation and age of occupant. The basis for this approach is that households within a particular area exhibit similar purchasing behaviour. The implications of geo-demographic segmentation for financial services organizations is significant in that it allows them to profile users and potential users for a service and then target customers who match these profiles. The profiling will seek to identify the propensity to purchase specific financial services. Geo-demographic segmentation has improved the ability to discriminate markets efficiently and effectively for financial services. Particular areas within cities/towns/rural areas can be used to target direct mailing activity.

4. *Behaviour segmentation*, which is where the marketer aims to distinguish the market in terms of user status, for example,

heavy, medium, light and non-users of a service, and then determine whether the needs or wants differ. Financial services are advancing this through database-held information with the development of sophisticated segmentation models. Behavioural scoring is one example whereby predictions can be made on the likely future patterns of financial behaviour. This permits the accurate targeting of specific product offerings and a rapid response to any changes identified in usage patterns. To illustrate this approach a credit card company can determine through interrogation of its database how frequently a customer uses a credit card. Customers can then be segmented by their behaviour pattern and different marketing strategies formulated for the different categories of users.

5. *Lifestyle segmentation*, which is where consumer markets are segmented on the basis of broad attitudes determined by factors such as values, lifestyle, personality traits, attitudes, interests and innovativeness. For financial services organizations this method provides information on customers' attitudes towards a variety of services, for example their disposition towards savings, investment and use of credit. Whilst attitudinal data is more difficult to collect, it can be an effective base to use when developing and shaping communication messages which will attract and influence target customer groups. For example, when developing the promotional campaign for credit cards, it would be beneficial to understand the motivations and attitudes of the target group towards the services. So, for example, is a credit card just viewed as a substitute for cash/cheques or as a symbol of financial success and prestige?

Active relationship management requires a comprehensive knowledge of the customer as an individual. One route available to ensure efficient and effective management is to utilize sophisticated customer databases that are designed to deal with the complexities of the customer base and the significant volumes of customer data. These systems can facilitate an in-depth understanding of consumer behaviour. The utilization of database marketing techniques opens up new opportunities for cross selling by spotting timely sales activity.

The ultimate goal in segmentation would be to design and tailor products to the individual, and indeed this is often the strategy which is adopted in the corporate banking market. There are now similar developments in some consumer markets, and these are often discussed under the concept of mass customization. This concept is essentially concerned with making tailor-made products for each individual buyer. The rationale is that by employing mass customization systems, organizations can produce enough variety in products/service so that nearly everyone finds exactly what they want at reasonable prices (Pine 1993). Within the financial services sector, product variety and customization of products, such as cheque accounts and mortgages could be offered, given the sophisticated information technology systems which are now available to support such innovations.

The customer relationship lifecycle

There are several distinct phases in the development of the customer relationship. These can be termed the consumption process or buyer behaviour. A series of questions underpins the understanding of buyer behaviour (Wilson et al 1992):

1. What is the market and what is the extent of customer power with regard to the organization?

2. What do they buy?

3. Why do they buy?

4. Who is involved in making the purchase decision and the buying of the product/service?

5. How do they buy?

6. When do they buy?

7. Where do they buy?

Information on these areas is vital to the formulation of effective and efficient marketing strategies to gain competitive advantage. However, there are many influences on consumer behaviour, and the outcome in terms of purchasing decisions can be difficult to understand from a rational perspective, since both emotional and rational influence will impact on the purchasing decision for financial services.

There are, however, a number of distinct phases in the development of the customer relationship. Recruitment is the first stage where contact is made with a potential customer. Both parties will evaluate the benefits of forming the relationship (i.e. selling the service/taking up the offer). Following the purchase the onus is on the supplier to maintain and enhance the relationship in a way that will ensure the customer remains willing to do business with the organization and to purchase additional services.

Figure 5.1 illustrates the development of the customer relationship life cycle in which there are distinct stages where the customer can exit if not satisfied. If the customer is satisfied with the total service offered then there is an increased likelihood of a repeat purchase.

Figure 5.1: The Customer Relationship Life Cycle

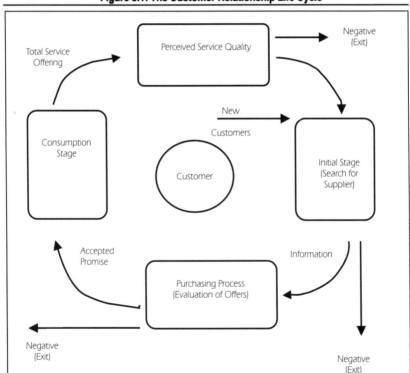

Source: Adapted from C Gronroos 1983

The importance of the life cycle model is that different strategies will be required at each stage. For example, at the initial stage emphasis should be on advertising and promotion to make potential consumers aware of and interested in the financial services organization and services on offer. During the purchase stage of a financial service the focus will be on the identification of the customers' needs/wants, and personal service will play a critical role at this point. The distribution channel is also important in that the experience of a branch visit or telephone call to the organization can cement or sever the relationship. Within the financial services industry, the success of purchase is often dependent upon the staff/customer interface. Staff have a key role in creating the sale, re-sale, customer retention and nurturing.

During the consumption stage there are many opportunities to fulfill or fail to meet the promises given to the customers. These opportunities are termed "Moments of Truth" by Carlzon (1987). This service encounter relates to the direct interaction between the organization and the customers, and can take various forms. For the financial services market the interaction could be:

- face-to face with an employee;
- by telephone;
- by letter;
- with a self-service machine;
- electronic via a PC or the Internet.

Service encounters have a high impact on the customer, and the quality of the encounter will be a critical determinant in the evaluation of the service received. Whatever the nature of the encounter this will impact on the customer's impression of the organization and the service. It is important to manage all the potential service encounters effectively to ensure ultimate customer satisfaction with the organization

The benefits an organization can gain from enhancing customer relationships is shown in the 'Relationship Management Ladder of Customer Loyalty' in Figure 5.2. The ladder provides an illustration of how the customer relationship develops, and how the customer progresses through a number of stages as the relationship becomes stronger. The philosophy of the Relationship Management Ladder is that as customers move up the ladder their affinity with the organization is enhanced. The underlying proposition is that the higher the customer moves up the ladder the less likely they will be to want to change organizations. Ultimately they could become 'Advocators' and 'Supporters', recommending the products of the organization to potential customers, and as such are rarely lost. In contrast 'Customers' are more vulnerable to poaching by the competition.

First Direct is an example of a financial services organization which has succeeded in moving customers up the 'ladder' to become advocators as a result of providing excellent customer services. A significant proportion of its business has been gained through word of mouth, and through recommendation by the advocators of the organization.

Figure 5.2: The Relationship Management Ladder of Customer Loyalty

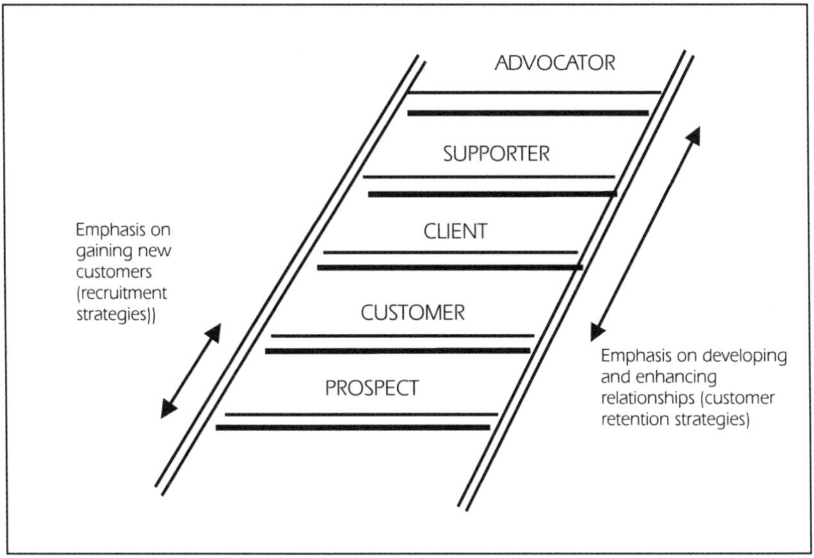

Source: Adapted from Christopher et al 1993

Customer retention strategies

An organization which only concentrates on the recruitment of customers can develop the 'leaking bucket effect' (Christopher et al 1993). That is to say, if an organization does not also concentrate on retaining existing customers all that that happens is that those recruited replace those who leave. The overall customer base will, at best, remain static, but the cost of the organization will be inflated by additional promotional expenditure required to attract new customers.

Recruitment through price led strategies may lead to the attraction of 'footloose' customers with no loyalty. These customers may not stay with the organization for long enough to become profitable. Therefore it can be an expensive strategy.

A key objective for a financial services organization should be to generate repeat purchases from its existing customer base. Customer retention should be regarded as a key business objective since a strategy of customer retention is cheaper than recruitment strategies. Research has suggested that it may be five times as costly to attract new customers as to keep old ones (Bartell 1993). Reducing defections or increasing retention by 5% can therefore dramatically improve profits:

- repeat customers may will be willing to pay a premium for the service if they value the organization;

- they may provide additional business to the organization through word of mouth recommendation.

The concept of customer loyalty suggests that a customer will remain loyal to an organization if that organization fulfills his or her needs and preferences. The organization can return the loyalty by becoming knowledgeable about the customer, enhancing the product offering, and providing greater value.

Loyalty stems from satisfaction and positive reinforcement, and leads to repeat purchases. Loyal customers offer their supplier the following benefits:

1. They visit the organization and are more likely to be receptive to a sales offer, and this reduces the costs of reaching them.

2. A good company that deals with a loyal customer has built up a relationship with them and therefore knows their requirements, and this encourages focused targeting.

3. A loyal customer is more likely to buy additional services, increasing customer longevity, and reducing defection rates.

4. Benefits of word-of-mouth recommendation lead to new business.

The establishment of loyalty schemes should be implemented to encourage customers to remain with the organization and to purchase additional products. "If customers have one product with your bank, there is a 15% chance that they will stay loyal to you for five years, With two products that rises to 45%, with three 80%. The commitment to customer retention must be everywhere, and employees must be empowered and in a position to make things right for the customer" (Bartell 1993). The degree of loyalty will be affected by:

- the perceived cost of changing organizations (switching costs);
- the availability of substitutes;
- the perceived risk of the purchase;
- the degree to which satisfaction has been obtained in the past.

Many organizations, including those in the financial services sector, are introducing incentive and loyalty schemes. To distinguish between the two:

a) *Incentive schemes* are also known as continuous sales promotion drives. They are designed to encourage customers to take out extra products or to increase usage of a specific product or group of products. Many of the credit card companies have incentive schemes such as offering airmiles or some other points system to encourage greater card usage.

b) *Loyalty schemes* are designed to reward customers who remain loyal to the organization, either by encouraging them to stay or by ensuring that products or funds are retained over a period of time. A number of the building societies offer a reduced interest rate on mortgages for long-standing customers as a reward for loyalty.

Customer focus and service quality

Ultimately, customer retention is driven by customer satisfaction, which in turn can be directly linked to service quality. Therefore, central to a relationship management strategy is the provision of a high quality of service. This is based on the premise that if a customer is satisfied with the service received, they will more readily consider the organization for other products and services and provide future sales opportunities.

Intense competition, compressed industry margins, an expanded array of providers and product options, and increased customer sophistication are all factors which have contributed to making quality a key strategic issue for financial services organizations. Customer service and quality should be viewed as key components of the overall 'offer', and as competitive weapons in the battle to provide differentiated and superior value to specific customer segments. In a marketplace where product features can be quickly copied, it will be quality where an organization can gain competitive advantage that is both sustainable and profitable. This is because price-led competition is becoming more difficult and customers are becoming much more demanding of the service they expect. Research amongst financial services organizations has shown that it is not only price-driven reasons which trigger the transfer of business. The factors are frequently also related to the service experience.

While over the last fifteen years or so many financial services organizations have introduced some form of customer care programme, these have often amounted to little more than short-term programmes, which were fundamentally flawed. The support processes were not in place to uphold a quality culture. Pursuing a quality of service strategy means pursuing a continuing journey, and not one-off programmes.

A quality strategy should not just be about focusing on customers and competitors, but should be expanded to include all stakeholders who have the potential to contribute to the creation of superior customer value. To provide the best value, the organization must bear in mind that the customer relationship can involve the buyer and seller in a network consisting of different parties, for example:

- suppliers;

- internal customers;

- influence markets (i.e. the government, regulatory markets, the media);

- referral markets (i.e. includes intermediaries, agencies, customer referral sources).

The whole network is part of the customer relationship and has an impact on the development of that relationship. There is a need to integrate activities both downstream to the ultimate customer, in terms of people and processes, and upstream to suppliers.

Quality of service must start with understanding the customer and the influences on buyer behaviour in order to determine how additional 'value' can be added to the service 'offering'.

The concept of value

Generally, customers prefer to have an ongoing relationship rather than continually switching between suppliers in search of value. Delivery of superior 'value' to the customer should drive the formulation and implementation of relationship strategies. Customers will remain loyal when they receive greater value from the organization compared to the competitors in the market. Perceived value relates to the customer's overall assessment of the utility of a service, based on the perception of what is received and what is given. Value reflects the growing customer concern of getting more for the money, time and effort invested (Zeithaml and Bitner 1996).

The customer's perception of total value will impact on their willingness to buy the service. However, value is an amorphous concept and means different things to different people. To create value the organization needs to understand, from the customer perspective, how value perceptions are formed, influenced and evaluated. For example, is value judged on the basis of quality, satisfaction, price or a combination of these factors?

A value-driven strategy must be based on some distinctive competence which will provide a source of unique and substantial competitive advantage. However, the organization must constantly monitor what constitutes value from the customer's perspective. The charge card/credit card market illustrates how value can change and the implications for the players in the market.

Traditionally, American Express has been positioned as a luxury card. Status and prestige were the critical 'value offerings'. However, whilst no other organization could successfully better American Express in its own positioning, during the 1990s rival cards have created new positioning more aligned to the 'value decade' by offering more for less. For example, a number of card issuers have dropped their interest rates and some are offering various incentive schemes such as Citibank who created a card that offered frequent flier miles. Compared to these value offerings the value proposition of prestige, which American Express had always adopted, was outdated. The result for American Express has been a declining market share eroded by competing cards (Zeithaml and Bitner 1996).

Components of quality

The term quality can mean many different things. For example, it is concerned with conforming to requirements, zero defects, getting it right first time and fitness for purpose. Essentially, service quality is about meeting customers' needs and requirements, and how well the service level delivered matches customer expectations. Expectations in this sense are concerned with the standard of performance against which service experiences are compared. They are based on what a customer believes should happen, and will be judged on the customer's subjective assessment of actual service experience. If there is a shortfall a service quality gap exists.

Extensive research has been undertaken to identify the key determinants consumers use in forming expectations about and perceptions of service (Parasuraman et al 1988). Figure 5.3 identifies the five key components which emerged as the criteria used by consumers, and which influenced their expectations and perceptions.

Figure 5.3: Key Components of Quality

Tangibles	The physical aspects of service such as the branch location, appearance of staff, style of plastic cards, statements, chequebook, equipment used, etc.
Reliability	Consistency of service and getting it right first time, and the ability to perform the promised services dependably and accurately. For example, accuracy of transactions
Responsiveness	Speed of service, availability of relevant information, willingness of staff to deal with problems/queries
Assurance	Knowledge and courtesy of employees, honesty and their ability to inspire trust and confidence
Empathy	Individualized attention

Source: Adapted from Parasuraman et al 1998

The dimensions vary in terms of how easy or difficult it is to evaluate them, for example, tangibles can be judged in advance, but most of the criteria relate to 'experience' qualities and can only be evaluated during or after consumption.

The same research identified five gaps which can prevent organizations from meeting or exceeding target market expectations. In this context Parasuraman (1988) defined service quality as the gap between consumers' expectations of the service and their perception of the actual service delivered by the organization (Gap 5). She proposed that this gap is influenced by other gaps (1-4) which may also occur in the organization. The five gaps are:

Gap 1   Difference between consumer expectations and management perceptions of consumer's expectations. Not knowing what the customer expects.

Gap 2   Difference between management perceptions of consumer expectations and service quality specification. Not selecting the right service designs and standards.

Gap 3   Difference between service quality specifications and the service actually delivered. Not delivering to service standards.

Gap 4   Difference between service delivery and what is communicated about the service to consumers. Not matching performance to promise.

Gap 5   Difference between performance and expected service.

It is important that financial services organizations identify the gaps which are in evidence in their organizations, determine the factors creating the gaps, and develop and implement appropriate solutions.

Measuring service quality

A critical factor in the successful delivery of a quality customer service is to have in place systems to monitor and evaluate the service quality over time. This could involve programmes of market research amongst customers and employees using focus group discussions. It could also use surveys and mystery shoppers to evaluate the perceptions of the overall service delivered against the service standards, and the overall satisfaction with service. In addition, the collection and analysis of customer complaints along with surveys of 'lost' customers is valuable information.

Perceptions of service performance should also be benchmarked. This is assessed relative to the performance of:

a) competitors to seek out opportunities for achieving competitive advantage through service leadership.

b) non-competitors to avoid complacency and identify opportunities for adopting innovative and up-to-date service strategies from outside the immediate industry.

A service quality culture

Whilst there is no one 'recipe' for delivering a quality strategy, there are some fundamental requirements which have implications across all of the business areas. These encompass systems, structures and products, and are underpinned by having competent and motivated staff who are committed to delivering service quality. So delivering service quality has implications for:

- top management;
- management structures;
- how work is organized and jobs designed;
- training;
- communication systems;
- recruitment and selection of staff;
- performance management and appraisal;
- reward systems;
- career development and promotion.

The foundation for creating a quality organization requires the right culture, along with a clearly stated mission and commitment by senior management who should lead by example. It must involve everyone in the organization. A quality service strategy must also include the consideration of product design and delivery, and focus on zero defects.

The mission statement for the organization should articulate the desired long-term direction of the organization by indicating products to be provided, markets to be served, and the means of servicing. There should be explicit reference to the concept of 'relationship'. The statement should be defined in a way which reflects customer needs rather than product features. It should also recognize the importance of customer service at a strategic level and that a relationship strategy is a means of achieving business strategy.

The factors underlying the development of a quality culture can therefore be summarized as:

- top management commitment;
- highly trained staff to build and nurture customer relationships;
- effective recruitment and training processes;
- process re-engineering to build superior services;
- measurement and reward systems which emphasize relationship building.

The organization must align these platforms behind a single coherent objective.

One approach to improving organizational effectiveness is a central focus on quality, or Total Quality Management (TQM), which was first introduced into Japanese companies in the post-war period by Deming and Juran. TQM is concerned with developing a long-term quality culture in the organization based on the principle that to achieve maximum profitability an organization must not only do things right, but do the right things right consistently, and focus on prevention of errors rather than correction of errors. The emphasis is on 'getting it right first time'. To achieve this quality must be perceived as a company-wide issue, involving all levels of employees with a commitment to total customer satisfaction through a process of continuous improvement.

To encourage commitment to a quality culture, a number of financial services organizations have introduced quality circles or quality action teams in order to generate employee involvement and ownership, and so improve customer service. The teams usually involve a small group of employees (say, five to eight members of staff) who meet on a regular basis. The purpose is to identify, analyse and suggest ways of improving service quality.

The role of staff in service delivery

Ensuring that the service delivered meets the specifications set depends upon all employees, who must be able and willing to deliver the desired levels of service. As Lewis (1994) states:

> *if an organization cares about its employees and their role in service delivery then success at managing internal service encounters will precede success in managing relationships with external customers.*

So employees play a critical role in influencing customer perceptions of service, and this is particularly the case in the financial services sector.

The concept of 'internal marketing' is fundamental to service delivery. This concept views employees as internal customers and jobs as internal products (Berry 1980), and is based on the proposition that the various functions of an organization have their own internal customers. Staff in different departments and sections should treat their employees as internal customers, because they are providing a service. In satisfying internal customers the organizations should be better placed to satisfy the needs of external customers and thereby maintain and generate new business. The aims of internal marketing are to develop internal and external customer awareness and remove barriers to organizational effectiveness. It is important to have the systems, structures and people aligned to delivering a quality of service to the ultimate customer.

The three objectives of internal marketing stated by Gronroos (1981) are:

1. *Overall* – to achieve motivated, customer conscious and care oriented personnel.

2. *Strategic* – to create an internal environment which supports customer-consciousness and sales mindedness among personnel.

3. *Tactical* – to sell service campaigns and marketing efforts to employees, which is the first marketplace of the company, via staff training programmes and seminars.

Quality standards

There are a number of quality standards and kite-marks which financial services have adopted.

ISO9000 (formerly BS5750) is one example of a quality assurance certification. This is an internationally promoted standard and aims to ensure that quality management systems of a suitable standard are in place. It does not cover every quality issue, rather it deals with quality systems. The British Standards Institution states the ISO9000 "sets out how you can establish, document and maintain effective quality systems which will demonstrate to your customers that you are committed to quality and are able to satisfy their quality needs".

The European Foundation for Quality Management (EFQM) Excellence Model is a quality framework used by a number of financial services organizations in their quest to achieve service excellence. The model consists of nine criteria, five of which are 'enabler' criteria and four of which relate to 'results'.

Enablers	**Results**
● Leadership	● People Satisfaction
● People Management	● Customer Satisfaction
● Policy and Strategy	● Impact on Society
● Resources	● Business Results
● Business Processes	

The "enablers" cover what an organization does and how it does it. The other four criteria relate to the "results" and cover what an organization achieves. The link between the two is that enablers cause results. Each of the criteria can be used to assess the organization's progress along the journey to excellence. The model suggests that customer satisfaction, people (employee) satisfaction, and impact on society are achieved through leadership which drives the policy, strategy, people management, resources and processes, which leads to excellence in business results.

Customer protection

Whilst many organizations are committed to a relationship management strategy, and provide a high quality of service, attaching great importance to amicably resolving customer complaints, there are sometimes situations where disagreements between the organization and the customer cannot be resolved. One way to pursue these is through the courts. An alternative would be to use one of the Ombudsman schemes such as the Banking Ombudsman, Building Society Ombudsman, Pensions Ombudsman or Insurance Ombudsman. The Ombudsman provides customers with the opportunity to have their case investigated without the costs that would be involved if done through litigation.

The Banking Ombudsman scheme was established in 1986 with the primary purpose of acting as an independent arbitrator between organization and customers in dispute. This scheme can be used by non-corporate customers and by small businesses for disputes where the amount does not exceed £100,000.

The Banking Ombudsman scheme can be used to investigate a wide range of areas within banking although the Ombudsman does not have any statutory powers. However, the Ombudsman can make awards of up to £100,000 which could include payments for damages or loss and also for any inconvenience caused. The Ombudsman cannot deal in any case relating to bank policies on commercial and lending decisions, nor in disputes over banks investment services which have to be referred to the Securities and Investment Boards or some other self-regulatory body.

In 1999 the different Ombudsman schemes will be replaced by a Financial Services Ombudsman scheme which will have a wider remit in terms of covering disputes across the financial services sector.

The Banking Code is a voluntary code followed by banks and building societies in their relations with personal customers, and sets standards of good practice which are followed as a minimum by organizations subscribing to it (The Banking Code). The underlying rationale is that the Code will allow competition and market forces to operate to encourage higher standards which will ultimately benefit the customer. The Code sets out eleven commitments which apply to the conduct of business for all products and services provided to customers. (Mortgages are covered in more detail in the Council of Mortgage Lending Practice.) The standards of the Code are encompassed in the key commitments. The subscribers promise that they will:

- act fairly and reasonably in all dealings with the customer;

- ensure that all services and products comply with the Code, even if they have their own terms and conditions;

- give the customer information on services and products in plain language, and offer help if there is any aspect the customer does not understand;

- help the customer choose a service or product which matches their needs;

- help the customer understand the financial implications of:

  - a mortgage

  - other borrowing

  - savings and investment products

  - card products;

- help the customer understand how accounts work;

- have safe, secure and reliable banking and payment systems;

- ensure that the procedures staff follow reflect the commitments set out in the Code;

- correct errors and handle complaints speedily;

- consider cases of financial difficulty and mortgage arrears sympathetically and positively;

- ensure that all services and products comply with relevant laws and regulations.

Summary

The marketing concept and relationship management views the buyer-seller relationship as continuous with the customer and as the focus for organizational strategies. Fundamental to the concept is developing a service culture and providing a quality of service which ensures long-term customer loyalty and results in more profitable customer relationships. As such, relationship management is a key strategic marketing concept for financial services organizations operating in a competitive environment.

References

The Banking Code (1997), 3rd ed. BBA Enterprises Limited

Bartell, (1993) 'Building Strong Customer Relations', *Bank Marketing*, Vol. 25, No.6

Berry L (1983) 'Relationship Marketing', in Berry et al eds. *Emerging Perspectives of Service Marketing*, American Marketing Association

Carlzon J (1987) *Moments of Truth*, Ballinger

Christopher M G Payne A & Ballantyne D (1993) *Relationship Marketing: Bringing Quality, Customer Service and Marketing Together*, Butterworth Heinemann

Christopher M G Schary P P & Skjoyy-Larsen T (1979) *Customer Service and Distribution Strategy*

Davidson H (1987) *Offensive Marketing or How to Make your Competitors Followers*, Penguin (2 ed)

Drucker P F (1973) *Management: Task, Responsibilities & Practices*, Harper & Row

File K M & Prince, R A (1992) 'Positive Word of Mouth: Customer Satisfaction and Buyer Behaviour', *International Journal of Bank Marketing*, Vol. 10, No.1

Gronroos C (1983) *Strategic Management in Marketing in the Services Sector*, Chartwell Bratt

Gronroos C (1994) 'From Marketing Mix to Relationship Marketing: Towards a Paradigm Shift' *Marketing Management Decisions*, Vol. 32, No. 2

Jain A K, Pinson C & Malhotra N K (1987) 'Customer Loyalty as A Construct in the Marketing of Banking Services', *International Journal of Bank Marketing*, Vol.5, No. 3

Keltner B (1995) 'Relationship Banking and Competitive Advantage: Evidence from the US and Germany', *Californian Management Review*, Vol. 37, No. 4

Kimball R C (1990) 'Relationship Versus Product In Retail Banking', *Journal of Retail Banking*, 12, 1 – Spring

Kotler (1991) *Marketing Management: Analysis, Planning & Control*, Prentice Hall

Levitt T (1960) 'Marketing Myopia', *Harvard Business Review*, July-August

Lewis B R (1991) 'Service Quality: An International Comparison of Bank Customers' Expectations and Perceptions', *Journal of Marketing Management*, Vol.7, No.1

Moriarty R T (1983), *Sloan Management Review*

Parasuraman A, Berry L L & Zeithaml V A (1988) 'SERVQUAL: A Multiple Item Scale for Measuring Consumer Perceptions of Quality of Service', *Journal of Retailing*, Vol. 64, No.1

Pine II B J (1993) 'Mass Customization, the New Frontier in Business Concepts', *Harvard Business School Press*

Webster F E (1994) 'Defining the New Marketing Concept', *Marketing Management*, Vol. 2, No.4

Wilson R M S, Gilligan C, Pearson DJ (1992) *Strategic Marketing Management*, Butterworth-Heinemann

Zeithaml V A & Bitner M J (1996) *Services Marketing*, McGraw Hill

Introduction to section two

Section Two is more concerned with 'management' than 'organization'.

Management as an academic topic is first explored through a necessarily historical approach which outlines the views of exponents of management theory. No particular stress is laid on the primacy of any one view of managerial activity since it seems to be generally recognized that in the complex, global, multi-cultural world of modern management it is sensible to take an eclectic approach. This point acquires even greater force when it is recognized that, with more and more managerial activity becoming concerned with maximising the usefulness of modern technology, and with change being the only constant, there will be no single body of management theory which is likely to be wholly and directly relevant to the world of work in the 21st century.

One of the great benefits of studying management is that the theoretical knowledge gained thereby may be applicable to practical situations encountered in a modern working environment. If such is the case, then the investment in studying the topic will be rewarded by a considerable saving of time, thought and effort, by applying knowledge gained in the past towards the resolution of current problems.

Chapters 6 and 7 look generally at the main schools of management thinking and in greater detail at the influential work of Fayol and Mintzberg. Not surprisingly it emerges that the ways in which theoreticians view the work of the manager is significantly dependent upon the precise context in which managerial activity is either experienced or observed. Furthermore the fact that it is usual and sensible to refer to 'schools' of management thinking suggests that there is much subjectivity used when generalising what constitutes 'management' and the work with which a 'manager' is involved.

Chapter 8 concentrates on the role of senior (board level) management in ensuring, or seeking to ensure, that organizations work to achieve their objectives effectively within the commercial, economic and regulatory environment in which they operate.

In contrast, Chapter 9 focuses on those problems which face all managers, i.e. the management of time, stress and careers, and attempts to relate traditional thought on these three elements of working life to the modern rather than the traditional world of work.

The distinction between what is referred to as 'management' and what is referred to as 'leadership' is difficult to determine with precision. Leadership as a topic is discussed in Chapter 7, and the discussion is then related to the exposition of the work on groups in Chapter 10.

It is fundamental to any managerial activity which involves human interaction that communication should take place, and it is probably not stretching things too far to say that an ability to communicate effectively is a key managerial attribute. Unfortunately effective communication is not easy to achieve for a host of reasons which are explored in Chapter 11.

6 The history of management

Objectives

In this chapter the different historical views on the development of management and the organization of work will be explored, from the views of the Classical school in the late 19th century to those of the Systems and Contingency schools in the mid to later part of this century. The objectives of this chapter are to:

- have an insight into the various functions of management;

- understand the historical development of management as a discrete activity;

- understand how the roles of managers change;

- appreciate the different systems of organising, such as bureaucracy and scientific management;

- examine the developments in management approaches, e.g. the Classical, Human Relations, Systems and Contingency schools.

Introduction

The role of management within an organization is to ensure that the production of goods and services is achieved as effectively as possible. This involves both managing the external boundaries of the firm and the internal environment.

Section 1 dealt mainly with managing the external boundaries of the firm and the organization's responses to that environment.

Sections 2 and 3 of this book look at the management of the internal environment.

Management in organizations

Organizations facilitate the achievement of things that could not otherwise be done by an individual alone. The role of an effective manager is to encourage and enable the transformation of the efforts of many individuals into corporate achievement.

Before considering the history of management and various contributions from different theorists, it is worth spending some time exploring the various definitions of a manager. Some appear to be more aligned to leadership than management, interpreting management as getting others to follow, rather than relating the role to the organization of work. However, most definitions do appear to have a common theme. Managers are those with the responsibility for getting things done through other people instead of doing the job themselves. In order to achieve organizational objectives and goals, they direct the use of human and other resources. Because of their key role and activities it is a critical area of study for those working in organizations. Managers do not only have to get things done but they also have to ensure efficiency and effectiveness in operations. Without this control, costs would escalate and work would not be co-ordinated or even resourced.

Today there is considerable interest in examining management as a specialist area in its own right. Research in the 1980s and 1990s by Charles Handy and others has led to increasing emphasis being placed on the education and development of effective managers. The Management Charter Initiative is one example of this. The Charter summarizes, in the form of competencies, the skills needed to perform the management role. All managers appear to face certain key problems, including the efficiency and effectiveness of operations, the clarification of aims and objectives, the designing of a suitable structure, and the carrying out of administrative functions. This is explored in greater detail in the next chapter.

Although research on the skills of management is ongoing t, research on organization, leadership and management has existed for several centuries. The development of management thinking, as known today, dates from the end of the 19th century, when large industrial firms were first established and the problems of managing these large scale resources was acknowledged. Before examining current thoughts on the role of management it is helpful to explore the historical development of management thinking and what might be termed management theory. Mullins (1997) emphasizes the importance of this study:

> *The application of theory brings about a change in actual behaviour. Managers reading the work of leading writers on the subject might see in their ideas and conclusions a message about how they should behave.*

The study of the development of management theory is helpful in understanding organizations. Knowledge of the writings of management theory assists in a wider understanding of the role of managers. An understanding of the development of the theory also helps to determine how management has progressed, and many of the findings and recommendations made in the earlier writings are still used and practised today.

For ease of study it is usual to divide the writers on the management of organizations into four major groups. The groups are distinguished by the basic differences in their approach. Thus the main trends and frameworks of analysis can be identified. However, within this framework, we can also identify a number of different strands. These show the complex nature of the theories and writings on management. Figure 6.1 below illustrates the four broad groupings or approaches.

Figure 6.1

Contingency: 1960s-present
Systems: 1950s-present
Human Relations: 1920s-1950s
Classical: 1880s-1990s

The oldest of these four groups or 'schools' is the Classical approach. This could be said to comprise three slightly different strands:

- scientific management;
- administrative management;
- bureaucracy.

As with all strands within one approach or school there are common threads. So the Classical approach examines the technical and economic aspects of organizations, but tends to neglect the behavioural, social and sociological aspects of management and organizations.

The second school or group is the Human Relations school, and this emphasizes the study of behaviour and the behavioural aspects of organization, examining specifically individual and group productivity, individual development and job satisfaction.

The Classical and Human Relations schools have now been replaced by more comprehensive approaches to the study of management and organizations in the Systems and Contingency approaches. The Systems school, which has its foundations in the biological theories of organisms (cybernetics), views organizations as systems – i.e. as an interrelated set of activities that converts inputs to outputs. It studies the key elements in an organization, how they interact with one another, and the influence of the environment on the organization. It therefore examines people, structure, technology and environment.

The most recent development has been termed Contingency, and is regarded by most writers, for example Mullins (1997), as forming a separate approach in its own right . This approach emphasizes the need to look at specific circumstances or contingencies when designing organizations or management systems.

The different approaches to management have developed very approximately in a chronological manner. Each approach has gradually expanded the theoretical base of knowledge and added to managerial concepts and ideas about the organization. Although these approaches can be distinguished from each other, it should be emphasized that the boundaries of each are not always clearly visible and the 'schools' can be difficult to define.

The classical approach

Certain common themes or features exist within each approach even though the areas of interest and recommendations may differ. The common features which appear in the classical writers approach are issues surrounding:

- the purpose and structure of organizations;
- the technical requirements of each job;
- the principles of management.

They also assumed that all behaviour in the organization was rational and logical. However, and despite these similarities, there are also significant differences in approach. These different approaches can be identified as Scientific Management, Administrative Management and Bureaucracy.

Scientific management

One of the best known and earliest writers within the Scientific Management school is Frederick Winslow Taylor (1856-1917). He is regarded as the father of work study and first published his ideas in a paper entitled, 'A Piece Rate System' in 1895. His ideas were later expanded in two books, *Shop Management* (1903) and *Principles of Scientific Management* (1911). Taylor believed that there should be a natural division of work into that performed by managers and that performed by employees.

Taylor stated that the major objective of management should be to obtain maximum prosperity for the employer, and maximum prosperity for each employee. This meant the development of all aspects of the organization to a state of permanent prosperity. For the employee 'maximum prosperity' did not just mean immediate higher wages, but physical and technical developments so that they could perform efficiently the highest grade of work of which they were capable. Taylor's work also encompassed job design and method, selection, training and payment systems, and he established four basic principles related to this. The four principles of management are:

1. The constant and intimate co-operation of management and men. There is a division of work and responsibility between management and workers. The management takes over all the work for which they are best fitted, i.e. the specification and verification of methods of working, time, price, quality and standards of the job, and the continuous supervision and

control of the employee doing it. The worker executes the task to the best of his ability.

2. The development of a true science of work. This involved establishing a 'large daily task', and was determined after a scientific investigation into the amount to be done by a suitable, selected and trained person under optimum conditions. For this each employee would receive a high rate of pay, much higher than in other 'unscientific' factories. Employees would also suffer a loss of income if they failed to achieve this level of performance as reward was linked to performance through piece work.

3. The scientific selection and development of the workman. To receive a high rate of pay, careful and scientific selection would occur to match the employee to the job. Taylor stated that it was the responsibility of management to then develop the workers by offering them opportunities for promotion, which would enable them to do the most interesting and profitable work of which they were capable.

4. The bringing together of this science of work and the scientifically selected and trained men so that employees could be specifically matched through recruitment and training for a job.

By claiming a 'science of work' Taylor meant to systematically observe and measure work. The development of this technique is referred to as work-study.

The insistence on maximum specialization was fundamental to Taylor's thinking. There are two aspects to this:

● the detailed division of labour so that complex tasks are split up into sub-tasks;

● the role of management in gathering this information and reducing it to rules, laws and formulae.

These two aspects mean that planning is performed by management and is separated from "the doing", which is completed by the workers. Taylor believed that the four management functions (production, finance, personnel and marketing) should be separated out and performed by different specialists. He called this system 'functional management', and likened it to the increased efficiency that can be obtained in a school where classes go to specialist teachers for different subjects, compared with a school where one teacher teaches all subjects. Taylor also formulated the 'exception principle' whereby all management reports were condensed, giving details only of exceptions to established standards or averages, and so providing an immediate picture of progress. This is now termed 'Management by Exception'.

Many others have followed Taylor's methods and principles in their research and writings, for example Gantt and Gilbreth. Indeed some of the principles established by Taylor are still followed by organizations today.

The advantages to employers of adopting his methods are considerable, for example:

- reducing the skill component can cheapen labour costs;
- streamlining the tasks can increase flexibility of labour;
- streamlining production systems means that unnecessary tasks are eliminated, physical layouts are improved and the work is speeded up.

The basic principles contained in Taylor's techniques have been adopted by many industries, including the financial services sector. The high degree of specialization and the maximum use of technology are principles widely adopted in processing centres, telephone call centres and similar business units.

Even in his lifetime, Taylor's ideas were widely criticized. He was viewed as trying to increase the employer's profitability at the expense of the employee, by establishing highly efficient work methods that required lower labour levels. Even today his views are often misunderstood. Few organizations, although willing to practice work-study, will introduce one of his basic tenets: that there should be no limit to the earnings of a high-producing worker. Taylor requires that:

> *both sides take their eyes off the division of the surplus*
> *as the all-important matter and together turn their*
> *attention towards increasing the size of the surplus.*

Many writers would claim that Taylor's views had severe limitations. Bravermann (1974), for example, has argued that Taylor's thinking characterizes a progressive degradation of work. With Taylor establishing a system of control by managers and maintaining discipline through labour method development, the workers are effectively left without any opportunity to make decisions about the way their work is to be carried out. This can lead to the deskilling of work.

Taylor was focusing on efficiencies in the workplace and, as Rose (1978) argues, although his principles may be effective it is important to consider how they are implemented. Although there may be one way to best perform a job, account needs to be taken of human behaviour. People need to vary their methods of working and to be allowed discretion over some of their working practices.

A more sophisticated philosophy was that of the Human Relations movement, which recognized the emotional and human needs of employees and which did not endorse the coercive work methods advocated by Taylor.

Administrative management

The second grouping within the Classical approach is that of Administrative Management. It is reflected in the writings of Henri Fayol (1841-1925), a French mining engineer. It was first translated from French into English in 1949 under the title *General and Industrial Management*. Fayol acknowledged, like Taylor, the importance of specialist commercial activities. He categorized these specialist activities under five groupings, again reflecting functional specialization:

- technical – production, manufacture and adaptation;
- commercial – buying, selling and exchange;
- financial – search for the optimum use of capital;
- security – protection of property and people;
- accounting – stocktaking, balance sheets, costs and statistics.

Fayol concentrated on the managerial aspects of organizations, which he felt had not been explored to date. He wrote about management's role in organizations, involving a series of activities which were common to all managers, whatever their role in industry. The common features were identified as:

- forecasting and examining the future;
- planning and following a path of action;
- organising and building up the structure and resources of an organization;

- commanding and maintaining activity;

- co-ordinating, bringing together, and harmonising activity and effort;

- controlling and ensuring that everything conforms.

Fayol also defined fourteen principles of management, which he believed should be applied in organizations if maximum efficiency is to be achieved:

1. Division of work. The work is to be divided amongst all within the organization so that the burden does not fall too heavily on any one person, i.e. work and responsibility should be shared, and this also allows for specialization and maximum productivity.

2. Authority. The right to give orders should be commensurate with responsibility.

3. Discipline. Employees should obey orders but only if management provides good leadership.

4. Unity of command. Employees should have to report to only one head.

5. Unity of direction. Everyone should be working towards the same end in the organization.

6. Subordination of individual interests to general ones.

7. Remuneration. Pay should be fair to both employees and the firm, although the goals of the firm are the most important ones.

8. Centralization. Control should be retained centrally for maximum efficiency.

9. Scalar chain. There should be a clear line of authority from the top to bottom of the organization, but lateral communication is also important. It is crucial leaders know what is happening.

10. Order. The organization should be ordered with a place for all employees and activities.

11. Equity. Employees should be treated fairly and equitably.

12. Stability of position. Employees should experience stability of position and long-term appointments, and no unnecessary change should be introduced even in management.

13. Initiative. All levels within the organization should be encouraged to show initiative.

14. Esprit de corps. A spirit of harmony and co-operation should exist within the organization.

Like Taylor, Fayol's writings have been influential in determining many of the concepts and ideas of management today.

Many of Fayol's principles of management continue to be respected as good management practice because they encourage sensible structures and practices for managers to follow. Some aspects of his work have been developed by later behavioural theories and this has led to additions and adaptations. For example when describing the role of management, it is now normal to include the concepts of motivation and communication.

The third aspect of the Classical approach focuses on structure and administration. It is termed Bureaucracy.

Bureaucracy

Max Weber (1864-1920) explored the concept of rationalization and bureaucracy. His major work was based around the concepts of power and authority, and his writings on bureaucracy developed from this. Originally Weber was interested in why people in organizations obey orders. He distinguished between power (the ability to force people to obey regardless of resistance) and authority (the right to expect obedience). He categorized the various types of authority shown in organizations as:

- charismatic authority, derived from the influence of one man on the organization (i.e. personality);

- traditional authority, based on precedent;

- rational-legal authority, based on the use of rules and procedures which are applicable to any office.

Rational-legal authority led Weber to develop the concept of bureaucracy as the ideal organization. The term 'bureaucracy' has negative connotations today, with images of red tape and unbending rules, but in management theory the term is used merely to describe the structural features of a particular type of organization.

Weber (1947), in fact, suggested that it was a superior type of organization:

> *experience tends universally to show that the purely bureaucratic type of administrative organization ....is from a purely technical point of view capable of attaining the highest degree of efficiency... it is superior to any other form in precision, in stability, in the stringency of its discipline and in its reliability.*

Weber identified the following as the main features of bureaucracy:

1. A hierarchy of authority exists within the organization and is assigned to various positions, not people.

2. Work is allocated to this hierarchy of positions. Each position has a defined sphere of competence.

3. There is a high degree of task specialization, with supervisors controlling the work of subordinates.

4. A formally established structure of rules and regulations ensures uniformity of decisions.

5. Officials are expected to administer impartially these rules.

6. Employment and promotion is based on objective criteria and promotion is usually on the basis of seniority and merit.

7. Reward for effort is regular payment on a fixed scale.

Weber maintained that the growth of bureaucracy had come about because of the increasing size and complexity of organizations. This dictated the need for specialization, which in turn led to a need for procedural rules. For Weber this rationalization meant that relationships became very impersonal. The organization has to achieve certain economic goals, and emotions and feelings have no part to play in this. However, this could mean that managers become merely administrators rather than people with initiative or discretion. Criticisms of bureaucracy as a structural term are related to this. It is governed by rules, a lack of responsiveness, a lack of flexibility and an inability to change.

As with the other classical writers, Weber takes no account of individual or group feeling in organizations. (1964), who is one of the major critics of the bureaucratic organization, claims that bureaucracies restrict the personal growth of the individual, stifle individualism, and cause feelings of frustration and conflict.

Gouldner (1955), who maintained that there was no anticipation of the later consequences of the widespread use of rules and control, provided further criticism of bureaucratic structures. Bureaucracies can lead to increased supervision to ensure that rules are carried out. As a consequence there is an increased emphasis on authority, and this can create greater interpersonal tension and resistance to change.

Gouldner further suggests an inherent contradiction within bureaucracies between a system of authority based on the appointment of experts, and authority based on hierarchy and discipline. The second authority arises from the office held by the individual, the first from superior knowledge. This represents an incompatibility in many professional organizations, where large numbers of employees may have more technical knowledge than their hierarchical superiors do.

Many financial services organizations have been said to possess bureaucratic structures, especially those in existence at head or regional offices where there are long lines of command, rules and procedures to be followed. Many would maintain (as has already been discussed in Chapter 3), however, that organizations are now moving away from a bureaucratic structure and towards a matrix or project structure .

The human relations approach

The Classical approach to management lacked any consideration of human behaviour in organizations. The Human Relations approach redresses the balance. It emphasizes the creation of an environment which encourages individuals to work towards organizational objectives. The study of organizations develops into a study of human behaviour, explaining how and why people behave and act as they do.

The Human Relations approach examines individual and group productivity, individual development and job satisfaction. The major areas of study can be grouped into:

- individual needs and motivation;
- behaviour of work groups;

- behaviour of supervisors/leaders;
- inter-group behaviour.

All of these will be examined later in this book in more detail.

The start of the Human Relations approach is generally assumed to be the Hawthorne Experiments at the Western Electric Co in Ohio, USA (1924-1932). The experiment was originally designed to examine the effects of the environment on productivity. Elton Mayo, as research supervisor, began by examining the effects of the intensity of lighting upon productivity. The results showed that productivity in the experimental groups increased even when lighting conditions deteriorated. Productivity also increased in the control group although lighting levels remained unchanged. Something, other than environmental conditions, had affected productivity. Other experiments then followed.

Six female employees (all friends) were transferred from their normal area of work to a separate room and a series of changes were made to their working conditions (hours of work, rest pauses and refreshments were all varied). An observer was also present. Productivity continued to increase after all but one of the changes. The researchers concluded that the extra attention given to the employees, and the increased interest in them shown by management, was the main reason for higher productivity.

Further experiments included trying a similar experiment with a group of men, and a series of interviews with employees about the work and their attitudes and feelings.

The Hawthorne Experiments are viewed as a significant milestone in management thinking as they emphasized the importance of people in an organization, and focused upon work groups, leadership and motivation, communications and job design, i.e. the social system. The experiments could be said to mark the start of the Human Relations movement, which stresses the importance of social factors in the workplace. The role of management should be concerned with providing a work environment which fulfils the social needs of employees, by providing interesting work and encouraging team building and co-operation as well as the task at hand. The writers within this school assume that management can manipulate social factors and use social needs to achieve managerial aims and objectives. It is not proposed to discuss this school of thought in detail in this chapter because the theorists and their writings on leadership, groups and motivation are explored later in the book in Chapters 7,10 and 15.

The major criticism that has been levelled at the Human Relations writers is that they may have been concerned with 'people without organizations'.

Bendix (1956) has argued that the Hawthorne Experiments concentrated on group processes and excluded organizational issues such as the influence of managerial power and the external environment. This led to the exclusion of attributing economic motives to the employees, as it was assumed that they were solely motivated by social needs. Bendix also questioned the extent to which the Human Relations philosophy and models have been accepted. Many examples of managerial control still tend to be founded upon Classical rather than Human Relations models.

The third argument is that the Human Relations theorists still represent a strategy of organizational control and not a new humane approach although control is based on manipulation and is more covert than the earlier Classical approach. However, it must be acknowledged that the Human Relations movement has affected certain areas of managerial activity, e.g. Human Relations practices and management training in terms of encouraging variety in leadership style, new job design, etc.

The Systems approach tries to some extent to remedy the criticisms of the Human Relations school, being concerned with the 'formal organization' of the Classical school as well as the 'people' of the Human Relations school.

Systems approach

In recent years attention has focused on an approach which views organizations as systems, and this has replaced the earlier Classical and Human Relations models. This new approach, which has its roots in cybernetics, sees organizations as an inter-related set of activities, which converts inputs to outputs (as system).

This view of organizations is set out in diagrammatic form in Figure 6.2.

Figure 6.2: Legal, Ethical, Political, Economic, Social, Technological and Competitive Influences

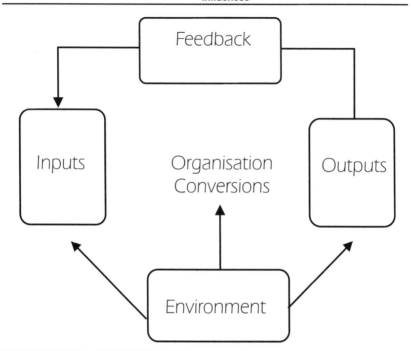

This approach studies the key elements in an organization, how they interact with one another, and the influence of the environment. It therefore examines people, structures, technology, the environment, and their effect on each other.

Organizations, by definition, are open systems because they interact and respond to their environment. A closed system does not interact with the environment. Each system is composed of subsystems. For example, the organization has financial, production and marketing subsystem and where each of the subsystems meet are interfaces. There are also decision-making, information and communication systems. The larger companies within the UK financial system could all be regarded as 'complex' systems. They are a conglomeration of a number of subsystems.

The work of the Systems school has developed from that of the

Human Relations school, which had investigated the relationship between job satisfaction and productivity. As no clear relationships between job satisfaction and productivity were demonstrated, other as yet unidentified factors obviously played a part. It seemed that there was one factor, technology, which could play a part in causing job dissatisfaction.

The Systems school developed these ideas, stressing that attitude and morale amongst employees was caused by a variety of factors, and not just one.

It is perhaps easiest to represent the Systems views in an historical format, following through the various authors. One of the first pieces of research published on the Systems approach was written in 1951 by two members of the Tavistock Institute of Human Relations, E L Trist and K W Bamforth, was entitled 'Some Social and Psychological Consequences of the Long Wall Method of Coal Getting'. Originally there was a 'hand-got' method of mining, which was based on a small group organization at the coalface, consisting of interdependent working pairs of colliers (a hewer and his mate), assisted by a boy trammer. The group would be allocated its own small face to work, and it was common practice for them to make their own contract with management. There were common pay bonuses shared equally between colliers.

This was replaced by increasingly mechanized methods of coal production known as 'conventional long wall'. The length of the coalface worked at one time was increased and there was an increasing degree of specialization. The work cycle of cutting, filing, pulley and stonework was now allocated to different groups operating on different shifts. However this system of working created distinct problems (a lack of co-operation between different shifts and an increase in absenteeism, etc.), and led to a need to try and preserve some of the advantages of composite work groups. The need to improve economic performance while retaining some work groupings was achieved by working a longer coalface using a three-shift cycle with the system continuing to use small groups responsible for a whole task along a limited section of the wall.

The group shared pay equally and became self-selecting. The influence of technology and work structure on productivity was thus established.

There are a number of advantages associated with the Systems approach to management:

- helps identify problem areas quickly within a system by revealing blockages at particular points;

- provides a means of systematising factors and influences in the organization;

- aids the understanding of the contribution of each part of the system to the whole;

- indicates the importance of communication and information systems;

- indicates the interaction of the environment with the organization.

However, a number of disadvantages can also be discerned such as:

- it is difficult to understand and apply directly to organizations;

- it is difficult to understand how a large complex organization works, and this needs a highly sophisticated approach;

- it is difficult to see how the subsystems interact and define the boundaries of each;

- when examining systems the people tend to be overlooked.

Contingency approach

The study of management and organizations has expanded further into what is known as the Contingency approach. Once again the focus is on structure and administration, but unlike the Classical teachers the Contingency school believe that there are no universal principles. Managers must face situations and then chose whatever seems appropriate in the circumstances. There is no one best way of designing organizations to meet objectives. The school therefore provides an insight into how to formulate responses in complex situations. Structure is one feature which must change to suit circumstances, as must technology. Organizations must adapt themselves to circumstances. This approach tries to identify links between causes and results, and particularly emphasizes the appropriate structure for certain circumstances already referred to in Chapter 3, when structures were discussed.

Like other schools there are a number of key writers associated with the Contingency approach. Burns and Stalker, who are well-known writers within the school, distinguished between two systems of organization: mechanistic and organic.

According to Burns and Stalker, the mechanistic system is characterized by a high degree of specialization, a rigid hierarchy of authority, and responsibility with clearly defined boundaries of rights and privileges. Communication is vertical (between superior and subordinate), rather than lateral. Loyalty and obedience are essential prerequisites for employment. This system was perceived by Burns and Stalker to be most appropriate to those firms operating in stable conditions, where everyone knows what is expected, what their responsibilities are, and the need for loyalty to the organization. It would be fair to say this type of structure has some similarities with bureaucracy.

The organic structure is more appropriate, according to Burns and Stalker, to conditions of change, because an individual's responsibility and job definition are never clearly described. The individual's job and role are seen as being directly related to the goals of the firm, to which the individual contributes their special knowledge or abilities. Responsibilities are given to those best qualified in the sense of knowledge and skill rather than position. Control, authority and communication operate in a network. Structure and responsibility are directed towards organizational goals and not individuals. A consequence of the flexibility of the organic structure is the sense of insecurity expressed by members, who can never be sure where their job and responsibilities end.

An organization has a need to gain the right structure for its particular circumstances. However a mechanistic organization, by its very history, is likely to experience resistance to change, and so be unable to make the transition to an organic structure if the need should arise. The organic structure can adapt to an uncertain environment.

Joan Woodward, another researcher within the Contingency school was involved in research between 1953 and 1958, examining the relationship between organizational structure, technology and performance in Essex manufacturing firms. She identified three major types of production systems that seemed to show some relationship to structure (already discussed in Chapter 3):

- unit and small batch;

- large batch and mass production;

- process production (continuous production as for chemicals).

The organizations using process production tended to use decentralization and delegation more than the large batch systems. It was also observed that the span of control of middle management (the number of subordinates reporting to one superior) tended to decrease with technical complexity (there were fewer people to report to one superior in process production). The more complex the technological process, then, the greater the chain of command. The span of control of the chief executive also increased with technical complexity.

The organizations which fell into the median range of their particular production system tended to be more successful than those at the top or bottom. Woodward's findings again emphasized the contingent factors influencing organizations.

Lawrence and Lorsch (1967) undertook studies of several firms in the plastics, container and consumer food industry. They were not only interested in structure, but also in how specific departments were organized to meet different aspects of the environment in which they operated.

They found in their study of six plastic industry firms that the most successful organizations were those with the highest degree of collaboration among departments and those whose managers responded well to the particular functional needs of their departments.

In their later research Lawrence and Lorsch concluded that the extent of collaboration and responsiveness would vary according to the demands of a particular environment. The mechanisms which the organization uses to make it successful vary. In mechanistic structures they are more likely to use policies, rules and procedures, whereas in the organic structure teamwork and mutual co-operation are used.

The Aston Studies (based at Aston University) developed research associated with Contingency theory and examined organizations as complex systems. They argued that there are four basic types:

1. Workflow bureaucracy: high standardization of procedures and specialization, e.g. the work at processing centres.

2. Personnel bureaucracy: some centralized procedures but production systems are localized. So within the financial services sector reward systems are largely centralized but

aspects of training and development can be localized.

3. Implicitly structured organizations: low standardization and smaller family run organizations.

4. Full bureaucracy: highly structured with high specialization. Banks have been said to fall into this category until recently. There was a slimming down of banks in the late 1980s, with fewer layers of management and less central control.

All the researchers and writers who could be said to belong to the Contingency school tried to establish links between causal factors and efficiency and effectiveness. They therefore developed the concept of the appropriateness of certain types of structures to technology.

Problems and advantages of the contingency approach

A number of problems could be said to exist with the Contingency approach. Child (1984) cites them as being:

- Causality – it cannot be certain that organizational performance does not have an effect on structure rather than vice versa;

- Measurement – the measurement of performance used in the contingency studies has not always been precise;

- Environmental influence – some organizations may be able to ignore environmental contingencies and still function effectively, e.g. those in a monopolistic position;

- Importance of different contingencies – although firms may be affected by a number of contingencies, it has not yet been established which are of importance to whom.

In defence of Contingency theory, Robey (1982) maintains that it has provided a wealth of empirical research and that it draws the attention of managers to factors that should be considered in organizational design. He concedes that one difficulty with the Contingency approach is that it emphasizes differences between organizations to the exclusion of similarities.

It could be concluded, as Mullins (1997) states:

That although there are limitations to the Contingency

*approach ... it does direct the attention of the manager
to the situational factors to be considered in the design
of organization structure.*

The Contingency approach draws attention to the situational variables which account for differences in the structure of organizations. It is more concerned with variances than similarities, and rejects the idea that there is one best structure. The success of the organization is more dependent upon the ability to assess situations and to respond accordingly.

Summary

This chapter has focused upon the development of management and organizational theory. It has reviewed the contribution of various theorists from the Classical, the Human Relations, the Systems and the Contingency schools. Although it is not always easy to define and separate the schools, there are clear differences in approach, with the Classical school claiming that there is one best way to organise a job, to manage individuals and to structure an organization. According to the Classical approach, there is no room for individuals. The Human Relations approach emphasizes the individual and the importance of people in organizations. The Systems approach discusses the impact of the environment and the relationship between different organizational subsystems, whilst the Contingency approach believes that there is no one best way to structure or manage organizations and individuals, but rather that different circumstances warrant different solutions. This chapter provides a useful beginning for the identification of trends and aspects of management theory and practice in the financial services sector.

The rest of this second section of the book examines the different management practices and approaches used in the areas of leadership, control, self-management, the management of teams, and communication.

References

Argyris C (1964) *Integrating the Individual and the Organization*, Wiley

Bendix R (1956) *Work and Authority in Industry*, Wiley

Bravermann H (1974) *Labour and Monopoly Capital: The Degradation of Work in the 20th Century*, New York Monthly Press

Burns T & Stalker G M (1961) *The Management of Innovation*, Tavistock

Child J (1984) *Organization*, Harper and Row

Drucker P (1974) *Management*, Pan

Fayol H (1949) *General and Industrial Management*, Pitman

Gouldner A (1955) *Patterns of Industrial Bureaucracy*, Routledge and Kegan Paul

Lawrence P R & Lorsch J (1967) *Organization and the Environment*, Harvard University Press

Lucey T (1987) *Management Information Systems*, DPP

McGregor D (1960) *The Human Side of Enterprise*, McGraw Hill

Mullins L J (1997) *Management and Organizational Behaviour*, Pitman

Robey D (1977) 'Computers and Management Structure', *Human Relations* Vol. 30, pp 963-976

Rose M (1978) *Industrial Behaviour*, Allen Lane

Taylor F W (1903) *Shop Management*, Harper Row

Taylor F W (1911) *Principles of Scientific Management*, Harper Row

Trist E L & Bamforth K W (1951) 'Some Social and Psychological Consequences of the Long Wall Method of Coal Getting', *Human Relations* Vol. 1, pp. 3-38

Weber M (1947) *The Theory of Social and Economic Organization*, Free Press

7 Elements of management

Objectives

The previous chapter explored the different approaches to management by thinking about the role of managers, job design and structures. This chapter continues this theme by examining in detail their position in an organization and how they can best manage the staff under their control.

The objectives of this chapter are to:

- appreciate issues of management authority and control;
- be aware of theories of leadership and management style;
- be able to analyse power and authority in organizations;
- appreciate the complexities of managing boss and subordinate relationships.

Introduction

The chapter begins by exploring the nature of managerial work, the common features of the managerial role and the differences. It then examines the skills required of a manager and the various interpretations of the role. The different historical approaches to leadership are examined (trait, style and process or contingency). Finally some of the concepts associated with leadership in organizations are explored, including power, empowerment, authority and responsibility.

The nature of managerial work

As has already been established, management is a key activity in the organization. During this century there has been a massive expansion in terms of the number of white-collar workers and managers, and a development of those industries (e.g. technical or professional) which employ managerial skills.

As stated in the previous chapter it is through management that the work of employees can be directed towards organizational goals. It is also through management that the different aspects of an organization are brought to fruition. The manager's role within the organization is therefore made up of a number of different aspects. These include responsibility for the individual and the group that is formed by these individuals, the tasks that the manager is assigned to carry out, and the organizational goals they must seek to attain.

As there are many different levels within the organization, so there are various managerial/supervisory levels, and the roles at each level vary accordingly. A senior manager may spend much of their time considering the long-term future direction of the business, whereas a branch or departmental manager will be most concerned with achieving weekly or monthly goals.

The nature of managerial work involves the performance of three key roles:

- securing resources (meeting clients, developing the business, etc.);

- managing projects or work teams;

- supervising or undertaking professional and technical work.

These have been commonly referred to as 'Finders, Minders and Grinders'. Each term reflects individual aspects of the role.

The managers of firms usually fulfil some aspect of all of these roles. The criteria for promotion to a supervisory/ managerial position is often based on a high level of technical knowledge which can subsequently be inappropriate. The future job may demand more interpersonal and project management skills.

This established career path has several implications. Many individuals have greater interest in the technical aspects of their work, and have no interest and sometimes little ability in developing broader managerial skills. However, they can often feel pushed into a managerial role because the organization offers only limited progression for technical specialists.

What then are these broader managerial skills that are required by organizations?

Managerial skills

The skills required of a manager fall into three broad areas:

1. *Technical skills* – these are generally job related but tend to reduce in importance as an individual progresses up the managerial ladder.

2. *Conceptual or process skills* – these include business planning, decision-making, financial control and analysis, change management and risk management.

3. *Interpersonal or people skills* – these include team working, motivation of self and others, leadership and interpersonal communication.

Many organizations use these broad categorizations of skills as a basis for management development and selection. A term which has been used to describe the combination of these skills is competencies. It has been defined by Boyatzis (1982) as:

> *An underlying characteristic of a person, which results in an effective or superior performance in a job.*

The concept of competencies embodies the ability to transfer skills and knowledge to new situations within an occupational area and so refers to technical knowledge as well as cognitive and interpersonal skills. This is further explored in Chapter 9 when career structures are discussed.

Competencies have two different aspects. Firstly, they can identify the skills needed to perform a job adequately, and secondly, they can also identify the skills needed to provide an excellent performance. Organizations view competencies as offering several additional advantages. Employers needs can be specified precisely when recruiting new members and a competency framework can then help identify those who require further development. A route using competencies can be developed for career progression. This is especially important when the number of upward promotional moves is severely limited because of delayering. In addition, it is possible to reward employees for the skills and competencies they acquire and demonstrate, and not just for the position they hold.

Managerial roles – the traditional view

As well as categorising the broad skill areas required of a manager, it is also possible to define the roles he/she will be involved in carrying out.

The earliest attempt at defining these roles was by Henri Fayol as discussed in Chapter 6. Many writers appear to agree on six main roles or functions for managers which are forecasting, planning, problem-solving, co-ordinating, controlling and monitoring, and communication. These are examined in more detail in the following paragraphs.

Forecasting

Most managers need to look ahead and anticipate events as part of their job. The extent to which they are required to do so varies according to their level of responsibility in the hierarchy. At the lower levels they are more concerned with the implementation of strategy rather than devising strategy themselves. In such cases, forecasting takes the form of deciding on possible future action to meet a target.

Forecasting implies both pro-active and reactive approaches. A pro-active approach is required when a manager examines and tries to anticipate the demands of the economy, customers, competitors and business development areas. This could be described as looking for opportunities.

A reactive approach could be described as looking for threats. Some UK financial services organizations have had reactive forecasting, for example, and have needed to respond quickly to threats like telephone banking and insurance systems by introducing their own systems in response to the strategies and initiatives of their more proactive competitors.

Planning

Strategic planning has already been discussed in Chapter 2, so this section is concerned with the nature of managerial planning. Planning implies that an organization is breaking down duties, devising a programme of objectives and allocating the work. It calls for forecasts, and demands that managers look ahead and anticipate future events.

Plans are important, even when change is introduced, to help establish key tasks, key result areas, targets and monitoring.

Planning involves a series of eight well-established stages:

1. *Determine the aims of the job.* A key area of activity is to communicate the aims to all those involved so that they know what is required of them.

2. *Estimate and secure the resources required.* Managers need to ensure the cost of the resources required in the plan will not outweigh the benefits. For one-off projects the task of securing resources can be difficult and not all the resources will be needed for the life of the project.

3. *Identify key result areas and the key tasks within them.* Key result areas are crucial to the success of change and within these certain key tasks need to be completed. For example, in order to take and pass an examination people have to enrol or plan a course of study, pay for entry to the examination and devote time to studying the subjects. All these could be regarded as key activities, which contribute towards passing an examination.

4. *Define success criteria.* This involves specifying how you will know you have succeeded, and can be broken down into specific stages. Taking an examination as an example, the first stage is being accepted onto a course, the next stage is purchasing a notebook, etc.

5. *Set standards of performance.* These give expected measures of performance whilst activities are ongoing rather than waiting for the end of the activity. These standards should be specific, measurable, achievable, relevant and trackable. (SMART is a useful mnemonic for remembering them.)

6. *Define short-term goals and first steps.* This needs to be completed so that individuals know where to start from and what to aim for.

7. *Set individual targets.* This is needed so that each individual

knows not only the overall objectives but also what is required for each person.

8. *Set up monitoring systems.* This is an important stage because it ensures that plans are proceeding smoothly.

In order to ensure that any planning is comprehensive and thorough, these various stages need to be worked through.

Problem-solving

This involves the manager identifying difficulties, preferably before they arise, and planning action to cope with the problem. Again there is a series of well-defined stages in the problem-solving process, which have some similarities to the stages in planning:

* selecting and defining the problem;
* gathering data about the situation;
* examining the situation to identify failings and irrelevancies;
* developing the new improved situation;
* installing the plan in action;
* maintaining the plan and modifying it where deviations have occurred.

Organising and co-ordinating

This means the organization and co-ordination of materials, equipment, and financial and human resources to ensure the production of goods and services. This is crucial where a project is involved, as all activities should proceed in a co-ordinated way. As activities increase across functional and departmental boundaries so there is an increasing emphasis on co-ordination.

Controlling and monitoring

This is concerned with evaluating performance and taking steps to bring it into line with plans. It presupposes that plans are already in place, otherwise there is nothing to control or aim for, or to measure performance against. From the plans targets are derived and performance can then be measured against these targets. Appropriate action can then be taken to eliminate the variance or to adjust the plan so that it reflects what can be achieved. There are four main ways of controlling:

1. By checking up on key events in a cycle and ensuring they are occurring at the right time.

2. By using milestones (reporting on all levels of activity at certain points) and management by observation, the manager can observe informally to make sure that actual progress matches anticipated progress.

3. By management by exception reports submitted if there is a variance between the plan and the performance. This principle was established by the Classical school.

4. By using budgets. This topic is explored in the next chapter as one of a number of techniques used to control output and expenditure.

Communication

According to Williamson (1981), communication is a process whereby messages are transmitted from one person to another. Communication as a topic area is fully discussed in Chapter 11.

In summary, discussions on the role of a manager can be found in the earliest organizational writings. Taylor and Fayol mention the principles of planning, organising, co-ordinating and controlling in the Classical school of theory. The ideas of problem solving and communicating are later additions from the Human Relations and Systems schools. The next section looks at some alternative views on managerial roles.

Managerial roles – alternative views

Other classifications exist which also attempt to describe the essential functions of a senior manager's job. As a result of a research study of five chief executives, Mintzberg (1979) classified the essential functions into ten different roles and divided them into three major groups:

1. Interpersonal roles – emphasising the relationships with others.

2. Informational roles – emphasising the gathering and dispersion of information.

3. Decisional roles – emphasising taking and implementing decisions.

These functions are illustrated in Figure 7.1 below.

Figure 7.1: Mintzberg's Managerial Roles

Interpersonal Roles
Figurehead
Leader
Liaison

Informational Roles
Monitor
Disseminator
Spokesperson

Decisional Roles
Entrepreneur
Disturbance Handler
Resource Allocator
Negotiator

Interpersonal roles

These arise from the manager's status, authority and relations with others. The manager is a figurehead representing the organization and its policies, i.e. signing documents, etc. The manager is a leader, responsible for staffing and for the motivation of subordinates. There is also a role to play in liaison with managers and others outside the manager's own unit.

Informational roles

The manager has an important communication role to play in the organization, which arises from his or her interpersonal role. Information must be monitored so that the manager can understand how the organization operates and the influence of the environment.

The manager also acts as a disseminator of information, passing on information from the environment to the organization and from senior management down to employees. The manager acts as a spokesperson communicating information to other departments, or to different levels in the organization, and outside the organization to suppliers, etc. This is a control type function, which emphasizes progress towards an objective.

Decisional roles

These involve the manager making decisions about the future of the organization and the department depending upon status, authority and access to information. In an entrepreneurial role the manager initiates and plans controlled change by solving problems, and by taking action to improve the existing situation. The manager can also act as a disturbance handler reacting to involuntary situations and unpredictable events. The resource allocator role involves the manager using formal authority to decide where effort will be expended, and making decisions about the allocation of resources. The negotiator role involves the manager negotiating activities with other individuals or organizations, for example a new agreement with a supplier, and emphasising the need to get things done.

Mintzberg (1979) suggests that to some extent this is an arbitrary division of a manager's role, and that the manager's work does not always divide itself neatly into these categories. It is merely one way of trying to group the manager's duties.

Although most models acknowledge similarities in terms of the roles a manager's job entails, others identify the differences in terms of demands, constraints and checks. Stewart (1976) classifies demands as what mangers have to do, constraints as the external/internal factors that limit manager's activities, and choices as what a manager is free to do but does not have to.

The job of manager and subordinate

All individuals come to work with certain expectations about what they can gain from the organization and their job. What distinguishes management from the individual employee is the responsibility of managers to manage, i.e. to get things done through others. Management is concerned with co-ordinating and directing action, and individuals in the organization should direct their activities towards the goals management has indicated. The employee's primary responsibility is for their own actions, whereas management is responsible for all their subordinates.

Associated with this directive and co-ordinating role of management is the leadership aspect of a manager's role, and it is this area which is examined in the following section.

Leadership

The job of a manager normally involves the leadership of some employees, but not all leaders are managers. To be an effective manager one must develop good leadership skills. The difference between leadership and management is that management involves co-ordinating activities and resources to achieve organizational goals, whereas leadership is more concerned with acting as a guide and motivator for others with the emphasis on interpersonal skills.

Acknowledging leadership as a key aspect of effective management has led to the development of research as to why some leaders are effective and others ineffective. One explanation is the individual's 'approach' to leadership.

Four major perspectives to this issue can be discerned. They correspond broadly speaking to four historical phases:

- trait or qualities approach;
- style of leadership approach;
- contingency/situational approach;
- functional approach.

Trait or qualities approach

This approach is the earliest attempt at explaining why some people are successful as leaders and others are not. It focuses on the individual occupying the post, and assumes that leaders are born and not made.

It suggests that leaders have certain qualities or traits which are innate and not easily developed or acquired, and that this distinguishes them from their followers. Attention should therefore be directed to selecting as leaders those people who possess these qualities, since the characteristics cannot be developed or encouraged through training.

However, researchers have found it difficult to identify the traits likely to lead to leadership effectiveness. Among the many that have been suggested are size, energy, integrity, decisiveness, knowledge, wisdom and imagination.

The problems with this approach are several:

- it may be that effective leaders learned to develop these qualities after becoming leaders, and that the ability to respond to different situations is the key trait;

- there is not much agreement among researchers as to which characteristics are important (McKenna 1991);

- this approach does not help in the development and training of future leaders.

Styles of leadership approach

During the 1950s a new explanation of leadership effectiveness began to emerge known as the style approach. This suggested that certain leaders were effective because of the behavioural style they adopted, and recognized that managers cannot merely rely on position in the organization to exercise leadership. The styles they can adopt range from autocratic to democratic. McGregor (1960) summed up these two extremes in his Theory X (authoritarian) and his Theory Y (democratic).

The traditional approach to leadership is expressed in Theory X:

1. The average person has an inherent dislike of work.

2. Because of this most people must be coerced, controlled and threatened with punishment to get them to put forward adequate effort towards the achievement of organizational goals.

3. The average person prefers to be directed, wishes to avoid responsibility, has relatively little ambition and wants security above all.

Fortunately, according to Theory X, not all employees are like this. There are some superior people, who can assume authority and control. These are destined to be managers.

A modern approach to leadership is expressed in McGregor's Theory Y, which he believed was more appropriate for today's manager:

1. Work is as natural as play or rest.

2. The average person not only accepts but seeks responsibility.

3. In modern industrial life people's potential is only partially utilized.

4. External control and the threat of punishment are not the only means of bringing about effort towards organizational objectives.

A leader adopting this set of premises is more likely to adopt a democratic approach. There are a number of other theorists who support the style approach.

White and Lippitt IOWA Studies (1939)

White and Lippitt's research was carried out in a boy's summer camp. The group leaders adopted and changed leadership styles between authoritarian, democratic and laissez faire. In the authoritarian style all policies were determined by the leader who dictated the jobs to be done by each member, and he was subjective in his praise and criticism. The democratic style meant that all policies were determined by joint discussion between the leader and the group. The division of tasks was determined by the group, and the leader was objective in his praise and criticism. The laissez faire style meant that the group alone decided the policies, if any, and the way tasks were to be divided. The leader gave only occasional comments on performance. Overall the democratic style proved to be the most effective in terms of group morale and productivity.

Tannenbaum and Schmidt (1973)

Tannenbaum and Schmidt developed a continuum of leadership behaviour along which various styles were placed ranging from 'boss-centred' (authoritarian leadership) to 'employee-centred' (democratic leadership), as illustrated in Figure 7.2. The continuum also included the degree of authority used by a manager and the degree of freedom for subordinates. This continuum of styles could be summarized by the phrase "tells, sells, consults, joins". At one end of the continuum leaders try to distribute power in decision-making using consultation, participation and delegation. At the other end the amount of decision-making by the supervisor or leader increases.

Figure 7.2: Tannenbaum and Schmidt Model

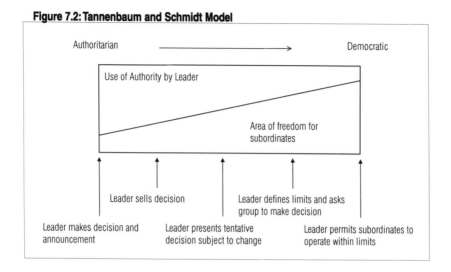

Blake and Mouton Managerial Grid (1984)

Rather than seeing the authoritarian and democratic styles at opposite ends of a spectrum, Blake and Mouton develop the views of Tannenbaum and Schmidt. They therefore see leadership as being two-dimensional, and place the styles on a grid as is illustrated in Figure 7.3.

The most effective leaders are those who rate highly on both dimensions, and who exhibit a concern for production and for people. Blake and Mouton found evidence that the supportive styles, i.e. concern for people scoring five or more were related to lower labour turnover, less inter-group conflict and high group satisfaction.

Reddin's Cube (3-D Theory)

Reddin (1970) takes the Blake and Mouton grid a stage further by introducing a third dimension known as 'effectiveness'. Reddin suggests that whether the manager's concern for task or people is high or low, they may still be effective or ineffective depending upon the situation. The four basic styles which can be used either effectively or ineffectively depending upon the circumstances are related, separated, integrated and dedicated, and the appropriate circumstances are determined by the nature of the task and the leader's relationship with their group.

Figure 7.3: Blake and Mouton Grid

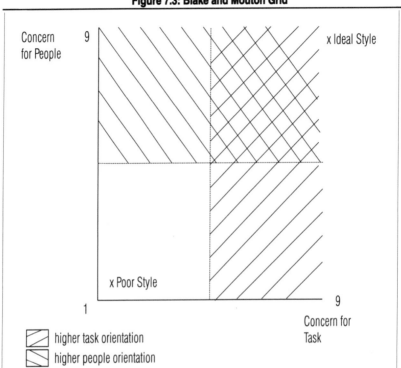

Concern for People

9

x Ideal Style

x Poor Style

1   9

Concern for Task

higher task orientation
higher people orientation

Ashridge Studies

A series of studies at Ashridge College in the 1960s and 1970s identified four styles adopted by leaders, similar to those described by Tannenbaum and Schmidt:

a) *The tells style* – where the manager makes decisions and announces them.

b) *The sells style* – where managers make decisions but rather than announcing them to subordinates they try to persuade subordinates to accept them.

c) *The consults style* – where the manager does not make the decision until the problem has been presented to the group, and advice and suggestions have been heard.

d) *The joins style* – where the manager delegates to a group (including themselves) the right to make decisions. The manager indicates the limits within which the decision must be made.

A survey was made of large multinational businesses. It revealed that the consultative type was most often preferred, although this varied according to the different categories of employee.

Unlike Blake and Mouton or McGregor, the Ashridge researchers do not suggest one ideal style, but rather maintain that the choice of style depends upon circumstances.

The contingency or situational approach

More recent views on effective leadership belong to what is termed the Contingency school, and develop from the concept that the most effective leaders have the ability to adapt their style according to the situation. Perhaps one of the most influential theories within this group is Fiedler's contingency theory.

Fiedler's contingency theory (1967)

Based on studies of a wide range of group situations, Fiedler explored the relationship between leadership and organizational performance. To measure the attitudes of a leader Fiedler classified a leader's orientation in terms of whether they enjoyed working with others, they were then said to have a high least preferred co-worker (LPC) score, or whether they were more production-orientated with a low least preferred co-worker score (LPC).

A questionnaire was issued to potential and existing leaders which, when completed, indicated whether they enjoyed working with others (a high LPC score) or whether they disliked working with others (a low LPC score).

Fiedler also attempted to identify key features in the situation including:

1. *Position of power* where the more formal the leaders' positions the greater the range of rewards and punishments at their disposal. In such positions power can then be judged strong or weak.

2. *Task structure*, where a high degree of task structure gives a more favourable situation for the leader as it means they can more easily monitor and influence the subordinate's behaviour.

3. *Leader member relations*, which asks whether the relationship between leaders and their followers is good.

All of these factors are combined in Fiedler's contingency model and indicate which situations are favourable to a particular type of leader.

When a situation is very favourable (with good leader-member relations, a structured task, and a strong position of power) or very unfavourable (with poor leader-member relations, unstructured task, and a weak position of power), then a task-orientated leader (low LPC score) with a directive, controlling style will be more effective.

When the situation is moderately favourable then a participative approach (a high LPC score) will be more effective.

Fiedler concluded that any leadership style may be effective depending on the situation. However, since some leaders may find it difficult to change their style, effectiveness can still be improved by changing the leadership situation. The position of power, task structure and leader-member relations can all be changed to make them compatible with the characteristics of the leader.

Hersey and Blanchard (1973)

Another model within the contingency school is the Hersey and Blanchard situational theory. This model is based on consideration of relationship behaviour and task behaviour. It suggests that the effectiveness of the leader is also affected by the willingness of the person the leader is attempting to influence.

Hersey and Blanchard suggest that leaders engage in:

- supportive behaviour which is concerned with the development needs of employees;

- directive behaviour which is concerned with directing and steering but allows the employee to perform independently.

A successful leader will select a style which is appropriate and which is based on the level of development of the employee.

Vroom and Yetton Normative Model (1973)

Vroom and Yetton have also contributed to the contingency approach to leadership. Their model assumes that decision-making is a key factor which determines the success or failure of a manager, and that there are three critical components which influence the overall effectiveness of the decision. These can be summarized as follows:

1. *Decision Quality* – which is the extent to which the decision meets the objective demands and requirements of the problem.

2. *Decision Acceptance* – which is the extent to which subordinates understand, accept and commit themselves to the decision.

3. *Timeliness* – which is the extent to which decisions are made according to schedule.

From their research with several thousand managers Vroom and Yetton believe that most managers can adjust their decision style to the situation and they provide a model which guides a leader towards effective behaviour. At certain key points in the decision process, the manager has to ask questions and his or her answer then determines his or her route along the decision tree. At the end of the path, a particular leadership style is recommended. There are five alternative decision styles the manager can adopt, and the model details which one is appropriate in a situation:

A1   *Autocratic.* The leader solves the problem or makes the decision himselves using the information available to him at the present time.

A11 *Autocratic.* The leader obtains any necessary information from subordinates, then decides on a solution to the problem herself. She may or may not tell subordinates the purpose of the questions or give information about the problem or decision they are working on. The input provided by them is clearly in response to the leader's request for specific information. They do not play a role in generating or evaluating alternative solutions.

C1   *Consultative.* The leader shares the problem with the relevant subordinates individually, getting their ideas and suggestions without bringing them together as a group. Then the leader makes the decision. This decision may or may not reflect the subordinate's influence.

C11 *Consultative.* The leader shares the problem with the subordinates in a group meeting. In this meeting the leader makes the decision which may or may not reflect the subordinate's influence.

G11 *Group.* The leader shares the problem with the subordinates as a group. Together they generate and evaluate alternatives and attempt to reach an agreement on a solution. The leader's role is very much like that of chairperson, co-ordinating the discussion, keeping it focused on the problem and making sure critical issues are discussed.

As well as the range of styles suggested by Vroom and Yetton, there are certain factors used to identify the type of decision. These fit the style and decision together and help the leader identify the most appropriate leadership style in a given situation.

Functional approach

This approach is the most recent and focuses on the function of leadership. It also views leadership in terms of how the leader's behaviour affects and is affected by the group they manage. This approach believes that the skills of leadership can be learnt and developed by concentrating upon the functions that lead to effective work performance. John Adair (1979) uses a functional approach in his guidance on how to train leaders which is known as action-centred leadership.

The effectiveness of the leader is dependent on meeting three areas of need within the work group:

- the need to achieve the common task;
- the need to maintain morale and build a team spirit;
- the need to meet the needs of the individual and the group.

This is illustrated in Figure 7.4.

Figure 7.4: Adair's Action-centred Leadership

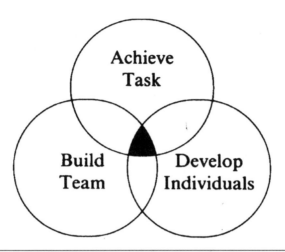

The action by a leader in any one of these areas of need will affect one or both of the other areas. The most effective leader will be the one who can meet all these needs and maintain a balance. This approach by Adair is further explored in Chapter 10 when examining groups.

Recent trends

The most recent trends in terms of leadership theory seem to group all the approaches described above into one category which are regarded as providing a transactional view of leadership. The newest approach assumes that a transformational view to leadership may now be the most effective for the circumstances which organizations face.

The transactional approach or more traditional approach to leadership assumes that a leader enters into transactions or relationships with subordinates and explains their requirements in terms of the contributions and the rewards they could receive. This situation can apply in circumstances of stability where established processes and systems are available to deal with this exchange and transaction.

However, in a turbulent environment with the advance of technology and ever-changing products and circumstances, leaders need to have vision and to be creative, innovative and capable of inspiring others to share their dreams. Leaders need to take calculated high risks, to establish high standards and to challenge the existing structure. Bass (1990) lists the characteristics these leaders need as charisma, intellectual stimulation and consideration of the emotional needs of each employee.

In addition, it has also been found that vision, creativity, and the selection and training of talented people is also desirable.

Changing environments means that theorists have once again looked at the traits and characteristics of effective leadership rather than just the style they may adopt and the situation.

Associated with the leaders position in the organization are a series of terms such as power, control, and authority, and it is these aspects of the managerial and leadership role that the final section of this chapter examines.

The leadership relationship

Leaders can be appointed or chosen either formally or informally, but their position and the regard in which they are held will be dependent upon the type and amount of power the leader can exercise over their group.

Power

Power is closely connected with leadership and management. However, it is a difficult term to define because of its constantly changing, complex and intangible nature. Power can mean the extent of control and influence. But it can also mean the type of influence. It is used to refer to the system of rewards and penalties of a formal and informal nature, which will ensure compliance to an organization's activities and policies.

For instance, has someone chosen to follow a course of action against their better judgement because of the power held over them, i.e. they were threatened, or because they understood the advantages of such a path.

The complex nature of power is also indicated by the use of a number of similar terms, for example authority, control and influence. These words are often used interchangeably, but in academic terms they have different meanings. Power is a subjective term in the sense that it is not always used but the fear lies in its anticipated use. In other words, it can be a threat.

There are two ways of viewing power either in terms of its process or in terms of its source. Various writers reflect these different perspectives.

Those representing the process view of power are first examined. Lukes (1974) developed a three-dimensional view of the process of power which described it as follows:

1. Power is observable in the clash of interests between decision-makers.

2. Certain groups are excluded from the bargaining arena and therefore from competing for power.

3. Certain groups are under the power of others and never really able to formulate their real interests.

Foucault (1979) emphasized the disciplinary notion of power as a process and categorized disciplinary power as integral to all social relationships and instigated in daily routines. This normalises behaviour and judgement, and so establishes the limits of behaviour and the standards to be achieved in organizational and societal relationships. Power was believed by Foucault to be the key governing the nature and types of social interaction. He is criticized because he is seen to have a pessimistic view of power assuming that it penetrates all social relationships and is the governing influence.

The second group of writers tries to define the source of power and therefore its nature. Weber (1947) perceived power to be a collective phenomenon. The power of managers came from the owners of the business and was exercised on their behalf. Similarly departments or groups can wield power.

Etzioni (1975) and French and Raven (1959) have similar definitions of the sources of power:

- *institutional* – this rests on external social and economic structures;

- *reward* – the ability to give rewards;

- *coercive* – the ability to punish;

- *legitimate* – based on the leader's position, and acknowledged by the recipient of authority;

- *referent/charisma* – admiration for the power holder;

- *expert* – this emphasizes the specialist knowledge or skill, and is crucial to the organizations survival (Pettigrew (1973) and Crozier (1964)).

The concept of political power is also used in some texts, and refers to a knowledge of the internal politics and working of the organization.

Empowerment

Over the last decade the term empowerment has been much used in organizations. Many companies have tried to introduce or support empowerment programmes as a way of improving competitiveness and dealing with customer requirements more effectively.

It is difficult to find a definition which encompasses the various forms empowerment has assumed. Empowerment implies giving an employee the opportunity and authority to take more responsible decisions and a greater say in the operation of the business. The aims of empowerment can be summarized as:

- increasing an organization's effectiveness through quicker decision-making;
- more responsiveness to customer needs;
- cutting costs through the reduction of management layers;
- coping better with the rapid changes required;
- enabling staff to be more creative and make greater use of skills.

Empowerment is also perceived to offer benefits to employees:

- it can provide greater opportunities for development;
- it can give greater responsibility to the individual for achievement.

Despite these advantages, problems can be created by introducing empowerment as it strips out a layer of management and redistributes the power to former subordinates. Empowerment can also cause a withdrawal of resource by reducing the number of managers and investment in training, and other human resource systems are needed to support its development. There can also be problems in ensuring consistency of standards across the different business units and departments which have been empowered. Resistance from senior staff may also result because they perceive a loss of individual power as a result of empowering subordinates.

Despite these difficulties, empowerment techniques have still been introduced in many organizations over the last decade.

Authority

Authority as a term used in organizations is closely related to power, and is the subject of research and study by many writers including Weber. It is associated with the position held in an organization. Authority as a type of social control means that others accept the power of senior officials.

Authority is a legitimate means of social control and, according to Weber (1947), there are three types:

- *charismatic* – based on respect and admiration;

- *traditional* – established by custom and rule;

- *rational* – legal occupancy of senior positions. This is widely used in modern work organizations especially bureaucracies.

The similarity in terms and definitions often make it hard to distinguish authority from the concept of power, especially where the power emanates from the position of the leader or their personal charisma.

Control

As mentioned by Fayol (1949) organizational achievement and structure implies that control has to exist to direct and co-ordinate work, especially since not all employees in the organization share the same corporate goals. There has been much writing about the conflict between managerial control and workers resistance. Child (1984) emphasized two managerial tasks, control and integration, which are the basic structures of authority and the division of labour.

There is the issue of control to maintain direction in the organization versus control stifling initiative and adaptation. There are often situations where major policy decisions are centralized; there are also situations where operations are delegated in order to maintain control but also to encourage initiative.

Part of the key to control is understanding individuals and assigning to them the type of work they enjoy. Control is therefore the interface between behaviour and the process of management (Mullins 1997).

Control through assessment and remuneration is explored in Chapter 15, and control through financial and accounting systems is developed in Chapter 8.

Summary

This chapter has explored the role and functions of a manger and how managers can be most effective in terms of their management of employees. The final section has examined the terms most commonly used in connection with leadership and management, namely those of authority, power, empowerment and control. Management is a constantly evolving and changing role, and although a historical perspective is still regarded as relevant most writers and researchers would accept that the changing nature of work and organizations has created new demands upon this key role and activity.

References

Adair J (1979) *Action Centred Leadership*, Gower
Bass B M (1990) *Bass and Stodgill's Handbook of Leadership*, Free Press
Blake R R & Mouton J S (1984) *The Managerial Grid*, Gulf Publishing Company
Boyatzis R (1982) *The Competent Manager*, John Wiley
Child J (1984) *Organization*, Harper and Row
Crozier M (1964) *The Bureaucratic Phenomenon*, Tavistock
Etzioni A (1975) *A Comparative Study of Complex Organizations*, Free Press
Fayol H (1949) *General and Industrial Management*, Pitman Publishing
Fiedler F E (1967) *A Theory of Leadership Effectiveness*, McGraw Hill
Foucault M (1979) *Discipline and Punish*, Penguin
French J R P and Raven B (1959) 'The bases of social power' in D Cartwright ed. *Studies in Social Power*, Institute for Social Research
Hersey P & Blanchard K H (1973) *Management of Organizational Behaviour*, Prentice Hall
Lukes S (1974) *Power: A Traditional View*, Macmillan
McGregor D (1960) *The Human Side of the Enterprise*, McGraw Hill

McKenna E (1991) *Business Psychology and Organizational Behaviour,* Lawrence Ehrlbaum

Mintzberg H (1979) *The Structuring of Organizations,* Prentice Hall

Mullins L J (1997) *Management and Organizational Behaviour,* Pitman

Pettigrew A M (1973) *The Politics of Organizational Decision Making,* Tavistock

Reddin, W J (1970) *Managerial Effectiveness,* McGraw Hill

Stewart R (1976) *The Reality of Management,* Pan

Tannenbaum R & Schmidt W H (1973) 'How to choose a leadership pattern', *Harvard Business Review* May- June, pp 162-175

Vroom V H & Yetton P W (1973) *Leadership and Decision Making,* University of Pittsburgh Press

Weber M (1947) *The Theory of Social and Economic Organization,* Free Press

White R K & Lippitt R I (1939) 'Patterns of aggressive behaviour in experimentally created social climates', *Journal of Social Psychology,* Vol. 10, pp 271-299

Williamson R J (1981) *Business Organization,* Heinemann

8   Control in organizations

Objectives

This chapter examines, both theoretically and practically, the ways in which people working within organizations are controlled.

The detailed objectives of the chapter are:

- to explore general concepts relating to organizational control;

- to suggest a framework within which issues relating to organizational control can be discussed;

- to outline specific requirements of some systems of organizational control;

- to suggest issues which may impact upon the ways in which organizations are controlled in future.

Introduction

The essence of 'control' in an organizational sense lies in ensuring that the members of the organization behave in a way which 'conforms'. This statement, of course, begs the question 'to what should the members' behaviour conform?' There is no simple answer to this. In Chapter 1 the concept of the stakeholders in an organization was introduced, and through the use of the Le Pest & Co mnemonic the various pressures which can impact upon an organization were explored. There is the possibility that each stakeholder and each of the components of Le Pest & Co will have different interpretations of the types of behaviour which qualify as conforming. The broadest definition of 'control' in relation to organizations must therefore cater for not only the requirements of the organization itself, but also for those of interested bodies outside the organization which have (or could have) mechanisms for ensuring that the organization conforms.

To illustrate this point consider one of the requirements of a government: that there should be an orderly and consistent approach to the way in which organizations conduct themselves. This is achieved primarily through legislation. For example, in the UK the Companies Act is periodically updated and reissued in much the same way as basic primary tax legislation. Contrast this control mechanism with that which may result from one of the requirements of an organization's customers, that the organization's products should give value for money. This can be controlled through market competition, but only where the products are subject to numerous purchasing decisions (e.g. the decisions to buy a particular brand of coffee or to use a particular supermarket). In the case of products which are not frequently bought, control is less secure, but it can still be achieved, over time, through the operations of consumer pressure groups such as the Consumers' Association, who are the publishers of *Which?*.

Irrespective of the requirements of an organization's stakeholders, the organization needs to be in control of the operations of its members to the extent that it can ensure that those operations are conducive to the achievement of the organization's goals. There are therefore both internal and external influences that in part determine the mechanisms by which an organization is required to control its operations. Given the number of these influences and the extent of possible control mechanisms it is sensible to confine this exploration within defined limits. The structure of this chapter will therefore be:

- the definition of some key concepts in relation to control in organizations;
- the development of a framework for thinking about control in organizations;
- a discussion of some specific aspects of control mechanisms;
- the identification of some possible future trends in organizational control.

Key concepts

In order to develop a rational approach to the discussion of control within organizations it is helpful to define a number of terms

Control

The literature dealing with control in organizations tends generally to concentrate on the ways in which management ensures that labour is productive in terms of the organization's objectives and conforms to the organization's norms (e.g. Fincham & Rhodes 1988). For the purposes of this chapter this is too narrow a definition since, in keeping with modern trends, businesses must not only control their own productivity, they must also ensure that they work within the legal, regulatory and social framework imposed on them by the states, markets and societies in which they operate.

Accordingly the definition of 'control' must be expanded to include the organizational structures and systems designed to establish, monitor and correct performance in respect of internally and externally established criteria. Such a definition encompasses aspects of corporate governance, compliance with legislation and the requirements of regulatory organizations.

Aspects of control in organizations

Prudential

Regulation of the financial services industry in particular is concerned with ensuring that organizations exercise prudence in relation to the commitments into which they enter. This is not simply a matter of protecting investors through the requirement that a level of capital is maintained within the business to meet calls on the organization's use of capital. It extends to the maintenance of the financial system in which the organization operates. This is so the organization, its correspondents and its competitors can have confidence in the longer-term viability of the system.

Parties external to the organization are therefore concerned to ensure that not only does the organization maintain a level of prudential capital in accordance, for example, with the Basle Accords, but also that it has sufficiently robust systems for monitoring the use of its capital base and for assessing, evaluating, monitoring and managing the risks associated with the use of capital.

Conduct of business

In addition to considerations of prudence, external regulators are also concerned with the ways in which the organizations they regulate conduct their businesses. This is for two basic reasons:

- to ensure protection of consumers;

- to promote orderly markets.

It is important to note that in this context the term 'external regulators' can have a wide interpretation and does not need to be limited to formally established regulatory bodies. The operation of market forces may be sufficient to ensure appropriate levels of consumer protection. In instances where no ready market exists, such as with the quasi-monopolistic, and recently privatized suppliers of public utilities (power and transport in the UK, for example), the trend of late has been to ensure consumer protection and orderly markets through the medium of official regulators.

This trend is important since it establishes a norm for the regulation of organizations which depends, at least in part, upon an informed dialogue between the regulators and the suppliers of products and services. This is an important aspect of the regulation versus legislation argument.

Nature of control

Control measures can be divided into three categories: preventive, detective and corrective.

Preventive controls are those which are designed to prevent a risk having a material impact on the business or an employee exhibiting wrong behaviour. Examples of preventive controls include sanctioning procedures, procedures manuals and the establishment of a budget.

Detective controls are those which seek to establish that aberrant behaviour, either on the part of a system or of an employee, has occurred or is about to occur. Examples include exception reports, 'whistle-blowing' procedures, and variance analyses of actual versus budgeted financial performance.

Corrective controls are those which are designed to return the organization, as near as possible, to an equilibrium state in the event of aberrant behaviour or of the manifestation of a material risk. Examples of corrective controls are insurance policies, hedging activities, business resumption plans and budgetary or performance adjustments. In the case of corrective controls there is often an irrecoverable cost involved which is nevertheless acceptable given the potential impact of the risk which is to be guarded against.

Risk in relation to control

Effective management of risk involves:

- analysis of the risk in terms of both the probability of its occurrence and the impact on the business should it occur;
- quantification of the risk;
- recording of the objective data which has loaded into any decision taken in relation to the risk;
- the determination of the reward which is to be sought commensurate with the acceptance of the risk;
- decision whether or not the risk should be accepted;
- the establishment of feedback mechanisms designed to monitor the effectiveness of decisions taken in relation to the risk;
- feedback to and adjustment of the risk analysis methodology.

In the context of control, the organization is not so much interested in the analysis and quantification of individual risks as in the calculation of the impact and probability of impact on the business as a whole. It is also interested in understanding the systems with which it interacts (such as the financial system), and of the occurrence of specified events either singly or in combination.

This point was illustrated by Howard Davies (1998) when referring to lessons to be drawn from the difficulties experienced by the hedge fund Long Term Capital Management:

> risk concentrations are not always apparent when market conditions are settled. Changes in sentiment can result in counterparties which have previously been regarded as unconnected being viewed as much more homogenous in terms of risk. This can change risk profiles very markedly and lead to the rapid drying up of liquidity.

Even under stable conditions, a prudent organization will monitor the impact on its assets and those of its investors, customers and suppliers of the threats to which its operations are or may be exposed. As the probability of those threats materialising increases, so should the organization take precautions or corrective control measures to minimize the impact.

A framework for considering control in organizations

The above should suggest that the topic of control in organizations is complex. It therefore helps to break down the areas interested in organizational control into three categories:

- general external influences;
- specific external influences;
- internal influences.

One can then describe how the organization relates the internal influences to the external influences.

General external influences

There are probably four major elements within this category:

1. **Suppliers** who have an interest both in the prudential and the conduct of business aspects of control. Suppliers need to know that they will be paid for the goods and services that they supply and that they will be paid in a timely fashion. On a preventive basis suppliers should be careful about the nature of their commitment to the organization, and they should take steps not to become, effectively, part of the organization by maintaining links with other customers. They will also no doubt have established detective and corrective systems to ensure payment within agreed timescales.

2. **Consumers** who, in quasi-monopolistic or oligopolistic markets, need on a preventive basis to form pressure groups in order to influence organizational outcomes (e.g. the Shell/Brent Spar episode). On a corrective basis consumers in many industries are now able to rely on industry watchdogs or ombudsmen in order to obtain redress for shortfalls in organizational control.

3. **'Small' investors** who have a direct, though not very effective,

channel of influence through the medium of the Annual General Meeting. In combination, however, these can become a significant thorn in the flesh of the organization's executive if they believe that the organization is not consistently exhibiting 'comforming behaviour'. Examples of the effectiveness of such actions include the National Trust's adoption of the ban on stag hunting (and its possible reversal under pressure from the counter-lobby), and Barclays acceptance of the need to institute an alternative disputes resolution procedure under pressure from the Struggle Against Financial Exploitation.

4. *Major shareholders* who have often in the past been criticized for relying too much on their ability to dispose of their holdings rather than accepting any direct responsibility for influencing the organization away from aberrant behaviour. It is possible to detect moves away from this traditional position now that, following the reports of the Cadbury, Greenbury and Hampel Committees, there is an acceptable set of criteria against which to judge the effectiveness of many of the key control mechanisms within companies. The moves since the Cadbury report to ensure the separation of the roles of chief executives and chairmen have often exemplified the pressure exerted by major institutional shareholders.

Specific external influences

1. *Government*. It is generally true to say that governments can only effectively influence organizations over the medium to long-term, through legislation. Although there can be no denying the force with which legislative measures are felt within the world of company administration, there are many drawbacks to a reliance on legislation as a means of controlling organizations.

Shortly after it came to power in 1997 the Labour Government in the UK began the process of consulting on reforms which might be introduced into Company Law. This was done despite the probability that it would not be able to find Parliamentary time to introduce such legislation until the Government's second term. The outcome is that the Companies Act 1985 is likely to be the basis of Company Law in the UK for up to 20 years. During this time there have been many changes in the thinking which underlies the ways in which companies are administered (such as the Committee reports), and which it may be wise to adopt but which can only be done on a voluntary basis.

Further drawbacks with legislation as a means of controlling organizational activity include:

- the need for legislation to be interpreted prior to its precise effect being determined. This often leads to doubts as to what precise actions a company needs to take in order to comply with the legislation (consider for example the conflicting advice offered at the time of the Blue Arrow episode);

- the inflexibility of legislation once introduced. Given a Companies Act is passed every 20 years it is difficult for legislation to be changed to reflect changes in actual practice. The result is that legislation is often seen as needlessly inhibiting;

- conflict between different bodies of legislation to which companies are at least potentially subject. This is becoming more of a problem as UK companies anticipate the effect of European Directives and find themselves needing to establish systems which allow them to comply with UK and EU requirements which may differ in small but significant ways.

2. **Regulators**. Given the drawbacks to the use of legislation as a control mechanism, it is little wonder that in recent years the reliance upon regulatory regimes has become greater. This is particularly relevant to the financial services industry in the UK where what was hitherto a plethora of regulators has been amalgamated to form the Financial Services Authority (FSA).

    One of the benefits of the formation of the FSA illustrates one of the chief advantages of control through regulation rather than legislation. Before its formation different businesses within a major financial institution were likely to be regulated by each of the constituent bodies which subsequently went to make up the FSA. Thus the financial institution would have to establish relationships with regulators within the Bank of England, the Securities and Futures Authority, the Securities Investment Board, the Insurance Directorate of the Department of Trade and Industry, the Investment Management Regulatory Organization, and the Personal Investment Authority. The nature of a regulatory regime, in contrast to one dependent upon legislation, is that it is capable of evolution. In such a model, as market practice develops so regulatory requirements can change to take account of these developments. This means that a body of precedent builds up within each regulator, raising the possibility that the requirements of different regulators will develop in often diverging and possibly conflicting ways.

Furthermore, as new products are developed, or changes in a business are implemented, it is common for the regulator to be consulted upon what effect these developments will have on the regulatory requirements. This implies that relationship management between the business and the regulator is important to both parties, and it therefore makes sense if this relationship is developed through a single channel rather than through a multiplicity of channels.

The way in which the FSA proposes to structure itself and approach its work is worth closer examination. This is partly because it has published numerous consultation documents which spell out the approach with considerable transparency, and partly because it exemplifies many of the key aspects of a regulatory regime.

The **aims** of the FSA (1997) are:

1. To protect consumers of financial services which it will achieve by:

    ● setting, monitoring and enforcing high standards of integrity amongst those it regulates;

    ● ensuring that consumers receive clear information about services products and risks;

- ensuring that consumers are not exposed to risks that they should not reasonably be expected to assume, while recognising that consumers do have to accept responsibility for their own decisions.

2. To promote clean and orderly markets which it will achieve by:

- promoting fairness, transparency and orderly conduct in financial markets and by looking to markets and participants to set and enforce high standards;

- taking action where standards are not adequate or are not enforced.

3. To maintain confidence in the financial system which it will achieve by:

- setting, monitoring and enforcing high standards of financial soundness and probity for financial services businesses;

- ensuring that the failure of individual financial institutions does not undermine the overall stability and soundness of the financial system.

Amongst the major areas of work with which the FSA will be involved are:

1. Policy Development, which is driven by factors such as the European Union, market innovation, actual experience and changing consumer needs.

2. Authorization, vetting and registration of current and potential participants in financial services.

3. Supervision (both prudential and conduct of business), which involves the continuous oversight of firms and requires knowledge of their strategy and business.

4. Assessment of competence and promotion of training in order to maintain high standards.

5. Enforcement which involves routine and special investigations of practitioners' activities, appropriate interventions which

could be both short- and long-term, and imposition of
sanctions and 'policing the perimeter'.

The FSA (1998) has already articulated the way in which it will
operate as far as setting standards is concerned namely by:

- making rules;

- stating principles;

- making evidential provisions;

- endorsing codes;

- issuing guidance.

Such an approach exemplifies the flexibility of a regulatory regime
operating within a developing marketplace, and points to the way in
which the policing of the market will develop out of dialogues between
regulator and participants. This in turn argues that organizations which
are subject to regulation need to be clear regarding their own control
mechanisms and how these will interrelate with the regulator.

Internal influences
Organizational model

Organizations vary, and even within organizations of a particular type
there are likely to be found many variations. Thus the way in which,
for example, a branch of a supermarket operates control mechanisms is
probably quite different from the way in which a firm of solicitors
approaches control. Similarly the nature of the control mechanisms
within joint stock companies will vary from organization to organization.
Recently, and particularly in the UK, there has been a concentration of
effort on determining the basis for control within corporations. This
has been based on a model of an organization which contemplates that
the direction of the organization, and therefore the control of its
operations, will be the responsibility of a board of directors who are
accountable to the shareholders of the organization. Many of the lessons
to be drawn from a consideration of this work can be applied to other
types of organizations.

Figure 8.1 illustrates a typical structure for the top levels of a UK
company. However, it can instantly be seen that this is too simplistic an
illustration. In the UK both the chairman and at least some of the

executive will be members of the board, the chairman may also be an executive of the organization, and the board may comprise both executive ('internal') and non-executive ('external') directors.

Figure 8.1

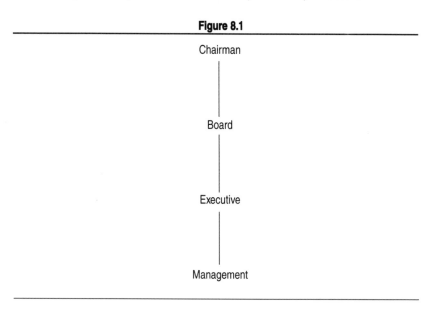

In June 1988, the Hampel Committee on Corporate Governance built upon the work of two previous committees (the Cadbury Committee and the Greenbury Committee), and produced 'The Combined Code'. This articulates certain principles to which UK-listed companies should aim to conform and also identifies best practice in specific areas of corporate governance. The code states *inter alia*:

A.   Directors
A.1   The Board
Principle Every listed company should be headed by an effective board which should lead and control the company.

A.2   Chairman and CEO
Principle There are two key tasks at the top of every public company: the running of the board and the executive responsibility for the running of the company's business. There should

be a clear division of responsibilities at the head of the company. This will ensure a balance of power and authority, so that no one individual has unfettered powers of decision.

Code Provision

A.2.1   A decision to combine the posts of chairman and chief executive officer in one person should be publicly justified.

A. 3   Board Balance

Principle The board should include a balance of executive and non-executive directors (including independent non-executives), so that no individual or small group of individuals can dominate the board's decision taking.

Code Provision

A.3.1   The board should include non-executive directors of sufficient calibre and number for their views to carry significant weight in the board's decisions. Non-executive directors should comprise not less than one third of the board.

A.3.2   The majority of non-executive directors should be independent of management and free from any business relationship which could materially interfere with the exercise of their independent judgement. Non-executive directors considered by the board to be independent in this sense should be identified in the annual report.

Accordingly the model of the top structure of the organization should be modified to conform more closely to that in Figure 8.2. It will be recognized that in this model the chairman can be either executive or non-executive and still conform to the Hampel principle provided that there is a recognized, articulated and clear division of responsibilities between the chair and the CEO.

Figure 8.2

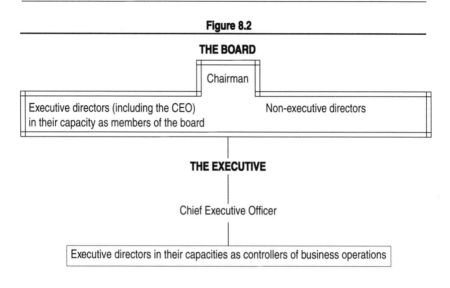

This principle of a clear division of responsibilities should be carried further to define the roles of the executive directors, be they operational (i.e. the heads of businesses) or functional (e.g. HR director, finance director). The reason for this lies in the concept of accountability. If serious problems arise in the running of the business (which, in the case of a listed company would necessitate a public disclosure), it is a function of the board as a whole to recognize those problems and take action on behalf of the company to redress them. Although this implies an element of collective responsibility, it is nevertheless important that individual members of the board are held to be accountable if only so that stakeholders can be reassured that the board is taking appropriate action.

This point was emphasized by Sir Andrew Large (1997), then Chairman of the Securities and Investments Board, who said:

> *The regulators have to be able to call individual senior managers to account where the controls and systems that they are responsible for implementing and maintaining are inadequate or fail, and where investors can lose out. We believe the key to this is to make more*

> *explicit what the duties of senior management are. If*
> *people know specifically what they are going to be held*
> *responsible for then it should be easier for all concerned*
> *– boards, management, regulators and the investing*
> *public – to establish where responsibility lies when major*
> *failures occur.*

The above extract implies that prime accountability will rest amongst the executive directors, but this does not diminish the role which the non-executive director is expected to play. Within the UK it is the quality of the non-executive directors on the board of a listed company which will be fundamental to its success in fulfilling the four roles for the board which have been suggested by the Institute of Directors (1995):

1. The board must simultaneously be entrepreneurial and drive the business forward whilst keeping it under prudent control.

2. The board is required to be sufficiently knowledgeable about the working of the company to be answerable for its actions, and yet able to stand back from the day-to-day management and retain an objective, longer-term view.

3. The board must be sensitive to the pressures of short-term, local issues while also being informed of the broader trends and competition which is often of an international nature.

4. The board is expected to be focused on the commercial needs of the business whilst acting responsibly towards its employees, business partners and society as a whole.

The proposition stressed by both the Cadbury and Hampel Committees is that within the UK the presence of high quality non-executive directors will ensure that the board does have a broader perspective than the immediate or parochial needs of the business. This will obviate any requirement, for example, that companies within the EU should conform to the German model of a two-tier board.

A two-tier board system effectively distinguishes between executive and non-executive directorial functions. The management board (which in a typical German company would meet weekly) 'runs' the company but is appointed by and reports to a supervisory board (which under German law must meet at least twice a year). German law also allows for an annual meeting of shareholders. The main benefit of the two-tier board system is that it facilitates the participation, albeit through representation, of shareholders and other stakeholders in the running of the company. Thus in Germany companies are required to have representatives of their shareholders on the supervisory board, and also, if the company is above a certain size, representatives of employees. The main criticism of the system appears to be the inhibiting effect that it has on the running of the company without necessarily adding anything by way of control. For example, the supervisory board failed to recognize and/or correct a number of control weaknesses in the derivatives operations of Metallgesellschaft with the result that there were major losses experienced.

The Cadbury and Hampel Committees did not recommend the adoption of a two-tier system in the UK, preferring to rely on balancing the powers of the executive directors through the quality of the non-executives on the board.

Board committees

A further recommendation of the Hampel Committee is that, for certain aspects of their work, boards should operate through committees. Three such committees are detailed in the Code of Best Practice. Each of these committees should consist of at least a majority of non-executive directors. The committees are detailed as:

- *Audit Committee*, comprising only non-executive directors. This has the responsibility to keep under review the scope and results of the audit by the company's external auditor, its cost effectiveness and the objectivity and independence of the auditor;

- *Nominations Committee*, comprising a majority of non-executive directors. This is responsible for making recommendations to the full board on new board appointments;

- *Remuneration Committee*, comprised of independent non-executive directors. This is responsible for recommending to the board the framework for remuneration of the company's executive and determining the specific remuneration packages of individual executive directors.

It can be seen that if the recommendations of the Hampel Committee are implemented, then there will exist the means by which a company's operations can be controlled or brought under control at least to the extent of satisfying the company's major investors. In turn, the investors will often bring pressure to bear to ensure that companies adhere to the principles of the code.

Relating internal and external influences on control

In addition to the roles of the chair, the CEO, the board and its committees, there are other elements within an organization which exercise or are designed to facilitate a control function. Some of these are internally oriented and some are externally oriented.

This point emphasizes one of the key difficulties in delineating control within an organization. Any employee operating within an organization which conforms to Weber's description of a bureaucracy, or within one which has an effective scalar chain of command as advocated by Fayol, should have no difficulty determining the limits of his or her power. Such organizations are not often encountered (at least in the UK and USA) in these days of delayered, organic organizations with empowered staff, and there is often confusion as to the extent to which any individual employee is capable of committing the organization. Internally this is best dealt with by the publication of a document which charts the ways in which authority is spread throughout the organization.

In theory all the authority within an organization rests in its members who delegate to the board power to run the company. This power is subject only to written resolutions made by all its members (an unlikely occurrence in the case of a listed company) or through the medium of a properly constituted general meeting. The board is thus effectively the repository of the organization's authority which it delegates to individual directors, empowering them to sub-delegate to others with similar powers of sub-delegation. Each delegation of authority can be limited so that subordinates have less power to commit the organization than their superordinates. Because changes are likely to occur in the ways in which the business operates (not least because of inflation), it is probably better to articulate the levels of authority in central documentation, such as an 'Authorities Manual', rather than in individual job descriptions.

The existence of such a manual, however, only deals with part of the problem since its contents are unlikely to convince people external to the organization that the employee with whom they are dealing has the authority to commit the organization. This is an example of the way in which law does not keep pace with practice. Legally the organization is committed when documents such as contracts are sealed with the corporate seal, or are signed by two directors or one director and the company secretary. Given the impracticality of directors of listed companies undertaking such document execution, however, companies are habitually committed by those who have control over the company seal and who, in all probability, have no knowledge of the underlying transaction. It is thus necessary, from the control point of view, for organizations to be able to establish that those who are empowered internally to commit the organization have the ostensible authority to do so. This is most conveniently done by ensuring that the person committing the organization has been given a properly constituted and executed Power of Attorney by the organization. This would convey either general or specific powers to commit the organization to a particular transaction. This represents another way in which a party external to the organization (in this case the party with whom the orgnization is contracting) exercises control over an aspect of the organization's operations.

The principal internally oriented control elements are:

a) **The organization's budgetary system**, which is designed to establish how, within a given time period, the organization's revenues are expected to be generated and its resources utilized.

Budgets are forecasts which specify the financial resources which have been allocated to an organization's activities or to the achievement of its objectives for a given period of time.

If properly prepared they form the basis of a plan against which the performance of the budgetary unit can be monitored and any variance analysed so that appropriate action can be taken.

Within a large and complex organization they are important because:

● they concentrate upon an area which it is important to control, namely costs;

- variances between forecast and performance can usefully be analysed;

- they set very clear and relevant standards of performance;

- they are directly comparable with the statistics produced by the organization at the end of the period;

- they simplify the production of end of period accounts;

- they are useful for cross-organization comparison (and negotiation in the competition for resources), because they are stated in terms which are common throughout the organization;

- they give senior management the opportunity to compare, co-ordinate, control and prioritize a wide variety of organizational activities.

Budgets present managers with two basic difficulties. Firstly, they often take a long time to compile and agree, and secondly, and possibly because of this investment of managerial time, they tend to take on the aura of rigidity.

Time investment
The budget setting process is often tortuous particularly in a large and complex organization because budgets are ideally built 'bottom up'. This means that each individual manager is asked to forecast his requirements for the forthcoming year and on the basis of these forecasts bid for a proportion of his boss's budget. The boss amalgamates the bids of all subordinate managers and passes the combined up to the next layer of management, and so on until the total of the bids for the corporate budget is established.

Generally at this point it is clear that the organization cannot afford to do all that its managers want to do and so in some way the bids have to pared to match what the organization reckons it can afford. This can be done either on a pro rata basis, or on some system which allows prioritization, or on a combination of both approaches. Naturally it is preferable that a prioritization mechanism is used because this allows the organization to decide the order of priority in accordance with its strategic goals and its long-term plan.

Whatever method is used the resulting figures are then passed down through the layers of the budgetary hierarchy, and at each stage managers trim their original budgets in accordance with the amount of the resources which are to be made available to them.

Set out in this way the budgetary system does not appear to be too onerous or difficult to operate provided that all management are available to go through the budget setting exercise at more or less the same time each year. Unfortunately things don't always work out like that, and so the length of time during which the budget is set tends to extend over a far longer period. Typically the managers in a large organization with accounts up to 31 December will start setting budgets in September or August, and this involves forecasting up to 16 or 17 months ahead.

Rigidity
Budgeting works well for stable organizations operating within a stable environment. Where, however, the organization or the environment are not stable it is often not feasible to expect management to be tied down to budgets which were agreed more than a year before, and which were based on assumptions made months before the agreement.

This is not to say that managers in such circumstances should not be required to budget. It does, however, suggest that the budgetary system itself should be susceptible to controlled flexibility. If it isn't then there will tend to be a move amongst managers to abuse the system and provide flexibility within their own budgets.

b) **Management information systems ('MIS')**, which refers to the gathering, processing and representation of data derived from sources which are internal to the organization and from sources which are external. In the context of this definition 'processing' involves the analysis of data, comparisons with similar data from other areas, comparisons with past data to identify trends, integration of data from diverse sources, and the marshalling of that data into strategically relevant information.

Essentially MIS is an aid to corporate decision-making at the strategic level where most problems concern the future. The quality of the strategic decisions made by an organization both in an absolute sense and in comparison with the decisions made by that organization's actual and potential competitors will to a large extent determine whether that organization has a competitive edge. In turn the quality of those decisions will be based upon two fundamental aspects:

- the quality of the information loading into the decision;
- the ability of the senior management to use that information.

The use of an MIS should help in both of these aspects, and is likely to do so if it contains the following key elements:

- adaptable to meet the changing needs of the organization;
- capable of meeting the needs of all potential users whatever their level in the organization;
- geared to the future rather than to the past or the present;
- able to encompass all areas of the organization's activities, and all its products/services and all its functions;
- interlinked with all the other information systems within the organization, e.g. the budgetary system;
- user-friendly, easily accessible and capable of presenting information in an easily digestible form.

c) *Internal Audit*, which is the principal agent through which directors can apply detective and corrective controls on the running of the business. Internal Audit departments should be geared to operate on both a reactive and a proactive basis. They should react to events which are indicative of control breakdowns and be proactive by identifying and correcting areas of control weakness prior to breakdown.

The proactive operations of an internal audit department are most effective if they are integrated into the organization's strategic planning process so that risks which are associated with planned developments are identified and articulated at an early stage. Subsequently they can be investigated by the internal auditor against the background not only of the organization's culture and operations but also of the best practice guidelines and methodologies which are available outside the organization.

A typical proactive internal audit process would conform to the following:

● determine the business objectives;

● identify the risks relevant to each process involved in the achievement of the business objectives;

● list the controls which already exist to aid the management of the risks;

● ensure that the organization's monitoring systems will link existing and future controls to the risk associated with the business objective under investigation;

● identify gaps in the control and monitoring systems;

● decide the extent to which these risks will be accepted, avoided, shared, transferred or diversified;

● formulate an action plan to manage the risks to the extent that they are to be accepted;

● document and monitor the effectiveness of the control mechanisms.

The principal externally oriented control elements are:

a) *The organization's annual report and accounts.* These must, by law be published to all members of the organization, as well as being lodged with governmental and regulatory institutions. The format is constrained by legal, regulatory and accountancy requirements and the document is prepared subject to an external audit. The auditor would normally present a report to the board's Audit Committee (which comprises non-executive directors), and the accounts are approved by the full board.

In relation to the topic of control, it has become a feature of the post-Cadbury environment in the UK that the Listing Rules of the London Stock Exchange are adjusted, possibly after representations from institutional shareholders. Listed companies are therefore now required to state in their reports and accounts the extent to which they comply with guidelines and codes of practice (such as those issued by the Hampel Committee), and explain any instances of non-compliance.

b) *Relationship management with institutional investors.* Listed companies are conscious of the need to maintain good communications with the major investing institutions so that corporate actions which have affected the share price can be discussed and explained. Naturally great care has to be taken to avoid the investor gaining possession of price-sensitive information. The major dialogues will therefore occur after the company has made an announcement but, from the control point of view, the establishment of communication channels facilitates the influence which investors can bring to bear on the organization.

c) *Compliance functions.* Most organizations which are subject to regulation have built up substantial specialist compliance functions to manage the relationships between the organization and the regulators. Compliance departments are primarily concerned with preventive control, and seek to ensure that the organization's systems are such that it will comply with the regulator's requirements. As occasion demands (for example in the period following the pensions mis-selling in the UK), compliance areas will also become heavily involved in corrective control by ensuring that the company's systems are adjusted to cater for what has been identified as a control breakdown.

Possible future trends in organizational control

It seems clear that in keeping with the development of more sophisticated systems of internal control, organizations will, in future, be subject to a greater degree of pressures for control from external sources. This results partly from the development of communication systems on a global basis, and partly from the shift to a control regime based on regulation which can therefore be both more flexible and more rigorous than one based on legislation.

The ease with which global communication can now be accomplished has attracted firms into different markets, and hence into different regulatory regimes. It has also facilitated the development of global standards, such as the Basle Accords, and the exchange of concepts of best practice from one market to another.

Additionally it facilitates communication amongst interested parties so that the formation of pressure groups becomes ever more likely. Bob Garratt (1998) has suggested that small shareholders and other stakeholders "are learning to form pressure groups, especially through the Internet, to gather proxy votes and allow them to speak inside the [company meeting] rather than demonstrate outside the door".

The development of investment funds which are designed to replicate exactly the performance of a particular share index will (as such funds become an increasing part of the portfolio of investing institutions), inhibit the ability of major investors to display their dissatisfaction with company performance by selling their shares. Dialogue between major investors and the companies in which they invest should therefore increase.

Summary

This chapter has taken a broad look at the ways in which organizations are controlled. The emphasis has been on the complexity of control and the interaction between internal and external control mechanisms.

Given the work of the Cadbury and Hampel Committees, and following the formation of the Financial Services Authority, it seems probable that within the financial services industry consideration of this topic will grow rather than diminish in significance.

References

Davies H (1998) *Long Term Capital Management*, Chartered Institute of Bankers

Fincham, R & Rhodes P S (1988) *The Individual Work and Organization*, 2nd ed., Weidenfeld & Nicolson

The Financial Services Authority: An Outline, (1997) FSA

Meeting our Responsibilities, (1998) FSA

Garratt R (1988) *Changing Values in Corporate Governance*, Gower

Committee on Corporate Governance   *The Combined Code*, (1998) London Stock Exchange

Institute of Directors (1995) *Standards for The Board*, London

Large Sir A (1997) *Effective Regulation and Responsibilities of Senior Management* – speech to The Cardiff Business Club, April

9 Self-management

Objectives

This chapter examines the methods of self-management and attempts to relate them to the modern world of work. In doing so it considers the usefulness of studies on aspects of self-management in relation to the rapidly changing working environment.

The detailed objectives of the chapter are:

- to outline the techniques of the management of time, information, stress and careers;

- to discuss the relevance of academic studies of these areas;

- to develop a rationale for approaches to the management of these areas for the current working environment.

Time management

The classic approaches to aiding the individual in the management of his own time include the following.

P. & O. Priority and Organization.

When faced with a number of tasks which have to be completed, how do you decide the order in which they should be tackled?

In the context of work it is essential to know what are the most important aspects of your job. Generally these will be found within your Key Results Areas and Key Tasks. All these tasks can be classified according to their **importance** and their **urgency**. Establishing that there is a difference between urgency and importance is significant, since there is a tendency for us to prioritize urgent matters over less urgent but more important items. This is a sensible approach provided that we do not spend too much time on less important matters.

An analysis along these lines is helpful in establishing the correct priority which should be given, both in terms of time allocation and the order in which tasks are to be completed, to outstanding work.

Tasks from a typical working day can be categorized using the following matrix:

	Important	Trivial
Urgent	*Schedule to ensure they are given quality time*	*Do them early without taking up too much time*
Not urgent	*Schedule to do them before they become urgent*	*Do them when they can be fitted in or delegate*

P.M.T. Paper Management Techniques

Many time management problems arrive in the form of paper. The fundamental rule of paper management to which we should all aspire is that each piece of paper should be handled once and once only. Realistically this is not possible but it is a good idea to keep this concept at the back of one's mind. Should paper find its way into your hand then the last place in which you should subsequently deposit it is your 'in tray'.

There are four ways in which to dispose of each item of paper:

● *Deal* with it, i.e. take whatever action is necessary;

- *Delegate* it, i.e. pass the responsibility for dealing with it onto somebody else;

- *Diarize* it, i.e. don't deal with it now but specify the time when you will deal with it and schedule that activity at the appropriate time in your diary;

- *Dump* it, i.e. recognize the paper as worthless and ensure that it is not allowed to disturb the time management of any of your colleagues!

Modem communication mechanisms, and particularly e-mail, add to the time management burden because they make communication itself easier and reduce response times. The 4D approach can, of course, be applied to e-mails.

B.B.C. Better Bandit Control

'Time Bandits' are those people and events which disrupt your time schedule. Imagine that you have a piece of work to do which you estimate will take two hours. As a good time manager you will have scheduled two hours in your diary in order to complete this task. What are the chances of those two hours being uninterrupted by colleagues, customers, bosses, subordinates and telephone calls? Any such interruption will tend to prolong the actual time, as well as the elapsed time, that will need to be devoted to the task in hand.

These potential interruptions could be dealt with by many methods including the following:

- Make yourself **unavailable**. Don't work at your usual work station. Instead book a room elsewhere in which to accomplish this task and make sure that nobody knows where you are! Alternatively, why not work from home?

- Operate a **half open door** policy. One of the mistakes which many of us make is to proclaim that our doors are always open to customers and staff alike. This gives permission to others to interrupt us at their discretion. It is often far better to proclaim that you are available to them only between certain hours, or that you are not available at other definite times. Having made such a statement you must not, of course, break your own rules by allowing interruptions outside the appropriate time.

- In an open plan office operate a **red time** system. This involves giving those who are likely to interrupt you a visible signal that you will not entertain such an interruption.

- Use all the facilities of modern telephone systems. Calls can be diverted relatively easily. If it is possible to do this for an interview it is possible to do the same thing to secure some uninterrupted time.

- Use your secretary (if you have one) as a gatekeeper. This will mean that incoming calls and visitors must initially be vetted by the secretary who will then schedule a time for any required meeting to take place.

These suggestions are counsels of perfection. Many managers, particularly in a customer service industry, do not take kindly to the idea of not always being available to their customers. Experience shows, however, that when customers, colleagues and subordinates are given a scheduled appointment, they actually feel more important and are likely to be better prepared and more businesslike when the scheduled meeting takes place.

The point which it is worthwhile to stress is that it is not necessary to apply these techniques consistently over time. It is essential to effective managerial performance, however, to have a command over them so that they can be applied as circumstances demand.

What do managers do?

The classic work on the way mangers use their working time is *The Nature of Managerial Work* by Henry Mintzberg (1973). What Mintzberg found was that the single most consistent feature of the way in which his research subjects spent their time at work was interruption.

> *Jumping from topic to topic, he (the manager) thrives on interruptions and, more often than not, disposes of items in ten minutes or less. Though he may have fifty projects going, all are delegated. He juggles them, checking each one periodically before sending it back into orbit.*

Not surprisingly, with '50 projects going', Mintzberg found that managers spend about 75% of their time 'communicating'. Furthermore, he concluded that the communication most valued by his subjects was that which was informal, since they seemed to shun reports and periodicals and tended to process their mail, picking up information by informal means, and often relying on gossip and hearsay.

Findings such as these call into question the work of Fayol (1949) who proposed that managerial work involves planning, organising, commanding, co-ordinating and controlling. This in turn suggests that what is important is not only the length of time devoted to a 'managerial activity' but also the quality of the input. It is possible to postulate that Mintzberg's managers were able to control their 50 projects by virtue of the quality of the planning and organising.

Mintzberg (1975) himself was at pains to point out that it was crucial to recognize what managers actually did rather than what they were supposed to do:

> Without a proper answer, how can we teach manage-
> ment? How can we design planning or information
> systems for managers? How can we improve the practice
> of management at all?

Is Mintzberg's analysis relevant?

In assessing the usefulness of any management theory or model, it is essential to analyse the nature of the objective evidence on which conclusions have been drawn and then to ask whether it is right to apply those conclusions to another time and space.

The subjects of Mintzberg's research were the Chief Executive Officers of five organizations (a school system, technology company, consulting firm, hospital and consumer goods company), and Mintzberg spent a week in observation of each in the early 1970s. Nevertheless, it seems that Mintzberg's analysis has to a large extent been unquestionably accepted. In a helpful article, Titus Oshagbemi (1995) has sought to establish the extent to which the actual use of managerial time had been the subject of academic investigation. His research found a total of 64 studies whose results were published between 1981 and 1993. Combining some of these with earlier studies, with a view to drawing conclusions from comparable data, he was able to list 25 studies undertaken between 1963 and 1990 which had addressed the question of the allocation of managerial time between various work activities.

Of these 25 studies, eight were of five or fewer managers, six were of between six and ten managers, three were of between 11 and 25 managers, and the remaining eight studied the time allocation of 26 or more managers.

From these Oshagbemi undertook a further analysis to ascertain whether there was any discernible pattern to the way in which the subjects distributed their time between 'deskwork', 'meetings' and 'phone calls'. The outcome in terms of the average time spent on these activities was:

Deskwork	Meetings	Phone calls
%	%	%
25	53	7

However, the average is not necessarily a sensible measure on the basis of which to draw conclusions. The range in the results was as follows:

Deskwork	Meetings	Phone calls
%	%	%
7 – 44	32 – 73	1 – 11

The respective standard deviations were as follows:

Deskwork	Meetings	Phone calls
%	%	%
9	10	2.5

This suggests that approximately 70% of managers spent between 16% and 34% of their time on deskwork, 43% and 63% at meetings, and 4.5% and 9.5% on the telephone.

It is also interesting to note that the way in which data was gathered might also have influenced the result. In an article written in 1996 Christopher Orpen analysed the discrepancy which is possible between various methods of collecting the data. Admittedly the subject of the study was a single individual, but the outcome is nonetheless instructive. The manager was asked first to estimate how his time was allocated between a number of categories of activity. He subsequently kept a time-log of the way his time was spent over a two week period during which he was observed. The results were as indicated in Figure 9.1:

Figure 9.1

Activity:	Working alone	Letters	Dictation	Meetings	Socialising at work	Meals	Phone	Reading/ producing reports
Estimate %	45	10	5	15	10	3	6	6
Time-log %	32	5	3	24	15	6	8	7
Observation %	34	5	3	22	14	6	7	9

Oshagbemi's study and Orpen's report together indicate that it is both difficult and dangerous to draw conclusions to the way in which managers allocate their time on the basis of any study which does not rely on some element of objective reporting. Even then it is likely that the results may be specific to the type of industry, organization or individual.

Furthermore it is also likely that any objective study of the distribution of management time is specific to the era in which it was conducted. The convenience of modern communications technology is such that it suggests that the volume of face to face work done by the manager of today and of the future will probably lessen, particularly if humans become accustomed to interacting socially via an electronic rather than an oral exchange.

The roots of this are already in place. We have heard much in recent years of the possibilities of home-working, tele-stations and the virtual office to suggest that the harnessing of IT as the fundamental method of communication may not be too far away. For time management, particularly within the financial services industry, this has profound implications, since many financial services organizations operate across time zones and cultures, and are basically dependent upon the flow of information in order to develop business. Thus the traditional patterns of work will become more stressful and a greater premium will be placed on the ability to manage the receipt, digestion, storage and retrieval of information.

Management of stress

More and more organizations are taking an enlightened attitude to the management of stress. This is not necessarily because there has been an increase in the amount of stress related illness. It is more because it is now recognized that in times of unprecedented change work becomes more stressful. Therefore the more that individuals are able to manage their own stress the more likely they will avoid stress related illness.

What is stress?

Stress is a concept which is known to engineers, doctors, psychologists, chemists, biologists and no doubt to many others, including managers. Each group will come up with its own definition of what constitutes stress, and there is no universal easily accessible definition. In the world of management it is probably easiest to think of stress as being present when an individual has 'more than he or she can cope with'.

This results from the presence of 'stressors' to which the individual reacts, producing behavioural differences which are the symptoms and the effects of stress.

The stressors which operate in our lives are likely to be different from one individual to another but they will fall into one of four broad categories:-

1. *Overload*, whereby the individual has too much work to do or too many 'roles' to play.

2. *Underload*, whereby the individual has too little work to do or too few 'roles' to play.

3. *Frustration*, whereby the individual is unable to control his own environment to the extent of being able to achieve his objectives.

4. *Change*, whereby the individual finds that the stability of his existence is disrupted by things beyond control.

The categorization of stressors outlined above was a product of the time before the IT revolution which, if anything, will have added to rather than detracted from the level of stressors available to assault the individual.

Not only is change implicit within the 'electronic office' it is also apparent that the altering patterns and methods of working have an impact upon the other categories. The speed of communication both increases the amount of work which can be done and decreases the time which it takes to do it. This can lead to either or both overload and underload.

Extensive communication systems, from the World Wide Web down to the office Local Area Network, increase the number of relationships to which the manager of tomorrow is likely to be party, hence increasing the chances of role overload.

The changing attitude to working life, and the ending of the cradle to grave philosophy, implies that there will be more frequent job changes than was the case hitherto. In terms of stressors each move away from a job/office/department/organization is a significant unbundling of relationships with the implication of role underload.

One of the most significant factors leading to individual stress within the financial services industry is the extent to which organizations are being restructured.

At the organizational level restructuring can result from an acquisition or a merger. This has been a trend in the financial services industry, since 1986, because the opportunities to realize synergistic amalgamations of businesses within the industry have been easier to achieve. Within organizations themselves the march of IT has been such as to drive restructuring both to achieve process re-engineering and economies in resource management.

In relation to the categories of stressors described above, any such restructuring will probably result in a significant amount of stress within the organization concerned.

It is for reasons such as these that many organizations have offered counselling services to staff to help them to manage the impact of such stressors on their lives.

It is important for both the individual and the organization to recognize that the provision of such support mechanisms must be general rather than specific to any particular stressful event.

The reason for this is twofold. In the first place individuals do not react to stress in a uniform and predictable way (though there may be a common process of reaction. Secondly it is likely to be the cumulative effect of a number of stressors (from both inside and outside work) which leads to a chronic breakdown in health. This breakdown, if it ever occurs, then will not necessarily be related in time to the incidence of a stressor, which was a major contributory factor.

The extent to which each individual can cope with different stressors varies so that what may be a major stressor to one individual may have a barely perceptible effect on another.

The effect of a number of stressors on the life of any one individual is cumulative, so that an apparently trivial incident may provoke a traumatic reaction because it is the latest in a long chain of stressors.

Similarly the ways in which people exhibit symptoms of stress vary. Wilkinson (1987) in the British Medical Association booklet *Coping with Stress* cites the following as being among the most common reactions:

Feeling of being under pressure	Inability to relax
Feeling mentally drained	Feeling frightened constantly
Irritability	Conflict
Aggression	Inability to concentrate
Increased tearfulness	Increased fussiness
Increased indecision	Impulses to run and hide
Fear of fainting	Fear of failure
Lack of enjoyment	Fear of social embarrassment
Change in appetite	Change in sleep patterns
Increased headaches	Indigestion
Constipation	Diarrhoea
Back pain	'Butterflies' in the stomach
Nausea	Weakness of the limbs
Muscle tension	Tiredness
Sweating	Fidgeting

Notice that many of these reactions are contradictory, and that they are not the exclusive province of stress as they can each be the symptom of some other disorder. This implies that recognising stress both in ourselves and in others is not easy. However, the clues are likely to lie in significant behavioural changes over time.

Although the reaction to stressors varies from individual to individual, it has been suggested (Mirvis 1985)) that the process of reaction to stressors in an organizational context mirrors that commonly associated with sudden bereavement or other personal loss. This process involves four stages: Denial, Anger, Depression and Acceptance.

1.   Denial and/or disbelief

During this stage the individual will refuse to accept that the merger, acquisition, restructuring, etc. will take place and, when this becomes undeniable, will deny that the *status quo* will be disrupted as a result. Thereafter there will be a tendency to believe that the resulting changes will not impact upon the individual.

2.   Anger, rage and resentment

The second stage is characterized by an uplift in energy levels which are not always positively directed. The result is often a major and/or extended expression of anger or resentment against those considered responsible.

3.   Depression

In contrast to the second stage, the third stage is characterized by a lowering of energy levels as the individual begins to recognize the impact upon himself of the change which has triggered the reaction. Fear and uncertainty as to what the future holds may push the individual into a clinically depressed state.

4.   Acceptance

In the final stage, the individual begins to recognize the changed order and to work positively to improve his own position within the context of his new environment.

Interestingly this process of reaction, though common in terms of the stages through which the individual passes, is not completed within a uniform timescale. In the case of some individuals or some incidents the entire process may be over in a matter of minutes whereas with others it may take months or years for the entire process to be completed – always assuming that the individual does not get stuck in an earlier stage. Thus for organizational support mechanisms to be successful they must be accessible at times which are not directly connected with the apparent trigger of the stress.

It is also worth noting that a certain amount of stress is worthwhile because it is likely to enhance performance. This suggests that stress is not something to be avoided so much as managed effectively.

Strategies for managing stress

Awareness   Be aware of what for you constitutes a stressor, and of what your typical reaction to stress is. If you know how you typically react, then you can watch out for those reactions and from them determine what it is that stresses you.

Diet   A sensible diet helps to limit the chances of succumbing to stress-related diseases and the effects of such illnesses. The main principles are to eat to maintain a sensible body weight, to eat less fatty foods, to increase dietary fibre, to eat more cereals, pulses, fruits and vegetables, and to to eat less sugar and salt. A watch should be maintained on the consumption of caffeine through drinking coffee and tea.

Fitness   It is preferable to maintain a reasonable level of fitness by taking some exercise on a regular basis. A 20-minute session, three times a week is what is recommended as adequate. The principle behind the approach to the exercise is that it should stimulate the heart and therefore leave you moderately 'puffed'. It should also address suppleness and build up muscle tone in those muscles, apart from the heart, that are important, principally the leg muscles.

Balance   Getting an appropriate balance between the various areas of life is particularly important. You have responsibilities to your family, to other close relationships, to your employer, but most of all to yourself. Stress often arises when the balance between these areas goes astray, and it is therefore important for each individual to sort out what really matters to them in their lives. These priorities may, of course, change at different stages in life.

Support   One of the most effective ways of managing stress is to ensure that there is strong and reliable social support available where daily problems can be expressed. This is most often found within family relationships, but if these are not available then friends and mutual support groups may provide what is needed. The key contribution which is made by the supporter is simply listening to what is said. There does not need to be any attempt to solve problems because the major benefits flow from the simple articulation of one's feelings about whatever may act as stressors.

Abuse   Tobacco, alcohol and drugs of dependence are not helpful in combating the effects of stress. Tobacco and drugs should be avoided completely, and the consumption of alcohol should be carefully managed.

Tactics for managing stress

As noted above, some stress in our lives is probably beneficial because it enhances our performance. Therefore it is useful to acquire techniques which help to control stress whilst it is present. Amongst the best ways of doing this are:

Breathing   Watch sports players who are about to perform some important individual feat (e.g. a penalty kick in soccer, a goal kick in rugby, a serve at tennis). As part of the preparation the player will often take a couple of deliberate deep breaths. The effect of this is to calm the mind since the concentration is on breathing, momentarily at least. This stimulates the body physically since more oxygen is being made available both for the muscles and the brain. The same technique can be applied to any anxiety provoking situation, e.g. an important interview, a meeting or presentation.

Relaxation   This involves the deliberate attempt to relax muscles by initially tensing them and then allowing them to relax completely. Again there are twin benefits in that not only is there a general release of tension within the muscles but also, because there is a need to concentrate on the exercise, the mind relaxes. This is a useful technique for coping with that modern stressor the tailback!

Assertion   Much stress is caused because of our tendency to give too much credence to the rights of other people over the rights of ourselves. Thus when the boss dumps work on us late in the evening we accept it and subsequently castigate ourselves for having acquiesced and perhaps missed an opportunity to do something else. Also we tend to criticize ourselves for not seizing opportunities to project our own viewpoints. Assertiveness teaches that in situations such as these we have a choice, and as long as we positively exercise that choice (which may mean that we choose not to say anything, or that we choose to accept the work from our boss) we are less likely to move into a spiral of self-criticism and thus are better able to manage stress.

Careers

The working definition of career as provided by Wilensky (1964) is "a succession of related jobs arranged in a hierarchy of prestige, through which persons moved in an ordered (more or less predictable) sequence."

It is fundamental to this idea of a career that there should be upward linear motion from one job to another, with the jobs being in some way related. The relationship between the successive jobs can derive from either the nature of the work or the organizational connection between the jobs. Thus an individual can pursue a career by periodically making a move from a job with one organization to a 'higher level' job in the same sphere of work in the same or another organization. In such cases the individual generally transports skills, knowledge and experience from the first job onto the second. Alternatively, with the active or passive agreement of the organization, the individual can pursue his or her career by moving from one job to another within the same organization but in a different work sphere. In this situation transferrable skills, knowledge and experience of the organization (as opposed to the work) are transported.

What is less likely to have happened in the past was a movement from one organization to another which was not bridged by some connection between the different spheres of work being undertaken. Such a move was more likely to be described as a 'career change'.

In this sense the concept of the career is inherently connected with the concept of the organization. The vast majority of the self-employed and 'traditional professionals' (doctors, dentists, lawyers, etc.) would not be seen as having careers in the sense defined above.

This means that, because we are currently experiencing what is likely to be a sea change in the ways in which organizations are structured, there will necessarily be profound changes in the ways in which careers are managed, both by the individual and by the organization.

The ideal organization for a careerist is one which has numerous layers to its hierarchy. Although it is a gross oversimplification it is illustrative to consider such organizations as conforming to two basic patterns: the 'inverted drawing pin' and the 'tall divisional' structures.

The inverted drawing pin is typical of hierarchies in which discipline and control are important, such as the armed forces, police and clearing banks. Their structure can be represented as in Figure 9.2.

This diagram shows (approximately) the structure of Barclays Bank in the early 1980s when there were about 21 hierarchical levels before the grading of 'Senior Executive' was reached. This structure was maintained until 1990 when the number of levels was reduced to 14. It has since been reduced further to eight.

The usually accepted explanations for the anomalous bulges at levels 11 and 17 are that level 11 was the first 'managerial' grade and at level 17 managers qualified for the company car. This suggests that it was better to plateau at these levels rather than at the level beneath.

The tall divisional structure may have as many levels as the inverted drawing pin but it will also have breadth throughout much of its structure. This is illustrated in Figure 9.3.

An inverted drawing pin structure is predicated on the proposition that the organization is delivering a single basic product which increases in complexity as it uses more of the organization's resources. In the case of the police, for example, the deployment of personnel brings more layers of the hierarchy into the delivery process. In the case of a traditional bank, the level of control increased in proportion to the level of finance required by the customer.

A tall divisional structure would be found in organizations which are multi-functional, multi-product or multi-site, but which still felt

Figure 9.2: Inverted Drawing Pin Structure

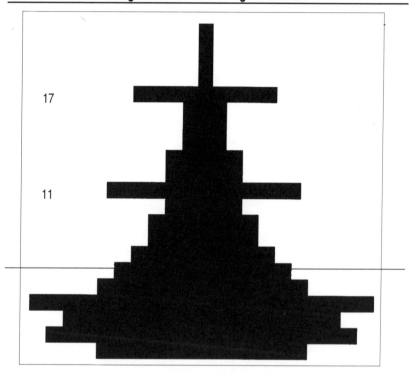

17

11

Figure 9.3: Tall Divisional Structure

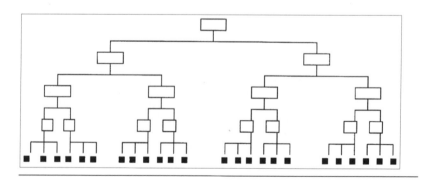

the need for there to be a measure of strong central control of resources. An example of this would be the hierarchy within a region of a clearing bank's operations.

Organization structures are more fully discussed in Chapter 3. The above illustrations are merely for the purpose of considering the effects of structures on career management.

Working within a heavily layered hierarchy the careerist needed only to perform to the organization's satisfaction to expect reward by promotion to the next level. The organization could plan to grow it's own future higher level managers by selecting the best candidates from each level for promotion to the next higher level. In the tall divisional type of structure the organization also had to worry about building the experience of the whole organization into the career path of its future general management by ensuring that at least some of these paths crossed departmental and divisional lines.

Reward systems within such organizations tended to offer a 'fair day's pay for a fair day's work' at each level within the hierarchy, and rewarded greater experience within any level by age or 'time in job' related increments within a band. As such, and once the environment in which the organization was operating was considered relatively stable, the bargain made between the organization and the individual was judged clear. The Psychological Contract (what employers and employees want of each other, as described in Chapter 12) though implicit was well understood by both parties. It can be summarized as follows:

If the employee	then the employer will	and the consequence will be
• is loyal	• provide a secure job	• a steady state
• works hard	• with regular promotion	organization
• conforms	• giving financial security	• in a steady state industry

Organizations which offered such psychological contracts attracted employees who had 'security' as a significant motivation factor.

The work of Michael Porter (1979) lists four forces governing competition in an industry:

1. Bargaining power of suppliers.

2. Bargaining power of customers.

3. Threat of substitute products or services.

4. Threat of new entrants.

In relation to the last of these he describes six major sources of barriers to entry

- economies of scale;

- product differentiation;

- capital requirements;

- cost disadvantages independent of size;

- access to distribution channels;

- government policy.

In 1986, the UK Government policy with respect to the financial services industry effectively changed. At the same time it became abundantly clear to the UK clearing banks that they had not managed the past introduction of IT to their systems particularly well, and that their current management of IT was not sufficiently sophisticated to take advantage of the opportunities which IT afforded. As a result the banks found all six of the barriers to entry into the industry under threat. To survive, it was deemed necessary to dismantle all aspects of being a steady state organization in a steady state industry, and the psychological contract was amongst the casualties.

The post-deregulation environment demanded that organizations within the financial services industry were responsive to changes demanded by customers often dictated by innovative products or services introduced by competitors. There was thus no premium to be placed on traditional knowledge and skills, nor on attitudes which were conducive to success within the traditional culture. Once IT had been effectively harnessed to serve the purposes of *inter alia* senior management there was little need for hierarchical controls. This was because they could be maintained through the use of effective management information systems (though they had to be understood by senior management *vide* Barings). The result was that spans of control could be broadened, layers of management stripped out and organizations flattened, as is illustrated in Figure 9.4.

Figure 9.4

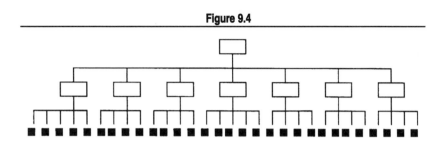

A flat organization such as that depicted in Figure 9.4 does not have the same scope for the careerist as did a taller organization. This poses problems both for the individual careerist and for the organization.

Organizational perspective

In the old style hierarchies there was plenty of scope for an organization to nurture its own talent. The consequence of the flatter structure is that with fewer positions into which talent can be promoted there is less chance of retaining high quality careerists if remuneration systems are designed to reward depth of experience. Furthermore with fewer hierarchical levels there will be fewer salary bands, and although the bands will be wider there will still be less scope for incremental payments to be given to talented people.

The solution which the majority of organizations have moved towards is to design remuneration systems which reward performance rather the experience. The theory is that talent will be retained because, by definition, it will produce desired results. In turn, talent will reap rewards which exceed those which can be anticipated by transferring allegiance to another organization.

The principle objective of Manpower Planning (see Chapter 13) is to have the right staff with the right attributes in the right place at the right time. Within an inverted drawing pin structure it was relatively easy to achieve this in respect of future senior managers because staff would, in their early careers, pick up the basis of the operations and in their subsequent careers graft deeper levels of understanding onto this secure basis. In such cases, the selection for promotion was likely to be founded on direct competition with peers who would all have the requisite attributes. In the tall divisional structures it was more likely that the seedcorn for future senior managerial appointments would be found within a cadre of fast-track employees. These employees were explicitly or implicitly managed by the organization to ensure that there would always be a sufficient pool of suitable candidates from which to chose each senior role with the benefit of some competitive element.

In the modern world of flatter organizations the development of future senior management is a more complex business. One obvious solution is to 'buy in' the talent at the relevant level. This can be accomplished through suitably constructed and disciplined recruitment and selection procedures (see Chapter 13). However, such an approach necessarily involves the acceptance of two risks:

a) that the new hire may meet all the objective selection criteria but may not be sensitive to the organization's culture – a fact only to be discovered when the individual and the culture have co-existed for some time;

b) a firm that is prepared to attract talent from another firm must, in turn expect its talent to be similarly poached by rivals.

In view of these dangers many flattened organizations have sought to retain a fast-track approach which in turn has meant that the attitude towards career development has had to become more sophisticated. This is illustrated by the words of ICI's Group Human Resources Development Director:

> *In the past, however, we sought to give our high-flyers as much functional and geographical experience as possible. As a result, they tended to become like spinning tops, moving rapidly between appointments throughout the world. While they gained great experience in a short time, one may question whether it was good for the customer base, for the style of the organization when its leaders chopped and changed, or for the individual who gained a scattering of knowledge but never stayed in position long enough to deal with the consequences of his or her decisions.*

The strategy now is to give careerists longer 'dwell time' in each new position with the expectation that they will be able to make a greater upward transition into the next job. Reward mechanisms can then be geared to the results produced during the dwell time, while the risks accepted in taking the next job are recompensed by a commensurate hike in salary and/or benefits.

A more subtle change in the area of career management is the shift of responsibility away from the organization to the individual. In the past decisions about career moves were often made behind closed doors by the organization before being presented (and, if necessary, sold) to the individual. However, a characteristic of the new approach is a far greater degree of openness about what jobs are on offer, on the one hand, and what positions are desired, on the other.

This is not a one-sided approach. Surveys conducted in the late eighties/early nineties in Britain show that young people who have been raised and educated in an atmosphere of peace and relative affluence have as one of their primary concerns the quality of life. They are judiciously critical of employers and authority seeking jobs which challenge them. They value independence, imagination, tolerance and responsibility whereas their parents (those over 50 in the survey) were more likely to emphasize the Protestant work ethic as a prime motivator (see Harding (1991)).

The presence of a greater proportion of women in higher value jobs has also placed a greater premium on jobs designed to give the worker greater autonomy and flexibility.

The inevitable outcome is that a new form of the Pyschological Contract is emerging often with many of the following features:

- organizations demand of employees not only that they do their work but that they improve their operations, contribute to the learning of the organization and manage their own development;

- organizations no longer assume a caretaker role in respect of the employee's immediate and long-term personal income (a feature of this is the move towards portable personal pensions);

- the outward signs of success have been eroded or changed, and gone are the automatically increasing income, job security and status which was accorded age and experience;

- promotion is no longer the currency of motivation, since this has shifted towards job enrichment and personal development;

- reward is more and more based on what the employee contributes to the employer;

- the norm for contracts is becoming that they should be either short-term or 'transactional' (i.e. for the achievement of specific objectives) as opposed to a 'job for life' approach. This sees its ultimate expression in the adage of Jack Welch, the CEO of General Electric, to the effect that GE offers its people a 'one day contract'. The employees will be employed only so long as the attributes which they can contribute are useful to the firm (see Mirvis & Hall (1994)).

The emerging Psychological Contract can be summarized as:

If the employee	then the employer will	and the consequence will be
• adds value • accepts responsibility for improving things and for self-development	• provide interesting work with the resources and freedom to facilitate performance and pay which reflects the contribution made, and development opportunities to enhance employability	• flexibility for both the employer and the employee

Individual perspective

The shift in the balance of responsibility for career management from the organization towards the individual implies that the worker of today needs to adopt career management competences which will cater for both vertical and lateral job moves, as well as for short-term and longer-term contracts. These competencies should also cater for moving into and out of particular organizations, and for moving into and out of the world of work.

Ben Ball (1997)suggests that these should encompass four areas:

- optimising career prospects;

- using a career planning cycle;
- undertaking personal development;
- balancing work and non-work.

Optimising career prospects

It is probable that the careerist seeks advancement as a means of satisfying self-esteem, as well as achieving recognition and enhancing feelings of self-worth. If this is true then the attainment of advancement is likely to be a basic motivational force and its absence will lead to frustrations and feelings of failure. This implies that careerists need to develop strategies which will enable them to adopt:

- a goal-directed approach to career planning;
- predict developments which are likely to affect their chosen working environment;
- anticipate significant life events;
- promote their own career interests.

This implies that such individuals should develop mentoring relationships with seniors within their organization or sphere of work. They should also build networks of contacts, again both inside and outside their current organizations, and be prepared to accept jobs, tasks, projects, assignments, etc. which add to their portfolio of experience without necessarily adding to their remuneration package.

Using a career planning cycle

Ball postulates a career planning cycle which is close to the 'learning cycle' suggested by Kolb (1984):

It is essential for the careerist to keep the relationship between his career aspirations and the working environment under review since both are susceptible to change.

The individual needs to be able to assess accurately the current state of his attributes and experiences before exploring options for future career development. This may then identify a gap between current and anticipated requirements which, with planning leading to appropriate activity, can be eliminated.

Figure 9.5

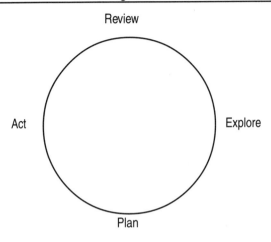

Review

Act

Explore

Plan

Undertaking personal development

Whereas in the past organizations may have dictated the ways in which their employees developed, through the provision of planned training or development activities, it is now increasingly incumbent on the individual to arrange access to those opportunities which will enhance his career. Since organizations are not necessarily seeking to maintain their link with the individual for the long term it is not in their direct interest to resource individual development. It is however in the indirect interest of the organization to do so for two reasons:

- it facilitates movement out of the organization of individuals who have outlived their current usefulness;

- it encourages the creation and maintenance of a pool of developed labour from which the organization can select its new hires.

It thus becomes a symbiotic relationship between the employer and the employee whereby the employee seeks to channel the employer's resources towards the satisfaction of his own development requirements.

Balancing work and non-work

In Western society, someone leaving the education system at the end of the twentieth century will have radically different prospects with regard to both life expectancy and the length of working life than his parents and grandparents would have had. Given the prospect of living for another 50 years (18,250 days) and an assumption of full employment (i.e. 230 days per year) the proportion of days devoted to work will be less than 40% of the projected lifespan. If the calculation is done in terms of hours devoted to work (say 12 per working day) then the proportion of work time to total time drops to about 19%. Much of the non-work time will be spent in sleep. Nevertheless this kind of calculation implies that a substantial part of the individual's life will be devoted to domestic, spiritual, leisure or developmental pursuits. It is odd therefore that most of the thrust behind modern day education is that it should operate as a preparation for work rather than as a preparation for non-work. This is not surprising since the education system was devised and hitherto maintained by people for whom the prospect of full employment throughout a full working life was seen not only as a realistic expectation but also as a right.

In *The Future of Work* Charles Handy (1989) points out that the norm for the post-World War II and previous generations of 100,000 hours (or 47 hours per week for 47 weeks per year for 47 years) is not sustainable in a modern Western economy, and that the norm is likely to shift towards a 50,000 hour working life with those 50,000 hours being distributed in a disjointed way over the period from the beginning to the end of an individual's employment. Thus the worker of the future has to expect and be prepared for periods of non-employment before employment finally ceases.

The expectation is that these periods will be devoted to activities other than work. The most obvious being child-rearing but other possibilities will include caring, reassessment of personal goals, personal development, voluntary work, return to education, re-skilling, self-employment and unenforced early retirement.

The key point made by Ball in this connection is that it is the responsibility of the individual (and clearly it is a responsibility that cannot lie elsewhere) to take an integrated approach to balancing the many aspects of work and life outside work which compete for portions of the individual's time. It is not sufficient to simply to comparmentalize the years from say 25 to 55 as those to be devoted to work and during this period it is important, even for a careerist, to pay attention to non-work issues and activities.

Summary

This chapter has been concerned with the management of time, stress and careers which are of specific concern to modern managers.

Studies of the ways in which managers are reputed to spend their time have been critically examined.

References

Ball B (1997) 'Career Management Competences: the Individual Perspective', *Career Development International*, Vol. 2, No. 2 pp 74-79
Fayol H (1949) *General and Industrial Management*, Pitman
Handy C (1989) *The Future of Work*, Blackwell
Harding S (1991) *Employee Attitudes towards their Employers: a European Perspective*, International Survey Research
Kolb D A (1984) *Experiential Learning: Experience as a Source of Learning and Development*, Prentice-Hall
Mintzberg H (1973) *The Nature of Managerial Work*, Harper and Row
Mintzberg H (1975) *The Manager's Job: Folklore and Fact*, Harvard Business Review
Mirvis P & Hall D (1994) 'Psychological Success and the Boundaryless Career', *Journal of Organizational Behaviour*, Vol.15, pp. 365-380
Mirvis P H (1985) 'Negotiations after the Sale: the Roots and Ramifications of Conflict in an Acquisition', *Journal of Organizational Behaviour*, Vol. 6, No. 1 pp 65-84
Orpen C (1996) 'Managing Time Effectively', *Competency*, Vol. 3, No. 4
Oshagbemi T (1995) 'Management Development and the Managers' Use of their Time', *Journal of Management Development*, Vol. 14, No. 8
Porter M E (1979) 'How Competitive Forces Shape Strategy', *Harvard Business Review*, March-April
Tudhope G (1997) quoted in Oliver J 'The New-Look Fast Track', *Management Today*, March, pp. 86-89
Wilensky H L (1964) 'Varieties of Work Experience', in Borow H ed. *Man in a World at Work*, Houghton Mifflin

Wilkinson G (1987) *Coping with Stress*, Family Doctor Publications

10 Managing groups

Objectives

Group working is becoming an increasingly important feature of financial services organizations, with many organizations investing in team-building activities.

People rarely work in isolation in organizations, most interact with others and most activities need some co-ordination through group work. If an organization is to function effectively and efficiently good team work is needed. This chapter seeks to provide an understanding of the theory and practice of group working by:

- exploring the meaning of groups;

- explaining the reasons why groups are formed and the different types of groups which exist in organizations;

- identifying the characteristics which influence effective group performance;

- investigating the managerial implications of groups in terms of communications, decision-making and managing conflict.

Introduction

The power and authority in organizations is moving away from the individual to the team (Belbin 1981). As organizational structures change, group working and the quality of team members is becoming increasingly important. This is evident in the financial services sector where the changing nature of structures and tasks, including flatter hierarchies, reductions of layers of middle management and moves to more employee involvement, mean that there is a greater emphasis on groups.

The overall success of organizations operating in this sector is significantly influenced by the interactions of a number of different groups who may facilitate or inhibit the attainment of organizational goals. Group working can be viewed as having the dual benefits of improving productivity and morale.

It is therefore crucial that managers have an understanding of the nature and impact of group dynamics on the performance of the organization if they are to influence the behaviour of people in the workplace. The key managerial issue, then, is how to build and develop teams. To be successful, members of groups must work together as teams sharing a sense of unity and purpose. However, group performance is both complex and dynamic, with a number of different variables influencing and constraining the behaviour of the group and its members. All of these variables will ultimately influence organizational effectiveness and performance.

This chapter will start by providing a definition of groups followed by an investigation of the important characteristics of effective groups. The managerial implications of groups are then explored with reference to decision-making, job design and managing group conflicts. The terms 'groups' and 'teams', for the purpose of this chapter, are used interchangeably.

The meaning of groups

Before examining why groups are formed in organizations it is important to define what is meant by the term 'group'. There are in fact many different definitions available, with no single, all-embracing and accepted definition. However, the definition provided by Schein (1988) is a popular one and combines some of the common characteristics of other definitions. He states that:

> *a psychological group is any number of people who:*
> a)   *interact with one another;*
> b)   *are psychologically aware of one another;*
> c)   *perceive themselves to be a group.*

A useful framework for analysing the characteristics of groups is provided by Adair (1986), who suggests a work group to be:

> *a collection of people who share most, if not all, the following characteristics:*
> - *a definable membership;*
> - *group consciousness;*
> - *a sense of shared purpose;*
> - *interdependence;*
> - *interaction;*
> - *an ability to act in a unitary manner.*

From the above definitions it is apparent that an essential feature of a group is that individuals perceive themselves as being members of the group. So a collection of people having lunch in the work cafeteria would not fulfil the criteria of a group, but those working together in the mortgage application section would.

Reasons why groups are formed

It is suggested that organizations function best when members act not as individuals but as members of highly effective work groups (Leavitt 1951).

The reasons why groups are formed in organizations are many, but in broad terms these can be divided into the achievement of work tasks, and the need to fulfil social needs. Therefore, the goals of a group can be both task and social in orientation.

From a task perspective, groups are formed as a consequence of the formal organizational structure and arrangements of the work tasks. For example, certain tasks can only be performed through the combined efforts of individuals working together. Therefore, groups are formed for reasons relating to the fulfilment of organizational functions, the division of tasks, and the structure and pattern of work processes and technologies. They are also formed with a view to making boring and routine work more palatable and interesting in order to enhance job satisfaction.

Handy (1986) identifies the following functions groups might perform from a task perspective:

- distribution of work;
- management and control of work;
- problem solving and decision-making;
- information processing;
- information and idea collection;
- negotiation or conflict resolution.

Working in groups should also increase people's skills, job satisfaction and motivation. So groups can be thought to fulfil social needs, and can be formed to provide an outlet for companionship, support, role identity, affiliation and recognition, and to give a sense of belonging to individuals. These reasons can all be identified with the Human Relations approach to management (discussed in Chapter 6) which gives recognition to the importance of group values and norms when providing guidelines on generally accepted behaviour.

It is clear from the above that groups are a key force on the behaviour of individuals at work, and provide potential sources of motivation and job satisfaction.

Types of groups in organizations

Many different distinctions and classifications of types of groups exist. Most research on groups makes the distinction between formal and informal groups. This is an important distinction in terms of the management of groups because of the different agendas in terms of task and social needs, both of which will influence the behaviour of individuals

The division and organization of work activities into different sections gives rise to the formation of formal groups in the organization. Formal groups are deliberately created by the organization to perform specific tasks and are part of the formal organizational structure. This type of group is created with the explicit objective of achieving organizational goals and objectives, and is governed by organizational rules, regulations and job descriptions. Objectives and roles of the members of the group will be predetermined.

Formal groups can be permanent or temporary. A permanent group may be a section or department in an organization. While the formal group is a permanent feature of the organizational structure there may be changes in terms of the actual membership. A temporary group could be a task or project group consisting of employees who work together to complete a specific task after which the group will be disbanded. This type of group is a common characteristic of a matrix organizational structure.

Informal groups develop in a more spontaneous way, and are often based on personal relationships, friendship or common interests, where membership is voluntary. Schein (1988) suggests that informal groups almost always arise if the opportunity exists. They are not explicitly set up by management and do not figure in the formal hierarchy, but, rather, they are formed to satisfy needs beyond those of doing the task. According to Feldman and Arnold (1985) these could include:

- the need to enhance one's own career;
- the need to sustain friendship;
- the need to satisfy affiliation needs and to enhance one's own personal status.

Informal groups develop across or outside the formal structure of the organization, and whilst they tend to be with people of the same status (that is horizontal), vertical and mixed groups can also be formed. Research studies by Festinger, Schachter and Back (1950), indicate that informal relationships and groups are most likely to develop when people meet in the course of other activities outside of work.

Informal groups can work to support or obstruct the achievement of organizational goals. The potential problems of informal groups arise from them serving a counter-organizational function, for example by resisting changes to work. Also, when their norms are inconsistent with those of management conflict can arise.

The benefits of informal groups include the fact that they provide social satisfaction for individuals, and they can aid the communication process in terms of providing informal information channels. However, these informal 'grapevines' can result in unnecessary anxieties for individuals as unfounded rumours can sometimes develop.

A further categorization of groups is that between primary and secondary groups. Primary groups are usually smaller and exist where members are in regular contact, for example in work teams/sections. Secondary groups are larger in terms of membership, the degree of dependency between members is less and they are often more formal. Within the organization context it is important to focus on both primary and secondary groups since both have a role to play in individual behaviour and performance.

Another category of groups is the reference group, which may not always constitute a real group. Individuals may wish to join this type of group because they want to identify with them in some way. So a reference group may influence an individual's behaviour without the individual actually being a member. For example, an individual may be an aspiring chartered accountant who is influenced by the persona of chartered accountants, even though not yet a member of the professional body (McKenna 1994).

Groups can also take different forms according to the needs of the organization. Holbeche (1998), for example, identifies the following types of teams:

1. *Senior management teams* who are responsible for determining the strategic focus of the organization and for putting the overall business needs ahead of any one function or department.

2. *Project teams* who are brought together for a specific business project, and bring skills and expertise from different business functions. They are essentially multi-functional, and usually having a temporary existence. Team members will still report to their line manager and return to their original role once the project work is completed.

3. *Process teams* have become popular in financial services organizations where Business Process Re-engineering (BPR) projects have meant the need for greater collaboration between different areas of the organization handling different parts of the process. Process teams are therefore created to ensure the smooth operations of managing various processes.

4. *Self-directed teams* are teams who work together without any direct supervision, and who have developed as organizations have downsized and reduced the levels and numbers of managers. This type of team is responsible for making its own decisions, setting its own goals and organising their own work.

Characteristics of effective group work

A key concern for all managers is to ensure that members of groups co-operate and work effectively together in order to achieve the results expected of them, and to give maximum benefit to both the organization and the individual.

Indicators that a group or team is working well include both qualitative and quantitative measures. Co-operation, belief in common goals and aims, commitment to the group, support of individual members, good communications, participation by all members, and conflicts resolved by the members themselves are examples of qualitative measures, and suggest that a group is working well.

In addition, the more quantitative benefits of lower levels of labour turnover, accident rates, absenteeism, errors and complaints may be evidence that a group is working effectively together. The positive outcome for the organization is higher levels of productivity and the achievement of targets.

Factors influencing the behaviour and performance of groups

There are many interrelated variables that influence and constrain the behaviour of groups, and contribute to the effectiveness of group working. The different factors can be considered under the headings of:

- cohesiveness of group members;
- group norms and values;
- group formation, development and maturity;
- group roles;
- group interactions.

Cohesiveness of group members

A key concept to understanding group effectiveness is that of cohesiveness. This can be described as how much members of the group like each other and want to remain members (Shaw 1981), and can be determined by the strength of commitment to the group and its goals. It is an important concept because the cohesiveness of a group will be a powerful determinant on the effectiveness of the group.

There are many different sources of cohesiveness. Firstly, the level of contact and interaction between members of the group, which can relate to both physical and functional distances, will impact on cohesiveness. Secondly, shared goals in terms of agreeing the group's purpose and direction will also lead to a more cohesive group. Evidence suggests that when group members participate in the setting of goals, higher cohesiveness will be achieved (Feldman and Arnold 1985).

A third source of cohesiveness, discussed by Aronson (1976) as one of the strongest sources, is the similarity and compatibility of attitudes and values of group members. Factors influencing the homogeneity of the group include shared backgrounds and interests, and similar attitudes and values. This source is of significance in the context of the organization's recruitment and selection policies and procedures.

Groups whose members are supportive of others also tend to be more cohesive. Constructive criticism can be helpful to the progress of the group whereas destructive and excessively critical comments tend to destroy rapport.

Mullins (1996) suggests that group size will impact on the level of cohesiveness. Whilst it is hard to be prescriptive about the optimum size of a group, cohesiveness is difficult to achieve where a group exceeds 10 to 12 members. As a group increases in size problems emerge in terms of communications, co-ordination and supervision, and a large group may end up splitting into smaller units.

Organizational factors such as management and leadership style and organizational culture will also contribute to the cohesiveness of groups. A supportive culture and participative management style will encourage a cohesive group to flourish.

A highly cohesive group should lead to the group becoming more effective at meeting its objectives. To ensure this is of benefit to the organization, Moorhead and Griffin (1992) state that there is a need for goal congruence. That is, the group's goals should be compatible and aligned with the organization's goals. Robbins (1991) goes on to identify another key variable in the relationship between cohesiveness and productivity: that of performance-related norms, for example, in terms of output, quality and co-operation. From the organization's perspective the aim would be to foster high group norms on these dimensions.

However, the outcome of cohesiveness on organizational performance will depend on how cohesiveness emerges. The relationship between performance and group cohesiveness can have both a positive and a negative impact on productivity, depending upon the group norms that regularize group behaviour (Seashaw 1954). A highly cohesive group may be considered desirable because the theory is that satisfied workers will lead to higher performance. This brings benefits to both the individual, in terms of a more enjoyable work climate, and to the organization in the achievement of objectives. With a highly cohesive group, factors such as lower absenteeism, lower turnover, good communications and participation and fewer problems with intra-group conflict are evident. This underlies the content theories of motivation, based on the assumption that there is a direct relationship between job satisfaction and job performance, and will be explored in greater depth in Chapter 15.

One disadvantage of strong group cohesiveness is that of managing change. A group's resistance to change in attitudes and behaviour is probably stronger than an individual's. This is of significance to management when faced with an environment where constant change is necessary for survival. The requirement is for individuals who are flexible and adaptable in the way they operate.

The negative aspects of cohesiveness will also emerge when there is conflict between the organizational norms and values and those of a highly cohesive group. The concepts of norms and values are explored in the next section.

Group norms

Group norms are the standards or ideas to which the group will conform. They can be formalized and written, or implicit and unwritten, and can be inferred from observation of behaviour. Norms will relate to the task process, social arrangements and allocation of resources. Each group will evolve a unique set of norms that reveals its nature, with no two groups developing the same set of norms.

The concepts of group norms and values have implications for the manager since they will directly affect organizational performance, work practices, rewards and the achievement of work targets. In a highly cohesive group, the norms will have a strong impact on an individual's behaviour within the workplace. The link between cohesiveness and performance is in fact tenuous, for whilst research shows that cohesiveness will reduce the variance of productivity between group members it does not necessarily increase the productivity of the group.

The Hawthorne Studies, already discussed in Chapter 6, provides research evidence on the potential negative impact of group norms on the performance of the task. In the Bank Wiring experiments it was shown that group performance norms on output were stronger in influencing individual performance than financial incentives for greater output. The experiments revealed that the output performance norm of the group was lower than in fact the group was capable of producing. The outcome was that the organization was not achieving its full potential in terms of productivity.

Action was taken by the group to ensure that conformance to 'task' norms occurred and the 'proper' behaviour of individuals was observed. Deviant behaviour resulted in the withdrawal of communication, or social pressures being exercised by isolating the non-conformist (ostracising) and binging (a hard blow on the upper arm). Behaviours not tolerated included over performance ('rate buster'), under performance ('chiseller'), reporting to the supervisor any information that might be harmful to the group ('squealer'), and being officious (that is a person with authority over group members should not take advantage of their seniority).

The work by Asch (1952) illustrates that group norms do not only affect behaviour but can also exert a significant influence on the judgement of individuals, not always to the benefit of the organization. This well-known study involved asking groups of individuals to compare a series of standard lines with various alternatives. They were then asked to state which of the alternative lines was the same length as the standard line. In each group all but one of the members were in collusion with the researcher and offered the same incorrect answer. In over a third of cases the genuine member of the group was swayed by the responses of other members, conforming to the norm. The result was of course wrong. In other words they succumbed to group pressure. Those who did not conform to the group pressure did state, after the experiment, that they experienced stress and discomfort.

Whilst a highly cohesive group with strong norms can have benefits for organizational performance, a potential problem is that it may lead to inter-group conflict. This occurs when there is disagreement between members of different groups over issues such as goals, authority or resources. Inter-group conflict may be desirable in some instances, for example to develop a team with low group cohesion. However, in other situations it may have negative consequences, such as a lack of co-operation and communication between groups. This could ultimately lead to the ineffective operation and communication of the task for the organization. The issues concerning group conflict are explored more fully later in this chapter.

In order that the organization can take advantage of the positive attributes of a cohesive group, the manager needs to be in a position to manipulate norms by selling task norms at the group formation stage.

Group formation, development and maturity

The level of group performance is affected by the manner in which groups come together. Whilst a number of people can be brought together to undertake a task, it cannot be assumed that the group will immediately work together effectively. To build an effective team it is important to acknowledge that it must be allowed to progress through the developmental stages and to go through a period of growth.

Tuckman (1965) describes a general model of group formation which suggests that to be effective, a group must progress through a number of stages, which have a linear relationship. He identifies the successive stages of group development as forming, storming, norming, and suggests that it is only when these stages have been successfully passed through, that the group can concentrate on the attainment of its purpose and on performing the task.

Forming	This period involves the initial formation of the group and brings together a number of individuals who establish parameters and formulate the initial objectives of the group. This stage is a period of testing individuals in terms of acceptable behaviours and codes of conduct, before roles begin to emerge. Members are attempting to create their identity within the group.
Storming	This period can be characterized as a period of internal conflict and high emotion. As people begin to know each other so they start to present their views to the group and disagreements and arguments begin to occur. This may lead to conflict and hostility, and even the collapse of the group.

If this stage is successfully passed through then new objectives and operating procedures for the group can be established with more meaningful structures and procedures.

Norming   As the conflict is resolved so new guidelines and standards of behaviour will be established. Group cohesion develops, and norms of what is acceptable behaviour are set which will govern members' behaviour. Norms are standards of behaviour to which members will conform and are unique to each group.

This stage is important in establishing agreed standards of performance. However, these can work against effective organizational performance, as for example in the case of the Hawthorne experiments discussed earlier in the chapter.

Performing   When the group has successfully progressed through the three earlier stages it will have created the cohesiveness to operate effectively as a team. At this stage the group will finally be able to concentrate on the achievement of its objectives and will be at its most effective because energies are focused on the task.

Tuckman suggested that the effectiveness of a group may be adversely affected if time constraints are put on each stage of progression. However, more recent research suggests that Tuckman's model, which presents the different stages as a linear progression is too simplistic. For example, it is assumed that any intra-group conflicts have been resolved at the storming phase. In reality these conflicts often resurface later on in the life of the group, having a detrimental impact on group performance.

The permanence and stability of group members is important in terms of group development and maturity. It does take time for group spirit and unity to develop, so group cohesiveness is more likely where members of the group are together for a reasonable period of time. Constant and frequent changes of group membership can have an adverse effect on group performance. Therefore, where changes do occur, with individuals leaving and new members joining, the group should be allowed to go through the group formation process before it can be fully effective.

Other issues which are important to nurturing an effective team relate to the group structure and processes. These include consideration of the nature of group functions and roles, since these factors will have a bearing on the behaviour of individuals in group situations.

Group roles

A factor that will influence the performance of a group is the roles individuals play, which will start to emerge in the forming stage of group development. The development of an effective group, therefore, involves the identification of distinct roles for members. Role differentiation is important when determining the structure and functioning of the work group and the relationships between members. Mullins (1996) defines a role as "a set of expected patterns of behaviour attributable to a person occupying a particular position".

Both situational factors, such as the requirements of the task and style of leadership, and personal factors, including values, attitudes, motivations, ability and personality, will influence an individual's role within a group. The role will determine the 'expected' behaviour of that individual. The implication of this is that an individual may play a role in one work group which is different from a role in another group.

A group can combine all the necessary qualities for success which an individual alone cannot possess. For example, research by Belbin (1981) was based on the hypothesis that a balance of skills and expertise is needed for the formation of an effective team. His research was concerned with analysing what team members' roles are essential for effective performance. He identified eight different roles, each of which is associated with a particular personality. The combination of having a mix of these different roles, Belbin asserted, has a major bearing on a team's ability to achieve its objectives. Unsuccessful teams can be improved by analysing their role profile, identifying any gaps and making appropriate changes.

In the follow-up to his original research, Belbin (1993) described the key team roles as follows:

1.   Co-ordinator

The co-ordinator controls the way a team moves towards achieving the group objectives, making best use of available resources, and recognising and ensuring that best use is made of each team member's potential. Typical features of the co-ordinator are that they are calm, self-confident and controlled but reasonably extrovert.

2.   Implementer

The implementer turns plans and ideas into practice and carries out plans efficiently and systematically. Individuals occupying this role tend to be hardworking and have a common sense and practical approach. They are usually conservative, dutiful and predictable in nature but also hard working and self-disciplined.

3.   Completer/Finisher

The completer/finisher makes sure that the team is protected as far as possible from mistakes and searches for the work which needs more attention. They have a sense of urgency about things, always conscious of deadlines. Characteristics of this type include being conscientious, anxious, paying attention to detail, and tending to be perfectionists.

4.   Monitor /Evaluator

The monitor/evaluator analyses problems, and evaluates ideas and suggestions, so that they can then make an informed decision and perform well in a quality role. Typical features of this role type include being unemotional, clever, detached, prudent, and shrewd in one's judgement.

5.   Plant/Innovator

The plant/innovator is a good source of ideas for the group and is imaginative and creative but may need to be encouraged by other members to contribute. They tend to be individualistic in nature and serious-minded but knowledgeable.

6.   Resource Investigator

The resource investigator explores and reports on ideas, developments and resources outside the group, and excels in conducting negotiations. The characteristics of this role type are extrovert, enthusiastic and curious, with individuals having good social skills and enjoy exploring anything new.

7. Shaper

The shaper shapes the way team effort is applied, directs attention to objectives and priorities, and seeks to impose a structure on discussions and their outcomes. Individuals in this role tend to be high achievers, and are usually outgoing but impatient. They are dynamic, have drive and like to win.

8. Team worker

The team worker supports members and promotes team spirit. Characteristics of the team worker are that they are responsive, and sensitive but may be somewhat indecisive. They are socially oriented.

Belbin, in his latest research, identified a ninth role, the specialist, which recognizes the significance to the team of the combination of professional expertise, particularly in project work. To be effective, the team should have a balance of all these roles. Some members will adopt a primary role and others may have what Belbin refers to as a back-up team role as well as their primary role. It is important to note that the different roles have both positive qualities but also weaknesses. Other members of the team should compensate for these weaknesses. Belbin's work has managerial implications for the recruitment and selection processes in the building of new teams and in recruiting new members to existing teams.

Benne and Scheates (1948) also classified different roles within a group, and recognized the need for a balance between task, maintenance and social dimensions. They can be summarized as follows:

- task orientated
  - initiator – contributor
  - information giver
  - co-ordinator
  - evaluator;
- maintenance orientated
  - encourager
  - harmoniser
  - gate-keeper
  - group observer;
- self-orientated
  - aggressor
  - blocker
  - playboy
  - help seeker.

It is important that role definitions are clear because inadequate or inappropriate role definition can lead to role conflict, and this can have a detrimental impact on the behaviour of individual members and the group. Role conflict can emerge in different forms, including role incompatibility, role ambiguity, role overload/underload and role stress.

a) Role incompatibility may arise where contradictory expectations are made on an individual and where people feel 'caught in the middle'.

b) Role ambiguity arises when people are unclear about their duties, responsibility and authority. For example, if an individual has insufficient guidance on hir or her job description.

c) Role overload occurs when an individual is at one extreme inundated with work and therefore finds it impossible to perform the expected roles well. At the other extreme role underload is when an individual feels the role is undemanding and they have capacity to undertake more roles.

d) Role stress can arise because of the conflict between the different demands made on individuals by other people, and can cause tension and inability to perform. This will influence levels of job satisfaction and work performance.

Group interactions

The levels of interaction within a group will influence group behaviour, group performance and the satisfaction derived by individuals. A key factor on the level of interactions is the structure of channels of communication. Research by both Leavitt (1951) and Shaw (1964) investigated communication networks in terms of problem solving, member satisfaction and leadership when different systems of communication were imposed on the group. Five different structures of communication networks were identified: the wheel, the chain, the Y, the circle and the all-channel. These different networks are illustrated in Figure 10.1.

Figure 10.1: Communication Networks

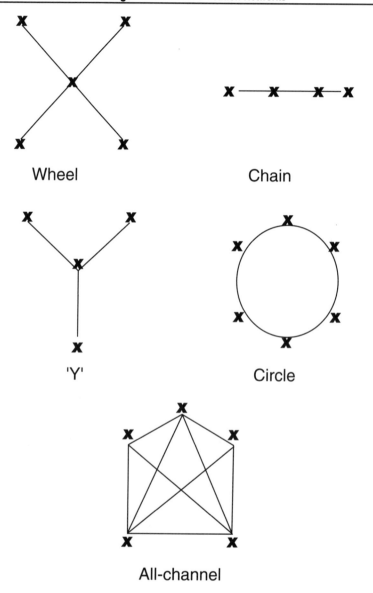

Wheel

Chain

'Y'

Circle

All-channel

The basis of this research was to examine performance depending upon the different levels of freedom of communication and the degree of centralization of leadership.

Referring to the different structures identified in Figure 10.1, the wheel is the most centralized network with the link person at the centre of the network acting as the co-ordinator for activities and information flows and restricting communication access. The circle is an example of a more decentralized network with decision making involving some degree of member participation. The all-channel involves full discussion and high levels of interaction amongst members and is the most decentralized network. The Y and the chain are intermediate forms. The more centralized channels restrict communication access, whilst the decentralized channels provide the maximum flow of information.

The research findings revealed that simple problems are best solved, and with fewer mistakes, by centralized networks, for example the wheel. However, more complex tasks were found to be more effectively performed by the less highly centralized groups, such as the circle or all-channel networks where everyone communicates with everyone else.

The researchers concluded that the greater the amount of inter-connectiveness of the communications network the higher the levels of satisfaction. So although the central person in the wheel network experiences high levels of satisfaction, for members on the periphery the wheel is the least satisfying network.

However, in reality any of the systems could have an adverse effect on the motivation of group members. Consideration must be given to the preference of group members for a particular network. The nature of the task must also be taken account of, as well as the physical location of a group.

The managerial implications of the research are that if a work group is faced with a variety of tasks and objectives then no single network will be effective. The choice of communication channels will involve a trade-off between the performance of the work group and the satisfaction of its members (Mullins 1996). For example, whilst the wheel is effective and efficient in the accomplishment of simple tasks, it can result in low job satisfaction and the low motivation of group members.

Group decision-making

Another concept related to the behaviour of individuals and groups is linked to the decision-making process of groups. There are some clear advantages of group decisions which Mullins (1989) identifies as:

- the pooling of resources;
- more knowledge and expertise available;
- interaction which can provoke future thoughts/ideas (snowballing effect).

In addition, where members are involved in decision-making they are more likely to be committed to the decisions and their implementation. Whilst group decision-making does offer many benefits for both the organization and individuals there are certain situations when individuals working alone may be more efficient. This is because group decision-making is:

- more costly;
- time consuming;
- can create conflict or be a compromise decision;
- lacks confidentiality;
- tends to be more risky.

Whereas individual decision-making tends to be:

- cheaper;
- quicker;
- confidential;
- risk aversive.

A number of the disadvantages of group decision-making can be examined by reference to the concepts of 'groupthink' and 'risky shift phenomenon'.

'Groupthink' relates to the exclusion of divergent views in discussions that can diminish the decision-making capability of the group. It emerges in long-term, highly cohesive groups that are isolated from external pressures. Consensus behaviour dominates, and diminishes creativity and innovation in preference for conformity. In such situations there is the demise of alternative actions.

Characteristics of 'groupthink' have been identified by Janis (1972) and include:

- invulnerability leading to over-optimism, and the taking of risky decisions since the group effect will reduce anxiety;
- correctness of judgement leading to ignorance of moral/ethical consequences;
- negative views of competitors;
- sanctity of group consensus;
- unanimity leading to minimising critical thinking and testing reality.

The 'risky shift' phenomenon relates to the view that some groups will take greater risks than an individual would since individuals can hide behind the anonymity of the group (Stoner 1961). Coexisting with 'risky shift' is the notion of 'cautious shift', which suggests that decisions may be made in a cautious direction. These two concepts can be referred to as group polarization and will to some extent be determined not only by group membership, but also by the culture of the organization.

The consequences of both 'risky shift' and 'groupthink' can lead to poor decision-making and can have a dysfunctional effect on group performance.

The psychological pressures resulting from individuals working closely together can also undermine some of the advantages of group decision-making. This view recognizes the groups emotional impact on individual behaviour in terms of conformity of behaviour, loyalty and identification and reaction to the group. McKenna (1994) asserts that when acting alone, an individual will have a greater reality orientation and be more efficient intellectually rather than when operating within the stultifying effects of group interaction. This concurs with the findings of the research undertaken by Asch (1952), discussed earlier in this chapter.

The factors which will ultimately influence whether decisions are made by either the group or by an individual are often interrelated, and will be determined by issues such as the urgency and time available, the need for specialization, the need for confidentiality, whether the decision is a routine/non-routine decision, and the cost implications of group decisions.

Work environment and organizational factors

The factors explored so far have tended to emphasize the internal processes such as group norms, group development and group roles on effectiveness. In understanding group behaviour attention must also be given to the contextual factors which can influence group performance. Sundstrom et al (1990) identify the following contextual factors:

- the physical work environment;

- organizational culture;

- technology and task design;

- group autonomy;

- reward systems;

- performance feedback;

- training and consultation;

- external threats.

All these factors will impact on the level of the performance of groups. Where, for example, members of groups work in the same location, in close proximity to each other, this will usually help group effectiveness. However, if members work at different locations but constantly need to communicate and interact regularly to complete their tasks, then this will also have a positive impact on group cohesiveness and performance. Similarly where the members share a common task the group is likely to be more effective than when individuals are working in close proximity but are involved in discrete activities.

If groups are to work effectively together then the different human resource policies such as the reward systems, performance measures and feedback mechanisms must be designed to complement group work rather than operate against it.

The nature of technology and work systems influence group behaviours and performance, with new information systems leading to new patterns of work organization and the structure of groups. This is characteristic of changes occurring in many financial services organizations where new technologies have significantly changed work processes. Effective group working is crucial to the activities of, for example, centralized processing centres and telephone call centres.

Encouraging the performance of groups

It is important that groups are effectively managed and motivated. When encouraging a group to perform more effectively the manager plays a crucial role. Building on the actions proposed by Braddick (1991), a manager should seek to:

- establish clear objectives for the group, since a common purpose will unite the group. However, objectives must be realistic and time scales for achievement given;

- good planning, to ensure the group has clear targets and members are involved in the process, thus building commitment. The manager should ask whether priorities established are realistic and relevant, and whether future direction is established with steps to get there identified;

- structure, the group should be well structured with tasks organized effectively with all members clear as to what is required from them;

- motivate the group, the members of the group need to be recognised and feel that they are making a contribution to performance. Attention should also be given to developing team spirit and comradeship;

- decision-making, where appropriate decisions should be made jointly through group participation encouraging inputs from all members;

- provide feedback and evaluation, the group needs to know their progress and can be given coaching or training if appropriate. Feedback should be honest but constructive;

- ensure resources and external support are available, this includes both physical and financial resources;

- provide effective leadership, both in relation to the task orientation but also in supporting individual group members;

- openness, in terms of encouraging constructive problem-solving rather than a blame culture. The group should be open and honest in communications between themselves, and should communicate appropriately beyond the team;

- rewards, the group should be rewarded and successes should be celebrated.

Managing the dynamics of groups is complex and more challenging then managing individuals. One of the most useful models developed to achieve effective performance is that proposed by Adair's action centred leadership. This model, already discussed in Chapter 7, suggests that effectiveness revolves around the balance between concern for the task, concern for the group and concern for the individual. The manager must be aware of three critical needs: to achieve the task, to build the team, and to develop each individual.

Team-building

The notion of team-building is developed from work on organizational development, which is essentially concerned with trying to fulfill the twin objectives of organizational goals and satisfying individual needs. Thus, team-building can be defined as 'the process of enhancing the effectiveness of the team'. Attention is focused on both work procedures and interpersonal relations. Enhancing the effectiveness of a team requires attention to characteristics such as, cohesiveness, norms, group development, roles and interactions, along with communications, involvement and decision-making. In other words to all the factors already discussed above.

Effort should be focused on integrating group cohesiveness and norms with productivity and commitment to the task. Team-building activities should be developed to take advantage of the benefits of strong group cohesiveness whilst using tactics to minimize any negative impact.

Team-building is concerned with encouraging team spirit and a feeling of belonging. In achieving this team members should be encouraged to support and help each other, Team meetings and team briefings are important activities in developing team spirit.

Many financial services organizations are making conscious attempts to develop managerial teams, investing in team-building training activities. A whole range of techniques can be used to encourage team development and the bonding of members, some of which are based on non-work task exercises, for example Outward Bound courses. Individuals are provided with the opportunity to learn more about themselves and their impact on others. The desired outcome of these activities is to develop effective and high performance teams with the ultimate goal of improving organizational performance.

High performance teams was the basis of the research undertaken by Margerison and McCann (1991), advancing the work of Belbin on group roles. They developed a team management wheel based on linking job functions with the roles team members are expected to perform. This is based on necessary behaviours such as exploring and controlling, and explored preferred roles in terms of advisers and organisers. These preferences are based on how people prefer to:

- relate with others;
- gather and use information;
- make decisions;
- organize themselves and others.

The roles the researchers identified as being key to a high performance team include:

- Reporter-Adviser who performs a supporting role, collecting and using information;
- Creator-Innovator who is creative generating new ideas;
- Explorer-Promoter who seeks out resources and establishes outside contacts;
- Assessor-Developer who identifies the best way to develop ideas practically and assesses the viability of proposals;
- Thruster-Organiser who ensures that appropriate procedures are in place and sets objectives;
- Concluder-Producer who focuses on ensuring that work is completed adhering to deadlines and quality considerations;
- Controller Inspector who ensures that a job is done in the correct way;
- Upholder-Maintainer who seeks to develop social systems and relationships;
- Linker who links people together within the team and acts as a representative in dealing with other teams.

The membership of a group is not static, so team-building must be a continuous activity. This has implications for the indoctrination and socialization of new members to the ways of the team, specifically the team's values, norms and expectations. The indoctrination is necessary to reduce role ambiguity, to increase the feeling of security and to create more behavioural uniformity. Bowditch and Buono (1990) identify indoctrination as a three-stage process starting with anticipatory socialization, followed by organizational or group encounter and finally acquisition of group norms and values. Successful indoctrination will have a positive influence on individuals productivity and commitment to the group.

Groups and job design

Where work is not intrinsically motivating and fails to generate group commitment to the task, this can negatively affect performance. This has implications for the design and structure of group tasks, and the style of management.

Given that the formation of groups in organizations is a consequence of the pattern of organizational structure and arrangements for the division of work, then this will clearly also have ramifications for the design of work. Job design is discussed more fully in Chapter 15, but essentially it is concerned with the relationship between workers, the nature and content of their jobs, and their task functions. It attempts to meet people's personal and social needs at work, through re-organization or restructuring, to enhance job satisfaction and make the best possible use of the 'human resource' (McKenna 1994).

The notions of job enlargement and job enrichment can be used within the design of work for groups to enhance the effective completion of the task and job satisfaction. Integrative work teams involve job enlargement where a large number of tasks are assigned to the group and provide the benefits of task diversity, team work and co-operation. Employees are still supervized, but employees can decide how work is allocated.

Autonomous work groups can provide job enrichment. The group has a goal to achieve but is free to decide how it will accomplish it, enjoying a high degree of autonomy and control over aspects such as the pace and scheduling of work, member selection, etc. This job design will require a cohesive team, and to be effective it must have group task norms which are congruent with organization objectives.

Where quality is a key performance criteria for an organization the use of quality circles can promote quality performance norms for groups. Quality circles involve members sharing responsibility and problem-solving on quality issues.

Managing group conflict

An organization is made up of a series of groups operating at various levels in the hierarchy. However, wherever there is interaction between individuals and groups it is inevitable that conflict will emerge and some of the negative consequences of this have already been discussed. Two broad categories of conflict can be identified, intra-group conflict and inter-group conflict:

1. Intra-group conflict arises when there are hostilities *within* the group, and where disagreements and differences between members occur. This type of conflict may emerge in the 'storming' stage of group formation proposed by Tuckman (1965) because of factors such as opposing norms and values, deviant goals and objectives, and disputes over roles.

2. Inter-group conflict is concerned with conflicts between different groups or teams.

Negative consequences of conflict involve the lack of co-operation and communication between members either *within* a group (in the case of intra-group conflict) or *between* groups (inter-group conflict).

Rather than focusing on eliminating conflict, which given the dynamics and nature of the work organization is probably unattainable, managers should decide what actions they can take to minimize conflict. Emphasis should be on:

● the setting of a superordinate goal. This is one all groups can aim for and one that will require increased communication;

● relatively greater emphasis being given to total organizational effectiveness;

● high levels of communication between groups;

● bringing the leaders of groups into interaction, and also encouraging a high degree of interaction between members of different groups through project working and also through inter-department social activities;

● frequent rotation of staff between sections and departments should be encouraged in order to stimulate a higher degree of understanding;

- the reallocation of tasks and responsibilities;
- inter-group training;
- locate a common enemy, such as a competitor or possibly another area/department in the organization;
- avoid win-lose situations, since groups should not have to compete for scarce resources and rewards should be shared between departments.

Inter-group conflict should not always be considered to be necessarily dysfunctional. Inter-group conflict can be encouraged in certain situations to encourage competition. As discussed earlier, Schein (1988) suggests that this can have the positive outcome of encouraging stronger cohesiveness within the group. Each group becomes more tightly knit and elicits greater loyalty from its members. The group also tends to become more highly structured and organized, as well as more task orientated. A number of financial services organizations have encouraged inter-group competition, for example by setting up sales league tables on performances between teams both within and between branches and rewarding the best performers. However, actively encouraging competition between teams must be carefully managed to avoid potential negative outcomes. Where a team is in the losing situation this can result in members finding ways to attribute the failure to others and the group can splinter, with intra-group conflict surfacing.

Summary

The organization needs to ensure that groups work as effectively as possible in order to achieve maximum benefits to the organization, in terms of effective and efficient completion of the task, and the achievement of organizational goals. It should also work for the benefit of the individual, in terms of fulfilling individual and social needs.

An analysis of the variables that influence group and individual behaviour reveals a multiplicity of factors that are difficult to disentangle by way of their individual impact on behaviour. The focus of this chapter has been on analysing the characteristics and processes of groups. Overlaying these factors are the influences of the individual and organizational factors.

There is no doubt that groups exert a major influence on organizations, and that this influence can be both positively and negatively directed at achieving targets and goals. Effective group working can also have both positive and negative effects on an individual's satisfaction and performance, and on task aspects of productivity and quality. Therefore, the psychology of groups is a key issue for managers and should complement the knowledge of individual behaviour.

References

Adair J (1986) *Effective Teambuilding*, Gower

Aronson E (1976) *The Social Animal*, Freeman

Asch S E (1952) 'Effects of group pressure upon the modification and distortion of judgements', *Readings in Social Psychology*, Swanson, Newcombe and Hartley

Bales R F (1950) 'A Set of Categories for the Analysis of Small Group Interaction', *American Sociological Review*, Vol. 15

Belbin R M (1981) *Management Teams: Why They Succeed or Fail*, Butterworth Heinemann

Belbin (1993) *Team Roles at Work*, Butterworth Heinemann

Benne K D & Scheates P (1948) 'Functional Roles of Group Members', *Journal of Social Issues*, Vol. 4

Bowditch J L & Buono A F (1990) *A Primer on Organizational Behaviour*, Wiley

Braddick W A G (1991) *Management for Bankers*, 2nd ed., Butterworths

Feldman D C & Arnold H J (1985) *Managing Individual Behaviour in Organizations*, McGraw Hill

Festinger L, Schachter S & Back K (1950) *Social Pressures in Informal Groups: A Study of Human Factors in Housing*, Harper and Row

Handy C B (1986) *Understanding Organizations*, 3rd ed., Penguin

Holbeche L (1998) *Motivating People in Lean Organizations*, Butterworth Heinemann

Janis J (1972) *Victims of Groupthink: A Psychological Study of Foreign Policy Decisions and Fiascoes*, Houghton Mifflin

Leavitt H (1951) 'Some Effects of Certain Communication Patterns on Group Performance', *Journal of Abnormal and Social Psychology*, Vol. 46

Margerison C J & McCann D (1991) *Team Management: Practical Approaches*, Mercury Books

McKenna E (1994) *Business Psychology & Organizational Behaviour: A*

Student's Handbook, Lawrence Erlbaum

Moorhead G & Griffin R W (1992) *Organizational Behaviour: Managing People and Organizations,* 3rd ed., Houghton Mifflin

Mullins L J (1996) *Management and Organizational Behaviour,* 4th ed., Pitman

Robbins S P (1991) *Organizational Behaviour: Concepts, Controversies and Applications,* 5th ed., Prentice Hall

Schein E H (1988) *Organizational Psychology,* 3rd ed., Prentice Hall

Seashaw S (1954) *Group Cohesiveness in the Industrial Work Group,* Ann Arbor: Institute for Social Research, University of Michigan

Shaw M E (1964) 'Communication Networks', in *Advances in Experimental Social Psychology,* Vol. 1, New York Academic Press

Shaw M E (1981) *Group Dynamics: The Psychology of Small Group Behaviour,* 3rd ed., McGraw Hill

Stoner J A F (1961) 'A Comparison of Industrial and Group Decisions Involving Risk', Unpublished, School of Industrial Management, MIT thesis, quoted in Brown R (1965) *Social Psychology,* New York: Free Press

Sundstrom E, De Meuse K P & Futrell D (1990) 'Work Teams: Applications and Effectiveness', *American Psychologist,* February

Tuckman B W (1965) 'Development Sequence in Small Groups', *Psychological Bulletin,* 63

11 Communication

Objectives

This chapter examines communication particularly as it relates to modern organizations. The detailed objectives of the chapter are:

- to discuss the process of communication and the difficulties encountered in attempting to achieve effective communication;
- to identify the communication channels prevalent in organizations, and to explore problems related to particular channels;
- to explain the basic techniques of the management of meetings.

Communication

Luciano Pavarotti is perhaps most famous for his performances in concert before vast audiences. It is said that one of his key attributes which helps to make these performances so successful is the accuracy with which he is able to position himself so as to maximize the effectiveness of the sound transmission system. This illustrates a key point in relation to communication by highlighting the idea that the singer and the technicians are not so much concerned with the sound which leaves Pavarotti's lips as with the sound which arrives in the ears of the audience.

Communication amongst humans involves the transmission of some idea, concept, thought, etc., from the mind of one person into the mind of another. What has been referred to as the 'conveyor theory of communication' (see Gerloff 1985)) holds that we can transmit meaning as easily as we can transmit a physical commodity. Thus, for example, a manager can relay his requirements to a subordinate simply by reducing them to writing and passing them to the subordinate. This theory suggests that what is in the mind of the manager (the 'transmitter') is commoditized by its realization in symbolic form and moved by a medium appropriate to the symbols chosen to the subordinate (the 'receiver') who is able to understand the message by decoding the symbols.

When Pavarotti sings in concert the sound which leaves his lips is encoded into a series of digital symbols which are relayed via cables to a decoder which converts the digital symbols back to sound for the benefit of the listeners. The conveyor theory would suggest that communication has thus taken place. Pavarotti would argue that the communication is successful only if an entire subtext of musicality, lyricism, artistry, interpretation, emotions, etc., which he has worked hard to incorporate into the sound which leaves his lips is appreciated by the audience. In the more mundane world of organizations the essential subtext is meaning, and the objective of communication is to move meaning from the mind of the transmitter into the mind of the receiver.

The process of communication

The process by which an attempt is made to transfer meaning from one mind to another can be represented as follows in Figure 11.1.

Figure 11.1

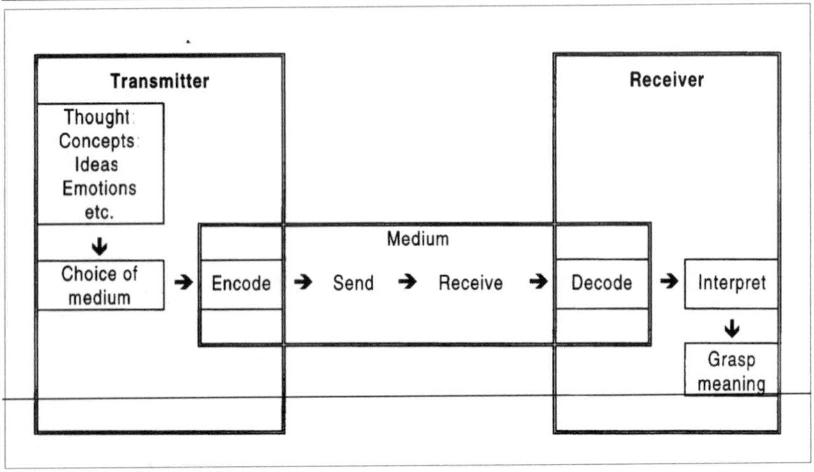

Barriers to effective communication

Given the differences between human beings and the idea that no communication system yet devised is entirely free from interference or noise, it is not surprising that successful communication is difficult to achieve consistently.

Humans have inhabited the earth for a period of time (say more then two million years) which is considerably longer than the period since writing was invented (say seven thousand years). The importance of writing in this context is that it was the first medium through which humans could communicate more complex messages when the transmitter was physically removed from the receiver. The significance of the time span during which humans existed but were unable to communicate, except when in relatively close proximity, is that it suggests that any genetic component to our communication skills is likely to predispose us to favour face-to-face communication.

Face to face communication has the advantage that the transmitter can in most cases receive immediate feedback putting one in a better position to judge the success of communication. This feedback can come not only in any oral contribution made by the receiver but also through the non-verbal signals given by the receiver which our genes and culture predispose us to interpret with some accuracy.

John Adair (1983) makes the point that communication in humans grows more problematic the further the medium of communication is removed from basic face to face. But even when it is possible for two human beings to see each other there are still many difficulties which can get in the way of good communication. Many of these are discussed in detail in Chapter 13 in relation to selection. However some are mentioned below.

Choice of words

Even when two humans are able to see each other, it is not guaranteed that communication between them will be successful. For example, the differences between the transmitter and the receiver are quite likely to mean that a word chosen by the transmitter will not have precisely the same meaning for the receiver. There is therefore the possibility of distortion in the message as interpreted by the receiver.

To illustrate this point consider what words represent the opposite of the words in the following list:

abstemious

black

fanatical

mercenary

studious

tardy

Compare the list you have generated with that generated by a colleague. Similarly compare your response with that of a colleague to an activity in which you are asked to list three words suggested to you by each of the following words:

bank

concert

corrupt

examination

jealous

mosquito

It is very unlikely that the responses of any two people to these exercises will match precisely.

The importance of this relates more to the 'subtext' of the message, since the exercises indicate that irrespective of the precision with which words are chosen they will each have different nuances for the transmitter and the receiver. Therefore the overall message which leaves the mind of the transmitter will not equate to the overall message that reaches the mind of the receiver.

Context

Interpretation problems go beyond the consideration of words in isolation since meaning is imported into words by the context in which they are set. Consider your interpretation of the aural signal which in the following sentences I have encoded in the symbols 'ataks':

The Chancellor of the Exchequer spoke about ataks on children.
The Home Secretary spoke about ataks on children.

Whether you see (or hear) 'ataks' as 'a tax' or 'attacks' is probably governed by the words which precede it.

It is not only in the involvement of individuals that the process of communication is fraught with difficulties. These can arise at each link in the process and in the stages themselves.

Choice of medium

The choice of medium may in itself be part of the message, and if it is inappropriate may introduce a distortion into the process. Thus, for example, routine matters requiring a decision are probably best presented in written form with the choice between memorandum, electronic mail and fax being determined by considerations of the required speed of response. It may be better to discuss matters which are not routine, and the choice between a telephone call and a meeting might again be dictated by considerations of speed and/or complexity. What is important is that there should not be a lack of congruity between the medium and the message. This occurs most often when there is a mismatch between the oral and the non-verbal signals in face to face communication. It can also occur in more remote forms of communication when the medium chosen does not match the level of urgency required. The availability of voice-mail is often a barrier in this respect since the initial choice of medium made by the transmitter (telephone) might not be matched by the medium actually imposed by the receiver which is the equivalent of a bulletin board or a letter and which is accessed at the instigation of the receiver.

Encoding the message

The two basic elements for the transmitter to consider relate to the format and the language of the message.

It is important that the message should conform to the norms expected by the receiver, the medium and the organization. Thus, regardless of whether messages are internal or external, they should conform to the 'house style' of the organization. This is a reinforcement of the concept of the medium being part of the message.

Communication with those external to the organization is generally couched differently, in terms of style, modes of address and formality of language, from internal communications. However, as the use of direct electronic means of communication (e.g. electronic mail) develops there is a likelihood that the conventions developed by pioneers of these media may come to dominate most aspects of communication, and impose a different formality on both internal and external communications.

The written English language is different from the spoken English language. One has only to contrast the text one would use when writing a message with the text one would use to deliver the same message by telephone (even to voice-mail) to appreciate this point. It is important therefore that the message is composed in the appropriate language. In the days before word processors it was necessary for the transmitter to translate spoken prose into written prose before committing thoughts to paper. Often speeches are written first in written English and then have to be translated by the transmitter (who may not be the same person as the writer) into his or her own version of spoken English.

Further complications can arise when the transmitter chooses to use a language which is hard for the receiver to understand, or uses a language which is emotionally charged and which will therefore produce an emotional rather than a rational response.

Noise during the transmission of the message

Noise in this context means anything which interferes with the clarity of the message which is introduced by the 'system' (or the whole of the methodology of transmission). Included within this definition are not only mechanical difficulties occasioned by the use of complex technological systems (downtime, machine breakdown, gateway overload, etc.), but also problems of a more human nature (interruptions, background noise, distracting conversations, etc.).

Decoding

The moment when a message is sent is generally a matter of choice for the transmitter. Although there may be elements of choice as to when the message is accessed, the moment of receipt is not usually the choice of the receiver. There may therefore be a difference between the time and effort which the transmitter is prepared to devote to encoding the message and the time and effort which the receiver is able to devote to decoding it.

In most modern forms of business communication the decoding of a message is not a matter of particular concern since that decoding relates to the translation of signals from a form conducive to the medium (usually digital) to symbols which are meaningful to the recipient (usually words or sounds). In modern communication this function is usually done automatically by a machine at the receiver's end of the communication process (e.g. a workstation, a fax machine or a telephone). Nevertheless this step in the chain should never be forgotten, as anyone who has ever experienced the frustration of not being able to download messages successfully will testify. There are two important points to make in relation to decoding:

- there is a responsibility on the transmitter to ensure that the choice of medium and the mechanism of encoding is one which can be accessed by the receiver;

- the transmitter should be careful never to assume that a message has been successfully decoded.

Interpreting the message

Similarly there will always be doubts as to whether a message which has been successfully encoded, transmitted, received and decoded will be correctly interpreted. The framework within which the message is interpreted which includes the mental and physical demeanour of the receiver, may not be conducive to the accurate interpretation of the message where accuracy is measured by the meaning imparted by the transmitter.

Thus the receiver might make insufficient effort to reach an understanding of the message. Alternatively, the receiver might base understanding on emotional as opposed to rational responses such as bias against, or in favour of, the transmitter, or might undertake to interpret the message when tired or otherwise not fully receptive.

Communication in organizations

Studies of communications in organizations vary in the importance which is attached to communication, and range from those which regard communication as being of fundamental significance (e.g. Barnard 1938 who sees the 'structure, extensiveness and scope of the organization' as being 'almost entirely determined by communication techniques'), to those who hardly dwell upon the subject (e.g. Lawrence and Lorsch (1967).

The significance of communication systems within organizations is probably dependent upon the context and the precise part of the organization being investigated. Thus, for example, organizations which are dependent upon the transference of information around the organization, such as many modern-day fast moving, multi-product retailers and financial services organizations, need organization-wide communication systems for the control of stock and delivery, in the case of retailers, and credit in the case of banks. Other organizations will have tried and tested communication systems in some sections, but these will not necessarily link the work outposts and the centre. For example a hospital must have systems for transferring information from one ward shift to another, but does not necessarily need to gather and reprocess this information centrally.

Harold Wilensky (1967)suggests that there are four factors which determine the importance of communication to the organization:

1. The external environment, which measures the degree of conflict with, or competition prevalent within the external environment.

2. The internal environment, or the extent to which the organization's relationship with the external environment is dependent upon internal support and unity.

3. Stability, which measures the degree to which the in-ternal and external en-vironments are predictable and therefore subject to planned influence.

4. The organization itself, including the organization's size, structure, goals, control mechanisms, and heterogeneity.

This suggests that communication is of greatest significance in organizations which are themselves complex,which deal with uncertainty, and which are dependent upon a valuable flow of information forwards and backwards across the organization.

This may however give too narrow a definition of communication, particularly as relates to information which flows vertically within the organization. Good communications systems are generally found within well-established, hierarchical and mechanistic bureaucracies operating in the stable conditions which have allowed them to develop and refine.

Communication within organizations is therefore most often

categorized according to the direction of the flow of information and can be usefully analysed by comparing those organizations which Burns and Stalker characterized as mechanistic with those they characterized as organic (see Chapter 6).

One of the difficulties in applying the outcomes of past studies of organizational communication to modern organizations is that they have generally been undertaken before the 'information revolution' and are thus concerned with methods of communication which are not based upon IT. Nevertheless it is clear that a traditional analysis is still germane to many modern institutions.

Channels of communication
Downward

Downward channels tend to reflect the hierarchy of the organization and are used to facilitate the information flows from the top or centre of the organization to the staff. They tend to be concerned with transferring the requirements of the organization to those who will ultimately deliver those requirements. However they can also be concerned with giving feedback on performance.

Katz and Kahn (1966) specify five elements which may bear upon the importance of downward communication to the organization:

1. Job instruction, whereby subordinates are informed as to what they are expected to do with the intention of producing reliable job performance. The more complex the task the more uncertain the outcome, and the more experienced the subordinate the less specific will be the instruction.

2. Rationale for the task, whereby the subordinate's task is placed in context by virtue of its relationship to other tasks which are being accomplished within the organization. This is, in fact, a complex area since although it can be argued that it is always necessary to place any task in the correct context and to make that context known to the worker, it is equally important to limit the information passed to the subordinate to that which the subordinate can fully understand. The potential for chaos if members of an organization are given information which they are unable to comprehend or accept is high. Equally dangerous is the possibility of alienation among the workers if they are

given too little information to allow them to perform effectively.

3. Procedures and practices, whereby the ways in which task elements are performed are made known to the workforce. This element is important in the control of quality within the organization, as well as in co-ordinating activity as work flows across the organization, and capturing data which is important to the organization so as to make it available for analysis.

4. Feedback, since it is advisable for an organization to have a mechanism for giving individual workers information about the way in which the organization views their performance.

5. Ideology, Katz and Kahn see the indoctrination of the workforce, which is aimed at securing an emotional involvement in the work required of them, as an important element of downward communication.

Included in the media whereby downward communication is achieved are the following:

- Mission statements
- Performance indicators
- Job descriptions
- Policy statements
- Information circulars
- Procedures manuals
- Training sessions
- Technical circulars
- Business objectives
- Strategy papers
- Evaluation reports
- Rule books
- Codes of behaviour
- Cascades
- Pay cheques

It is a feature of organic organizations that they tend to have few downward channels of communication. This is largely because the nature of the organization does not lend itself to the level of stability which is inherent in the media listed above.

One of the difficulties within large modern organizations, such as banks and building societies which have an extensive, if not trans-national geographical spread, is that they have grown to their present size partly by virtue of their use of typically mechanistic downward communication channels whilst current market forces compel business units within the organizations to adopt typically organic approaches to operation. There is therefore the potential for tension between the communication systems emanating from the centre and those generated by local management, and for considerable distortion in the communication.

Upward

Upward communication is a feature of both mechanistic and organic organizations. In the mechanistic organization there is a need for feedback to ensure that performance is matching established plans. To meet such a requirement upward communication will take the form of periodic work reports, stock inventories, sales figures, transportation statistics, etc.

Additionally, it is probable that the organization's budget will be built around a combination of downward and upward communication. This will not necessarily be built upon a basis of consultation but more as an iterative exercise to develop a realistic budget in line with organizational goals.

In an organic organization the relative level of upward communication is likely to be higher given the emphasis on teamwork. It is also probable that the chosen channels will be less formal and less likely to be documented than in a mechanistic organization. Informal upward communication will occur whenever a subordinate consults with a superordinate colleague.

A feature of mechanistic organizations, and particularly those which have 'tall' hierarchical structures, is the extent to which messages flowing up the organization are filtered at successive levels of the hierarchy so that top executives receive only encapsulated summaries. This feature is probably of dwindling significance in organizations which have a heavy investment in IT, since the information passed on to senior management will be drawn from cuts, i.e. particular interrogations, of the data available within the organization. These can be readily reorganized to garner fresh information to suit the actual needs of the senior manager rather than the chain of subordinates' subjective prediction of those needs.

Lateral

All organizations will require some element of lateral communication generally in parallel to the flow of work across the organization. Burns and Stalker argued that in an organic structure there will be an emphasis on lateral communication and a corresponding de-emphasis on downward communication. A further feature is that the method of lateral communication in an organic structure will probably be less formal than in a mechanistic organization where the emphasis will be on administrative control.

Routing slips, work orders, schemes of work and processing vouchers are all examples of formal methods of lateral communication. At a slightly less formal level will be interdepartmental meetings, co-ordination meetings and project groups, while organic structures will make greater use of personal contact between leaders and operatives of different teams.

The impact of information technology on communication in organizations

The traditional institutions within the financial services industry evolved as effective mechanistic bureaucracies with well refined formal communication systems. Since the deregulation of the industry, which coincided with the restructuring of IT-based communication systems, organizations have had to revise their approaches to internal communications in order not to suffer competitive disadvantage and to keep pace with market demands. This has not led necessarily to the dismantling of traditional communication systems, but it has brought to the fore some of the problems inherent within them.

A burgeoning problem is that occasioned by the extent to which data is now available. The ease and speed with which data can be generated and transmitted is such that any individual within the organization is in danger of overload. This is not of particular importance until the distinction between data and information is recognized.

Data comprises statistics, facts, opinions, figures and estimates which are as yet unmarshalled and therefore of little interest or direct relevance. When data is presented to the right person, at the right time, in the right context, and in the right combinations to allow inferences to be drawn, it becomes information. In the context of the communication process 'data' comprises the commoditized elements that can be transmitted while 'information' connotes the understanding by the receiver of what has been communicated. The danger with overload arises because the extended use of IT-based communication systems means that a large quantity of data can be transmitted and stored. When related to the conveyor theory of communication this implies that communication has taken place but so long as the information remains unretrieved from the data there has been no effective communication.

The spread of IT-based communications systems also means that the time taken to process much of the work within the financial services industry is shorter than would otherwise be the case. This in turn implies that individuals have the resources to take on more elements of work than their predecessors and have a correspondingly greater appetite for information. This emphasises the need for retrieval systems that assist the individual and the organization in the management of their information.

A further problem brought about by the greater dependence on IT relates to the relationship between formal and informal communication systems.

In essence many of the IT-based communication systems have the trappings of informality if only because of their speed. However, yet they are becoming the standard method of transferring information around the organization and, increasingly, between the organization and other stakeholders (e.g. customers, regulators and suppliers). Studies of the ways in which managers gather information show that this is most frequently done by personal contact and by informal means. The implication is that as IT-based systems become more and more a part of the fabric of the modern organization, the pattern of information gathering, processing and communication will alter radically.

Management of meetings

One of the ways in which communication within an organization is manifested is through the medium of a meeting.

Meetings with which an organization is involved range from the company's Annual General Meeting to meetings between two individuals. In the latter case both individuals may be employees of the organization, or one might represent the organization to the other, who as an individual or as the representative of some other concern interacts with the organization as a customer, supplier, regulator or some other category of interested party.

Between these two extremes there are many types of meetings, including press briefings, discussions with analysts, consultations with advisors, project meetings, interdepartmental committees, staff briefings, and target settings and appraisals.

In order to explore something of the nature of meetings and how they can best be managed it is helpful to focus on meetings which involve several participants (say between six and twelve) each of whom is likely to represent a separate viewpoint and to be able to add value to the process of the meeting. A sensible example of such a meeting would be an interdepartmental meeting which has a particular purpose to pursue.

The point about the meeting having a purpose is of paramount importance since if there is no purpose the meeting is a waste of time for all of the participants. That having been said, it is sometimes not obvious what the purpose of the meeting is. This applies particularly to meetings at which senior members of a company are briefed on aspects of the company's activities or plans, such as a board meeting or a meeting of an executive committee. At some such meetings an impartial observer could accurately assess that all participants were often fully aware of the items on which they were being briefed and thereby suggest that they were not using their time effectively. Such an observation misses a fundamental point, which is that in an instance such as that described it is the fact that the meeting is scheduled to happen which ensures that the work which has had to go into the briefing is actually completed. If the meeting does not take place as scheduled then the preparatory work does not get done.

This illustrates a fundamental point about meetings, which is that they are or should be concerned with generating actions which move the organization towards a goal state.

Naturally the action does not happen during the meeting but the essence of the meeting remains to ensure that appropriate action takes place.

To put this idea into an appropriate context it is helpful to think of meetings in relation to models for training and development. Most approaches to training can be categorized as being based on 'thinking', 'feeling' or 'doing'. Instructional courses, lectures, demonstrations and most discussion groups are therefore examples of training where the individual is changed by reference to his or her thought processes. Instruction manuals, computer-embedded training, practical lessons, experimentation and action learning are examples of training based on action and gestalt. Transactional analysis and T groups are methodologies whereby the individual develops by reference to his or her own feelings.

Relating this to the whole process of a meeting it can be recognized that the 'doing' element, or the action, should follow the meeting.

A frequent cause of lack of productivity within a meeting occurs when the individuals attending are required to think through their basic positions on some point of interest whilst they are in the meeting . This is because they have not had the opportunity to do this before the meeting. Any meeting which is to engender serious discussion or lead to the enlightenment of participants or to a decision being made is likely to be sufficiently taxing for the participants making their contributions without their having to develop those contributions as the meeting progresses. Thus a fundamental aspect of a well-conducted meeting is that the participants have had the opportunity to prepare and to have prepared themselves. The period before the meeting should therefore be devoted to 'thinking'. By implication it is during the meeting itself that 'feelings' may have to be dealt with.

While this may for many meetings be overstating the case, it is as well for those primarily involved in meetings to bear this model in mind. It should be remembered that communication between human beings involves not only the transmission of the text of the message but also the transmission of a subtext. If this subtext is to appear anywhere within the process of a meeting, then it is best if it appears when all the participants are together. In addition, it is often the case that there is a desire within a meeting which has the objective of reaching a decision for all participants to be bound into that decision. This is more likely to be achieved if the participants can be both rationally and emotionally committed to the decision. The consequence of not gaining the emotional commitment may be that only lip service is paid to the decision. Alternatively, and within organizations this is a serious drawback, the effectiveness of the decision can be sabotaged by the actions (or inaction) of discontented participants.

It is usual to think of attendees at a meeting as falling into at least one of three categories:

a) the person who is to control the meeting, i.e. the Chair.

b) the person who is to administer the meeting, i.e. the Secretary.

c) the participants, and this category can include the Chair and the Secretary.

Prior to the meeting

All three categories have a role to play in ensuring sound preparation. Participants who are contributing papers should have them written well in advance The Secretary is usually charged with the responsibility for compiling and distributing the papers, and it may be necessary for the Chair to bring to bear the weight of his or her authority to ensure that the distribution takes place as planned. Documents should be circulated in sufficient time for them all to be digested prior to the meeting.

The other key contribution of the Chair, in conjunction with the Secretary, prior to the meeting is the determination of the agenda. Frequently, and particularly with formal meetings, the agenda tends to follow a set pattern. In meetings which are more contentious, and where there are a number of topics to be discussed, the structure of the agenda is a matter to which some considerable thought should be given.

Where possible the early items on an agenda should be those which will enable all participants to make individual oral contributions. This will ensure that a level of comfort with making some contribution has been reached by the time the key issues are to be discussed. Agenda planning should also take into account the likely time scale to be devoted to each topic to ensure that participants are not faced with a session of detailed and serious discussion which extends beyond normal attention spans. It is a fair tactic to attempt to limit the discussions during the meeting by specifying in the agenda the length of time that each item is expected to take. This at least indicates to the participants where their greatest contributions will be expected.

Chairing the meeting

The role of the Chair is probably of greatest significance during the meeting itself. While it is true to say that all attendees have obligations to their colleagues the onus in ensuring that there is a productive meeting rests mainly with the Chair.

Generally participants should be prompt, attentive, willing to share their views yet concise in their contributions, respectful of the contributions of others and of procedural decisions made by the Chair, and accurate in their reporting of the meeting.

Control of the process of the meeting

The Chair has responsibility for the process as opposed to the content of the meeting. Accordingly it is the Chair who should state the purpose of the meeting and ensure that the meeting is conducted so as to achieve that purpose.

It is useful, if the agenda is lengthy, for the Chair to indicate early in the meeting the key topics for discussion and thus inform participants as to those items which should be dealt with relatively swiftly.

The Chair should also structure the discussion on any particular topic in such a way that participants are able to weigh opposing views constructively. This in turn involves the Chair knowing the likely contributions of the participants, which may mean preparatory contact with individual attendees. Similarly the Chair must be watchful of the entire meeting in order to gauge who amongst the participants wishes to contribute so as to bring those contributions into the discussion at the appropriate time.

Ultimately, it falls to the Chair to ensure that topics, and particularly controversial topics, are fully explored before the meeting arrives at a decision. There is therefore often a tension between the need to move the meeting along and the need to ensure a sufficiently deep discussion on important agenda items.

Summarising

This process is facilitated by the Chair summarising agreed elements as they emerge from the discussion to form part of the consensus towards which the meeting is building. When done skilfully, such summaries serve to indicate to participants that discussion of that particular part of the topic is now closed and it is time to focus on another aspect. Bearing in mind that the meeting is concerned, at least in part, with the management of emotions, skilful Chairs will not summarize until they are satisfied that the feelings of all of the participants, and particularly those representing minority viewpoints, have been given adequate and appropriate opportunity for expression. This is important not only in securing the commitment of all participants to what emerges as the collective decision but also in respect of the management of the meeting itself, since views which have been suppressed are likely to find an outlet later in the meeting at a point when it will be counterproductive to revisit that aspect of the topic.

Recording the meeting

The most important outcome of a meeting are the decisions taken and the action points agreed upon. The Secretary should record these accurately and they should form the minutes of the meeting. That having been said, it is sometimes necessary for the minutes to indicate how a decision was reached and what matters were taken into account when formulating such a decision. Whether it is necessary for the minutes to be expanded in this way is largely governed by who will eventually read the minutes. If these readers include people who were not present at the meeting but are necessary recipients of the minutes (for example senior employees in departments who are affected by the outcomes of the meeting, or persons or bodies external to the organization), then the minutes may need to be more expansive.

Consensus building and decision-taking

Again, it is the responsibility of the Chair to build the consensus of the meeting towards its decision and to formulate and clearly state what that decision is. It is not necessary for decisions to be voted upon. It is perfectly legitimate for the Chair to 'take the sense' of the meeting, and to articulate his or her conclusion as to what decision the meeting has reached, and to seek agreement/disagreement with that conclusion.

Given what has been said above about the importance of meetings as vehicles for the management of emotions and for the development of decisions, it may seem odd to advocate that the minutes of a meeting should be written in advance. Whether this is advantageous or not depends on whether the minutes will be required to reflect the discussion, but where the minutes are essentially recording decisions it is often helpful for all participants to have them available in draft in advance of the discussion. This does not imply that they should predict the outcome of the meeting. For example a draft minute could read:

> *After full and careful discussion it was agreed that the company would [not] invest £?,000,000? in a new computer system to be supplied by firm A/firm B/firm C.*

There are two advantages to drafting minutes in advance:

1. It helps to ensure that all elements of a decision are dealt with. This is particularly relevant when a decision is complex in nature and requires subsidiary or ancillary matters to be dealt with. But it can also be helpful in relatively simple decisions. The above example indicates that the meeting must address

questions as to whether to invest, how much to invest and from whom to purchase.

2. It enables the Chair to focus the attention of all participants on each element of the decision, with participants having freedom to agree amendments to the decision/minute as drafted.

After the meeting

After the meeting has concluded the Chair has the responsibility of approving the minutes and action points as drafted by the Secretary prior to distribution to the participants. The Chair also has responsibility for securing completion of the action points from those to whom they were assigned.

Summary

This chapter has looked at the basic components of communication within organizations and emphasized the importance of this topic.

The ways in which communication is channelled within organisations have been explored at a general level, and the particular use of meetings as a medium of effective communication has been investigated in greater detail.

References

Adair J (1983) *The Art of Leadership*, Gower

Barnard C I (1938) *The Function of the Executive*, Harvard University Press

Gerloff E A (1985) *Organizational Theory and Design*, McGraw-Hill

Katz D & Kahn R L (1966) *The Social Psychology of Organizations*, John Wiley and Sons

Lawrence P R & Lorsch J W (1967) *Organization and Environment: Managing Differentiation and Integration*, Harvard Graduate School of Business Administration

Wilensky H L (1967) *Organizational Intelligence: Knowledge and Policy in Government and Industry*, Basic Books

Wofford J C, Gerloff E A & Cummins R C (1977) *Organizational Communication: The Keystone to Managerial Effectiveness*, McGraw-Hill

12 Human resource management

Objectives

Human Resource Management (HRM) has received widespread usage amongst certain industries, including the financial services sector, as the new term for managing people. The aim of this chapter is to introduce the concept of Human Resource Management by:

- determining what is personnel and what is HRM;

- considering the different perspectives of HRM;

- exploring the relationship of HRM with business strategy;

- considering the implications for HR policies of pursuing alternative strategic directions;

- examining the roles of the HR specialist and the line manager;

- investigating the changing employment relationship and psychological contract in the financial services sector.

Introduction

At a simplistic level the terms personnel and HRM can be used to describe the functional area responsible for achieving the most effective use of human resources. They are both concerned with the policies and processes involved in the management of people, and include the key human resource systems associated with:

- recruitment and selection;

- training and development;

- performance management;
- appraisal;
- rewards.

In addition, they are both about the development and application of policies governing all aspects relating to the terms of the employment relationship, and the negotiation and application of agreements on pay and working conditions. The wider human and social implications of changes to methods of working, and the economic and social changes in the wider environment, should also be the concern of Personnel and HRM.

This chapter seeks to explore the nature of HRM by looking at the traditional role of personnel and how HRM differs, the strategic nature of HRM, and the changing employment relationships in the financial services sector. The subsequent chapters will consider, in depth, the different HR systems in terms of HR planning, recruitment and selection, training and development, reward systems and employee legislation.

The traditional role of personnel management

Traditionally in organisations the personnel function developed from a welfare role, and was concerned with managing the interface between the organisation and the individual. It was generally recognised as occupying a supportive/paternalistic role. Personnel tended to operate as a tactical fire-fighting activity, having a short-term perspective, reacting to changes in the external environment, such as employment legislation, labour market conditions, trade union actions and other environmental influences.

To a large extent personnel was involved with designing efficient systems to ensure equitable policies for selection, rewards, discipline, dismissal, redundancy, etc. Personnel management was operational in nature, and was concerned with the administration and implementation of policies.

One definition of personnel management proposed by the Institute of Personnel Management is as follows:

> *Personnel Management is that part of management concerned with people at work and their relationship with an enterprise. Its task is that of ensuring the optimum use of human resources to the mutual benefit*

> *of the enterprise, each person and the community at*
> *large to enable them to make their best contribution to*
> *its success.*

Torrington and Hall (1995) suggest that personnel management is essentially workforce centred, and takes into account the views and aspirations of the workforce rather than being totally identified with management interests. They state that:

> *Personnel Management is a series of activities which*
> *first enable working people and the business which uses*
> *their skills, to agree about the objectives and nature of*
> *their working relationship and, secondly, ensures that*
> *the agreement is fulfilled.*

Both of these definitions suggests that people have a right to be treated as human beings whilst at work, and that they will only be effective when their job-related needs are met.

Human resource management

In recent years there has been an increasing tendency to use the term Human Resource Management (HRM) to replace personnel management. This trend is evident in the financial services sector. The term HRM has, however, been in use for the last 30 or 40 years. It came to prominence in the United States around 1980 when American industry faced intense Japanese competition in both its domestic and international markets. The principles on which HRM was built reflected the deficiencies in American organisations competing with Japanese firms. It was felt that American working practices, classified as "Type A" values, which stood for short-termism and lack of teamwork, compared unfavourably with Japanese or "Type J" values, which encouraged worker commitment, adaptability and high quality (Ouchi 1981).

In the UK, HRM came into prominence in the mid-1980s when many industries, including financial services organisations, were facing an increasingly complex and turbulent environment. Operating within this climate organisations started to recognise employees as a key strategic resource, which could be utilised in pursuit of gaining competitive advantage.

Introduction to section three

The final section deals with the different policy areas involved in the management of what are arguably an organizationtion's most important assets, its employees. Therefore, the theme of the final section is to ensure that managers make the best use of the human resources of the organization.

Human Resource Management (HRM) has become an influential approach to the management of employment and Chapter 12 seeks to introduce the concept by distinguishing between HRM and personnel. The strategic nature of HRM is examined in terms of its relationship with business strategy. It is proposed that all HR systems should be aligned with business strategy. The remaining chapters consider the translation of HR strategy into HR plans and examine the contribution of the different HR policy areas.

Chapter 13 starts by looking at the HR planning process, and includes an examination of the approaches to recruitment and selection. Following on from this, Chapter 14 explores the issues surrounding the importance of education, training and development. Linked to this the role of appraisal systems is examined.

Chapter 15 focuses upon how to motivate employees in order to encourage high performance, and examines the different approaches to motivation. It then moves on to look at the relationship between job design and job satisfaction and investigates alternative reward systems.

Finally, Chapter 16 deals with the legal aspects governing the nature and management of the employment relationship, and specifically examines the terms of employment, health and safety at work, discrimination, managing diversity, and grievance, and disciplinary procedures.

There is much debate regarding the characteristics and philosophy of HRM, and it remains an ambiguous concept raising many questions. Torrington and Hall (1995) view HRM as essentially resource-centred, in contrast to the workforce orientation of personnel management. In other words HRM is directed mainly at management needs, rather than the needs of employees. Beardwell and Holden (1997) suggest that four broad perspectives exist on HRM:

1. HRM is merely a re-naming of the personnel function with nothing to distinguish it from personnel.

2. HRM represents a fusion of personnel management and industrial relations, and therefore creates a new management discipline and function that takes a holistic approach to the management of people.

3. HRM represents a resource-based approach that stresses the potential of the individual employee in terms of an investment rather than a cost, and focuses on the role of the individual rather than collective employment models. This perspective, in conjunction with the second point, has its roots in the Human Relations school, and emphasises the need for personal development in order to gain the commitment and motivation of employees.

4. HRM can be viewed as part of the strategic business function in the development of business policy. Thus it is concerned with matching employment policies to organisational strategies. The strategic nature of HRM is explained by Armstrong's (1994) definition:

    Human Resource Management is a strategic and coherent approach to the management and organisation of an organisation's most valued asset, the people working there, who individually and collectively contribute to the achievement of its objectives for sustainable competitive advantage.

The above definitions and perspectives suggest that HRM can be viewed as a strategic approach to acquiring, developing, managing and motivating people, with policies which should match the organisation's business strategy. It is concerned with creating a positive culture and encouraging the commitment of employees to the goals, objectives and values of the organisation.

Whilst HR strategies must be developed to support the achievement of business objectives it must be recognised that people cannot be treated just like any other resource. People are individuals and have their own needs and expectations which may or may not be consistent with those of the organisation. So HRM must be both *business*- and *people*-oriented.

Developing this theme Storey (1992) distinguishes between the 'soft' and 'hard' dimensions of HRM. 'Soft' HRM emphasises the 'resource' part of HRM and is rooted in the Human Relations school with a focus on employee development, communication, motivation and leadership. The 'hard' form of HRM is concerned with managing the human resource in a rational way (as for any other economic factor) "employees are just another figure in the input/output equation" (Armstrong 1994). This version tends to emphasise the business needs rather than the needs of the individual. It is a cost-effective approach seeking to improve employee utilisation.

HRM practitioners are often torn between the hard (management) and soft (developmental) aspects of HRM. This can be applied to the financial services sector where hard HRM has been in evidence in terms of the downsizing and de-layering activities of organisations, while at the same time a soft approach has been used to provide a high quality service.

Characteristics of HRM

If HRM is considered to be more than just a task performed by specialists in the organisation then the following key features should be identified (Armstrong 1994):

- it is a top management-driven activity;
- the performance and delivery of HRM is a line management responsibility;
- it emphasises strategic fit, in other words the integration of business strategy and personnel strategies;
- it involves the adoption of a comprehensive and coherent approach to employment policies and practices;

- great importance is attached to a strong culture and to strong values;
- it lays great emphasis on the attitudinal and behavioural characteristics of employees;
- employee relations are unitarist rather than pluralist, individualist rather than collective, and involve high rather than low trust;
- the principles of the organisation are organic and decentralised with flexible roles and reliance on teamwork;
- rewards are set according to performance, competence or skill.

There are a number of assumptions which underpin these features:

1. People are the most important assets an organisation possesses. Organisations exist to deliver value to their customers and it is the human capabilities which distinguishes successful organisations from the rest. This could be said to be especially true for financial services organisations. Organisations should utilise people to their full capacity and potential.

2. Organisational success is better achieved if people policies are linked with and make a contribution to business objectives. This will enable management to achieve organisational objectives through its workforce and develop a coherent set of personnel and employment policies that jointly reinforce the organisation's strategies for matching resources to business needs and improve performance. Because HRM is of strategic importance it should be considered by senior management in the formulation of business objectives and strategies.

3. Corporate cultures, values, organisational climate and managerial behaviours exert an influence on achievement. Culture must be managed, starting from the top, to get values accepted and acted upon. The culture should be aimed at achieving flexibility, creating commitment and innovative teamwork,and focusing on reducing total quality management in the pursuit of excellence. HR policies should be integrated with business plans to reinforce appropriate culture or to modify an inappropriate culture. Commitment must be fostered from the individual since their performance is fundamental to the success of the organisation.

4. Continuous effort by senior managers and line managers is required to encourage organisational members to work together towards the achievement of common goals. There are common interests between employers and employees and as such adversarial confrontation should not exist.

A theory of HRM

The assumptions described above are embraced in the UK theory of HRM proposed by Guest (1987). He presents HRM as a particular approach to employee management and identifies four dimensions of HRM: integration, high commitment, flexibility/adaptability and quality.

1. Integration "is the ability of the organisation to integrate HRM issues into their strategic plans, to ensure that the various aspects of HRM cohere and for line managers to incorporate an HRM perspective into their decision-making".

2. High Commitment "is concerned with both behavioural commitment to pursue agreed goals and attitudinal commitment reflected in a strong identification with the enterprise".

3. Flexibility "is primarily concerned with what is sometimes called functional flexibility, but also with an adaptable organisational structure with the capacity to manage change and innovation".

4. High Quality "refers to all aspects of managerial behaviour, including management of employees and investment in high quality employees, which in turn will bear directly on the quality of goods and services provided".

Ultimately, with the support of key leadership, and with the development of a strong culture and the pursuit of a conscious strategy, the achievement of these outcomes should lead to positive organisational outcomes. However, some researchers suggest that there are inherent tensions with this theory. Legge (1989), for example, comments on some of the problems with integration:

● if an organisation is operating in diverse product markets can it have a company-wide mutually reinforcing set of HRM policies;

- if the business strategy dictates the choice of HRM policies some strategies will dictate policies which fail to emphasise commitment, flexibility and quality.

Integration of HRM with business strategy

The integrative characteristic does, however, support HRM as a strategic activity that should both contribute to and determine strategy. It implies that the successful achievement of business objectives depends upon the effective use of human resources, along with financial and physical resources. Thus, HRM policies are inextricably linked to the formulation and implementation of corporate strategy. HRM should not be carried out in a vacuum. It must align with the strategic objectives of the organisation and will, to some extent, be governed by the external environmental factors, such as the LePest & Co influences discussed in Chapter 1. Figure 12.1 provides an illustration of the 'matching model' of HRM with the business environment.

The key to successful integration of HRM with business strategy is based upon:

- understanding how business strategy is formed;
- understanding the key business issues which have an impact on HR, for example, growth or consolidation, increasing competitive advantage through quality;
- developing a performance-oriented culture, through empowerment, involvement and team working.

To achieve this, a good fit is needed between business strategy and Human Resource strategy so that the latter supports the former. In practice there are difficulties in achieving this 'fit' for a number of reasons:

1. The diversity of strategy for different sections of the organisation means that HR strategies must vary. This has implications for setting consistent HR policies throughout the organisation. One of the key difficulties of managing HR at a strategic level for many financial services organisations is that HRM policies are often set at head office level for the whole organisation or group, but these may not be appropriate or fit with the HR strategies required for specific business units.

Figure 12.1

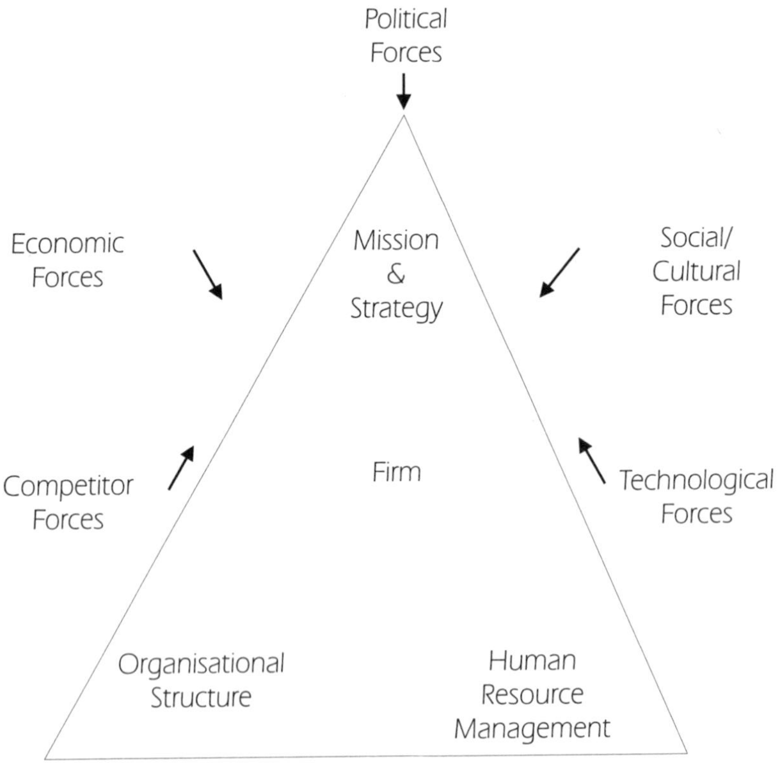

Source: Adapted from 'The Matching Model of HRM' (Devanna, Fombrum and Tichy (1984))

2. The changing and evolving nature of business strategy which makes it difficult to develop relevant HR strategies.

3. The absence of clearly written and transmitted business strategy, which exacerbates the problems of clarifying the strategic business issues which HR strategies should address.

4. The qualitative nature of HR issues can conflict with business strategy that is often quantifiable (e.g. market share,

profitability, etc.). Some HR areas are quantifiable, for example resourcing, but it is more difficult to measure the impact of complex variables such as commitment, good employee relations, morale, etc.

5. Financial orientations can be incompatible with the policies described as imperative to the practice of HRM.

6. Tensions between 'soft' and 'hard' HRM. As a strategic activity HRM can be 'hard' in that people will only come first when it is economically advantageous to pursue such a strategy but it could be argued that equally important is managing the 'softer' people issues. The softer aspects are critical to encourage greater employee participation and the liberation for employees from bureaucratic systems, thus giving individuals greater autonomy and responsibility.

The 'Investors in People' standard (IiP), which many financial services organisations are seeking to achieve, explicitly links business strategy with the management of people. This is best summed up in the statement provided by Investors in People UK:

> An Investors in People makes a public commitment from the top to develop all employees to achieve its business objectives. Every business should have a written but flexible plan which sets out business goals and targets, considers how employees will contribute to achieving the plan and specifies how development needs in particular will be assessed and met. Management should develop and communicate to all employees a vision of where the organisation is going and the contribution employees will make to its success, involving employee representatives as appropriate.

HRM and strategic capability

Everything from the corporate mission and corporate values has implications for HRM, so it is ideal if the HR Director is involved at top management level with the formulation of business strategy.

A critical stage in understanding the strategic capability of an organisation is having a knowledge of the resources available. Human resources are a key resource for financial services organisations along with the other resources that can be grouped as physical resources, financial resources and intangibles. The skills and motivations of employees and the way they are deployed can be a major source of competitive advantage. Thus, a crucial part of identifying the strategic capability of a firm is closely linked with the people it employs. An assessment of HR should be undertaken, as part of the internal audit referred to in Chapter 2, to identify the number and types of different skills within the organisation and the adaptability of the HR.

The strategic intent for organisations has an impact on the way HR are selected, appraised and rewarded. Of key importance is the close alignment of employment systems with business strategy. This is a view supported by Guest (1989) who states:

> The effectiveness of the organisation rests on how strategies interrelate and how HRM issues are integrated into strategic plans – the various aspects of HRM cohere and line managers incorporate an HRM perspective into their decision-making.

HR strategies are primarily about making business strategies work and should set the agenda for a whole raft of HRM activities:

- resourcing;
- skills acquisition and development;
- culture, values, attitudes;
- communications;
- productivity;
- performance management;
- rewards;
- employee relations.

When deciding its business direction an organisation has a number of alternative strategic directions which it could take to achieve its corporate objectives. The alternative directions for development include, for example, withdrawal from the marketplace, consolidation, market penetration, market development, product development and diversification (related and unrelated).

For each of the alternative directions there are a different method for development:

- Internal Development;

- Merger and Acquisition;

- Strategic Alliances and Joint Ventures.

The alternative routes and methods, which were discussed more fully in Chapter 2, have implications for HR policies. For example, an organisation pursuing a policy of diversification could do so by either acquisition or internal development. Each would have ramifications for human resources. In the case of internal development, the organisation would have to consider the human resource requirements in terms of the numbers of people, types and levels of skills. If new skills are required then the selection procedure may have to change.

In the case of diversification via a merger, a key consideration in assessing the suitability of this option would relate to the cultural 'fit' between the two organisations.

Thus, different business objectives will have implications for HR policies in terms of:

- recruitment and selection;

  How can we acquire, retain or shed the right number and quality of people to meet the forecast needs of the organisation or department?

- developing and training;

  How can we train and develop employees to ensure that they respond to change and the resulting demands for different skills and abilities?

- performance and reward management;

  How can we ensure that we have a fully committed and well-motivated workforce, and that those worth retaining stay with the business and reward those who deliver the desired results?

The successful implementation of strategy will also have implications for HRM, as already explored in Chapter 4. HR policies must be developed to encourage and support organisational change.

The formulation and implementation of HR strategies and business strategies must take account of both external and internal factors. Key external issues which impact on HR policies include, for example, demographic factors that are changing the shape of the workforce. There is a declining number of young people entering the workforce and organisations must consider their recruitment and selection strategies in order to attract young people and those from alternative groups such as women returners. Technological changes are also significant in that they are changing the structure of work. New employment legislation on areas such as equal opportunities and work time will also affect HR strategies.

Internal factors include managing and developing human resource policies in the context of:

- cultural change;
- maturing workforce;
- workforce diversity;
- job design;
- pressures on quality of life;
- pressure for education;
- continuous learning and skills development;
- redundancy;
- morale and motivation.

All of these factors are pertinent to what is occurring in the financial services sector.

Duties and responsibilities of HR managers

The above sections have considered the issues surrounding HRM as a strategic activity, and raise questions regarding who is responsible for HR. Research amongst financial services organisations does indicate that many organisations have elevated HR to a strategic position, setting up strategic HR departments and having HR representation at board level.

Another trend to emerge is that financial services organisations are devolving personnel activities to line managers at local level. The role of line managers is expanded so that it incorporates people responsibilities as well as technical responsibilities. An increasing proportion of management time will therefore be taken up with 'people' management issues. Fundamental to this is the view that managers must develop skills that are not just technical and task-oriented and must be rewarded for the 'people management' activities of their role. Increasingly, these softer skills are becoming important key competencies needed for progression within the organisation.

There is, of course, still a role for specialist HR staff who are needed to provide guidance and support on all matters relating to the employees, such as providing guidance on issues relating to employee legislation. Specialist HR staff may also take an active role in procedures such as recruitment and selection, training and development, and assessments for promotion decisions. The aim is to ensure that management deals effectively with everything concerning the employment and development of people (Armstrong 1995).

The various areas of HR activity in developing, revising or implementing policies include:

1. **The Design of Jobs**. This involves analysing, designing and structuring, and will mean measuring and deciding upon the content of jobs in order to evaluate their worth and relationship with other jobs and functions. Job design will be looked at in detail in Chapter 15.

2. **Recruiting and Selecting Staff**. This involves the planning and forecasting of the numbers and types of employees required both now and in the future, looking at the supply both in the organisation and outside, and drawing up plans to close any gaps between demand for employees and supply. In addition it involves understanding the requirements for a job in terms of the competencies required to do it successfully. Finally, it involves choosing the most suitable candidate from those who apply using selection techniques as appropriate in the most reliable, valid and ethical way. Chapter 13 investigates HR planning and the processes involved in recruitment and selection.

3. **Developing Staff**. This involves determining the appropriate method of training or development and evaluating effectiveness. This will include analysing training needs at

corporate, division or individual level. Job analysis and HR planning will assist in the process of defining what is required.

4. **Performance Monitoring and Appraisal.** Managing performance is concerned with the design and implementation of performance management and appraisal systems. Developing staff and performance management are explored in Chapter 14.

5. **Rewarding Staff.** The activities here will include measuring the value of jobs, their position in the organisational hierarchy, and monetary value. Administering pay systems and the development and implementation of the wider staff benefits packages is also included. Also under this heading the external market rates and influences must be understood. Chapter 15 explores in detail issues relating to performance management, and the appraisal and design of reward systems used in the financial services sector.

6. **Employee Relations.** This involves the communication, participation and involvement of staff, and includes relations with trade unions, staff representatives and consultative committees.

7. **Social Responsibilities.** This would involve ensuring that statutory obligations relating to the Health and Safety at Work Act and any other employee legislation such as equal opportunities are fully discharged. The legal implications are explored more fully in Chapter 16.

8. **Administrative Responsibilities.** In addition to all the above responsibilities, records of individual employees must be kept up to date within the scope of the Data Protection Act. Guidelines on the policies and procedures for the conduct of affairs to ensure consistency and equability in their application across the organisation must be developed.

Changing employment relationships in the financial services sector

The multiplicity of changes occurring within the financial services sector as part of the drive for organisational survival and prosperity has led to fundamental changes to traditional HR policies. During the period from the Second World War up until the early/mid-1980s, organisations operating in the financial services sector saw prosperity and growth. Employees could anticipate lifetime employment and career progression with a single organisation. The culture tended to be one of 'the company will look after you'.

However, changes in market conditions, including intense competition and turbulent organisational climate, have provided the imperative for greater organisational flexibility and adaptability. Management practices have changed radically with the move away from a paternalistic culture to a flexible high performance culture. Within this context, organisations can no longer support the traditional HR policies which underpinned jobs for life and 'onwards and upwards' career progression.

With the move away from offering conditions of lifetime employment and job security, and the introduction of flatter organisational structures, the focus should now be on improving staff employability which is based on a flexible employer-employee relationship.

Essentially, employability is concerned with developing the competitive skills to gain and maintain jobs. Both the employer and the employee should share the responsibility for maintaining and enhancing individuals' employability inside and outside the organisation. The outcome will be employees who are constantly reviewing their skills base and updating their skills. The assumption is that individuals will accept less job security in return for opportunities to develop new skills and expertise.

Employability can be viewed by enlightened employers as having the dual benefit of encouraging employees to develop as a way of adding value to the organisation, but also as a hedge against unemployment. However, and notwithstanding the growing literature on the subject, it is still the case that the concept of employability has yet to be implemented on a wide scale.

Employability is tied up with the concept of 'the psychological contract' already referred to in Chapter 9. This is concerned with what employers and employees want and expect from each other, and the understanding people have regarding the commitment made between themselves and their organisation. In other words:

- the employer   -   What outputs they will get from the employees?
- the employee   -   What rewards will be given for investing time and effort?

Characteristics of the psychological contract are that it is voluntary, subjective, dynamic and informal. The implication is that the contract is one of exchange, and the idea embraces the promissory exchange of offers by the two parties and thus the mutual obligations to fulfill these offers.

The rapidly changing economic climate in which financial services organisations now operate has meant there have been pressures for change on both sides of the contract (employer and employee). Sparrow (1996) provides a useful summary of the old and new characteristics of the psychological contract, and Figure 12.2 identifies some of these factors.

Figure 12.2

Characteristics	Old	New
Change environment	Stable, short-term focus	Continuous change, intense competition
Culture	Paternalistic, time served	High performance where those who perform get rewarded
Focus	Security, job for life	Employability, lucky to have a job, no guarantees
Rewards	Paid on level, position, status, length of service	Paid on contribution linked to business strategy and objectives
Motivational currency	Promotion, onwards and upwards	Job enrichment, skills, competencies and personal development
Promotion basis	Expected, time served, technical competence	Less opportunity, horizontal/ lateral, new criteria for those who deserve it
Personal development	The organisation's responsibility	Individual's and employer's responsibility to improve employability

Characteristics	Old	New
Employer's key responsibility	Fair pay for good work	High pay for high performance
Employee's key responsibility	Good performance in present job	Making a difference
Employer's key input	Stable income & career advancement	Opportunities for self-development
Employee's key input	Time & effort	Knowledge, expertise, adding value
Redundancy/tenure guarantee	Job for life	Lucky to have a job, no guarantees
Trust employees project	High trust and commitment to organisation possible	Desirable, but expect to become committed to profession

Source: Adapted from Sparrow (1996)

The above chart illustrates that what is emerging is a very different psychological contract between employer and employee. The changes in the relationship mean that organisations are more demanding of their employees and the paternalistic culture no longer dominates. Organisations are becoming more ambiguous places to work where people will be utilised only when they have the required skill. Individuals need to plan their own development and manage their own careers because jobs for life and job security are disappearing. Job enrichment and development of new skills will be the motivational currency rather than promotion. Pay systems will be based on an individual's contribution to the organisation, for example through Performance Related Pay systems, not on grade position or status.

It is argued that new psychological contracts are a necessary part of the transformation process to improve organisational performance capabilities. However, there is the suggestion that the 'new' contract can be conceived as a degradation of the employment relationship and trust, and it is predicted that the quality of the contract will deteriorate.

Hendry and Jenkins (1997) argue that the psychological contract traditionally enjoyed by those working in the financial services sector has been disrupted and abrogated. Furthermore, it is reported that staff morale is at its lowest level and that trust in management is low (Storey 1995). Some researchers do disagree with this, stating that it is too simplistic an assumption. Herriot (1995), for example, suggests that employee attitudes will be a determinant on the way the new psychological contract is perceived and on the resulting behaviours. He states that staff understand the reality of why the changes are occurring but will act differently depending upon their attitude. He identifies the following groups and likely responses:

- flexers, who understand the reasons for and nature of change, and are willing to adopt flexible working patterns and lateral career progression;

- ambitious,who whilst understanding the implications for change they still see career and personal progression for themselves;

- lifers, who still hanker after the guarantee for job security, and who believe that experience and length of service are legitimate as the basis for reward;

- disengaged, who are those who have withdrawn, either explicitly or implicitly, from the organisation, with a desire to leave voluntarily or seek voluntary redundancy or early retirement. They no longer demonstrate in their behaviours commitment to the organisation.

The segmentation described above is problematic for HR practitioners since the categories are not necessarily determined by demographic variables, such as age, grade or length of service, but rather attitudes which are harder to recognise.

The Royal Bank of Scotland is an example of an organisation that has instigated change in the psychological contact through its re-engineering programme, 'Project Columbus'. One outcome from the project has been a rationalization of grade structures where staff have had to reapply for re-designed jobs. The new job roles have been advertised on the basis of competencies rather than grade and without reference to pay (Hiltrop 1995).

Different psychological contracts may exist for different groups of employees in financial services organisations, for example:

a) Senior managers will receive a high degree of support and investment which is necessary to ensure that they stay, or to attract new high calibre staff.

b) Highly skilled staff/specialists (possibly contract staff) are capable of managing their own careers and thus maintaining employability outside the organisation.

c) Other more general staff receive a high level of role specific training from the organisation but limited general and personal development. They are expected to take the initiative in maintaining much of their employability.

HR policies and processes will all impact on the relationship between the employer and the employee. The features of the psychological contract are central to the motivation of employees. Any changes will have implications for employee behaviour and the way careers, rewards and commitment are managed (Sparrow 1996). The critical issues for HR include:

- finding new ways to attract, retain and motivate employees;
- the psychological contract must evolve in line with the new characteristics and expectations of people entering the workforce;
- changes in management style;
- changes in organisational structures and roles;
- the building of cross-functional teams;
- creating challenging work experiences;
- provision of training;
- nurturing leadership talent;
- eliminating barriers to change.

The psychological contract must evolve, reflecting the changed business conditions and the expectations of people entering the workforce.

Summary

HRM can be considered to have a strategic focus, and has a close relationship with wider business policies. In this context HRM is integrated into business policy rather than being subordinate to it. Success is achieved through the effective management of human resources with the achievement of strategic goals. The changing business environment in which financial services operate has meant there has been significant changes in HRM systems and policies.

Having explored the philosophy and strategic nature of HRM, the following chapters will examine aspects of specific HR policy areas, starting with HR planning.

References

Armstrong M (1994) *Human Resource Management*, Kogan Page

Armstrong M (1995) *A Handbook of Personnel Management Practice*, 5th ed. Kogan Page

Beardwell I & Holden L (1997) *Human Resource Management: A Contemporary Perspective*, 2nd ed. Pitman

Devanna M A, Fombrun C J & Tichy N M (1984) 'A Framework for Strategic Human Resource Management', in C J Fombrun, N M Tichy & M A Devanna ed., *Strategic Human Resource Management*, Wiley

Guest D E (1987) 'Human Resource Management and Industrial Relations', *Journal of Management Studies*, Vol. 24, No. 5

Guest D E (1989) 'Personnel and HRM: Can you tell the difference?', *Personnel Management*, January

Hendry C & Jenkins R (1997) 'Psychological Contracts and New Deals', *Human Resource Management Journal*, Vol. 7, No. 1

Herriott P (1995) 'Psychological Contracts' in *Encyclopedic Dictionary of Organizational Behaviour*, Nicholson N (ed), Basil Blackwell

Herriot P & Pemberton C (1996) 'Facilitating New Deals', *Human Resource Management Journal*, Vol. 7, No. 1

Hiltrop J (1995) 'The Changing Psychological Contract: The Human Resource Challenge of the 1990s', *European Management Journal*, Vol. 13 No. 3

Legge K (1989) 'Human Resource Management: A Critical Analysis', in J. Storey ed., *New Perspectives on Human Resource Management*, Routledge

Ouchi W (1981) *Theory Z: How American Business Can Meet the Japanese Challenge*, Addison Wesley

Sparrow P R (1996) 'Transitions in the Psychological Contract in UK Banking', *Human Resource Management Journal*, Vol. 6, No. 4

Storey J (1992) *Developments in the Management of Human Resources*, Blackwell

Storey J (1995) 'Employment Policies and Practices in UK Clearing Banks: An Overview', *Human Resource Management Journal*, Vol. 5, No. 4

Torrington D & Hall L (1995) *Personnel Management*, Prentice Hall

13 Human resource plans and their implementation

Objectives

This chapter is concerned with aspects of organizational management relating to the implementation of an HR strategy.
   The detailed objectives of the chapter are:

- to discuss the problems of translating the HR strategy into an HR plan;

- to consider approaches to the informed recruitment and selection of human resources;

- to emphasize the key role played by effective induction in the management of human resources;

- to identify the problems encountered by commercial organizations in attempting to correct the size of their staff complements.

Human resource planning

Chapter 12 dealt with the relationship between business strategy and HR strategy. One of the key difficulties in the formulation of organizational plans which are designed to achieve a business strategy is that business strategies are generally couched in terms relevant to the use of and returns expected from capital rather than human resources. However, it is the inter-relationship between these two categories of resources that will determine the success or otherwise of the business strategy.

The function of the HR plan is to articulate how the organization's human resources will be deployed and managed in order to achieve the business objectives. The process of producing an HR plan which has a chance of satisfying that function is however so fraught with problems that its usefulness has long been questioned.

A significant factor concerns the timing of the beginning of the HR plan. If planning is an iterative process, then organizations tend to concentrate their iterations on 'getting the figures' right and then (if at all) advert to 'getting the people' right. As has been argued human resources are more complex, in terms of planning, than financial resources, for example, no homogeneity and people are difficult to commoditize. It is therefore little wonder that in the iterative process of business planning when human resources feature it is only as headcount figures.

This is not to imply that HR planning is necessarily a sterile process. It is well to remember Mintzberg's (1994) dualistic concept of 'planning' which:

● contributes to the development of the 'strategic vision';

● provides the basis of the mechanisms of the control process.

In an ideal world it may be best if HR planners contribute to the development of the business vision. However, this may not be essential, particularly given the complex nature of the resources. The prime virtue of HR planning may therefore lie in the discipline which the process will bring to the achievement of that vision. The plan is there so that progress can be monitored and effective corrective action taken.

It is too simple to think of human resources as 'people'. It is better to think of each individual as a combination of 'attributes', without ever forgetting their individuality. This is because the achievement of the business strategy through human resources is predicated on there being human resources of the correct calibre, which are able to contribute the right attributes and are available to the organization. In most organizations this will mean taking account of the human resources currently within the organization, and how those human resources are themselves organized, so that the drive to achieve the business vision may need to be tempered to take account of what is feasible and attainable. This in turn implies that HR planning involves much more than merely ensuring that the headcount is correct.

Essentially, HR planning involves a 'gap analysis' which is a comparison between 'where we want to be' (in accordance with the business vision) and 'where we are now'. This will identify the differences in terms of human resources and the plan will chart the way in which the organization will move from its current state to its goal state. The HR planning process will however have to take into account the influences of the internal and external environment. It is no good planning for a massive expansion of the operation in the north-east, for example, if the north-east will not provide a ready pool of human resources (with the necessary attributes) to be brought into the organization and the organization's existing human resources are not easily relocated from their current workplace to the north-east.

If the human resources are to be regarded as combinations of attributes, then it is necessary for the HR plan to articulate the attributes which the organization requires. This will involve consideration of factors such as:

- knowledge
- experience
- personality
- age
- mobility
- job needs

- skills
- attitudes
- cultural orientation
- re-employability
- development potential
- career aspirations

It may be that resources with the required attributes are already available inside the organization. On the other hand it may be that the organization's current workforce was ideal for the organization as it was but not what the organization will require in its goal state. Thus an assessment of the attributes of the current workforce will form part of the scanning of the internal environment.

In assessing the internal environment it will also be necessary to take into account the ways in which, at an 'organizational' rather than a 'managerial' level, the human resources are organized and managed. This will involve the consideration of such factors as:

- work locations
- reward systems
- career systems
- exit systems
- turnover
- management

- unionization
- development systems
- appraisal systems
- communication systems
- promotion systems
- succession plans

The significance of reviewing the internal environment can be illustrated by returning to the Boston matrix, and by contrasting the differing HR requirements of a company categorized as a 'Star' (high market share: high market growth) with those of a company categorized as a 'Cash Cow' (high market share: low market growth).

Given that the Star needs to be able to accommodate a stabilising product base, while remaining alert and being able to exploit new developments so as to be able to protect its market share, it is not surprising to find that the resource requirements are quite different from those of the Cash Cow, which operates in a less volatile marketplace.

Table 13.1: Star vs. Cash Cow

	Star	Cash Cow
Management	Stability but with entrepreneurial overtones	Steady State backed by ability to control costs
Staff	Differentiated because of the need to take advantage of technological changes while marketing a well received product	Structured and stable marketing a stable product
Unionization reward systems	Probably growing Differentiated reflecting different work requirements. Controlled at business level	Probably well established Structured and centrally controlled
Communication systems	Tailor made for various operational requirements	Formal and uniform
Performance control systems	Concentration on investment returns	Concentration on minimising costs
Training systems	Need for rapid response to developments in technology and/or markets	Inductee training well established little need thereafter

Additionally, the Cash Cow may have established internal 'social' and 'welfare' organizations aimed at employee maintenance.

It is instructive to use the above format of analysis to consider the changes which have been experienced within the UK financial services industry since deregulation. With the collapse of the barriers to entry, as well as in response to other competitive pressures, the UK banks in particular have gone through the painful process of dismantling structures and systems which were conducive to life as a Cash Cow. These have been replaced with less bureaucratic and more flexible approaches to the management of human resources.

The above illustrates the proposition that HR planning and management is not simply about having 'the right people in the right place at the right time'. It is more about having the 'right number of people with the desired attributes supported by the right HR systems in place in order to compete for the jobs which the organization will have available'.

Approaches to the identification, selection and retention of people with the desired attributes will be dealt with later in this chapter, while consideration of the development of those attributes within the existing workforce will be discussed in Chapter 14.

Amongst the other aspects of HR planning which need to be considered are the following:

1. **Establishment plans.** It is unlikely that the existing internal supply will match the predicted demand of the goal state in which case plans will need to be made in order to regularize the position. This may involve at one extreme a recruitment campaign, whilst at the other an exercise in 'rightsizing', i.e. shedding employees in order to meet future establishment needs.

   Alternatively, manpower needs might be satisfied from the existing workforce provided that it is possible for them to be relocated. Furthermore, it is not difficult to imagine situations (e.g. as different products reach different stages in the product life cycle) where each of these approaches would need to be combined in order to achieve the overall objective.

   In each case the exercise should be planned in a way that is sensitive to the organization's long-term requirements. Thus an organization which is shedding part of its workforce, but wishes to retain the remainder, should aim to handle the severance in such a way as to induce those being retained to maintain their relationship with the organization.

2. **Organizational structure plans.** It is inevitable that in an organization of some size, tasks will have to be grouped. The classical distinction between a 'product' organization and a 'functional' organization is probably too simplistic to match up to the reality of the structure of any modern complex organization. It thus becomes a key element of planning that the actual tasks to be performed by the various groups within the organization are specified.

   This is of particular importance to HR since many of the HR functions are as capable of being performed at divisional or departmental level (e.g. manpower planning, recruitment, job evaluation) as they are from the centre. The dismantling of HR bureaucracies has been a trend since the 1980s, with many of the functions formerly performed from the centre being redistributed throughout the organization. An approach such as this clearly has advantages where it is appropriate for HR functions to be executed in different ways in different parts of the organization (e.g. remuneration policy). However, these advantages must be balanced against the diminution of the homogeneity of the organization. A fully centralized HR function is likely to be the only element of an organization with which all employees will have a relationship.

3. **Performance Management plans.** There are three strands to the management of the performance of the organization's HR each of which will need to be considered in the formulation of the Performance Management plans, and each of which may have plans of their own. These are:

   a) *Performance.* The articulation of targets is a key element in the process through which the strategic vision is to be achieved. But performance plans may also relate to 'softer' issues such as the behavioural characteristics required of the staff of the organization as it will be in the future. Performance plans must also deal with methods of monitoring and measuring performance.

b) *Reward*. Reward plans must not only deal with the quantum of rewards at various levels and in various parts of the organization, but also with the contexts in which rewards will be generated. For example, if profit is the key element of organizational performance then rewards are likely to be geared to the development, marketing, sale and administration of profitable lines. On the other hand, if relationship maintenance is the key element of performance then rewards should match approaches which satisfy both new and established customers rather those which simply maximize profit in the shorter term.

c) *Training and Development*. In so far as there is a gap between the current reality of the organization and its strategic vision, or a gap between required performance and actual performance, there is at least a prima facie case for training and development plans designed to eliminate the gap.

4. **Communication plans.** Even within a simple organization it is necessary to pay due attention to the methods of communication within the organization. At a basic level communication systems are necessary to enable management to relay to employees what is required of them. Communication systems should also incorporate the means by which upward communication can be accomplished, if only to facilitate the achievement of organizational goals in the light of the real problems encountered at the time of implementation. In more complex organizations it is necessary to establish communication systems which can facilitate the flow of required information across the organization.

5. **Employee relations plans.** As the complement of an organization grows it becomes increasingly difficult for management to accomplish what is needed in terms of individual relationships with the result that consideration must be given to the ways in which unavoidable conflicts of interest between the organization and its employees are to be discussed, negotiated and resolved.

This illustrates the fundamental difficulty of HR planning, since there are so many strands which need to be taken into consideration and which cannot necessarily be viewed in isolation. This in turn suggests that the formulation of the business strategy and business plan in terms of financial resources alone is probably beneficial, for otherwise the planning process would probably expand to the extent that it would inhibit any movement towards implementation. On the other hand it is important that the complexity of HR planning is not forgotten, and that due regard is given to the resource that will be needed to draft and perfect the HR plans prior to the launch of a new business strategy.

Recruitment and selection

In the late 1980s in the UK there was much talk of the 'demographic time bomb', a phrase which implied that the demographics of the workforce were changing so dramatically that it was widely predicted that there would not be enough current and potential employees to fill all jobs. The reality has turned out to be somewhat different. Although, following the end of the recession of the late 1980s, the general trend of unemployment has been downwards, many employers have been shedding rather than recruiting employees. This observation when coupled with the unemployment trend suggests that jobs have been expanding within the economy rather than within organizations. It also suggests that the main candidates for downsizing were those organizations which traditionally operated on a basis of large complements, such as those within financial services.

This exemplifies another aspect of the general trend for both employers and employees to want to do away with the 'cradle to grave' mentality. The concept of a 'job for life' implied that the job would last longer than the working life, and that therefore whenever the current jobholder ceased to do the job he or she had to be replaced. A more modern approach is to question the necessity of the job, and to ponder whether, even if the job does add value to the organization, there is not some more effective or cost-effective way of achieving that same added value.

One of the most significant changes in working life between the late 1980s and the late 1990s, particularly in the service industries, has been the lessening of the dependence on mainframe computing capacity and the growth in the concept of the workstation as the basic tool of many jobholders. The result is that fewer workers, equipped with greater computer power, can often accomplish more work in a shorter time than had hitherto been the case.

When a jobholder leaves a necessary job, the first question the manager or HR function should ask is not 'how do we go about securing a replacement?', but rather 'can the job be redesigned in such a way as to do away with the need to find a replacement?'. This may mean that jobs other than that of the job holder are also affected as work is redistributed. As a result there is a great premium placed upon flexibility within both the workforce and the organization's systems.

There are numerous ways in which necessary work can be restructured to ensure that there is no need to find a direct replacement for an outgoing jobholder. These include:

- *mechanization*: the introduction of new equipment, not available when the post was last filled, may render replacement unnecessary;

- *alteration in the hours worked (temporal flexibility)*: the essential work could be done by increased overtime, increased part-time work, staggered hours, job sharing, etc.;

- *alteration in the contractual relationship (financial flexibility)*: the work may be covered by placing it outside the organization by means of a definite move towards outsourcing or by sub-contracting to another entity which does not work full-time for the organization such as a consultant or an agency.

When, however, it is decided that a replacement has to be found then it is best if the task is approached in a structured way. This in itself gives rise to difficulties because elements of a structure tend towards rigidity rather than flexibility. As a result many organizations, or parts thereof, develop their own approaches.

Figure 13.1 shows the elements which should feature in a complete selection process and exemplifies the dangers alluded to above. The usual approaches to the development of job analysis, job description and person specification begin by detailing what is involved in the current job and what sort of person is needed to do it. Because selection is necessarily about the future of the job then the above approach, can be seen as an attribute of the cradle to grave philosophy which is obviously inappropriate in a climate of change and advancing technology.

Figure 13.1

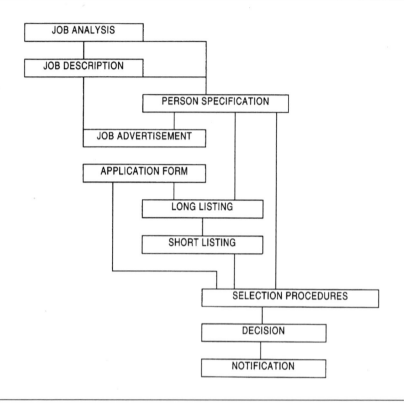

The key elements in each stage of the process are as follows:

1. *Job analysis.* Job analysis entails a rigorous examination of the
   job in order to determine in detail what it involves. It is not an
   easy undertaking and an approach with some form of structure
   is therefore helpful. Such an approach is likely to identify:

   ● objectives of the job;

   ● responsibilities of the jobholder;

   ● decisions to be made by the jobholder;

   ● relationships in which the jobholder will be involved (e.g.

with bosses, subordinates, peers, customers etc.);

- attributes helpful to the successful completion of the job;

- environment, i.e. what is the nature of the geographical, physical, social and financial environment in which the job is done?

2. *Job description.* It is axiomatic that all employees within an organization should have a job description since it forms the basis of the management of their performance. Typically it will encompass:

- job title;

- job grade or evaluation;

- reporting lines;

- main areas of responsibility;

- resources controlled;

- specific responsibilities, even to the level of key tasks;

- limits of authority;

- working conditions.

Because job descriptions tend to become out of date with some rapidity, managers should keep them under review. However, it is important to distinguish between developments in the job and developments in the jobholder.

3. *Person specification.* The person specification describes the type of person who is required to do the job. In many cases, particularly when selecting for a new or 'future' job, it is the key element in the decision-making process since it is against the attributes listed in the person specification that competing candidates are judged. The person specification aims to describe the jobholder in terms of the knowledge, skills, qualifications, experience and other attributes which are essential or desirable for the successful completion of the job. Again a structured approach is useful. Rodger's (1950) seven point plan directs attention to the following areas:

- physique, health and appearance;

- attainments;
- general intelligence;
- special aptitudes;
- interests;
- disposition;
- circumstances.

4. *Job advertisement.* There are three decisions to be taken in respect of the job advertisement:

- in which media will it appear?
- how will those media be approached?
- what will form the text of the advertisement?

Possible media include:

- internal advertisement;
- local press;
- national press;
- technical press;
- the Internet.

The choice is an important one since the objective of advertising is to produce a competitive field of candidates from which an appointment can be made. Placing the advertisement in the 'wrong' medium may produce insufficient candidates with the desired attributes to provide sufficient competition which may then lead to the job having to be re-advertised. Conversely the wrong choice of medium may produce too many apparently suitable candidates so that the process of narrowing the field is wasteful of resources.

If a medium external to the organization is chosen, then a decision is needed on whether the organization will place the advertisement directly or use an agency. The work involved in booking space, preparing layout, checking proofs, managing the media and processing applications is considerable, and can often be usefully outsourced.

The text of the advertisement should be designed to attract only candidates with appropriate attributes as determined by the job description and person specification. Care must be taken to ensure that the text does not narrow the field of candidates unduly. Thus many advertisements require that applicants should be graduates but do not specify the subject of the degree. This is because it does not always have a bearing on the job.

It is also necessary to avoid listing subjective criteria such as 'considerable' experience which can be interpreted in different ways by different potential applicants. It is far better to specify, for instance, 'at least five years experience' if this is thought to be essential to the successful execution of the job.

5. *Application form.* Most organizations which undertake large-scale or regular recruitment will have developed a standardized application form which may or may not be helpful in respect of a particular post. The essential elements of the documents which candidates are asked to submit are that they should enable candidates to:

   ● provide information about themselves on the criteria on which selection will be based;

   ● encourage candidates to describe themselves in relation to the areas which can profitably be explored during selection. This should elicit evidence as to whether the candidate either does or does not have the attributes sought for the job.

6. *Long listing and short listing.* These processes are required to reduce the number of candidates to those who will provide a competitive field from which the required number can be selected. It should be done by comparing the documents submitted by candidates against the criteria for selection as specified in the person specification. Long listing can be undertaken by those remote from the decision, such as an agency or an HR function, whereas short listing should involve at least some of those who will make the decision.

7. *References.* Practice varies as to when in the process these are

taken up. Clearly, if they are to be part of the informed decision taking they should be available before the decision is taken and certainly before any offer of employment is made.

8. *Selection procedure* – See below.

9. *Decision.* As intimated above, any decision made at any stage of the selection process should be based upon a comparison between the evidence available and objective selection criteria. It should also be well documented. Not only does this mean that the decision will be made as part of a procedure which conforms to best practice. It also means that the decision is more likely be justified and justifiable should it ever be called into question, say by an industrial tribunal.

10. *Notification.* Notification should take place as soon after the decision has been made as is practical. Naturally both successful and unsuccessful candidates must be notified and it is good practice to specify the reasons for rejection, or to be prepared to discuss them with the unsuccessful candidates.

Selection procedures

		Candidates for a position who ...	
		SHOULD be selected	SHOULD **NOT** be selected
Candidates for a position who ...	ARE selected	✔	A very costly experiment
	ARE **NOT** selected	A garden of missed opportunities	✔

The above table suggests the reasons why making correct selection/ rejection decisions are of vital importance to organizations. In reality the position is not as dire as the table suggests, because someone who is selected but should not have been may nevertheless:

● have been the pick of a bunch of unsuitable candidates for a post which needed to be filled;

● be capable of doing much of the job;

● may grow into the whole job.

The additional costs of developing the individual or covering the parts of the job which cannot at first be done remain with the organization. In a sense these costs can be measured, and if they can be measured they can be managed.

The costs which cannot be measured, in normal circumstances, are the opportunity costs of turning down people who would have been better than those selected. This is the organizational equivalent of 'The man who sold the Beatles'.

It is not surprising therefore that over the past 20 years the level of sophistication of selection methodologies which are used by organizations has risen substantially. This in turn suggests that making correct selection/rejection decisions is not easy, and that the reason for this is that the decision is normally made by a human being and human beings are not 'wired' to make these decisions readily. This is because we have a remarkable facility to attribute qualities to other people based on the flimsiest of information.

An example of this is to be found when we meet someone for the first time having had numerous telephone conversations with that person beforehand. How many times are we shocked to find that the person does not match up to the mental image which we have created?

Another example will be provided by your answers to the following questions about me:

1. What newspaper do I read?

2. To what level am I educated?

3. What sort of car do I drive?

4. What leisure pursuits do I enjoy?

What is interesting is not the answers which you articulated and which will probably have been 'I cannot possibly say', but the images which flashed into your mind as you saw each question. If you capture those you will probably recognize a certain consistency amongst all four answers, and that they say more about you than they do about me and that they are readily available to you.

It is likely that humans have evolved with this facility because of the benefit to our ancestors in being able to make relatively rapid judgements when faced with the 'new'. However these benefits are counter-productive in the modern context of making correct selection decisions.

There are four 'barriers' which selectors need to overcome before they can be reasonably secure about the rectitude of their judgements concerning the people they are selecting.

a) **Forward information**. Faced with application documents a selector has substantial amounts of information which helps to colour his or her judgement about a candidate. This runs from hard facts about the candidate (name, geographical details, career history, etc.) to less tangible, but nonetheless powerful image creating stimuli such as handwriting, sentence construction and presentation.

b) **First impressions**. Generally in the process of selection, and before a decision is made, there is a meeting between the selector and the candidate. At such times both the selector and the candidate are busy constructing their own versions of each other's personality. Child (1968) has proposed that 'personality' refers to "more or less stable, internal factors that make one person's behaviour consistent from one time to another, and different from the behaviour other people would manifest in comparable situations". From the selectors' point of view, it is important to be able to judge what are these stable personality factors. It is unfortunate therefore that it appears that these judgements are made rapidly and rarely subsequently questioned.

c) **Self-fulfilling prophecies**. Having rapidly constructed the personality of someone we have just met, we then spend time confirming that the impression which we have created is the correct one. This is not to say that we test the assumptions which have been made, but rather that we seek out clues which establish the rectitude of our judgements.

The process is even more subtle than that. The judgements which we make about other persons determine the way in which we behave towards them, and this in turn helps to determine the way in which they react towards us.

d) **Criteria for judgement**. The process by which we implicitly judge people is governed by many things including our own past experience and self-perception, and the feedback which we have received from others. These elements determine the dimensions in respect of which we choose to judge others, and the way in which we assess others in relation to each of these dimensions. For example let us say that a judgement dimension which is important to me is 'flexibility'. If I am implicitly judging another person on this dimension then I never have to articulate precisely what the word flexibility means to me. Let us say further that, within this context, the opposite of flexibility is steadiness. As a selector, I would judge a candidate on the basis of the following dimension:

$$1 \quad 2 \quad\quad 3 \quad\quad 4 \quad 5 \quad\quad 6 \quad 7 \quad 8 \quad 9 \quad 10$$
Steadiness<————————————————————————>Flexibility

Where I see a candidate on this dimension will depend to a great extent on where I see myself. If I regard myself as 'high' on flexibility, say between eight and nine, and I judged the candidate as significantly closer towards steadiness than me, I might place the candidate somewhere between two and three. Another selector, who saw him or herself as 'steady' rather than flexible, might judge the same candidate as being high on flexibility. Similarly the candidate, on his or her own construct of 'flexibility', may see him or herself as being somewhere in the middle. Each of us would be at a loss to understand the others' assessments in the absence of a discussion as to how they were reached.

Our tendency is to make judgements of another person based on a number of criteria which are of significance to us, and to build an overall impression of the personality of the individual which is consistent with both the judgements we have made and our past experience of others whom we have similarly judged.

Carried to extremes this enables us to stereotype whole categories of individuals. By way of illustration, ponder what would be the first impression that comes to mind if, when on holiday in Europe, you saw in the early morning a beach towel draped across a sunlounger!

The barriers described above apply only if the selection/rejection decision is made by a human and they depend in the main on there being a meeting between the decision-maker and the candidate. However it is rare that such decisions are made either by totally mechanical means or without a meeting taking place. As a consequence most of the selection methodologies which have been developed and which are now widely used are designed to increase the level of objectivity which loads into the decision.

The following are amongst the techniques currently in use:

1. Biodata analysis   Biodata has been defined (Anderson & Shackleton (1990)) as 'historical and verifiable pieces of information about an individual in a selection context usually reported on application forms'. Such information is compared with known information about current job holders, who are both good and poor performers, so that the presence within the biodata of information which is typically matched by good performers is an indication that the candidate is likely to succeed in the job. Conversely the presence of information which is associated with poor performers is a contra-indicator. Biodata analysis is particularly useful in long and short listing where there are many applicants for many positions (e.g. graduate recruitment). In these circumstances the likelihood of gathering good information on current jobholders is relatively high because there are large numbers of them and the use of biodata analysis is cost effective in narrowing down a wide field of candidates. If this technique is to be used, then the application form or the form from which the biodata is to be gathered will have to be designed specifically to give candidates the chance to display information relevant to the job.

2. Telephone interviews   Again, when a large number of candidates need to be screened it would be inordinately expensive for them all to be interviewed by means of a meeting. Much of this potential expense can be saved by seeking standardized information in a standardized format through a telephone interview. Telephone interviews are most productive if they are set up in advance rather than operated as a 'cold call'. The candidates are advised of the time they will be called and given some indication of the type of questions they will be asked so that they have an opportunity to prepare and to ask questions of the interviewer.

3. Aptitude tests   As with biodata analysis the efficacy of aptitude testing depends upon the validity of the method as a predictor of success within a job. Thus information on current and past job holders, both in terms of their performance in the job and their performance in the tests, is vital. If it can be shown that there is a correlation between a particular range of performance in a test and good performance in the job, then the use of the test will increase the level of objectivity that can impact upon the decision. A danger with reliance on test data is that the extent of the match between the test result and performance in the job, although statistically valid, may not be great. The relationship between test scores and job performance is expressed as a correlation coefficient (r). If $r=1$ then there is a perfect match between the test scores and job performance. Conversely then, if $r=0$ then there is no relationship at all between the two elements. Statistically, and for sound mathematical reasons, a correlation coefficient of $r=0.4$ is regarded as good. This nonetheless implies that reliance solely on test results which correlate to this extent with job performance is still more likely to lead to an incorrect decision than a correct one. It should be noted however that the correlation coefficient for performance at interview as a predictor of success in a job is as low as $r=0.2$. This argues that reliance on a single technique in making a selection decision is not as likely to lead to a correct decision as basing the decision on a combination of several approaches.

One of the main criticisms against the use of aptitude tests is that they may not be clear of bias. The essential mechanism of testing is that all tests are taken under a strictly standardized procedure (covering the way in which the test is introduced, the environment in which it is taken, the instructions which are given and the time taken). The scores are then compared with the scores of a 'norm' group each of whom took the test under the same standardized procedure. If the norm group from which the comparative scores were obtained was biased in any way (say by an over representation of one gender or an under representation of one race), then conclusions drawn from the test results will tend to reflect that bias. Once recognized this difficulty can be readily overcome by constructing a different norm group which reflects the population under test. Not so easily adjustable is any bias which has crept into the formulation of the questions used in the test. In accordance with statistical requirements and best practice these are rigorously trialled before a test is published for use. However if they have been trialled on a population which is biased in any way then difficulties may arise when the questions are presented to candidates drawn from elements not reflected in that population.

4.Personality *inventories* Personality inventories or questionnaires are often referred to as 'Personality tests'. Strictly speaking, this is incorrect, since although it may appear to be a test, it really seeks to establish:

- the way in which the individual judges him or her self on a number of dimensions;

- a comparison between those self-perceptions and those of a norm group.

Personality inventories are thus not administered under standardized conditions and do not depend on comparisons of performance in response to specific 'items'. Instead they depend upon comparisons of self-perceptions in response to specific items. Personality inventories tend to be used more in assessing candidates for immediate or future managerial roles than for assessing for manual, clerical or ad-ministrative jobs. Qualification to use them in the UK is governed by rules introduced by the British Psychological Society and gaining the relevant qualification is relatively expensive. This generally means that the administration and interpretation of inventories (and aptitude tests) tends to be the province of the HR professional rather than the ultimate decision-taker. The outcome is that the usefulness of inventories in increasing the level of objectivity in selection decisions has been questioned (Fletcher 1990)). Best practice suggests that the detailed outcome of a personality inventory be used to explore certain aspects of the self-perceived personality of the candidate at a subsequent interview.

5. *Assessment* Assessment Centres have been defined (Fletcher 1982))
   centres as 'the assessment of a group of individuals by a team of judges using a comprehensive and integrated series of techniques'. Whether, in practice, the techniques used are comprehensive and/or integrated may be questioned, but Assessment Centres do have the advantage of not being reliant on one technique only. They have the serious disadvantage, however, of being expensive and difficult to arrange since they necessarily involve finding a fit in the diaries of the panel of 'judges' who may be relatively senior people. Amongst the techniques commonly found in Assessment Centres are:

- *Group exercises,* which can take a variety of forms, such as business games, the requirement for the group to undertake a task, and a leaderless group discussion. Essentially such exercises should be designed to explore how individuals react in a group, but they can also provide evidence of leadership, persuasiveness, oral communication, and inter-personal skills in general.

- *Role plays,* in which candidates may be observed undertaking a particular type of communication activity such as an appraisal interview.

- *In-tray exercises,* in which candidates are faced with a number of problems to be dealt with in what is probably an inadequate amount of time. Such exercises can be designed to illustrate the candidates' approaches in a number of areas, such as grasp of detail, written communication, managerial style, analytical ability, approach to subordinates, etc.

As usual, the outcome of the exercise should be debriefed and can provide a rich basis for discussion. In addition Assessment Centres frequently involve some or all of the other techniques outlined above.

6. Selection For the reasons which were given above, when discussing *interviews* the barriers to making sound selection/rejection decisions, the selection interview is fraught with difficulties. Nevertheless the interview is the most widely used selection technique, and it is extremely unlikely that a manager or an organization would want to appoint or employ someone unseen. The objectives of the interview are threefold:

- to discover evidence of the candidate's attributes or lack of the attributes required to do the job;

- to leave the candidate with a good impression of the organization;

- to ensure that the candidate feels and recognizes that he or she has been treated fairly.

In *Decision-making in the Employment Interview* Webster (1964) concludes that:

- interviewers make their decision early in the interview and spend the remainder of the interview seeking confirmatory evidence;

- interviewers place more weight on unfavourable evidence than on favourable evidence since they are looking for reasons not to select rather than reasons to select;

- having made a decision early in the interview, the interviewer's behaviour then betrays the decision to the candidate and this in turn determines in part the behaviour of the candidate setting up a 'self-fulfilling prophecy'.

For these reasons selection interviewers should approach their task with caution. The interviews themselves should be seen as one element in a selection procedure which ideally draws on the structure outlined above and involves other judgement methods.

Documentation and evaluation

Selection procedures should in all cases be fully documented. Thus the reasons why particular attributes appear on the person specification should be identified. A clear and trackable system should be installed for dealing with applications and for communicating appropriately with both successful and unsuccessful candidates at each stage of the procedure.

In particular it is necessary to articulate and record the reasons for selecting and rejecting candidates, and to offer and be prepared to give feedback to candidates on their performance in aspects of the procedures. This is a requirement in the case of aptitude tests and personality inventories. Personality inventories often indicate, in the case of successful candidates, areas for development (the personality will not change but behaviour may be capable of modification) or management concerns which, with the permission of the candidate/employee, could be worked upon.

If it is important to organizations to be able to repose confidence in the correctness of selection decisions, it is surprising that little attention appears to be paid to checking on whether their selection methods used actually work. Few, if any attempts are made to check whether there is any correlation between the selection method used as a predicator of performance in the job and the actual performance of the candidate selected.

As a matter of course those who are responsible for the administration of selection procedures should discuss the performance of those selected with the appropriate line management after management has had an adequate opportunity to assess performance.

Where standardized selection techniques are used to select relatively large numbers of employees, as with graduate recruitment, it is possible to investigate the extent to which there is any correlation between performance on the job and performance in one or more elements of the selection procedure. If a statistically significant correlation can be found, then that particular element should be given greater weight in future selection decisions. On the other hand if little or no correlation is found, then there is an indication that the element is not adding value to the procedure and should in future be dropped or replaced by a different technique.

Induction

Once personnel have been recruited or selected internally into a new job, it is vitally important from the organization's viewpoint that they are inducted effectively. This is because of the costs involved which include:

● the costs of recruitment;

● the costs of re-recruitment;

● the costs within the existing workforce and within the labour market of the formation of an adverse reputation as an employer.

In addition, employers need to take account of the following:

Legal obligations, since effective health and safety training is required by the Health and Safety at Work Act. There is a duty on the employer to treat staff fairly which amongst other things implies that effective job training should be supplied to the employee if a performance standard which is acceptable to the employer is to be reached.

Culture, since recruitment is often a matter of choosing people who will fit in with the "culture" of the organization they are joining. Part of this culture is the set of values that those who belong to it "buy into" or exhibit. Effective recruitment procedures will ensure that many of these values are in place in the recruitment strategy, but for those values which need to be developed the first few months of employment are crucial. If no attention is paid to the newcomer, then this in itself is an exhibition of a cultural value which may be interpreted as "new staff don't matter", or "in this company you have to make your own way", or "you have to prove yourself before you get accepted", or in other ways.

Every exit is an entrance somewhere else. Conversely, every entrance is itself an exit from elsewhere. It is as well to remember this when thinking about the problems of induction from the inductee's viewpoint. At the moment of selection the future inductee is on a high! This state of euphoria is likely to continue for the period between selection and taking up the new position. Then the doubts will begin to creep in:

- "Will I be able to do the job?"
- "Will my new colleagues respect/like me?"
- "Will I respect/like them?"
- "Will I break any of the rules?"
- "Will I get on with my new boss?"

These are some of the major concerns of new employees, and many of them are confirmed in the early days of employment not because of what actually happens but because of what the inductee perceives to be happening.

Accordingly, it is important for the inductee's boss and colleagues to pay more attention to the inductee during the early days of employment than would normally be the case with an established employee.

Planned induction

There are two approaches to planning an induction process, and these should be considered in parallel.

Firstly, from the organization's perspective, it is important to consider what needs to be achieved in order to bring the inductee up to speed and to satisfy the organization's obligations. A useful guide is that provided by ACAS which lays particular emphasis on the importance of specifying whose responsibility it is to carry out each induction task.

Secondly, from the inductee's perspective, it is important that there exists an induction plan which is visible, tangible and available to him.

Induction starts as soon as selection is completed and once the future employee has accepted the job offer which was made. It is not something which can be postponed until the arrival of the inductee. Therefore, the induction plan should chart what needs to be achieved during a timescale which runs from before arrival until a date on which induction can be said to be complete.

The plan should specify requirements in terms of knowledge, tasks and people contact. It will thus help gain the commitment of the inductee by giving him or her targets for achievement.

Combining the ideas of targets and achievements suggests a matrix format. In the following table some possible activities have been included in the boxes as examples:

	SEE	KNOW	DO
BEFORE ARRIVAL	History and rules of the organization	When to arrive	Who to report to
1ST DAY	Induction Plan Manager Immediate workmates	Local rules regarding lunch-time, personal telephone calls, tea breaks, etc.	Locate toilets and canteen, coffee machine, etc.
1ST WEEK	Local or Central Personnel Manager Manager	Completion of an on the job training module	Completion of a work-related self-contained task

What actually loads into each box depends upon many factors such as the nature of the job, the familiarity of the inductee with the organization, the availability of more senior or more remote management to meet the inductee, etc. The matrix can, of course, cover a longer period than up to the end of the first working week.

The important point is that by taking an approach such as this planned induction is ensured. This may turn out to be inadequate, but that can then be rectified the next time there is to be an induction. This emphasizes another point: that at the end of the induction period the inductee should be encouraged to give feedback to the organization regarding what went well and what went not so well with respect to the induction.

Inclusion

Many recruits leave within the first 18 months of employment. There are three broad categories of reasons for this exodus:

1. **Drop out.** This denotes the recognition of a mistake having been made, either by the recruit who realizes that this employment or this employer is not for him or her, or by a

combination of recruit and organization who jointly realize that there is a mismatch. Naturally, given the costs involved, one of the aims of the company's recruitment procedures is to keep the drop out rate as low as possible.

2. **Induction crisis.** This is the term given to a recognized trend which occurs across industry and commerce whereby there is a peak in labour turnover during the first few weeks or months of employment. It is attributed to the discomfort and the feelings of inadequacy which are often experienced by recruits when they begin to realize that the job entails more than they had originally thought. People undergoing an induction crisis should receive a greater amount of managerial attention until the necessary adjustment in their situation has been made.

3. **Lack of inclusion.** Those recruits who do not experience an induction crisis, or who survive it, but nevertheless leave within the first 18 months often cite as their reason for leaving that they were never made to feel that they belonged. Management should respond by asking, belonged to what? Section? Office? Department? Branch? Region? Division? Company?

The answer could, of course, be any or all of the above. However, it is most likely to be the geographical unit in which they worked. This implies that there is a responsibility on all work colleagues to help to include the newcomer as one of the team. It also means that, from the managerial standpoint, there is a positive advantage in the promotion of a reasonable amount of unit-based socialization to which newcomers could be encouraged to contribute.

Rightsizing

The changes which have impacted on the financial services industry particularly since 1986 are well rehearsed. These changes have had a major impact on all business strategies, and have had significant implications for the deployment and management of human resources. As financial services organizations have struggled in the face of competition to manage their labour-intensive cost bases, while at the same time attempting to exploit fully their investment in information technology, there has emerged a need for a radical change in the internal structure of such organizations.

A major change resulting from re-structuring (including the outcomes of mergers and acquisitions) has been the reduction of the workforce. In essence organizations have had to 'downsize'. Cameron (1994) defines downsizing as being "explicitly associated with the strategic impetus to improve organizational productivity, effectiveness and efficiency through an integral set of activities which result in a reduction in employee numbers which also affects work processes." In essence, the cutting of costs by reducing the headcount.

For many financial services organizations while downsizing is a relatively recent experience it is a growing trend. Many organizations in the sector have lacked the necessary techniques to manage downsizing effectively. Much of the literature on downsizing has tended to focus on procedures and technical issues rather than the strategic implications and the 'softer' people issues.

If job losses are a necessary part of re-structuring then the period of re-structuring is likely to be traumatic for all involved. It should be remembered that work not only provides the means for economic existence but also provides many individuals' needs for socialization and status. As a result, any programme of redundancy will disrupt the work and the social lives both of those whose jobs cease to exist and of those who survive within the organization.

Handling Downsizing

Research has demonstrated that the way redundancy is handled can ameliorate the potentially adverse effects. Bailey and Sherman (1988) state that "if handled rationally downsizing can lower costs and increase profitability by eliminating unneeded layers of management, ridding the company of duplication and overlaps, and streamlining decision making".

Before embarking on a downsizing programme, organizations should consider its inevitable costs which include:

- severance packages, early retirement programmes, etc.;
- legal costs (following litigation from disgruntled employees/ unfair dismissal cases);

- replacement costs;

- training costs for personnel who are left but do not have the necessary skills.

Some organizations have failed in their downsizing efforts because they have taken a simplistic approach (e.g. an across-the-board reduction of headcount) which can result in superficial changes rather than challenging how a company does business in terms of reassessing business processes. A broader approach to downsizing involves reviewing all aspects of work processes with a view to a fundamental reassessment of how the firm conducts its business and, where appropriate, a redesign of work processes to produce improved productivity. Essentially, downsizing should be part of a comprehensive change process.

In managing a downsizing strategy the impact on different 'stakeholders' should be considered. These include:

- *victims*, i.e. those who will lose their employment;

- *survivors*, i.e. those who will remain in employment with the organization;

- *implementers*, i.e. those charged with the often stressful task of delivering the unwelcome news to employees;

- *suppliers and customers*, whose relationships with the organization may be disturbed by the personnel and process changes.

The effects on the employees remaining in the organization are often not considered. Redundancy situations can have a dramatic impact on those staying. This is a phenomenon called 'survivors syndrome', and can result in problems for the organization as a result of feelings of guilt, animosity towards management and fears about future job security. All of these factors can undermine the desired outcome of increased productivity.

There is the possibility that a mishandled rightsizing exercise will result in a demotivated and overworked workforce which is untrained in all the tasks it is now expected to perform. In the short term, following a redundancy programme, there may be undesirable effects, such as a decrease in productivity, loyalty and commitment, and an increase in staff turnover as employees spurred by feelings of insecurity seek alternative positions.

The way in which a redundancy policy is implemented impacts upon the survivors whose attitude to their employer will be coloured by their perceptions of the way the redundancy of their former colleagues was handled. This suggests that the more open the organization can be about its redundancy policy, whereby all staff are seen to be treated fairly and sensitively, the more likely it is that surviving staff will wish to retain their link with the organization. It is therefore important that the redundancy strategy is consistent with the corporate culture which includes sensitive management of the firm's human resources.

During a redundancy process account should be taken of each of the following considerations:

a) *Decision mechanisms*: how will the organization arrive at the names of those who will be made redundant?

b) *Communication mechanisms*: how, precisely, will the communication both to potential leavers and survivors be handled?

c) *Packages*: if a redundancy payment which is more than the organization is required by law to offer is to be made available, then the quantum of the payment and the details of any ancillary elements (such as outplacement services) should be determined and, as appropriate, negotiated with the employees' representatives.

d) *Counselling*: if this is to be made available to those affected.

e) *Timing of departures*: a sensitive approach will take into account the requirements of each individual with regard to the timing of severance.

f) *Documentation*: it is imperative that the entire process is seen to be fair and this implies that each stage should be carefully and fully documented.

In making the decision as to which staff should be offered redundancy, the organization should take into consideration not only the skill sets which it will be losing but also the potential age profile of the surviving workforce. In organizations where continuity is important, it is unwise to build a 'generation gap' in the workforce since this could result in a cohort of skill and experience retiring more or less simultaneously at some future date.

Managing rightsizing

As with most other aspects of management activity, it is simplest if rightsizing is approached in a structured way. Applebaum et al (1987) have developed an approach with the following components:

1. Problem recognition and initial decision that greater productivity needs to be achieved.

2. Consideration of solutions which do not involve redundancy. These could include:

   - re-deployment;

   - reduction in overtime;

   - temporary lay-offs;

   - voluntary early retirement;

   - ceasing to use contractors and non-permanent workers (i.e. temporary, casual, fixed-term contracts, self-employed, agency);

   - natural wastage and recruitment restrictions;

   - re-training;

   - reducing bonus levels;

   - permanent reduction in hours.

3. Specific action plans designed to produce the slimmed down future organization replete with the skill sets and age profile necessary for the business to continue.

4. Downsizing programme components, including decision-making, communication, documentation and facilitation mechanisms.

5. Communications and implementation.

6. Assistance to displaced employees.

7. Follow up and rebuilding of the organization.

Throughout this proves the organization's aim is to ensure that the remaining workforce is made up of those skills and 'personalities' which fit with the new-style organization, and that those whose contracts which are to be terminated are dealt with fairly and sensitively.

Summary

This chapter has looked in general at the problems of implementing plans concerning an organization's human resources. It has dealt in detail with the processes involved in the selection, recruitment, induction and reduction of staff.

References

Anderson N & Shackleton V (1990) 'Staff Selection Decision-making into the 1990s', *Management Decision*, Vol. 28, No.1
Applebaum et al (1987) 'Downsizing: The Ultimate Human Resource Strategy', *Business Quarterly*, Vol. 52, No. 2
Bailey G, Sherman D & Tomasko RM (1988) 'The Downside of Downsizing', *Management Review*, Vol. 77, No. 4
Cameron K (1994) 'Strategies for Successful Organizational Downsizing', *HRM Special Issue on Downsizing*, Vol. 33, No. 2
Child I L (1968) 'Personality in Culture', in Borgatta & Lambert ed., *Handbook of Personality Theory and Research*, Rand McNally
Fletcher C (1982) in MacKenzie Davie D & Harris M ed., *Judging People*, McGraw Hill
Fletcher C et al (1990) 'Personality Tests: The Great Debate', *Personnel Management*, September
Hussey D (1982) *Corporate Planning: Theory and Practice*, 2nd ed. Pergamon Press
Mintzberg H (1994) 'The Fall and Rise of Strategic Planning', *Harvard Business Review*, January/February
Rodger, A (1950) National Institute of Industrial Psychology
Webster E C (1964) *Decision Making in the Employment Interview*, Eagle

Wood R & Barron H (1992) 'Psychological Testing Free from Prejudice', *Personnel Management*, December

14 Training, development and appraisal

Objectives

This chapter examines issues surrounding the need for individuals over time to expand their areas of expertise to meet both their own needs and those of their employers.

The detailed objectives of the chapter are:

- to discuss the respective roles of employees, employers and the State in relation to education, training and development;

- to discuss in detail a model for an organizational approach to training and development;

- to emphasize the importance to employees of the link between development and appraisal.

Anyone leaving the education system at the turn of the 20th/21st century can, if able to maintain a relatively full working life, expect to retire around the year 2030. It may be foolish to make such a prediction. What is not so foolish is to predict that the products, services, tools and working methodologies from which that person retires will be radically different from those with which his working life began.

The past 30 years have seen two paradigm shifts in the world of work in Western economies. Firstly came the acceptance of the computer as a key part of many operational systems; secondly came the shift from the mainframe to the networked personal computer as the basis of technology in the workplace.

If there is a single comparable paradigm shift over the next 20 years then employers will make demands of the workforce which are the equivalent of current requirements for computer literacy. This is something which many years of education could not equip the employee for, and for which little useful formal training is available.

This raises important questions in relation to the personal development of employees in the future, including what do we mean by the terms 'training', 'development' and 'education'?, and who has responsibility for ensuring that the workforce continues to develop in ways supportive of the economy?

Training, development and education

Part of the difficulty of describing the differences between these three terms is that from the point of view of organizational systems each term describes what is essentially the same process. Traditional analyses identify that all three are concerned with the inculcation in the individual of knowledge, skills and attitudes and that each, in systemic terms, involves the model:

input $\Rightarrow$ process $\Rightarrow$ output

In the above model **input** can take one or a combination of many forms, including lecture, tutorial, individual reading, overhearing a conversation, watching a television programme, receiving a provocative question, being presented with a challenge, etc. **Process** is the element during which the individual incorporates the input element into his or her frames of reference, and **output** is the way in which what has been learned manifests itself.

The model itself can be applied to all sorts of learning situations from the trivial (for example the incorporation of a new joke into one's personal repertoire), through the somewhat more important (for example driving a car, performing in the workplace or preparation for a university or professional exam), to the absolutely essential (such as working out how to maximize the use of the latest piece of technological wizardry).

As suggested above, an analysis of what has to be learned can be broken down into requirements in terms of knowledge, skill and attitude.

Knowledge is what the learner needs to know in order to achieve specific learning objectives. A generally recognized universal example of this is knowledge of the Highway Code, which is necessary to achieve the status of 'driver'. **Skill** is what the learner needs to be able to do adeptly in order to accomplish the objective, such as stop a car without stalling the engine. **Attitude** dictates the behaviours which it is advantageous for the learner to exhibit in order to accomplish the objective. In the learning to drive example this would be represented by an attitude of respect for other road users.

Most texts on training and development will define knowledge, skill and attitude in terms broadly similar to the above (e.g. Torrington and Hall (1987)). According to Whyte and Plenderleith (1990) a training consultant, Tim Russell, has added a further category of learning which he labels **judgement**. Russell defines this as "the ability to use one's knowledge and skills in such a way as to be able to deal with novel or ambiguous situations. Judgement is the ability to add up all the facts and the issues involved and to come to a decision". A driving example of judgement in action would be the decision on when precisely to begin the manoeuvre of turning from a minor road onto a major road.

Russell further sub-divides skills into mental, physical and social skills, and differentiates between knowledge and skills, on the one hand, and judgement on the other by pointing out that whereas in the case of both knowledge and skill there is always a right answer, and hence a multiplicity of wrong answers, in the case of judgement there is no necessarily correct answer. This concept may be difficult to grasp in relation to skills since different people do things in different ways. Nevertheless in terms of organizational approaches to the training, development and education of personnel, it is useful to be able to distinguish those situations for which it is possible to specify a correct answer or approach from those which call for the exercise of judgement.

Such an analysis is a reminder of the need to define and differentiate between training, development and education. Buckley and Caple (1989), drawing on a number of sources, including the 1978 edition of the Department of Employment's *Glossary of Training Terms*, define these words as follows:

Training: "A planned and systematic effort to modify and develop knowledge/skill/attitude through learning experience, to achieve effective performance in an activity or a range of activities. Its purpose in the work situation is to enable an individual to acquire abilities in order that he or she can perform adequately a given task or job."

Development: "The general enhancement and growth of an

individual's skills and abilities through conscious and unconscious learning."

Education: "A process and a series of activities which aim at enabling an individual to assimilate and develop knowledge, skills, values and understanding that are not simply related to a narrow field of activity but allow a broad range of problems to be defined, analysed and solved."

Relating each of these definitions to work situations and to the expressions defined above, training will be predominantly concerned with ensuring that the learner has sufficient knowledge and skills, coupled with the appropriate attitude towards such things as safety, company procedures, and communication with colleagues to perform in a current job. Development, on the other hand, will aim to equip the employee to move beyond a current job and into a higher-level activity, and thus will concentrate on enhancing skills, inculcating attitudes towards company policies and cultures, and increasing the individual's propensity to make useful judgements in relation to work.

Education, as the definition suggests, has connotations of strategy as opposed to tactics, and will be primarily concerned with knowledge and judgements, and may not be regarded by the employing organization as falling within the ambit of its responsibilities to the employee.

This in turn raises the question as to where responsibility for training, development and education lies, given that the learner must always accept some element of that responsibility.

Possible contenders to be charged with this responsibility in the work, as opposed to the academic, environment include: the State; Research Institutions; the Industry (through for example Industrial Training Boards, Training and Enterprise Councils and Professional Associations); the Employing Organization: Departments/Divisions within that organization; the Employee's line management; and the individual employee.

Many of these elements combine in respect of particular learning experiences, such as the pursuit of professional qualifications. However, in a general sense, it may be reasonable to suggest that:

- the State and research institutions are primarily concerned with education;

- the industry is concerned primarily with training and to a lesser degree with development;

- the organization (given that it is large enough to have departments and/or divisions) is more concerned with development than training;

- the department/division and line management will probably focus on training and discourage (either overtly or covertly) development, since this will promote the idea of job movement beyond the boundaries of the department and thus be wasteful of resources;

- the individual is obliged either to accept responsibility for his or her own training, development and education, or conversely to accept the consequences of ignoring opportunities to become more learned.

The next sections of this chapter will deal with ways in which organizations and individuals can aim to meet their responsibilities in this area.

Organizational approaches to training and development

Given size and complexity, organizations need to develop systemic approaches to the training and development of their employees. However, it should never be forgotten that, unlike other resources at the disposal of the organization, the resources to be trained and developed have their own contributions to make to the process. Therefore, in order for the process to be regarded as successful, these contributions must be taken into account. This naturally gives rise to a difficulty since individuals behave and learn in different ways, some of which will be less conducive to the organization's systems than others.

A good training system will take these individual differences into account and is likely to conform to the pattern shown in Figure 14.1.

The approach to the problem

Ironically it is probably true to say that the key element in the training system is the decision as to whether or not a recognized problem necessitates a training solution. Stripped to its simplest terms, consideration of this question will lead to one of three basic responses:

a) do nothing;

b) resolve the problem by methods which do not involve training;

Figure 14.1

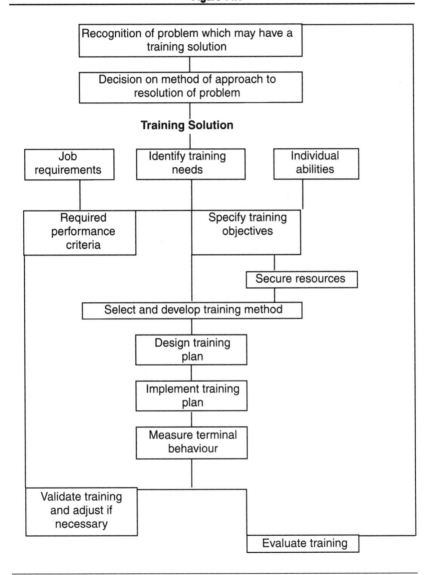

c) resolve the problem through training.

The first of these solutions often appears to be the most attractive since it is presumed to have zero costs. However this argument is often countered glibly by training professionals who state, "if you think training is costly, try ignorance!". Davies (1971) points out the following as possible costs of pursuing this solution:

● additional on-job or other forms of supplementary training;

● slowing down of production;

● under-utilization of machines and equipment;

● increased wastage of materials and damage to equipment;

● increased demands on supervisor's/manager's time;

● increased Health and Safety risks;

● job dissatisfaction;

● poorer service to customers, and thus more time spent in handling complaints and erosion of the customer base;

● decrease in sales.

There is a wide range of possible approaches apart from training which may provide the solution to a work-related problem. These include:

● re-defining work objectives;

● adjusting procedures;

● changing the working environment;

● repairing or improving equipment;

● re-positioning equipment;

● re-allocating work

● re-designing jobs;

● improved supervision;

● replacing untrained staff with trained staff.

Buckley and Caple (1989) suggest that there are fundamental conditions which must apply before it can be concluded that the problem should be solved through training. These conditions are:

1. Training in some form is either

   a) the most effective and appropriate way of overcoming a current or anticipated shortfall in performance, or

   b) training will result in current performance objectives being achieved more economically.

2. Present and future job objectives are clearly linked to the organization's corporate objectives.

The crucial nature of the second condition can be readily appreciated. There is little point in expending resources on developing or improving performance in areas which are not in line with organizational requirements. This in turn emphasizes the importance of the organization determining its strategy, articulating that strategy and developing plans which aim to implement that strategy. Such plans should incorporate the satisfaction of relevant training and development needs.

Organizations are thus concerned with both current and future training needs, where current needs address a particular and identified work problem, and future needs cope with an anticipated problem or a planned change.

An example of a technique which can be employed to determine whether or not a training solution should be applied is a *D I F analysis*. This aims to assess the task in accordance with its level of **D**ifficulty, its **I**mportance (in terms of work or organizational objectives) and the **F**requency with which the task is to be performed.

Figure 14.2 illustrates how DIF might be applied, though the conclusions as to whether or not to train may differ depending on more sophisticated analysis of the three criteria. In this way a DIF analysis might be used to differentiate between different levels of training. Thus a task which was of great difficulty, high importance and low frequency (for example, emergency landing of an aircraft) might require training to the highest level and refreshing training at specified intervals, whereas a task which was of little difficulty, high importance and performed very frequently (for example, the procedural checks to be undertaken prior to an aircraft taking off) might require training to a more moderate level with no formal periodic reinforcement since it is effectively reinforced by frequent repetition.

Figure 14.2

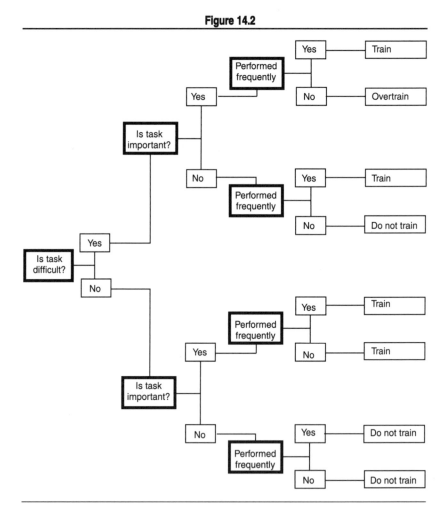

Identification of training needs

Where a decision has been made that a current or anticipated problem is susceptible to a training solution, it becomes necessary to analyse the problem in such a way that training objectives can be specified in terms of knowledge, skills and attitudes (judgements being more in the sphere of development rather than training).

Robbins (1984) puts forward four questions which need to be answered in order to achieve this:

1. What are the organization's goals (note that this can apply both to current problems, where it relates to the performance objectives attached to jobs or to tasks currently undertaken, and to strategic considerations)?

2. What tasks must be completed in order to achieve these goals?

3. What behaviours are necessary for each job holder to complete the assigned tasks?

4. What is the gap between the knowledge, skills and attitude of the current target trainees and those required to exhibit the necessary behaviours?

'Behaviours' is a word with pejorative connotations, particularly in relation to training and development. By emphasising knowledge and skills, elements which in Russell's analysis are capable of being categorized as 'right' and 'wrong', the training need is expressed in ways which are measurable both in an absolute sense and relative to the performance criteria which indicate successful, or better, completion of the task.

Specification of training objectives

In order to stress the importance of an accurate specification of training objectives, it is necessary to outline one of the major obstacles to training being fully effective. This is an obstacle which is well recognized amongst training professionals, but not much appreciated by those who employ them.

It is well known that, in the absence of any planned programme to redress the problem, trainees will fail to retain much of what they have absorbed during a training session. Consequently, within well constructed training programmes, considerable resources are devoted to the reinforcement of what has been learned. In the context of training to perform workplace activities, however, reinforcement adds little value. This is because, although the trainee may retain more whilst undergoing the training, it is of no value to the employer unless what is retained is carried back to the working environment. The issue of 'transfer of training' relates to the difficulty which trainees experience when trying to transfer what they have learnt whilst undergoing training to their workplace.

Positive transfer occurs when the trainee can apply to the job the knowledge, skill and/or attitude gained whilst being trained. Negative transfer arises when performance on the job is hindered by the knowledge, skills and attitudes which have been acquired. Between these extremes is a wide area of 'neutrality', where an enthusiastic trainee returns to the workplace and carries out his or her tasks as if the training had never been undertaken.

Two theories have been advanced to explain the problem of 'transfer of training' (see Buckley and Caple 1989).

1. The 'transfer through principles' theory stresses that during training the trainee should absorb or develop conceptual or behavioural principles which can then be generalized and accessed in order to guide behaviour in the workplace.

2. The 'identical elements' theory holds that the extent to which positive transfer takes place depends fundamentally on the degree to which there are common or virtually identical stimulus and response elements in the training and work situations. Thus if the stimulus experienced in the training situation is exactly the same as the stimulus experienced in the work situation, then it is far more likely that the trainee will reproduce in the work situation the response inculcated during the training.

The 'transfer through principles' theory points to the importance in training programme design of devoting some element of the resources to the 'process' element, and ensuring that trainees have the opportunity to internalize what they are learning. Such an approach would ensure that trainees are themselves guided through all the stages of the 'learning cycle' (see page 361 below).

It is in relation to the 'identical elements' theory that the importance of the correct specification of training objectives can best be illustrated.

As Brian Livy (1988) points out:

> It is not sufficient to describe training objectives in broad, umbrella terms, for example 'to understand how a radio works' or 'to understand an electrical system'. Such statements are vague and ambiguous. What are required are clear and specific

details, preferably formalized as a written statement and spelt
out in precise behavioural, observable and measurable actions
described by an action verb. This means that the desired
terminal behaviour should be specified by name or kind thus:

● *Performance – what the trainee has to be able to do;*

● *Condition – under which the performance has to take place;*

● *Standards – or the level of performance expected.*

An example of specified training objectives which conform to Livy's
criteria would be that by the end of the training, the trainee should be
able to: describe Abraham Maslow's ideas on human motivation during
a written exam, taking no more than five minutes and writing on less
than one side of A4, accurately labelling the behavioural drives and
giving relevant examples of each.

The above example which illustrates a training objective at, say, level
2 also serves as an example of the importance of selecting an apposite
verb. If the same subject were to be treated at, say level 5 (first degree
level), the training objective might be specified as follows. By the end
of the training, the trainee will be able to: **explain** Abraham Maslow's
ideas on human motivation and **apply** them to a case study under exam
conditions, showing a clear understanding of the theory and an ability
to present counter-arguments.

It should be clear that a trainer faced with the second training
objective would construct a radically different training event than if
faced with the first objective.

Secure resources

It is in the nature of organizational training that resources need to be
secured prior to the selection of training methods, although it is perfectly
feasible for the spend on training to be determined only after the format
of the training has been worked out. Ideally these two activities will
proceed in parallel, although it is probably better from the point of
view of discipline if the budget informs the choice of methods rather
than the reverse. This position should be adjusted in the light of any
Difficulty: Importance: Frequency analysis.

Select and develop training methods

The choice of training methods, though possibly constrained by the availability of resources, should be dictated by the training objectives and the analysis of the training need. The knowledge, skill and attitude components which the trainee is required to display following the training should be related to the model:

input   ⇒   process   ⇒   output

Moreover, a training method should be chosen either for each individual component or on the basis that one method will accommodate all the required elements. As an example refer back to the second of the Maslow training objectives above.

Component	KSA?	Input	Process	Output
Maslow's ideas	K	Lecture	Trainees question and absorb	Trainees explain and discuss
Apply	S	Case study	Trainees prepare and present ideas	Trainees critically discuss presentation
Present counter-argument	S	Trainer facilitates challenge to presentation points	Trainees discuss theory and challenges. Trainer encourages generalization	Trainees present conclusions and assess usefulness of Maslow's ideas
Under exam conditions	S (+K)	Trainer sets case study question	Trainees marshal and apply learning	Exam script

Given the precise nature of the training objective it is imperative that a case study is used as the training method relating to the skills of applying Maslow's ideas. It is not essential that the knowledge input is accomplished by a lecture. This could be done through required reading, by showing a video, or by having the trainees build up the theory for themselves through a carefully structured series of questions based, for example, on the order in which Robinson Crusoe satisfied his needs.

The above training programme takes account of another key factor in the process of learning, namely the contribution made by the trainee by virtue of his or her individual learning style.

Early theories of the way in which learning is acquired tended to be founded upon the concept of a stimulus and response mechanism whereby the trainee was trained to produce a specific behaviour in response to a stimulus. Skinner (1953), in experiments with pigeons and rats, showed that the link between a stimulus and the desired response was strengthened if exhibited responses were followed by reinforcement on the part of the trainer (reward for the correct response, punishment for an incorrect one). Skinner's ideas underlie many of the modern approaches to education and training within organizations, particularly programmed training which is habitually designed to give the trainee frequent rewards.

Rival ideas to the stimulus and response school were developed most usefully in the work of Kolb and Fry (1975), who investigated the ways in which people seek and use information in developing concepts. Kolb (1981) developed this work into a 'Learning Style Inventory' which identified four distinct components of a 'learning cycle':

- *Concrete experience* – Learning from experience: relying, as a learner, more on feelings than on thought processes;

- *Reflective observation* – Learning from observation: weighing up different perspectives before making a judgement;

- *Abstract conceptualization* – Learning by thinking about new concepts, ideas, etc. and applying logic to develop intellectual understanding;

- *Active experimentation* – Learning through experimentation: taking a risk by trying something novel.

The theory maintains that each person blends aspects of each of these stages of the learning cycle into his or her personal learning style and that learning is richer if all aspects of the learning cycle are catered for during the training event.

Thus in the Maslow example the preparation for the presentation of ideas caters for concrete experience. During the critical discussion period there is opportunity for reflective observation. In the next discussion period the trainer encourages abstract conceptualization. Finally active experimentation is catered for when the trainee has the opportunity to express his or her ideas on Maslow in relation to a new case study.

Implement training plan

A good training plan will not only seek to achieve the training objectives it will also be designed to ensure that those objectives, when achieved, will be transferred back to the workplace. This means that training is not something which can profitably be considered as divorced from the job.

An effective training plan involves a partnership between the three areas which are fundamentally concerned with the training. These can be described both in an organizational and in a personal sense. They are:

ORGANIZATIONAL	PERSONAL
Line management	The trainee's boss
The training establishment (whether internal or external)	The trainer
Those who need the training	The trainee

The most important contributor to this partnership is the line manager/trainee's boss, who is often referred to as the 'Stakeholder'.

It is the stakeholder who is most interested in seeing that the right needs are identified, the right objectives set, the right training delivered, and that that training is transferred to the working environment of the trainee. Thus the training plan should be agreed with the stakeholder at the organizational level, and at the personal level the stakeholder should positively contribute to the training process by briefing and de-briefing the trainee.

Briefing involves discussing three things with the trainee:

1. Why the trainee is undertaking this training.

2. What the training objectives are.

3. What the trainee's personal objectives are.

De-briefing involves discussing with the trainee:

1. What objectives were achieved.

2. How the stakeholder can help the trainee to ensure that the learning is transferred to the workplace.

Measure terminal behaviour

The importance of the concept of the stakeholder to the success of organizational training is emphasized by the relationship between what gave rise to the training need and the behaviour exhibited by the trainee following the training. If all has gone according to plan then the trainee will have transferred back to the workplace his or her generalizations of the knowledge gained from the training coupled with an appropriate attitude and expanded skill set. If the trainee's behaviour does not match the required behaviour specified in the training objectives then there has been a failure, either of the trainer, or of the trainee, or of the training system. An isolated failure amongst trainees suggests that attention should be given to that particular trainee. General failures amongst a set of trainees suggest that the effectiveness of the trainer should be investigated, and if this is not found to be wanting then there has been some lapse in the administration of the training system.

This in turn stresses the importance to organizations of following a systematic approach to training since it will facilitate a constructive analysis in the light of apparent training failure.

Validation and evaluation of training

Where the two terms are used distinctly, validation of training essentially seeks to establish the extent to which the issue which gave rise to the training need has been effectively resolved. Evaluation seeks to assess whether or not the resolution of this issue has been conducted cost-effectively.

There is often a distinction to be made between internal and external validation. Internal validation is concerned with whether the trainees learned what they were supposed to learn whereas external validation is concerned with establishing whether or not that learning is being applied at work.

Hamblin (1974) and Kirkpatrick (1967) suggest that validation can be carried out at a number of levels:

1. *Reaction*, which is concerned with how the trainees reacted to the training and typically addresses their opinions on:
   - the content of the training (in terms of knowledge and skills);
   - the trainers and the training methods used;
   - the training environment;
   - the extent to which any attitudinal objectives have been met.

   Traditionally this information is collected immediately or very shortly after the training has finished, usually in the form of a tick sheet with very little chance for trainee reflection. More sophisticated methods of garnering reaction can be used, but essentially they are all open to abuse by the trainers whose knowledge of the training content and the structure of the feedback sheet enables them to structure training sessions to produce results which reflect well upon their efforts rather than on the ways in which the trainees have been changed by the training.

2. *Learning*, which is concerned with the extent to which the specific training objectives have been met in the immediate post-training period. Where used, this often takes the form of an end of course assessment which inevitably threatens not only the trainees, but also the trainers and possibly the training itself if it had attitudinal as well as knowledge and skill objectives.

3. *Job*, which is concerned with the changes in the trainees behaviour and performance which result from the training, and which are exhibited back at the workplace. If validation at this level is to take place then it is essential that the integrated approach to training which is at the core of a training system is adopted and that the stakeholder concept is adhered to. Validation at this level is unlikely to be carried out by those who were involved in the implementation of the training plan, and it is only by taking an integrated approach that the training plan and/or its delivery can be adjusted in the light of an unfavourable review at job level.

4. *Organization*, which is concerned with changes in organizational performance which can be attributed to the training undertaken. Inevitably validation at this level is more problematic given the greater length of time between the training and when results begin to manifest themselves. Hence the greater chance that factors other than the training will have influenced performance. Nevertheless there are instances, such as the need to bring about a cultural shift within an organization, or the launch of a new product, where the chain of causation between the training and the outcome is both relatively robust and short. In such cases, building a feedback loop from measured performance back to the issue which gave rise to the training need is likely to be productive.

Training, development, education and the individual

Although it is probably too broad a generalization there is some truth in the idea that, for much of the second half of the twentieth century in Western economies, 'education' was seen as very much the province of the State, while 'training' and, to a lesser extent, 'development' were seen as the responsibility of the employer and industry. In the UK this was achieved through the medium of such institutions as Industrial Training Boards, professional associations and Training and Enterprise Councils.

One of the thrusts of modern educational thinking, fuelled to a large extent by the emergence of communications technology, has been the transference of more and more responsibility for 'education' and 'development' away from institutions to the individual.

The State and institutions play their part in this movement in three ways:

- by the inculcation of the 'core skills of communication, numeracy and information technology' into the workforce of the future;

- by providing a broader based range of possible qualifications, with attainment being marked by awards which follow the successful completion of a number of modules. The next stage in this will be the development of increased co-operation between awarding bodies and deliverers so that increasingly wide combinations of modular studies will lead to the award;

- by providing opportunities for individuals to continue to develop themselves professionally.

The effect of this approach is that the individual is provided with the basic tools needed for him or her to undertake a 'pick and mix' programme of study in order to gain qualifications which are recognized by employers as having a certain level of validity, and thereafter to update their learning in areas which are relevant to their chosen field of work.

Responsibility for choosing modules for study and for continuing development will rest more and more with the individual. Although they may be guided by their employer, with the demise of the 'cradle to grave' approach to working life the principle stakeholder in the process is the individual.

This implies that the individual, equipped with core skills, should mark out an 'education and development' strategy as a framework for maintaining parity of qualification with a field of future competitors which is likely to be continually expanding as the age range of possible job holders widens.

There may then be a tension between the individual and the employer since the employer, in the capacity of the provider of 'training', may require greater and greater specialization, whilst the individual is looking for more and more diversification. This could be resolved by an enlightened attitude on the part of employers and by encouraging the 'development' of employees into their future role which may or may not be with that employer. An employer who seeks to bring in talent from outside the organization rather than develop it internally must logically encourage the maintenance of a pool of talent within the potential employees in the sector.

Amongst the components which are important to the individual in deciding the course of continued development will be an awareness of the match between the attributes which it is perceived the individual has and those which are perceived to be fundamental to the areas in which the individual wishes to seek future employment, whether within or outside the current organization. In this respect any appraisal system operated by the organization is of interest to the individual.

Appraisal

The traditional view of organizational appraisal systems is that they were designed to provide a linkage between performance and some other aspect of life within an organization, usually the organizations training system. Various methods of appraisal have been devised whereby some aspect of an individual's contribution to the organization is measured, with some attempt at objectivity, with a two-fold objective:

- to provide the organization with some information on the totality of its workforce;
- to provide individuals with some information on how they could improve their chances of succeeding within the organization.

As with training systems, there are three essential 'participating elements' in an appraisal system:

- the organization, which devises and administers the system;
- the appraisee;
- the appraiser, usually, but not necessarily, the appraisee's line management.

Torrington and Hall (1987) point out that:

> *We all constantly appraise, consciously or unconsciously, objectively or subjectively. When we appraise something we rate its worth, its usefulness and the degree to which it displays various qualities ... we appraise behaviour, personality and systems.*

Any organizational appraisal system imposes a level of formality on this process of informal appraisal between an appraiser and an appraisee, and as such may well add direct value to the appraisal itself.

Most organizational appraisal systems have however been designed not only to provide a linkage between these two aspects of organizational life, but also to serve additional organizational needs amongst which have been found:

- assessment for reward
- assessment of training needs
- career development
- identification of potential
- manpower planning

- motivation
- performance improvement
- performance management
- succession planning

Randell et al (1984) suggest that the organizational uses of appraisal can be divided into three broad categories which are concerned with:

- performance
- potential
- reward

They argue that, to be effective, an organizational appraisal system should be designed to satisfy only one of these categories. This implies that the whole of the appraisal apparatus (which includes forms, procedures, instructions, training, and contributions from employees) should be geared consistently towards meeting the requirements of the chosen category, and not be contaminated by having to satisfy the requirements of another category. This, of course, gives rise to problems. For instance, how many systems should an organization install, and if reward reviews are distinguished from performance reviews then how is performance to be linked to reward?

Figure 14.3

Uses of organizational appraisal system	Blue collar	%	White collar	%	Management	%
Concerned with performance	249	64.2	711	63.0	801	62.5
Concerned with reward	35	9.0	92	8.2	104	8.1
Concerned with potential	98	25.3	314	27.8	368	28.7
Other	6	1.5	11	1.0	9	0.7
Totals	**388**		**1128**		**1282**	

Figure 14.3 shows an interpretation of results obtained by Torrington and Hall (1987) from a survey of 350 organizations in answer to the question: "for which of the following purposes is your performance appraisal system used?". Organizations tended to appraise management and 'white collar' staff to a greater extent than 'blue collar' staff but, irrespective of the category of staff appraised, the appraisal systems seem to be used predominantly for concerns relating to performance (which included assessment of training and development needs). Note, however, that in the case of management, for example, a survey of 350 firms elicited more than 3.5 times that number of responses. This suggests that the appraisal systems served multiple purposes and thus did not conform to the design proposal of Randell and his colleagues.

Although it may seem cynical to suggest that this is the case, there is the possibility that the main justification for any organizational appraisal system is to ensure that an appraisal of its staff actually takes place. As Torrington and Hall point out, we all appraise. However to the extent that this is unconscious and subjective our appraisals may be of little use to the potential principle beneficiary, i.e. the appraisee. The requirements of an appraisal system will probably ensure that appraisals are articulated and made available to the appraisee who, amongst other things, will then obtain some guidance as to the areas in which to seek development and education.

Given the thrust towards the individual accepting responsibility for his or her development it seems probable that the future use of appraisal systems will be geared more towards satisfying the needs of the appraisees rather than those of the organization. In this respect, the traditional criticisms of appraisal systems (that they lack objectivity, measure the wrong thing, and are contaminated by the needs of other organizational systems, etc.) will no longer be relevant.

Summary

This chapter has examined critically the approaches taken by modern organizations to the training, developing and appraisal of employees. Emphasis has been laid in particular on the role of the individual in relation to his or her personal development.

References

Buckley R & Caple J (1989) *The Theory and Practice of Training*, Kogan Page

Davies I K (1971) *The Management of Learning*, McGraw-Hill

Hamblin A C (1974) *Evaluation and Control of Training*, McGraw-Hill

Kirkpatrick D L (1967) 'Evaluation of Training' in Craig and Bittel eds. *Training and Development Handbook*, McGraw-Hill

Kolb D A (1981) 'Learning Style' *Inventory*, McBer

Kolb D A & Fry R (1975) 'Towards an Applied Theory of Experiential Learning of Group Processes' in Cooper C L *Theories of Group Processes*, Wiley

Livy B ed. (1988) *Corporate Personnel Management*, Pitman Publishing

Randell G, Packard P & Slater J (1984) *Staff Appraisal*, Institute of Personnel Management

Robbins S P (1984) *Personnel: the Management of Human Resources* Prentice Hall

Skinner B F (1953) *Science and Human Behaviour*, Macmillan

Torrington D & Hall L (1987) *Personnel Management – a New Approach* Prentice Hall

Whyte I & Plenderleith J (1990) *Management* 2nd ed, Chartered Institute of Bankers

15 Motivating employees

Objectives

In this chapter the different approaches to rewarding and motivating individuals in the organization are explored. The chapter begins by examining the different historical approaches to motivating people at work and then continues by examining the different reward systems in operation in organizations.

The detailed objectives of this chapter are to:

- understand the theoretical framework of motivation and its application in the areas of job evaluation, work and job design;
- understand organizational reward systems;
- be able to grasp the significance of motivation and reward.

Introduction

The issue of motivation arises when trying to understand why people behave as they do. Motivation examines an individual's needs, motives, goals, drives and incentives. The study of motivation began several decades ago, in times of prosperity with low unemployment and a tendency for individuals to change jobs frequently. The studies tried to determine the features that could create a stable and contented workforce and thereby increase productivity and skill. Although relatively full employment is not a feature of the labour market today, the implications of motivation for skill and productivity have meant that it continues to be an area of research.

An efficient organization, it is believed, will have a well-motivated workforce so research has been directed towards discovering the conditions that create this type of employee. The later part of this chapter therefore concentrates on examining how organizations have sought to create this motivation in its employees, through payment systems, job design and fringe benefits.

Approaches to motivation

There have been many definitions of motivation. Mitchell (1982) identifies four common characteristics found in the many definitions:

1. Motivation is an individual phenomena because every person is unique.

2. Motivation is described as intentional and under the employee's control. They have choices for action.

3. Motivation is multi-faceted – the two key factors are what arouses people and the desire or force of the individual to engage in desired behaviour.

4. Motivational theories try to predict behaviour.

There are several groups of theories that have tried to discover what determines motivation as defined above. These now appear to form four major approaches:

- economic, traditional or utilitarian view of man, which is the earliest approach;

- human relations view (also known as social man);

- self-actualizing view;

- the complex man view or process theories.

It is also possible to group all these theories into two broader areas: content theories and process theories. Content theories are regarded as encompassing the economic, human relations and self-actualizing approaches whilst the process grouping refers to the complex man theories.

The content theories assume that all individuals possess the same set of needs, and recommend ways to satisfy individuals as well as characteristics that should be present in jobs.

The process theories stress that all individuals are different, and part of the skill of management is to grasp and accept the various aspects of temperament and ability and match these differences to job requirements so that the individual can achieve personal goals as well as organizational ones.

The next sections considers the content theories and then moves on to discuss the process ones.

Content theories

The economic, traditional view or utilitarian man

This traditional approach to motivation and encouraging a satisfactory level of employee involvement and effort is expressed in McGregor's Theory X already discussed in Chapter 7. In this view it was felt that people did not enjoy work and were only interested in earning money. McGregor (1960) put forward a series of assumptions that would support this view.

The assumptions can be summarized as follows: people need to be controlled and threatened before they put enough effort into work. It can be described as the 'carrot and stick' approach to motivation and is based on the belief that employees are motivated only by economic needs. This links back to the work of F W Taylor who believed that workers are motivated by the amount of their wages. This is also referred to as the rational-economic view of man.

The human relations view or social man

There are a number of theories which could be grouped under this broad heading. The earliest could be termed 'social man'. This view developed from the Hawthorne Experiments conducted by Elton Mayo which were described in Chapter 6. They supported the concept that man is a social animal who gains a sense of identity, self-respect and fulfilment from his social relationships. To rationalize work, and take out the social element, takes away the meaning of work. According to this theory there is a need to build social relationships into jobs and design organizations around work groups.

Self-actualizing man

These theories developed from the concept that man is self-motivated and self-controlled. This view maintains that the usual managerial actions tend to reduce autonomy and so reduce motivation, and can be summarized in McGregor's Theory Y (1960). People enjoy working and can exercise their own control over work. The writers in this group adopted a psychological orientation and focused attention on the content and meaning of the task in trying to make job content more satisfying.

Having outlined the various approaches of the content theories several key theories will be examined in some detail.

Maslow's hierarchy of needs (1943)

This is one theory that could be said to belong to the self-actualizing approach. Peoples' needs are arranged in a hierarchy, and once one need is satisfied individuals move on to the next level. Unsatisfied lower-order needs take precedence over higher-order needs and as the lower-order needs are satisfied, the higher-order needs begin to motivate behaviour. This is illustrated in Figure 15.1. The most basic need is physiological followed by security, social, ego and self-actualization.

The implications are that:

- management must find out where individuals are placed on the hierarchy;
- the organization will gain most by satisfying the lower-order needs, because then an individual will be motivated by praise rather than by money;
- organizations need to be able to satisfy different levels of needs for different individuals.

Although Maslow's theory is intuitively appealing, when closely examined a number of problems seem to present themselves.

1. Can the theory be put into effect? Since there is no timescale to indicate when satisfaction is supposed to occur at a particular level, the organization will need to be constantly checking and rechecking the satisfaction level of employees. Moreover many employees satisfy some of their needs outside of work.

2. Although Maslow implied that the needs pattern could vary between individuals, there is no acknowledgement that different individuals put different values on the needs, which are often shaped by personality and the environment.

3. It is difficult to fit motivators into categories, e.g. a company car satisfies both physiological and ego needs.

Figure 15.1: Maslow's Hierarchy of Needs

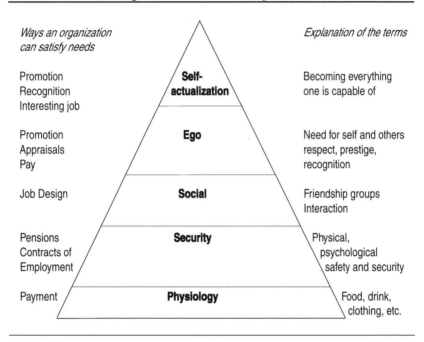

*Ways an organization
can satisfy needs*

Explanation of the terms

Promotion
Recognition
Interesting job

**Self-
actualization**

Becoming everything
one is capable of

Promotion
Appraisals
Pay

Ego

Need for self and others
respect, prestige,
recognition

Job Design

Social

Friendship groups
Interaction

Pensions
Contracts of
Employment

Security

Physical,
psychological
safety and security

Payment

Physiology

Food, drink,
clothing, etc.

4. Research carried out into Maslow's theory has found no empirical evidence to support his views. Lawler and Suttle (1972) found no evidence to indicate that 'satisfied' needs become any less important than 'unsatisfied' ones, or that the satisfaction of lower-level needs raised the importance of higher-level ones.

Despite these problems Maslow's framework is a convenient means of viewing the different needs and expectations.

Herzberg's two-factor theory

This theory evolved in the late 1950s from a survey undertaken among 203 engineers and accountants which asked them what made them feel exceptionally good or bad at work. The items falling into the former category were:

- achievement;
- recognition;
- work itself;
- responsibility;
- advancement.

In the latter category were:

- company policy and administration;
- supervision received;
- salary;
- interpersonal relations;
- working conditions.

Herzberg (1974) drew the conclusion that factors in the work situation fell into two categories:

1. Those that led to satisfaction and were intrinsic to the job: *motivators* (the first set of factors listed above).

2. Those that were extrinsic to the job: *hygiene factors*. Although these could prevent dissatisfaction to some extent, they never provided true satisfaction (the second set of factors above).

There are a number of implications for management of Herzberg's view. If managers wish to motivate employees they can only do so through job content. Pay increases or better working conditions cannot alone increase motivation, because it is a progressive need, and the employee can never become completely satisfied. Autonomy and responsibility for organizing and controlling one's own work is the real answer. No amount of environmental improvement can compensate for task impoverishment.

There are, however, some problems with Herzberg's two-factor theory:

- the theory is method bound, so if the same methodology is used the same results are always obtained, but if more searching questions are asked the results are not the same (King 1970);

- the two groups of factors are not as mutually exclusive as

Herzberg suggested. Motivators can also act as sources of dissatisfaction.

However Herzberg's contribution is still considered to be important as he established the theoretical basis for job enrichment and new job designs. This will be explored later in the chapter.

McClelland's theory

In another content theory, McClelland (1988), who developed his ideas in the 1970s, cited various needs and motives (over 40 in total) which are of importance to individuals and which act as factors to influence behaviour and reactions. Several needs, which McClelland claimed are of particular importance in today's work environment, include those for achievement, the power motive, the affiliative motive and the avoidance motive.

Individuals differ in the extent to which they experience the different needs and motives. In order to assess this, McClelland used TAT (thematic apperception tests), which are a mixture of pictures to interpret verbal questions and problems. The role of management is to determine the level of needs an individual possesses and assign organizational duties in line with this.

McClelland suggested that an effective manager should possess a high need for power but also be concerned with group goals. However, McClelland has been criticized because of the lack of empirical support for the theory. He has also been criticized for the unreliability of the TAT stories and pictures and the lack of attention given to the issue of how the needs interact with other organizational factors.

The complex man view or process theories

The more recently expressed views on motivation (from the late 1960s) accept that people may have hierarchies of needs, but maintain that these hierarchies can change as circumstances change. People are individuals with many needs and can respond to a variety of managerial strategies. Their reactions are dependent upon the situation and the need, which are dominant at the time.

This view of motivation, together with some of the problems associated with the earlier theories, gives an indication that simple content theories of motivation are not enough to account for behaviour in organizations. The earlier models do not explore individual contexts and how individuals understand, attach meaning to and interpret the work situations they find themselves in. As a result there have developed a series of theories that tried to explain motivation in terms of the process. One major theory in this area is the 'Expectancy Theory' developed by Porter and Lawler (1968). They describe motivation as a function of the relationship between effort expended and perceived level of performance, the expectation that rewards will be related to performance and the expectation that rewards are available. These relationships determine the strength of the motivational link as illustrated in Figure 15.2.

Figure 15.2: Adapted from Porter and Lawler's Expectancy Model of Motivation

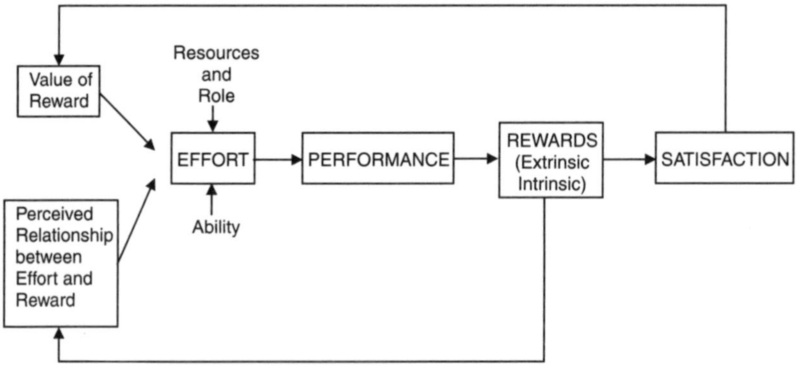

An individual has a need, say, for promotion. This leads the person to put in greater effort to secure promotion. However, performance is also influenced by his or her ability and role perception (the training the individual received, work delegated, whether the individual has confidence in his or her own managerial ability, etc.). If the individual receives the reward, i.e. promotion, satisfaction will be experienced and this leads the person to put in greater effort again. If there is no reward in the form of promotion, the individual will feel dissatisfied and motivation will fall.

The advantages of this theory of motivation are that:

● it is a comprehensive approach incorporating many variables. Instead of promotion it could be examination success, a company car, etc., as the need which is experienced by individuals;

- there is an emphasis on feedback and its importance;

- it takes account of the many intervening factors that determine motivation and attitudes to work;

- it draws attention to the complex nature of work motivation.

The theory states that people are only likely to exert some effort when they value the rewards and believe they will get these rewards as a result of performance. An individual's social background can greatly affect their valuation of different kinds of reward. Some groups may strive for improved social status, others will not. It cannot be assumed, and the theory quite rightly allows this, that work is the central life interest. The importance of work may vary with socio-economic background, and also with age, sex, etc. The theory also accepts that the people the manager is trying to motivate may not believe that their effort will result in the offered reward. Similarly the effectiveness of effort is influenced by their own skills, the resources available to them and their own perceptions of their role. The model also assumes that the theory only applies to behaviours under the control of the individual.

However, there are still a number of difficulties with the theory that have to be resolved:

- it has become very complex because it tries to incorporate so many variables;

- it tends to concentrate on prediction in terms of present events, e.g. how the needs relate to current work attitudes and behaviour, rather than how the needs arise in the first place. (Why does one individual feel the need to be promoted and another does not?)

Managers often hope that there is a theory of motivation which can be applied to unmotivated employees. They are usually disappointed. The value of studying motivation lies in helping people think about their own views (and perhaps prejudices) on the matter. The employees which managers are trying to motivate often see the world quite differently, and it may be the employees' perceptions that managers should consider more frequently.

Having explored the theories underpinning the area of motivation some consideration needs to be given to the methods used by organizations to try and motivate employees. These methods of reward management include both extrinsic and intrinsic factors.

Extrinsic rewards consist of salary, pay in kind and deferred pay such as pensions. Intrinsic rewards are associated with the satisfaction derived from work itself and have grown in importance over the last few years as delayering and tighter salary budgets have reduced the role played by promotion and pay increases as motivational tools. It is the area of intrinsic rewards that will be explored first.

Intrinsic rewards

Job design

The application of motivational theories has led to an increasing interest in job design and the effect of this on motivation and work performance. New job design tries to accommodate personal and social needs at work through the reorganization and restructuring of tasks. It therefore helps in enhancing personal satisfaction and makes best use of people (an expensive resource today.) The content theories of motivation, especially Herzberg, assume a direct relationship between job satisfaction and improved performance. The process theories recognize the complexity of individuals and consider the relationship between satisfaction and performance in more detail.

The level of job satisfaction can be affected by a wide range of variables including: the individual (personality, education, etc.), social factors (the relationship between co-workers, groups, etc.), cultural factors (underlying attitudes, beliefs and values), the organization (its nature and size, formal structures) and the environment (economic and social factors).

In Chapter 6 the issue of employee control over the environment was explored and how methods of work advocated by the Classical school could increase feelings of alienation and powerlessness. Much research work carried out in the 1960s and 1970s tried to develop new job designs and to increase the personal satisfaction of the employee derived from work, making the best use of people as a resource. In order to increase satisfaction these new job designs should emphasize, according to Hackman and Oldham (1980), three key areas:

- work should be experienced as meaningful, worthwhile and important;
- workers must experience that they are responsible for the work outcome and accountable for the products of their efforts;
- workers must determine how their efforts are working, the results achieved and whether they are satisfactory.

These three features are most likely to be achieved if there is present in the core activities of the job:

- *skill variety:* the degree to which a job requires the worker to perform activities that challenge a variety of skills and abilities;
- *task identity:* the degree to which a job requires the completion of a whole piece of work with a seen outcome;
- *task significance:* the degree to which the job has a perceivable impact on the lives of others;
- *autonomy:* the extent to which the worker has freedom in scheduling work and determining how it will be carried out;
- *feedback :* the degree to which the worker gets information about his efforts from the work or his supervisors;
- *development:* the opportunity to develop in the job.

There was a major research study carried out by the Department of Employment into job design in the UK during the 1970s, which was entitled, *On the Quality of Working Life.* The research involved establishing evidence about desirable task characteristics aimed at increasing job satisfaction and motivation. It suggested:

- combining tasks to create a coherent whole job, either using independent tasks or related ones, so that their performance makes a significant contribution to the job holder;
- providing feedback on performance both directly and through others;
- providing a degree of discretion and control in the timing sequence and pace of work and effort;
- including a degree of responsibility for outcomes.

Within the job there should be an opportunity for learning and problem solving within the individual's competence. It should be seen as leading toward a desirable future and provide opportunities for development in ways that are relevant to the individual. The job should also enable workers to contribute to the decisions that affect their jobs, whilst providing adequate resources and support and ensuring that goals and expectations are clear.

Within these criteria a number of different forms of new job design have evolved, including job rotation, job enlargement, group working and job enrichment.

Job rotation

This is perhaps the most basic form of individual job design. Job rotation involves moving a person from one job or task to another. It helps to add variety and relieve boredom in the short term because it offers a wider range of tasks to perform. Normally the tasks are very similar and once a routine is established a worker can become very bored again. Job rotation may add to the range of skills a person possesses, but they are not usually skills of a different level.

Some theorists would claim that it is not really job design because it does not attempt to restructure jobs, but rather gives a worker the opportunity to do different tasks.

Job enlargement

This emerged during the 1940s and 1950s as a response to high task specialization. It offers employees a greater variety of operations with longer cycle times, and it requires a wider range of skills. There is normally an enlargement of tasks horizontally as well as greater latitude given to workers to determine methods and procedures.

It is not always a popular technique when employed in organizations. Workers may view it as increasing the number of routine boring tasks, and as a means of increasing productivity and reducing the number of employees.

Job enrichment

The basis for this concept lies in Herzberg's two-factor theory of motivation. Motivators are intrinsic to the job and offer the opportunity for achievement, recognition, advancement, etc. Motivators determine the extent to which a person is satisfied by a job.

Job enrichment offers vertical job enlargement. Workers are given greater autonomy over the planning, execution and control of their own work. It increases the complexity of work and provides a more meaningful and challenging job. It would mean, for example, not only assembling a product but also pacing the work, receiving feedback on the product and checking its quality. It emphasizes greater control for the employee. As with job enlargement, some employees view this as worker intensification, rather than as an explicit organizational strategy of developing and motivating staff.

Group working

This emphasizes the achievement of the group through its work. The group assumes greater responsibility for the effective performance of the work. Specific goals are set, but the members decide how the goals are to be achieved and have greater choice and wider discretion over the planning and control of their work as a group. This technique ensures that the technological process is integrated with the social system and so becomes a socio-technical method.

The organization's choice of job design will ultimately depend on its philosophy and structure. Is it person-centred or job-centred? Does it aim to achieve technical efficiency or individual satisfaction through work? How much organizational control and managerial direction can be surrendered to individual authority and responsibility? These and similar factors will determine an organization's approach to job design and whether any change in redesign is truly possible.

More recently greater emphasis has been placed by organizations on autonomy and feedback rather than on other core dimensions of job design. Many organizations have introduced empowerment, and so given greater authority for action to employees. The area of empowerment has been explored in greater detail in Chapter 7.

Before focusing upon the extrinsic reward systems used by organizations and how they are implemented, the next section will examine the procedures which allow an organization to establish relative criteria for the value of a job. These processes are termed job evaluation systems.

Job evaluation processes

Job evaluation is defined by Armstrong (1993) as:

The process of establishing the value of jobs in a job hierarchy.

Although it is possible to determine job values by negotiation or on the basis of broad assumptions about market rates and internal relations, a more analytical approach can be adopted using a job evaluation scheme, with market rates and pay surveys. One of the major causes of industrial unrest is said to be the differential argument. Individuals or groups believe that they are not being fairly rewarded as individuals. A good job evaluation scheme should help to remove some of these major sources of conflict. However, conflicts can still arise over the value assigned to a job by the organization and grievance procedures can then be used to resolve such disputes.

The aims of job evaluation are to:

- provide a rank order of jobs for the organization. This can then be used to determine the salary level and the status of any job position;

- ensure judgements about job values are made on objective grounds;

- provide a continuing basis for assessing the value of jobs.

There are two major categories of job evaluation techniques: the quantitative and non-quantitative. The quantitative techniques involve allocating points or values to the various elements of jobs, which are then combined to form a whole, whereas the non-quantitative method involves the comparison of the whole or parts of jobs and places them in a rank order. There are two major non-quantitative schemes: job ranking and job classification, which is sometimes termed grade description.

Points rating

This system breaks down each job into a series of factors. Each factor is allowed a maximum number of points. Through the system of maximum points each factor is weighted to award importance. The total number of points awarded to a job will decide the grade of the job.

All systems of job evaluation use job analysis and description. It is only when a job has been analysed and its duties described that it can be accurately evaluated and placed in a rank order.

Similarly the benchmark jobs or an established system of grading like HAY/MSL can be used. The benchmark jobs represent a particular grade within the job evaluation system. These jobs are recognized as standard and have an agreed value assigned to them and so provide help with the position of other posts. The HAY/MSL scheme is one commonly used in the financial services sector. This concentrates upon know-how, accountability and problem solving as three key components in grading jobs.

Job evaluation does involve (whichever system is used) some subjectivity, as human judgement must be used to establish an order of jobs or assigning values to them. This in turn means that the job evaluation system must allow employees the right of appeal against a particular evaluation. It will normally be heard by a separate appeal panel who will check that the job has been evaluated correctly using information previously provided and any new evidence.

Job ranking

This ranks jobs by comparing whole job descriptions. A paired comparison method is sometimes used, where two jobs are compared. In such cases two points are awarded to the higher ranking post, one where each is considered to be of equal rank, and none to the lower ranking job.

Job classification or grade description

This job evaluation scheme begins with a series of hierarchical grades. Each one is then assigned a description or classification. The description has to cover the various duties that may be involved in the post, but includes enough detail to make the classification of jobs clear. It must detail the type of work as well as the level of ability and provide key jobs for the identification of grades. Each job within the organization can then be slotted into the appropriate grade.

The alternative quantitative methods of job evaluation aim to make the process as objective as possible.

Having considered the issue of job evaluation processes, the next section of this chapter will examine the issue of extrinsic reward structures.

Extrinsic reward structures

It has been widely acknowledged that a number of significant changes have occurred in the nature of extrinsic reward packages over the last ten to fifteen years (Armstrong 1993).

The traditional view of extrinsic rewards was characterized by:

- a belief in equity with maintenance of internal relativities;

- a tendency to focus on the pay arrangements for groups of staff rather than individuals;

- a concern for clarity and order with structured rigid pay schemes and clear rules for progression;

- a wide range of fringe benefits established to cope with the lack of differentials arising from the past incomes policies;

- an emphasis on job evaluation as a means of establishing new pay levels.

The new approach to extrinsic reward systems which has evolved over the last decade has emphasized:

- pay systems need to be market-driven, since external factors are more important than internal relationships in pay;

- individual rather than group focus, with individual contracts of employment and individually agreed levels of pay;

- flexibility with an ability to respond to organizational changes and to move in line with the business;

- integrated pay systems;

- a move away from fringe benefits to cash-based rewards;

- an emphasis on getting value for money.

Some of these elements have had much more of an impact than others. Paying for performance has been widely adopted in most financial services organizations but most still use a job evaluation system and have retained fringe benefits for senior staff.

There are a number of different pay systems in common use within the financial services sector, which can be broadly grouped into salary systems, and performance-related pay.

Salary systems

Most salary systems provide the opportunity for progression either according to age or to experience. This opportunity for progression provides motivation for improved performance in the future as well as encouraging high fliers to remain with the firm. In order to ensure that a progressive system is as efficient as possible and can be easily controlled, it needs to:

- be divided into defined areas or zones;
- have incremental systems to indicate the rates at which individuals can progress;
- have guidelines for determining merit increments.

Incremental systems can vary from rigid fixed procedures to flexible systems where management has complete discretion over the award. Within financial services organizations, the incremental system is fairly tightly controlled with a scale of increments according to performance.

There are a number of advantages and disadvantages associated with salary scale systems. It is perceived to offer several advantages, including:

- it is clear and available to employees;
- it is predictable, so budgets can be anticipated for employer and employee;
- it offers incremental rises;
- performance bonuses can still be incorporated.

However, it is acknowledged that problems also exist with their use:

- salary is paid irrespective of results and effort;
- pay structures are rigid;
- it encourages promotion because this is the only way of really increasing income substantially;
- there can be anomalies between grades.

Performance-related pay

With less opportunity for promotion and fewer layers of management, many financial services organizations have adopted performance-related pay (PRP). In this way good performance can continue to be rewarded and recognized when no promotion opportunities exist.

Although many organizations in the financial services sector have moved towards adopting a system of performance-related pay, there appears to be no agreement on how effective this system of payment can be. There are two main groups of opponents:

1. Those who believe that there is something fundamentally flawed about PRP, especially when it is used on an individual basis, and no amount of investment in its design and implementation will address this issue.

2. Those who believe that the system is basically sound, but that it is the failure to learn from and correct the faults that has caused problems to arise.

Those belonging to the first group would argue that the assumption that money motivates employees to higher effort is flawed, and that rather than motivating the whole workgroup only a few are favoured under PRP. This is seen to lead to a lack of motivation for the majority of the whole workforce. It is also suggested that PRP has been developed from payment schemes relating to the manufacturing industries, and that is not appropriate for roles where no quantitative judgements can be made.

The disadvantages of using PRP could be summarized as follows:

● it is not always easy to set targets for individuals to achieve since some are qualitative rather than quantitative measures, and this can be time consuming and costly;

● the setting, monitoring and evaluation of performance against targets is time consuming;

● it is not always easy for the employee to budget because income is uncertain;

● salaries cannot be published as there is no uniform standard or scale;

● it can be very difficult to judge performance objectively, especially where the employees' performance may be measured in qualitative terms.

However others would argue that PRP offers some significant advantages, namely:

● rewards should be related to effort;

- there is not the same necessity to promote in order to increase rewards;

- the system can be integrated with corporate goals and an MBO system;

- it is easy to incorporate into an organization if it can use quantitative targets to assess performance against;

- it can be used to reward correct behaviour;

- it encourages the achievement of targets and increased productivity can fund the increased pay.

Within the financial services sector as well as and linked to the move towards performance-related pay, there has also been a move towards broad banding of salaries in line with delayering. This move towards broad banding de-emphasizes status and grading, reduces the pressure for promotion and regrading, blurs the edges around pay decisions, and makes it easier to move people laterally across the organization.

Skill-based pay

Based on the concept that individuals are valuable to the organization if they are highly skilled, some organizations are considering a payment system based on skills or competencies. This system is not widely in use at the present time. Some of the problems which organizations need to address relating to it include, how to assess an individual's level of skill and how to prevent paying an individual for a skill they do not currently use in their job role, although they may have used it in the past.

Fringe or additional benefits

Within most salary systems there is a range of additional benefits which are available for different categories of staff, for example:

- bonus schemes, profit sharing;

- non-contributory pension schemes;

- low interest housing and assistance with transfers;

- sick pay;

- paid holidays;

- company cars;

- medical benefits.

Some organizations are now introducing cafeteria or flexible benefits systems to allow the employee to select an individually tailored package of benefits from those on offer. The hope is that this will benefit the employer in both recruitment and retention by providing a competitive edge.

Summary

Despite the vast numbers of theories and studies on the relationship between job satisfaction and work performance there are still conflicting views on how to best manage an organization so as to have high job satisfaction and high levels of productivity. It seems that there are three key recommendations:

1. *An individual orientation system* – based on traditional good management, and structuring work so that it is rewarding to the individual.

2. *Group orientation* – structuring work around groups and rewarding on a group basis.

3. *Organizational orientation* – gaining satisfaction from contributing to the welfare of the organization as a whole. There are few status differentiators and rewards are company-based with option bonuses and profit sharing.

The skill lies in managing these different levels of motivation and reward.

It is perhaps by viewing the areas of motivation, job design and reward systems holistically that there is the most to gain. The contribution of theory on a motivational environment needs to be considered in line with the rewards on offer, both intrinsically and extrinsically.

In the next chapter the issues of legislation and employee disciplinary and grievance procedures are considered.

References

Armstrong M (1993) *Managing Reward Systems*, Open University Press
Hackman J R & Oldham G R (1980) *Work Redesign*, Addison Wesley

Herzberg F (1974) *Work and the Nature of Man*, Granada Publishing

King N (1970) 'A Clarification and Evaluation of the Two-Factor Theory of Job Satisfaction', *Psychological Bulletin*, Vol. 74, pp 18-31

Lawler E E & Suttle J L (1972) 'A Causal Correlational Test of the Need Hierarchy Concept', *Organizational Behaviour and Human Performance*, Vol. 7, pp 265-287

Maslow A H (1943) 'A Theory of Human Motivation', *Psychological Review*, Vol. 50

McClelland D C (1988) *Human Motivation*, Cambridge University Press

McGregor D (1960) *The Human Side of Enterprise*, Penguin

Mitchell T R (1982) 'Motivation, New Directions for Theory, Practice and Research', *Academy of Management Review*, Vol. 7 No. 1, pp 80-88

Mullins L J (1996) *Management and Organizational Behaviour*, 4th ed. Pitman

Porter L W & Lawler E E (1968) *Managerial Attitudes and Performance*, Irwin

16 Employment legislation and policies

Objectives

This chapter focuses on some of the issues which influence employee relations, namely those relating to terms of employment, health and safety, equal opportunities, grievance and disciplinary procedures.
The objectives of this chapter are to:

- examine the theories and application in the following areas: equal opportunities, disciplinary and grievance procedures, employee relations policies;

- understand the significance of the managerial processes of exiting and counselling.

Introduction

The employment relationship is an important factor in managing people at work. Through the earlier chapters the nature of managing people, the role of human resource management, selection, training, development and the motivation of the employee has been explored. This final chapter seeks to examine the role and influence of legislation in determining the nature and management of the employment relationship. However, the area of employment legislation is vast and this chapter can therefore only focus on some of the key elements which manage the employer and employee relationship. It examines specifically terms of employment, health and safety at work, discrimination and managing diversity, grievance and disciplinary procedures.

The areas of employment law will be explored under three major headings:

- terms and conditions of employment;

- welfare and conditions of work;

- managing diversity and equality (especially the role of women employees).

Most employment legislation has been drafted over the last twenty to twenty five years, and it is during this time that there has been a considerable increase in the degree of protection awarded to employees by statute. Each of these aspects is explored in terms of the scope of the legislation and its impact on the employer/employee relationship.

Terms and conditions of employment

Under Section 1 of the Employment Protection Consolidation Act (EPCA) 1978, and the earlier Contracts of Employment Act 1963, employees have the right to obtain a written statement from their employer setting out their terms of employment. It must identify:

a) Job title.

b) The employer and employee.

c) The date the contract began.

d) When continuous employment began and if any previous employment counted towards this, e.g. maternity leave. This has an effect on redundancy payments, sick pay, dismissal, etc.

e) Methods used for calculating pay, including bonus, overtime payments and intervals of pay.

f) Holiday entitlement.

g) Working time.

h) Sick pay and provisions.

i) Pension provision.

j) Periods of notice, grievance and disciplinary procedures.

All employees also have a right to receive an itemized pay statement and should be informed of grievance and disciplinary procedures, especially what constitutes a dismissal. The organization must also inform employees where the health and safety requirements are displayed. Although these terms are specified there are other conditions of employment enshrined in common law which the employer and the employee are expected to observe, for instance duties of care, co-operation and loyalty. The conditions laid out in the terms of employment must, however, conform to individual rights of employment. For instance, every employee has the right to at least one week's notice.

Welfare and conditions at work

There are two major pieces of legislation that affect financial services organizations in the area of health and safety.

Office, Shops and Railway Premises Act (OSRP)1963
Health and Safety at Work Act (HASAW) 1974

Office, Shops and Railway Premises Act (OSRP) 1963

This Act extended the requirements of the Factories Act 1961 to people employed in offices, etc. The main requirements are:

a) Suitable and sufficient toilets and washing facilities provided and maintained with proper lighting and ventilation.

b) Stairs and gangways of sound construction with handrails and no obstructions.

c) Drinking water provided.

d) Places for hanging clothes.

e) Seats for employees.

f) Facilities for eating food.

g) No person under 18 years of age using dangerous machinery.

h) No one may lift a heavy load, which could cause injury.

i) First aid boxes should be provided.

j) No overcrowding of rooms with 40 square feet or 400 cubic feet for each person.

k)   Reasonable temperatures, no less than 16c after the first hour and thermometers to check the temperature.

Fire precautions and accidents should be reported. The Act also allows for a compulsory inspection of the premises by inspectors.

Health and Safety at Work Act (HASAW) 1974

In 1972 it was felt that a radical change was needed in the approach to health and safety at work. In 1973 1,000 deaths and 600,000 injuries were incurred at work. The law was complex and sometimes obsolete. As a result of the Robins Report, published in 1972, the HASAW 1974 was born. This is now the major piece of legislation governing health and safety at work. It consolidated the previous 30 Acts and 500 regulations covering safety at work. It had certain objectives:

- to secure health, welfare and safety for people at work;

- to protect others from risks arising at work;

- to control the use and storage of dangerous substances;

- to control the emission of noxious or offensive substances into the air.

The Act specifies a range of duties for both employer and employee which are enforceable through the criminal courts.

The employer's duties are:

> To ensure as far as is reasonably practicable the health, safety and welfare of all ... not only employees but those affected by your products or plant.

The employee's duties are also important because safety at work cannot be achieved without the interest and support of employees.

Trade unions have a right to appoint safety representatives to look at hazards and complaints and to make representations. The safety representatives should have at least two years work experience with the current employer, and should carry out inspections quarterly and immediately following an accident.

Employees have a duty to take reasonable care for their own and others safety. There are two offences "horseplay", and "deliberate disregard of safety requirements".

Employers must:

- provide information, training and supervision;
- issue a policy statement;
- consult the trade unions;
- establish safety committees.

In addition manufacturers are also expected to provide safe products, and test and provide information on them.

There are two Enforcement Agencies: the Health and Safety Executive and the Health and Safety Commission. The Health and Safety Executive consists of a director and members who supervize five industrial sectors (factories, mines and quarries, explosives, nuclear installations, and alkali works). The inspectors have the right to enter premises, examine them and question employees. However, the role of inspectors is to pursue the cause of safety and not just apprehend wrongdoers.

The Health and Safety Commission was established in 1974 and consists of a chairman, three representatives of trade unions, representatives of employers and three neutral representatives. They are responsible for issuing codes of practice, new regulations and general research.

Penalties can be invoked against a company or individual. Some directors and managers as well as safety managers can be prosecuted under HASAW. For the manager to be prosecuted it has to be shown that a breach has occurred through his consent, connivance or neglect. The remedies offered by the Act mean that contravention is a criminal act and can result in fines and imprisonment. This can be invoked for refusal to comply with a notice, breach of general duties, a grave or repeated breach of a relevant act. The imposition of fairly severe penalties was aimed at reducing accident and injury rates in UK industry.

Discrimination and the law

Discrimination is said to occur where an employer treats one person less favourably than another in the same or similar circumstances, whether intentionally or not, in respect of the employee's sex, race, colour or marital status. There are three major acts in this area: Equal Pay Act, Sex Discrimination Act, and Race Relations Act.

Equal Pay Act (EPA) 1970 (amended by the Equal Pay Amendment Act 1983)

This states that men and women should be treated the same where they are employed to perform like work or work rated as equivalent.

Employees should be paid the same and have the same rights if they are performing like work or work rated as equivalent or of the same value.

The situation becomes complex when defining jobs of equal value because the Equal Opportunities Commission has argued that the evaluation is more related to the sex of the job occupant than the job itself.

The Equal Pay Amendment regulations are significant because they followed a long dispute between the UK and EU. The 1983 Act widens the scope of the 1970 Act so that jobs can be compared even though evaluation is not available. This allows, for example, check-out operatives and warehousemen to be compared in terms of their value to the supermarket organization.

Sex Discrimination Acts (SDA) 1975-6 (amended by the Employment Act 1989)

There are three types of discrimination:

1. *Direct Discrimination* – where the employer makes it clear applicants of one sex will not be considered for the post (this discrimination was removed by the Sex Discrimination Act 1975).

2. *Indirect Discrimination* – where neutral conditions for employment or promotion mean they affect one sex more than another, e.g. height when it does not materially affect the performance of a job.

3. *Victimization* – when one employee is treated less favourably because they have instigated proceedings against the employer under the EPA (1970) or SDA (1975).

Race Relations Act 1976

This covers discrimination on the basis of colour, race, and nationality, ethnic or national origin. Once again discrimination can be termed direct or indirect or victimization.

Managing diversity

In recent years there has been a greater awareness of the need for organizations to manage proactively the diverse nature of their workforce. This concept of diversity complements equal opportunities, HR and quality management. It has three main purposes:

- to help employees who are perceived as different from the majority of their colleagues to succeed and develop their careers;

- to create an environment where all can work together combating prejudice, harassment, stereotyping and undignified behaviour, and to allow people to be valued as individuals;

- to help effect cultural change.

There are a number of factors driving this movement towards managing diversity:

1. The increasing age of the workforce. By 2001 one in three will be aged over 40 and yet there is prejudice about the employment and training potential of older people.

2. The increasing number of women in the workforce. Since 1975 the number of women in employment has increased by 34% to 12.2 million in 1995, whilst the number of men has fallen by 0.5% to 15.6 million. Between 1994 and 2001 male employment will only rise by 3%, female by 11% and women will make up 45% of the workforce.

3. The increase in part-time working. Between 1994 and 2001 part-time working increased by 22% and full-time decreased by 1%.

4. The acknowledgement of caring responsibilities for both children and the elderly with 2½ million men and 3 million women having caring responsibilities for elderly dependents.

5. Discrimination and harassment experienced by those entering or in employment.

As well as satisfying social and legal demands, the Institute of Personnel and Development (1997) claim that managing diversity should be encouraged for business reasons. This can be a means of improving customer care and market share by reflecting customer backgrounds, needs and attitudes in the workforce. It can encourage the development of organizational ethics and values as well as enhancing HR practices. Managing diversity reflects societal changes, ensures compliance with legislation, and leads to the adoption of best practice.

Some organizations have tried to introduce an approach to managing diversity by establishing value systems based on trust, fair criteria for HR systems and procedures, and ensuring that all forms of harassment and bullying are dealt with. These organizations are also seeking to address the diverse needs of customers and to ensure organizational awareness of international culture. Some organizations also have in place specific policies to address the issue of equality for female employees and it is this area which is discussed in the next section.

Women and employment

Although financial services organizations obviously abide by, and in some instances exceed, employment regulations as far as discrimination is concerned, the vast majority of managers are male (over 80%) although women form over 60% of the workforce. From the days of their earliest employment women in banking generally occupied clerical and secretarial roles, and even as late as 1967 it was expected that the banks were providing a limited period of employment for women until family commitments took over. For male employees banking was seen as a lifelong career. During the 1970s attitudes began to change with women taking less time off work to bring up children and the number of single parent families increasing. With the introduction of the Equal Pay Act in 1972, job evaluation and grading systems were also introduced. This enabled banks to introduce a career structure within clerical grades and people were paid for the work they did rather than according to age and sex. Maternity provisions, which were introduced in 1978, had little effect on increasing the number of women in senior posts, since most women with a baby wished to work part-time and the banks did not allow that. Only two fifths of women with a baby were doing paid work in 1979. However, over the last twenty years there have been significant improvements in terms of encouraging career progression and employment of women.

Steps have been taken within the industry by appointing staff to be specifically in charge of equal opportunities, and by introducing new family friendly schemes whereby some employees with children can have a five-year career break.

Recent statistics indicate that women are becoming an increasingly active section of the labour-market. Marriage now appears to have little effect on the economic activity of women with over 90% continuing to work. However, there is still a dip in activity rates for twenty five to thirty four-year-olds, reflecting the time when they have left work and are raising a family, although predictions indicate this will disappear (e.g. Fincham and Rhodes 1992). It is anticipated that fewer school-leavers will be available for work at the start of the next century (due to demographic trends) which means that employers will have to make increasing use of women returners. Organizations will try to project new models of the family friendly firm as employer's adopt new HR policies. The growth in the industry has been in terms of clean, quiet, less demanding jobs which women may find attractive.

The grievance and disciplinary process

It was during the mid to late 1970s that organizations first introduced disciplinary and grievance procedures. The impetus for the disciplinary procedures was the growing amount of employment legislation, especially that governing unfair dismissal. It was perceived to be an opportunity to formalize procedures, which had often been completed by negotiation and agreement with the representatives of staff, usually trade union officials. Whilst drawing up disciplinary procedures which could be invoked against an employee, most firms also drew up grievance procedures which employees could use when they felt that there was a problem, or that they had been treated unfairly by the employer. In summary, a grievance procedure is the specified procedure to be followed in an organization when an aggrieved employee wishes to take his or her grievance to the higher levels of the organization. The disciplinary procedure is that which must be followed when an organization feels an employee has not maintained its disciplinary standards.

It is necessary now for organizations to possess both a grievance and disciplinary procedure, according to the Contracts of Employment Act 1972 and the Employment Protection Consolidation Act 1978.

The procedures adopted by a company should conform to the guidelines contained in the Code of Practice issued by the Advisory Conciliation and Arbitration Service (ACAS). The code also contains information and advice about the operation of such procedures. A grievance or disputes procedure should describe the stages for dealing with disputes in the organization from when the issue is first raised until it is referred (if it is not settled at an early stage) to outside conciliation.

The procedures which organizations follow for dealing with grievance and disciplinary actions are to some extent determined by law, although each organization specifies its own particular procedure. The procedure exists for both union and non-union employees. It may be that for trade union members there is a national agreement between employer and union.

Operating grievance and disciplinary procedure is an area of employment law where managers may be frequently involved. It often causes anxiety amongst managers when they have to use grievance and disciplinary procedures, because of the fear of mistakes occurring.

Grievance procedures

The grievance procedure should be written down, specifying to whom the employee takes their grievance and their right to be accompanied. No industrial action should be taken until the procedure is exhausted and time limits should be set for completion of one stage in the grievance procedure before moving onto the next. (Five working days is normal.) The three stages are as follows:

Stage 1

All queries and grievances should be raised initially by the employee with the employee's immediate supervisor. An employee may choose to approach a Union or Staff Association representative first, so that the issue can be raised jointly or by the representative on the employee's behalf. The supervisor will do his or her best to resolve the issue and give an answer within five working days. If it cannot be satisfactorily resolved, the matter will be referred to Stage 2 of the procedure.

Stage 2

If the employee is not satisfied by the supervisor's answer, the issue will be referred to the departmental sectional manager. At the meeting there may also be in attendance, a trade union representative and the HR manager. The departmental manager, following discussions with the HR manager, should give an answer within five working days of the matter being raised.

Stage 3

If the union representative is not satisfied with the answer given by the departmental manager, the matter will be referred to a senior manager, who with the HR manager will discuss the matter with the union representative and senior union representative. Again five working days will be available before an answer is required.

In some organizations the procedure ends here, in others it is referred to a mediator or joint consultative body.

It is normal for the HR department to be informed when a grievance procedure starts. Everyone involved in a grievance procedure can then be treated in the same way. It is also the right of the employee always to have a representative present.

Disciplinary procedures

It is normal for an employer to have a disciplinary procedure for employees, as this ensures that standards can be maintained.

A key aim of the disciplinary procedure is to try and achieve a change in behaviour on the part of the employee so that further action is unnecessary (assuming that there is an indication that the problem is one of employee behaviour). Employees may be unaware of what is expected of them, so it is desirable that there is a general understanding of what constitutes a misdemeanour and what the consequences might be. Also individuals should be given warnings of what will happen if they fall below standard. The procedure also ensures that all individuals are treated consistently. The proceedings may indeed reveal mistakes by management in failing to communicate disciplinary rules, and it may be that after discussion it is felt to be unfair even to classify it as disciplinary action.

It is important that the procedure be followed in disciplinary action. Otherwise an eventual dismissal may be considered unfair if inappropriate action has been taken. In financial services organizations there are certain guidelines established:

- the procedure must be in writing;
- it must specify to whom it applies;
- it must provide for speedy action;
- it must allow employees the right to be accompanied;
- no action can be taken until the complaint is investigated, and employees must be given the right to state their case before action is taken;
- no employee can be dismissed for a first breach of discipline except in cases of gross misconduct;
- employees must be given an explanation of the penalty imposed and a right of appeal.

The reasons for dismissal of employees are given below (as contained in the Employment Act 1978):

- incapable of performing the job or appropriate qualifications absent;
- misconduct;
- redundancy;
- contravention of duties or restrictions imposed by law by continuing employment;
- other substantial reason to justify dismissal.

A dismissal is unfair if insufficient reason is given or the dismissal is not reasonable in the particular circumstances, i.e. the employee has not received a copy of the disciplinary rules. Under the 1980 Employment Act, the employee is entitled to a written statement giving reasons for his or her dismissal.

Disciplinary action can only be taken where there is clear evidence against the employee. The action can only be appropriate to the size of the offence and must be consistent. Employees should be represented and have the right of appeal, and the matter should be investigated.

The following stages constitute the disciplinary process:

Stage 1
A verbal informal warning is given to the employee in the first instance

or where it is a minor offence. The employee's immediate supervisor should give the warning.

Stage 2

A formal verbal warning is made by a supervisor or manager.

Stage 3

A written or formal warning is given to the employee by a senior manager when they commit a serious offence or after repetition of minor offences. This states the nature of the offence and specifies future disciplinary action which will be taken if the offence is committed again within the specified time period. A copy of the written warning is placed on the file of the employee's personnel record, but is destroyed in twelve months if the performance is satisfactory. The employee is required to read and sign the formal warning and has the right of appeal if he or she believes the warning is unjustified.

Stage 4

A final written warning is given by a senior manager and in some instances the HR department.

Summary dismissal

An employee may be summarily dismissed in the event of gross misconduct (as defined in the company rules). Only senior managers can recommend summary dismissal and action should not be taken until the HR manager has discussed the case and the appeal procedure has been carried out.

Appeals

In all circumstances, an employee may appeal against suspension or dismissal. The HR manager should be present and the employee may be represented. A member of management conducts the appeal. Appeals should be held as soon as possible.

If an appeal against dismissal is rejected, the employee has the right to appeal to the chief executive.

The HR manager and the employee representative may be present.

An employee can appeal against a dismissal they consider unfair before an Industrial Tribunal. Under current legislation the employer is required to demonstrate that the dismissal has been fair and reasonable.

Grievance and disciplinary interviews

A crucial part of both grievance and disciplinary procedures are the interviews, which are normally in the first instance conducted by the line manager. The interviews involve a number of different stages.

Preparation – In the case of disciplinary interviews the managers have time to prepare themselves. In the case of grievance interviews the managers may not have the time they would like to prepare for the initial interview. The managers should ideally carry out a full investigation into the circumstances of the case. This should be done speedily and the observations and memories of witnesses should be included. The managers should get as much information as possible so that they understand the facts. In the disciplinary procedure the employee should be interviewed to establish this version of events, and the representative should be told a disciplinary interview is to occur.

After the preparation the stages are the same as those introduced for other interviews:

- introduction;
- investigation;
- listen;
- close.

In the introduction the manager should explain the stages in the disciplinary and grievance procedure. They should also explain what the issue is, who is present and why, and what will happen during the interview. If the employee is not accompanied they should be reminded of that right.

The investigation in both the grievance and disciplinary interviews are concerned with establishing the facts. Hopefully in the grievance interview the manager may have some idea of the nature of the grievance, and they should aim to find out as much as they can. Braddick (1991) identifies several areas for investigation:

- background;

- circumstances;

- latent and manifest causes.

The manager must be aware that there are symptoms and causes. It is only by exploring the case that they can find the true cause and thereby solve the problem. It is for this reason that the manager should be prepared to keep an open mind, and ask open and probing questions.

The manager should listen to the employee and not try to offer solutions at this stage to the problem. Most grievance procedures include a time period for the manager to consider the situation before offering a solution. After the initial meeting the manager should consider the facts raised by the employee, the possible action paths and implications of each.

Reply and Close – After the various action paths have been considered the manager should call a further meeting to give a response, and to try to close the issue (although this may not be possible if the manager does not have the proper authority). In the closing solution the manager should aim for a win/win situation so that both employee and employer are satisfied. If the issue is not closed the further stages in the grievance procedure should be outlined.

In the disciplinary interview after the introduction the manager should give the reason for the warning and ask the employee to comment. The manager should specify standards, restate what the employee is required to achieve, and question the employee about any help needed to meet these standards. There is an expectation that the manager will listen to what the employee requires and agree to help. In closing the interview the manager should specify what the employee should do in order to have the warning removed, recap on the appeal procedure and ask if there are any questions.

In both grievance and disciplinary procedure a written record should be kept.

Summary

This chapter has summarized some of the key pieces of legislation that influence employment policies and a manager's role in financial services organizations. The employment legislation currently in existence has an influence on all aspects of a manger's role from the selection, induction training and development of employees to dealing with problems and disciplinary matters.

References.

Braddick W A G (1991) *Management for Bankers*, 2nd ed. Butterworths
Fincham R & Rhodes P S (1992) *The Individual Work and Organization*, Oxford University Press
IPD (1997) *Managing Diversity*, An IPD Position Paper

Index

3-D Theory 179
4-D approach 218-219
7 point plan 325
7 S Framework 104-105

A

AA 25
Abbey National 14, 45, 65
abuse 229
ACAS 339, 401
    Code of Practice 401
acceptability 46
acceptance 227
acquisition 44, 101, 225, 227, 305
action-centred leadership 184, 266
Adair, John 184, 246, 266, 275
    's Action-centred Leadership 185
added value 41
additional benefits 389
adhocracy 57
administrative management 148,
    152
adopting learning 107
advertisement 326, 327
advertising 116, 126
Advisory Conciliation and
    Arbitration Service see ACAS
advocators 127
agencies 88, 130
agency 323, 326, 327, 345
    staff 88
    workers 83
agenda 288

airmiles 129, 131
alienation 76, 77, 281, 380
    and technology 76
all-channel 259, 261
alternative directions 41
ambitious 312
American
    Express 131, 132
    management 69
analysis 117
ancillary work 89
Anderson N and Shackleton V 332
Andrews K 30
anger 227
Annual
    General Meeting 285
    hours 80
    report and accounts 213
Ansoff, H 5, 41
Anthony R N 49
Apollo 66
appeals 404
Applebaum et al 345
application form 327, 332
aptitude tests 333, 337
Armstrong M 297, 298, 307, 383,
    386
Aronson 251
artefacts 63
Asch S E 253, 263
Ashridge
    College 180-181
    Studies 180
assertiveness 230

assessment centres 335
assessor-developer 267
assets 14
assurance 132
Aston
    Studies 163
    University 61, 163
Athena 66
Atkinson J 80, 81, 83
    and Gregory D 83
atmosphere 116
attitude 350
attributes 316, 317, 325, 326, 327
audit committee 207, 213
auditor 213
authorities manual 208
authority 153-154, 189
    charismatic 189
    rational 189
    traditional 189
autocratic 183
autonomous work groups 268
autonomy 381
awareness 227

B

back office 24, 89
BACS (Bankers Automated Clearing
    Systems) 23
Bailey and Sherman 342
balance 228
Ball, Ben 238 ,239, 241
Bamforth 160
Bank of England 11, 12, 14, 21, 90,
    200
Bank of Scotland 45
Bank Wiring experiments 253
Banking
    Code 138
    Ombudsman 138
banks 35, 282, 399
Barclaycard Profile points 42
Barclays 65, 198, 231
Barings 234
Barnard C I 279
Bartell K M 128, 129
    and Martin 101

Basle Capital Adequacy Accord
    1988 9, 13, 194, 215
Bass B M 186
batch production 73-74
Beardwell I and Holden L 85, 297
behaviour segmentation 122
Belbin 244, 256, 258, 267
Bendix R 158
Benne K D and Scheates P 258
Berggren C 76
Berry L 136
bet your company culture 68
Better Bandit Control (BBC) 219
biodata analysis 332
BIS capital adequacy requirements
    14
Blake R R and Mouton J S 181
    Managerial Grid 179-180
Blauner R 76
Blue Arrow 199
Blyton P 323
benefits, fringe or additional 389
board 203, 205, 206, 208, 213
    balance 204
    committees 207
    two-tier 206, 207
bonus 389, 393
Boots 44
Boston Consulting Group (BCG)
    growth share matrix 37-38, 318
Bowditch J L and Buono A F 268
Bowman C and Asch D 35
Boyatzis R 169
Braddick W A G 71, 265, 405
branch network 59
Braverman H 77, 151
breathing 229
British
    Medical Association 226
    Psychological Society 334
    Standards Institution 137
broking firms 66
BS5750 137
Buckley R and Caple J 350, 354, 358
budgets 195, 173, 209-210, 211,
    283, 387-388
building societies 9, 10, 129, 282
Building Society Act

1986 8, 9, 11
1987 10
Building Society
    Commission 11
    Ombudsman 138
bureaucracy 65-67, 148, 154-156,
    162, 208, 280, 284, 320
Burns T and Stalker G M
    162, 281, 283
business
    environment 65
    level planning 49
    objectives 282
    Process Re-engineering (BPR)
    99, 249
    strategies 315
buyer behaviour 124

C

Coulson-Thomas, C 111
Cadbury Committee
    198, 203, 206, 207, 214
Cameron K 342
capital 14, 194
career 231, 235, 239, 242, 309
    change 231
    definition 230
    development 134
    prospects 239
careers 230
Carlzon J 126
carrot and stick approach 373
case study 360
cash 23
    Cow 38, 318, 319
casual staff 88
catalyst 109, 111
categorical imperative 16
causality 164
cautious shift 263
centralization 60-61, 153
centralized processing 24
CEO (Chief Executive Officers) 203,
    204, 205, 208, 221
chain 259, 261
chair 208, 287, 288, 289, 291
chairing 288
chairman 203-205

Chandler A D 70
change 224
    agent 109-110
    cultural 102
    discontinuous 95
    driving forces
        against 106
        for 105
    forces of 95
    four main triggers for 95
    fundamental 95
    hard and soft approaches 98
    incremental 94
    individual resistance to 106
    managing 93-113
    models for 97
    nature of 94
    organizational resistance 107
    planned 97
    resistance to 105, 108
    stages of resisting 107
    structure and 100
    successful 112
    transformational 95
    who should manage 109
changeability 5
CHAPS (Clearing House Automated
    Payment System) 23
charge card 131
Cheltenham and Gloucester
    Building Society 9
cheques 23
Chief Executive Officers see CEO
Child I L 330
Child J 57, 61, 164, 189
Christopher et al 127
circle 259, 261
Citibank 131
Classical school 148-149, 152, 154,
    156, 161, 173, 380
Clearing House Automated Payment
    System (CHAPS)
Clerical and Medical 45
Club culture 65
co-operation 149
co-ordinating 172
co-ordinator 256-257
Code of Best Practice 207, 208

codes of behaviour 282
cohesiveness 250, 251, 252, 264,
    266
Cole G A 73
collaboration 163
Combined Code 203
commercial 121
committed customers 120
communications 157, 161, 173, 269,
    273-291, 304, 335, 345
    and information technology 284
    channels 18, 281
        downward 281
    direction of the flow 281
    in organizations 279
    networks 259-260
    plans 321
    process of 274
    systems 134, 318
Companies Act 193
    1985 198
competencies 169, 238, 312
    definition 169
competition 130
competitive
    advantage 40, 49
        achieving 40
    influences 25
    rivalry 27
    scope 40
competitors 50, 106, 130, 134
completer 257
complex
    man 372
        view 377
    systems 159
compliance 214
    department 214
    functions 214
    -based ethical organization 18
computer viruses 25
conceptual or process skills 169
conciliation 401
concluder-producer 267
conditions at work 394
conduct of business 195
conflict resolution 247
consensus building 290

consolidation 44
consultant 109, 110, 323
    role of 110
    external 110
    internal 111
consultative 183
consumer 197
    behaviour 123
    buying patterns 118
    protection 195
Consumers' Association 193
consumption process 124
content theories 373
context 276
contingency
    approach or school 161, 162,
        164, 165, 181, 183
    theory 163, 181
continuous
    learning 306
    sales promotion drives 129
continuum of leadership 178
contract staff 88, 312
contracting 78
contractors 345
contracts 238
    short-term 238
    transactional 238
    nil hours 88
    of Employment Act
        1963 393
        1972 400
    zero hours 88
control 117, 189
    and risk 196
    corrective 195
    definition 194
    detective 195
    framework 197
    in organizations 192-216
    key concepts 194
    nature of 195
    preventive 195
    prudential 194
controller inspector 267
controlling 172
conventional long wall 160
conventionalist ethic 16

conveyor theory of communication
    273, 285
coping with stress 226
core
    business 89
    workers 81, 83
corporate
    appraisal 39
    banking 124
    clients 73
    image 63
    objectives 355
    strategy 30, 117, 301
cost leadership 41
Coulson-Thomas C 111
Council of Mortgage Lending
    Practice 138
counselling 344
cradle to grave 365
creator-innovator 267
credit
    card 123, 129, 131
    scoring 24
cross-selling 25, 123
cross-functional teams 313
Crozier 188
cultural change, four steps 102
culture 37, 47, 56, 62, 64, 96, 109-
    112, 236, 251, 297, 299-301, 304,
    309-310, 338, 344, 351, 398
    and organizational effectiveness
    69
    artefacts 63
    basic assumptions 63
    change 72
    classifications 65
    covert/implicit 64
    definition 62
    development 64
    four types 65
    levels 62
    managing 71
    norms 63
    of successful firms 70
    overt/explicit 64
    service quality 134
    sub-cultures 64
    values 63

custom and practice 8
customer 120, 127, 130, 285, 325,
    343
    attracting 119
    awareness 136
    bargaining power 27
    base 22, 128
    complaints 134
    data 123
    focus 129
    keeping 119
    loyalty 119, 128
    needs 106, 135
        and attitudes 21
    protection 137
    relations, managing 114-142
    relationship 125, 126
        lifecycle 124-125
        retention 128-129
        strategies 127
    satisfaction 129
    segments 130
cybernetics 148, 158

D

data 284-285
    processing 89
    Protection Act 308
Davidow W H and Malone M S 101
Davidson 115
Davies
    I K 354
    Howard 196
Deal T E and Kennedy A A 68
debriefing 362
decentralization 60, 61
decision making 48, 247
decisional roles 174, 175
declining sales 117
decoding 278
defence 107
delayering 14, 170, 244, 380, 389
delivery
    and product design, changes in
    24
    channels 22, 90
Deming 135
demographic 21, 81

influences 21
segmentation 122
time bomb 322
trends 400
denial 226
and confusion 107
Department of
Employment 350, 381
Trade and Industry (DTI) 12, 13,
200
dependents 398
depression 227
deregulation 8, 9, 25, 284, 319
description 98
deskilling 24, 76, 77
deskwork 222
Devanna et al 302
development 321, 351-
352, 355, 356, 365, 366, 369,
381
approaches to 352
definition 350
diet 228
DIF analysis 355, 359
differentiation 41
digital TV 24
TV banking 43
Dionysus 67
direct discrimination 397
Director General of Fair Trading 13
directors 203, 396
disbelief 226
disciplinary
interview 405-406
procedures 401-402
process 400, 403
discipline 153
disclosure rule 16
discrimination 398
and the law 396
disengaged 312
dislike of uncertainty 107
dismissal 402
disseminator 174
distancing 80
distinctive competencies 37
distribution channels 26, 43, 126
disturbance handler 174-175

diversification 43, 58
related 43
unrelated 43
division of work 153
divisionalized structure 57, 59
documentation 344
dog 38
downsizing 87, 322, 342-343, 345
handling 342
downward
channels of communication 282
communication 5, 281, 284
drop out 340
Drucker P 115

E

e-mail 24, 219
early retirement 312, 342, 345
economic influences 20
economics 20
economies of scale 26
education 351, 365, 366, 369
definition 351
effectiveness 179
electronic
mail 277
office 224
empathy 132
employee relations plans 321
employees, core 81
Employment Act
1978 403
1980 403
1989 397
Employment Protection
Consolidation Act (EPCA) 1978
393, 400
employment
legislation 392-407
structure of 78
empowerment 188, 383
encoding the message 277
enforcement agencies 396
entrepreneur 174-175
environment 4, 47, 161, 163, 211,
239, 252, 280, 325, 380
environmental
analysis 3

influence 6, 164
   audit 6
epicureans 15
Equal
   opportunities 306, 400
   Opportunities Commission 397
   Pay Act (EPA)
      1970 396-397
      1972 399
   Pay Amendment Regulations
      397
equality 399
equity 153
esprit de corps 154
establishment plans 319
ethical influences 15
Etzioni A 187
EU (European Union) 11, 14,
   15, 201, 206
   Capital Adequacy Directive 1996
      9, 12, 14
   Second Bank Directive 1993 9,
      11, 15
   Second Banking Co-ordination
      Directive 1993 9, 11
European
   Commission 85
   Community 8
   Directives 199
   Foundation for Quality
      Management (EFQM) 137
   Market Initiative 11
   Union (EU) see EU
ex-employees 88
excellence 70
exception principle 151
executive 203
   director 203, 205-207
existential culture 67
Expectancy
   Model of Motivation 378
   Theory 378
expert
   modelling techniques 25
   systems 24
explorer-promoter 267
external environment 65, 78, 158
   analysis of 36

external
   labour market 86
   regulators 195
   workers 83
extrinsic reward 386
   structures 385

F

Factories Act 1961 394
falling market share 117
family friendly schemes 400
far environment 6
Fayol H 57, 152, 154, 173, 189, 208,
   221
fear of the unknown 107
feasibility 46
feedback 68, 196, 275, 281, 282-
   283, 331, 337, 340, 364, 379,
   381, 383
   channels 19
Feldman D C and Arnold H J 248,
   251
Festinger et al 248
Fiedler F E 181, 182
   's contingency model 181-182
figurehead 174
finance 150
Financial
   flexibility 323
   services 5
   Services
      Act 1986 9, 12
      Authority (FSA) 13, 14, 199-
         202
      Ombudsman 138
   areas of work 201
   standards 202
Fincham R and Rhodes P S 73, 194,
   400
finders, minders and grinders 168
finisher 257
First
   Direct 44, 127
   impressions 330
fitness 228
   for purpose 132
five forces 36
fixed-term

contract staff 87
contracts 88, 345
flat
    management 309
    organization 235
flatter hierarchies 244
Fletcher C 335
flexers 312
flexibility 79, 309, 323, 331, 386
    definition 79
    financial 80, 90
    functional 79
    in financial services sector 85
    numerical 80
    objectives 83
    task 79
    temporal 80
    wage 80
flexible firm 101
    model 81
flexitime 80
flow or mass production systems 74
focus 41
    group discussions 133
Ford, Henry 74
Fordism 74
forecasting 170, 211
forecasts 171, 210
foreign exchange 12
formal
    communication systems 285
    organizational arrangement 55
formality 278
forward information 330
Fouccault M 187
fraud 25
Freeman R E 50
French W L and
    Bell C H 64
French J R P and Raven 187
fringe benefits 389
frustration 224
FSA see Financial Services
    Authority
full
    bureaucracy 164
    employment 241
    -time staff 87

functional
    approach 184
    specialization 58
future of work 241

G

Gantt and Gilbreth 151
gap 39
    analysis 317
Gaps, the 5 133
Garratt, Bob 215
General
    and industrial management 152
General Electric 238
General Motors 25, 44
    GM credit card 118
generation gap 345
Geo-demographic segmentation 122
geographic
    segmentation 122
    structure 58
Gerloff E A 273
getting it right first time 132
gilts bullion market 12
globalization 43
golden rule 16
Gouldner A 156
government 83, 84, 130, 198, 234
grade description 384, 385
grading systems 399
grapevines 248
Greek gods 65
Greenbury Committee 198, 203
grievance
    interviews 405
    procedures 401
        three stages 401
    process 400
Gronroos, C 125, 136
groups 245-271
    and job design 268
    behaviour and performance of
    250
    cohesiveness 250
    conflict 269
    decision making 262, 265
    definition 245
    development 266

dynamics 266
encouraging performance 265
evaluation 265
exercises 335
feedback 265
formation 254
formal 247
formation, development and
    maturity 254
interaction 263
interactions 259
leadership 265
management 244-272
motivatation 265
norms 252, 268
objectives 265
openness 265
planning 265
reference 249
roles 256
structure 265
support 265
types of 247
why formed 246
work, effective 250
working 383
groupthink 262, 263
Growth
    rate targets 36
    Vector Matrix 42
Grundy T 95
Guest D E 300, 304

H

habit 106
Hackman J R and Oldham G R 380
half open door policy 219
Halifax 9, 14, 45, 95
Hamblin A C 363
Hampel Committee on Corporate
    Governance 198, 203,
    206, 207, 208, 214
Handy, Charles
    62, 65, 66, 146, 241, 246
harassment 398
hard HRM 298
Harding S 237
Harrison 65

HASAW *see* Health and Safety at
    Work Act
Hawthorne Experiments
    157, 158, 253, 255, 373
HAY/MSL 385
head office 59, 301
Health and Safety 354
    at Work Act (HASAW) 1974 308,
    338, 394-396
    Commission 396
    Executive 396
hedonistic ethic 16
Hendry C and Jenkins R 311
Herriot P 311
Hersey P and Blanchard K H 182
Herzberg F 375, 376, 377, 380, 382
    's two-factor theory 375, 376,
    382
hierarchy 155, 162, 231, 233, 235,
    269, 281, 283
    of needs 374-375, 377
high performance teams 266
Highway Code 349
Hiltrop J 312
hire and fire policies 80
Hofer C H and Schendel D 47, 49
Hofstede et al 64
Holbeche L 249
home-working 223
Hong Kong 20
Hoskyns 90
house style 277
Household and family structure 22
HR (human resourece) 112, 158,
    247, 372, 399
    and changes in the financial
    services sector 308
    approach 156, 158
    managers, duties and
    responsibilities of 306
    movement 152
    school 148, 160, 173, 297, 298
    planning 315-347
    policies 400
    view 373
HRM (Human Resource
    Management) 50, 100, 103, 294-
    314

and business strategy 301
and strategic capability 303
characteristics 298
definition 294, 297
four dimensions of 300
hard 298, 303
soft 298, 303
systems 188
theory 300
HSBC 43
human relations 158, 372, 399
Human Resource Management *see*
HRM
human resources 83
Hussey D 316
hygiene factors 376

I

iceberg model 64
ICI 236
ideology 56, 282
implementer 257
implicitly structured organizations
164
importance of different
contingencies 164
in tray 218
exercises 335
incentive schemes 100, 129
inclusion 340-341
increasing competition 118
incremental systems 387
Independent Financial Services
Advisors 67
indirect discrimination 397
individual 244
indoctrination 268
induction 338
crisis 341
plan 339-340
planned 339
industrial
relations 297
Training Boards 351, 365
tribunal 328
industry margins 130
influence markets 130
informal 248

communication systems 285
information 284, 285
systems 68, 161
technology (IT) 88, 89, 90, 223,
224, 234, 284, 342
informational roles 173, 174
initiative 154
innovation 116
innovator 257
input 349
inspectors 396
Institute of
Directors 206
Employment Studies 81
Personnel and Development 398
Personnel Management 295
institutional investors 214
insurance
companies 9, 12
Directorate 200
Ombudsman 138
integrity-based ethical organization
18
inter-group
conflict 253, 269-270
training 270
interdepartmental meeting 286
internal
analysis 36
audit 212-213, 304
departments 212
customers 130, 136
development 44
environment 54-92, 145, 317
labour market 78, 86
marketing 3
internalize 107
Internet 23, 24, 43, 126, 326
interpersonal
roles 173, 174
skills 169
interpretation 276
interpreting the message 279
interview 336
intra-group conflict 269-270
intranet 24
intrinsic rewards 380
intuition ethic 17

inverted drawing pin structure 231, 235
investment
banking 68
banks 66
Management Regulatory Organization 13, 200
Investors in People (IiP) 303
ISO9000 137
IT see information technology

J

Janis J 263
Japanese management 69
Job
advertisement 326
analysis 323-324
classification 385
description 323, 325, 327
descriptions 282
design 157, 268, 306-307, 380, 382-383
enlargement 79, 268, 382-383
enrichment 79, 238, 268, 382-383
evaluation 320, 383-386, 399
systems 383
for life 322
instruction 281
or unique production 73
ranking 385
rotation 382
satisfaction 247, 380
security 309
sharing 323
-share systems 83
jobbing 73
Johns and Connock 16
Johnson J and Scholes K 5, 30, 45, 49, 51
joint ventures 45, 305
Judaeo/Christian moral concepts 15
judgement 350-351
Juran 135
just in time systems 75

K

kan ban 75-76
Katz D and Kahn R L 281, 282
KcKinsey 7S framework 71
Kelly J E 77
key
results areas 217
tasks 217
King N 376
Kirkpatrick D L 363
knowledge 95, 349, 351
Kolb D A 239, 361
and Fry R 361
Kotler 115, 116, 117

L

Labour Government 21, 198
labour
market 78
primary 78
secondary 78
markets, flexible 78
Labour Party 365
Large, Sir Andrew 205
lateral communication 283, 284
Lawler E E and Suttle J L 375
Lawrence P R and Lorsch J 163, 279
Le Pest & Co 6, 7, 36, 95, 192, 301
factors 7
framework 95
leader 174
leadership 157, 176, 313, 335
action-centred 184
authority 189
autocratic 183
consultative 183
contingency or situational approach 181
continuum of 178
control 189
empowerment 188
functional approach 184
group 184
power 186
relationship 186
styles of leadership approach 177
trait or qualities approach 176

transactional view 185
leaking bucket effect 127
learning
    categories of 350
    cycle 239, 358, 361
    Style Inventory 361
Leavitt H 246, 259
Leeds Permanent Building Society
    9, 45, 95
legal influences 8
Legge K 300
legislation 199, 392-407
    employment 392-407
Lewin K 97, 105, 108
Lewis B R 136
liaison 174
life
    cycle 122, 126
    stage 65
lifers 312
lifespan 241
lifestyle segmentation 123
line
    management 351, 362
    managers 306
linker 267
listing Rules 214
Livy, Brian 358, 359
Lloyds TSB 9, 65
Local Area Network 225
London Stock Exchange 214
Long Term Capital Management 196
longlisting 327, 332
lost customers 134
low-skilled 101
loyalty schemes 129
LPC score 181, 182
Lukes S 187
Luthans F 101
Lynch R 5, 37

M

Maastricht 20
Machiavelli 96
machine bureaucracy 57
McCalman J and Paton R 107
McClelland D C 377
    's theory 377

McGregor A 177, 181, 373
    and Sproull A 84, 95
McGregor D 374
MacInnes J 77
McKenna E 177, 249, 263, 268
McKinsey 71
McKinsey 7S framework 71
McKinsey Consultants 104
macro-environment 6
maintenance
    agent 109
    orientated 258
major shareholders 198
management 151
    administrative 148, 152
    and leadership 176
    by exception (MBO) 151, 173
    Charter Initiative 146
    definitions 146
    elements of 167-191
    four
        functions 150
        principles of 149
    fourteen principles of 153
    functional 150
    history 145-166
    in organizations 146
    information systems (MIS) 211
    matrix 66
    of groups 244-272
    scientific 148-149
manager and subordinate 175
managerial
    roles
        alternative views 173
        traditional view 170
    skills 169
    work, nature of 168
managers, what they do 220
managing
    change 93-113
    customer relations 114-142
    diversity 398
manpower planning 235, 320
manufacturing industries 20, 388
Margerison C J and McCann D 267
market
    development 43

growth 37
penetration 42
research 133
share 302
marketing 115, 116, 118, 150
   5 steps 116
   analysis, planning and control
   117
   definition 115
Marks and Spencer
   9, 25, 26, 44, 64, 70, 118
marriage 400
Marx, Karl 76
Maslow, Abraham 359-
   360, 361, 374, 375
   's Hierarchy of Needs 374-375
mass
   customization 75, 124
   production 74
   systems 74
MasterCard 42
matching model 301
maternity 87, 399
   leave 87, 393
matrix structure 59-60, 101
Maxwell pension scandal 19
Mayo, Elton 157, 373
MBO system 389
means to an end ethic 17
measurement 164
   and evaluation 103
measuring service quality 133
mechanization 323
mechanistic
   organization 162, 283
   structures 163
media 130, 326
medium, choice of 277
meetings 104, 222, 286, 288, 290-
   291
   chairing 288
   control of 288
   fundamentals 286
   interdepartmental 286
   management 285
   recording 289
   summarising 289
mergers 44, 101, 225, 226, 305

Metallgesellschaft 207
micro-environment 6
Middle East 20
middle line 56
Midland
   Bank 43, 44
   Choice 42
might equals right ethic 17
milestones 173
mining 160
Mintzberg, Henry
   30, 48, 56, 173, 175, 220-
   221, 316
   five Ps of 30
   ten roles of 173
minutes 291
   of a meeting 290
Mirvis P 226
   and Hall D 238
MIS 212
mission 47, 51
   statement 35, 135, 282
missionary organization 57
Mitchell 372
modelling techniques 121
moments of truth 126
monitor 174
   - evaluator 257
monitoring 172
Moorhead G and Griffin R W
   62, 251
morale 61, 76, 184, 303, 306
Morgan G 100, 101
Moriarty R T 119
mortgages 10, 42, 58, 124, 129, 139
motivation 157, 247, 371-391
   approaches to 372
   content theories 372-373, 377
   definition 372
   expectancy theory 378
   extrinsic rewards 380
   intrinsic rewards 380
   process theories 372, 377, 380
motivators 374, 376, 377, 382
motor insurance industry 119
movement/change 98
Mullins L J 55, 96, 101, 147, 148,
   164, 190, 251, 256, 261, 262

multi-skilling 79
multinationals 18, 20, 61
mutual status 11
mystery shoppers 133

N

Nat West 65
National Economic Development
    Office (NEDO) 79
National Trust 198
nature of
    managerial work 220
    work
        changes 24
        force 95
near environment 6
NEDO *see* National Economic
    Development Office
negotiator 174-175
network organization 101
new entrants, threat of 26
niche players 25
Nishiguchi 89
noise 278
Nominations Committee 207
non-executive director 203-207
non-work 241
norming 255
norms 63, 111, 248, 250-255,
    266, 269

O

Office, Shops and Railway Premises
    Act 1963 (OSRP) 394
Ohmae 48
ombudsmen 138, 197
On the Quality of Working Life 381
on-call staff 88
open systems 159
operating core 56
operational/functional level
    planning 50
opportunities and threats 32
optimism 107
options 98
order 153
O'Reilly J 86

organic
    organization 162, 283
    structure 163, 283
organization 4
    ethic 17
organizational control 192-216
    the future 214
    goals 65
    model 202
    perspective 235
    structure plans 320
organising 172
Orpen, Christopher 222, 223
Oshagbemi, Titus 221-223
Ouchi W 69, 296
output 349
outsourcing 78, 83, 86, 89, 323,
    326
Outward Bound 266
overload 224-225
overtime 80, 90, 345, 393
owners 50

P

paper management techniques
    (PMT) 218
Parasuraman et al 132
Parliamentary legislation 8
part-time 86
    staff 80
    work 22, 323
    workers 83-84, 86-87
participation of staff 99
Pascale R T and Athos A G 69
pattern 31
Pavarotti, Luciano 273
pay systems 311
PC 43, 126
    banking 24, 90
pensions 380, 393
    miss-selling 19, 214
    schemes 389
    Ombudsman 138
people skills 169
performance
    management 134
    management plans 320
    -related pay systems (PRP) 311,

386-389
performing 255
person
  culture 65, 67
  specification 323, 327, 337
personal
  development
    238, 239, 240, 307, 310, 313
  Investment Authority 13, 200
  pensions 237
personality 330
  inventories 334, 337
  tests 334
personnel 66, 150
  bureaucracy 163
  definition 294
  management 296, 297
  traditional role 295
perspective 31
Peters T J and Waterman R H 70
Pettigrew A M 62, 188
pharmaceutical research 68
phone calls 222
piece
  rate system 149
  work 150
Pine B J 124
plan 31
planning 5, 48, 117, 170
  gap 39, 40
Plant 257
plcs 11, 14
ploy 31
points rating 384
political influences 19
Porter,
  L W and Lawler 378
  Michael 36, 41, 233
Porter's five forces model 26, 36
position 31
positioning 117, 121
power 154, 186
  culture 65
  of Attorney 209
predictability 5
price 131
primary labour markets 78
Principles of Scientific Management

149
Priority and Organization (P&O)
  217
problem
  child 37
  solving 172, 247
procedures 282
  manuals 195, 282
process 72, 349
  culture 68
  production 74, 163
  re-engineering 135, 225
  skills 169
  teams 249
  theories 372, 377, 380
processing 211
  and money transmission,
  changes in 23
  centres 264
product
  development 42
  life cycle 319
  obsolescence 95
  options 130
  specialization 58
production 150
  systems 162
productivity 252, 343
professional
  associations 351
  bureaucracy 57
  ethic 17
professionals 231
profit
  centres 58
  targets 36
profitability 303
profitable segments 120
Project
  Columbus 312
  teams 249
  working 269
promotion 126, 134, 238, 311, 378,
  380, 387
psychological contract 233-234,
  237-238, 309-311, 313
Public Interest Disclosure Act 1998
  19

publicity 116
pull system 75
purpose of organization 35

Q

qualities approach 176
quality 131
    action teams 135
    circle 135, 268
    components 132
    culture 135
    key components of 132
    standards 137
question mark 37

R

Race Relations Act 1976 396-397
Randell G 368
    et al 367
rate for the job 80
rating agencies 21
rational-economic view 373
re-recruitment 338
retraining 345
reception area 63
recognized professional bodies 13
recruitment 134, 236, 251, 305-
    307, 319, 320, 322,
    327, 338, 345, 390
red time system 220
Reddin W J 179
    's Cube 179
redeployment 345
redundancy 306, 311-312, 343,
    344, 345, 393, 403
reengineering 99
references 327
referral markets 130
refreezing 98
regulators 195, 199, 285
regulatory markets 130
relationship 135
    management 118-120
    Management Ladder of Customer
    Loyalty 126, 127
relaxation 229
reliability 132

remuneration 153
    committee 207
    policy 320
repeat purchases 128
reporter-adviser 267
reregulation 8, 9, 12
resentment 227
reskilling 241
resource
    allocator 174-175
    investigator 257
    planning 46
resourcing 303, 304
responsiveness 132, 163
restructuring 86, 87, 106
retail 121
return on
    capital employed (ROCE) 36
    investment (ROI) 36
review, evaluation and control 47
reward 238, 308, 321
    management 305
    mechanisms 237
    systems 100, 134, 308, 318, 383
rewards 304, 310, 388, 389
rightsizing 319, 341
    managing 345
risk 68
    analysis 24
        methodology 196
    assessment 25
risky shift phenomenon 262-263
rituals, heroes and symbols 64
Robbins S P 251, 357
Robey D 164
Robins Report 395
Rodger A 325
    's 7 point plan 325
role
    culture 65, 66
    definitions 259
    differentiation 256
    play 335
roles 269
Rose M 152
Royal Bank of Scotland 45, 312
Rule books 282
Russell, Tim 350

S

sabotage 25
safety representatives 395
Safeway 45
SAGA 25
Sainsbury's 25, 26, 45
  Bank 45
salaries 388
salary 376, 387
  systems 386, 389
sales
  promotion 116
  volume 36
Sathe V 103
satisfaction 131
scalar chain 153
Schein E H 62, 70, 112, 245, 248, 270
science of work 150
scientific management 148-149
Seashaw S 252
secondary labour markets 78
secretary 287, 288, 289, 291
  of State for Trade and Industry 12
Securities and
  Futures Authority 13, 200
  Investment Board 12, 138, 200, 205
security 106
segmentation 121, 124
  behaviour 122
  demographic 122
  geographic 122
  lifestyle 123
  of tasks 86
selection 322, 329, 337
  documentation 337
  interview 336
  procedures 328
  perception 106
Self Regulatory Organizations (SROs) 13
self-
  service banking 24
  actualizing man 373
  directed teams 249
  employed 83, 231, 345

employment 241
fulfilling prophecies 330, 336
  management 217-243
  orientated 258
senior management teams 249
service
  delivery and staff 136
  industries 20
  quality 129
    culture 134
services sector 22
severance packages 342
Sex Discrimination Acts (SDA)
  1975-6 396-397
  1975 397
shaper 258
shared values 105
shareholders 50, 207
  major 198
  small 198
Shaw M E 250, 259
Shell/Brent Spar 197
shift
  work 80
  -working 90
shop management 149
shopping malls 24
short-term 84, 101
shortlisting 327, 332
SIB 13
Silverwieg S and Allen R F 102
simple structure 56
situational approach 181
size of market share 36
skill 105, 350
  -based pay 389
  shortages 81
  variety 381
Skinner B F 360
slow growth 118
small
  investors 197
  shareholders 215
SMART 171
smart card 23-24
social ethics 16
social
  influences 21

man 372, 373
    pressures 253
sociological influences 81
soft HRM 298
Sparrow P R 310, 313
specialization 57, 155
specialist 89, 110-111, 258, 312
    staff 87
speeches 278
spokesperson 174-175
stability 280
    of position 154
staff 105, 126
    and service delivery 136
    association 401
    representatives 308
stakeholders 50, 51, 106-107, 130,
    192, 193, 207, 215, 285, 343,
    362, 364
star 37, 318
state 106, 351
status 107
steering agent 109, 110
Stewart
    J 96
    R 175
Stock Exchange, London 9
stock-market dealing 68
stockless production 75
Stoics 15
Stoner 263
Storey 298, 311
storming 254, 269
strategic
    alliances 45, 305
    analysis 35
    apex 56
    choice 40
    implementation 46
    level 49
        planning 49
    management
        process 30, 32-33
            different approaches
            47
    planning 170
vision 316
strategy 104, 117

definitions 30
and
    planning, different levels 48
    stakeholder influences on
strategy 50
concept 30
process 29-53
streamlining 151
Strebel 94
stress 223-228
    definition 224
    management 223, 227
    tactics 229
    related illness 224, 228
stressors 224-226, 229
structural forms 70
structure 57, 61, 65, 96, 104,
    112, 163
    importance 61
    of
        employment 78
        the firm 55
*Struggle Against Financial
    Exploitation* 198
style 105
    of leadership approach 177
sub-cultures 64, 68, 71
subcontracting 89, 323
subcontractor 80, 83
subordinate 175, 176, 281, 335
subordination of individual
    interests 153
substitute products and services,
    threat from 26
subsystems 104, 159
subtext 274, 287
suitability 45-46
summarising 289
summary dismissal 404
Sundstrom et al 264
supermarkets 24, 25
superordinate goals 105
supervisor 401
suppliers 130, 197, 285, 343
    bargaining power 27
support 228
    staff 56
supporters 127

surveys 133
survivor's syndrome 343
suspension 404
SWIFT (Society for World Wide
    InterBank Financial 23
switching costs 129
SWOT analysis 39
systems 72, 96, 104
    approach 158
    school 148, 159, 160, 173

T

tactical ethics 16
takeovers 44
tall
    divisional structure 231, 236
    hierarchical structures 283
tangibles 132-133
Tannenbaum R and Schmidt W H
    178, 179, 180
targeting 121, 128
targets 73
task
    culture 65, 66
    orientated 258
    significance 381
TAT *see* thematic apperception tests
Tavistock Institute of Human
    Relations 160
Taylor 150, 151, 152, 154, 173
Taylor, F W 373
Taylor, Patrick Winslow 149
team 76, 244, 255, 258, 341
    building 266-267
    management 100
    spirit 266
    worker 258
teams 66, 245, 248, 249
teamwork 283, 299
technical skills 169
techno-structure 56
technological
    change 58
    influences 23
technology 76, 95, 106
    and alienation 76
tele-stations 223
telephone

banking 24, 43, 90, 126, 170
    call centres 264
    interviews 332
tells, sells, consults, joins 178
temporal flexibility 323
temporary 84, 101, 345
    staff 87
    work 22, 87
    workers 86
terminal behaviour 362
terms and conditions of
    employment. 393
Tesco 25, 45
    Personal Finance 45
    thematic apperception tests
    (TAT) 377
Theory
    X 177, 373
    Y 177, 374
    Z organizations 69, 70
thruster-organizer 267
Tichy N M and Devanna M A 95
time
    bandits 219
    management 217
    management 223
Torrington D and Hall L
    296, 297, 350, 367, 368
Total Quality Management (TQM)
    75, 135, 299
tough-guy Macho culture 68
TQM *see* Total Quality Management
trade unions 83-85, 308, 318, 395-
    396, 400, 401
trainee 360, 362-363
trainer 363
training 134, 188, 286, 305, 313,
    318, 321, 343, 351-366, 378
    and development 321
    and Enterprise Councils 351,
    365
    and the individual 365
    appraisal 366, 368
    approaches to 352
    definition 350
    development and education 349
    methods 359
    needs 356

objectives 357
plan 364
    implementation 361
    validation 364
    and evaluation 363
trait or qualities approach 176
transaction marketing 119
transcendental ethics 16
transfer
    of training 357, 358
    through principles 358
Treasury 12, 13
trends 118
Trist E L 160
Tuckman B W 254, 255, 269
Tudhope G 236
type
    A values 296
    J values 296

U

underload 224
unemployment 20, 322
unfair dismissal 342, 400, 403
unfreezing 97
unique production 73
unity of
    command 153
    direction 153
unmotivated employees 379
upholder-maintainer 267
upward communication 283
Urwick L 61
utilitarian
    man 373
    principle 17

V

value 40
    definition 131
    -driven strategy 131
values 64, 250, 299, 304
variance analyses 195
verbal informal warning 403
victimization 397
Virgin 9, 25, 44, 49, 118
virtual

memory 101
office 223
organization 101
reality 101
Visa 42
Vroom V H and Yetton P W
    183, 184
    Normative Model 183

W

Watzlawick P 330
Weber Max 57, 154-
    155, 187, 189, 208
Webster
    E C 336
    F E 120
Welch, Jack 238
welfare and conditions at work 394
Western Electric Co 157
wheel 259, 261
Which? 193
whistle-blowing 19, 195
White and Lippitt IOWA Studies
    178
wholesale money markets 12
Whyte I and Plenderleith J 350
Wilensky, Harold 230, 280
Wilkinson G 226
Williamson R J 173
Wilson et al 124
withdrawal 44
women 398
    and employment 399
    returners 400
Wood R & Barron H 334
Woodward 162, 163
words, choice of 275
work
    and non-work 241
    environment 264
    groups 157
    hard, play hard culture 68
    -study 150, 151
workflow bureaucracy 163
workforce 21
    nature of the 22
working time 80
workshop sessions 103

World Wide Web 225

Y

Y 259, 261

Z

Zeithaml V A and Bitner M J
    131, 132
zero defects 132, 134
Zeus 65